W9-AHB-186

The title of this book was originally *Essential Catholicism*. After some time and after hearing from various critics it was decided to change it to *Dynamic Catholicism*—the title I originally favored. *Dynamic Catholicism* I believe conveys much more accurately the flavor of this book, which tries to show how the church and its doctrines have been a dynamic evolving organism. Until Vatican II this truth was obscured by the prevailing myth of the changeless church—a myth fostered by inadequate attention to the history of the church.

By changing the title I also hope to deal with the complaints of some critics who felt that the title *Essential Catholicism* was misleading insofar as it seemed to promise a straightforward and authoritative account of the basic teachings of the church—a kind of updated Baltimore catechism. The main thrust of the book, however, is its focus on the attempts of current theologians to update the teachings of the church. They work on the frontier of Catholic theology; their theories and ideas are by their very nature tentative and exploratory and have not yet been incorporated into the received wisdom of the Catholic tradition.

*Thomas Bokenkotter.*

# DYNAMIC
# CATHOLICISM

RIORDAN HIGH SCHOOL LIBRARY
175 PHELAN AVENUE
SAN FRANCISCO, CALIFORNIA 94112

# DYNAMIC
# CATHOLICISM

## A HISTORICAL CATECHISM

## Thomas
## Bokenkotter

RIORDAN HIGH SCHOOL LIBRARY
175 PHELAN AVENUE
SAN FRANCISCO, CALIFORNIA 94112

IMAGE BOOKS
DOUBLEDAY
NEW YORK   LONDON   TORONTO   SYDNEY   AUCKLAND

94034

AN IMAGE BOOK
PUBLISHED BY DOUBLEDAY
a division of Bantam Doubleday Dell Publishing Group, Inc.
666 Fifth Avenue, New York, New York 10103

IMAGE and DOUBLEDAY are trademarks of Doubleday, a division of Bantam
Doubleday Dell Publishing Group, Inc.

First Image Books edition, titled *Essential Catholicism*, published
September 1986 by special arrangement with Doubleday; this Image Books
edition, re-titled as *Dynamic Catholicism*, published November 1992.

"The Creed—Faith Essentials for Catholics," © 1985 by St. Anthony
Messenger Press, originally appeared in the July 1985 issue of *Catholic
Update* and is herein reprinted with permission of the publisher.

*Library of Congress Cataloging-in-Publication Data*

Bokenkotter, Thomas S.
[Essential Catholicism]
Dynamic Catholicism : a historical catechism / Thomas
Bokenkotter.
p.   cm.
Originally published: Essential Catholicism. Garden City, N.Y. :
Doubleday, 1985.
Includes bibliographical references and index.
1. Catholic Church—Doctrines. I. Title.
[BX1751.2.B576   1992]
230'.2—dc20      92-11390
CIP

ISBN 0-385-23243-8 (pbk.)
*Copyright © 1985, 1986 by Thomas Bokenkotter*
ALL RIGHTS RESERVED
PRINTED IN THE UNITED STATES OF AMERICA

5   7   9   11   13   12   10   8   6

# CONTENTS

## PART II: JESUS THE CHRIST

## PART III: THE CHURCH

## Part IV: Liturgy and Sacraments

# PREFACE

Nearly thirty years ago, Doubleday published in its Image Books series a *Handbook of the Catholic Faith*, which had basically the same objective as this treatise, namely, to provide the intelligent Catholic with an explanation of the main doctrines and practices of the Church. A comparison of the two books, however, would reveal quite significant differences in their approach and in their content. The reason is quite obvious. The past twenty years have witnessed a tremendous burst of Catholic theological activity, unparalleled, in fact, in modern times. The groundwork for this theological renewal was laid at the Second Vatican Council. In a number of revolutionary steps, it gave a new direction to Catholic theology. Specifically it endorsed the historical-critical method in scriptural studies. It also acknowledged the possibility that its doctrinal formulations could be faulty and in need of correction, and in fact it revised a number of them.

But, above all, the Council in various ways helped to create a climate of intellectual freedom in the Church. Its authoritarian structures were kept intact, but much was done that offset their rigor. For instance, theologians who in the preconciliar days had been punished by the Curia for their progressive views were dramatically rehabilitated and given prominent roles at the Council. The Curia was also openly criticized by some of the bishops for its tyrannical use of authority. All of this was bound to have a liberalizing effect on the exercise of authority in the Church.

A theological renaissance occurred as theologians, liberated from tight control by the Curia, set to work on the problems engendered by the advance of secular thought. No doubt some of this theological speculation has little permanent value, but one can hardly deny that much positive work has been accomplished, especially in the fields of scriptural interpretation, history of doctrine and moral theology.

A great amount of recent research, therefore, is now available for those studying contemporary Catholic theology—most of it, however, hidden away in theological journals unfamiliar to the average lay person. My aim here has been to sift through it and select what seems most helpful and enlightening for those who seek an understanding of the essentials of Catholicism today.

In drawing up this account of Catholic doctrine today, I have put particular emphasis on the historical dimension. As the bishops said at the Council, we are passing from a static to a dynamic view of reality as we have become aware of how history has affected the expression of our ideas and doctrine. Vatican II, in fact, manifested a great openness to the totality of Christian and human history. In the words of Josef, now Cardinal Josef, Ratzinger, "Liturgical forms and customs, dogmatic formulations thought to have arisen with the apostles now appeared as products of complicated processes of growth within the womb of history."[1] Hence I felt it necessary to give a detailed account of the historical genesis of the main doctrines and liturgical forms.

I've also stressed the ecumenical dimension. Vatican II called for Catholics to engage in dialogue with other Christians so as to reach a truer understanding of the doctrinal differences that divide the churches. Since then, many such dialogues have taken place and their findings have been published. They constitute very valuable studies of many key doctrines. The scholarship they manifest is of a very high order indeed, and I have been able to make good use of many of these studies in my treatment of such topics as the papacy, the sacraments and Mariology.

A final point I want to emphasize is that this book is not aimed at those Catholics who simply want an account of the official teachings of the Church. I do try to state clearly in each instance what the official teaching is, but I frankly recognize the great amount of pluralism and dissent in the Church today. This pluralism is most evident today in the field of moral theology, where revisionists and conservatives are locked in an epic struggle for the Catholic soul.

*Caveat emptor!* This book is not for the Catholic obsessed with orthodoxy, or for the one who wants an uncomplicated version of the main doctrines of the Church. It is for the Catholic who wants to think through his/her faith and is often puzzled by the apparent conflict of faith with certain findings of modern science and who wonders whether the conflict is really as severe as some priests and teachers seem to imply.

1. *Theological Highlights of Vatican II* (Paramus, N.J.: Paulist/Newman Press, 1966), p. 99.

I have tried to write it in the spirit of the ancient saying *fides quaerens intellectum* (faith seeks understanding). It is also written, I hope, in the spirit of Cardinal Newman's motto found on his gravestone, *ex umbris et imaginibus in veritatem*—here below we dwell amid only the shadows and images of eternal truth.

# DYNAMIC
# CATHOLICISM

# I

---

## The Fundamentals

# 1

## Religion: Do We Need It?

There have been many attempts through the centuries to explain the origin of religion and why it is a universal phenomenon—no civilization without a religion ever having been discovered. Some have viewed it sympathetically as a response deeply rooted in the very nature of man, while others, such as the rationalists and skeptics (Voltaire, Rousseau, etc.), saw the various religions as distortions and degenerations caused by superstition and priestcraft. It was only in the nineteenth century that the study of religion took on the character of a science, as mere speculation was replaced by serious historical, ethnological and psychological investigations. Archaeologists excavated long-forgotten temples; anthropologists collected material on the religion of primitive peoples; philologists studied ancient myths and fables, in attempts to reconstruct the history of primitive religion.

### COMPARATIVE RELIGION

Max Müller (d. 1900), an Oxford professor and philologist, is usually considered the father of comparative religion. His interest in Eastern religions led him to publish a six-volume edition of the *Rig-Veda*. His *Essays on Comparative Mythology* (1856) was the first important book on comparative religion. Through analysis of language and of mythological texts, he claimed that man's fascination with the sun was at the origin of all myths. Since Müller's time, an immense amount of data has been gathered on the religions of mankind. Perhaps the most famous collection is James Frazer's *The Golden Bough*, a twelve-volume compendium of material covering most of the known religions.

Müller's philological approach was soon eclipsed by the evolutionary approach. Charles Darwin (d. 1882) established the dominance of the evolutionary approach not only in biology and the natural sciences but also in ethnology and comparative religion—with special help from Herbert Spencer, who made evolution the foundation of his *System of Synthetic Philosophy*. One of the most important evolutionary approaches to the study of religion was found in the work of Edward Burnett Tylor, a cultural anthropologist who claimed that religion had evolved in straightforward fashion from the Stone Age to the present. From Tylor's time onward it was assumed that the first stage in the evolution of religion was **animism**: the belief that everything was inhabited by spirits. Belief at this stage was then followed by a belief in many gods (**polytheism**), which was finally replaced by **monotheism**, or belief in one god. The evolutionary approach was largely abandoned after the First World War as too simplistic an explanation of a tremendously complex phenomenon.

One scholar who never subscribed to the evolutionary theory was Wilhelm Schmidt, S.V.D. (d. 1954), a missionary and linguist who was inspired by the work of the anthropologist Andrew Lang. Lang found evidence of belief in a Supreme Being among Australian and other aborigines —a fact impossible to reconcile with the evolutionary hypothesis. The scholarly world in general paid little heed to this unexpected piece of evidence. But Father Schmidt was the exception. Lang's discovery started Schmidt on research that culminated in a monumental work, *Der Ursprung der Gottesidee (The Origin of the Idea of God),*[1] a multivolume work that attempted to prove that, originally, primitive people believed in a high God or Supreme Being; only later did a degeneration set in as the image of the Supreme Being was overlaid by fantasies of lesser gods, ghosts, spirits and demons.

Actually, neither the theory of degeneration from monotheism nor the theory of evolution from animism or preanimism (another version) has gained general acceptance. As Mircea Eliade says, it is safer to assume that

1. Six vols. (Munster in Westf.: Aschendorffsche Verlagshandlung, 1926–35).

religious life was from the very beginning rather complex and that "elevated" ideas coexisted with "lower" forms of worship and belief.

One of the outstanding antagonists of religion was Sigmund Freud (1856–1939), whose eccentric views on the origin of religion were tremendously influential. Freud belongs to the company of those other great haters of religion Marx, Nietzsche and Lenin, who saw religion as an illusion of people who were either frightened, alienated, resentful or neurotic. His tremendous prestige as the discoverer of the unconscious lent exaggerated importance to his views on religion. His earliest work on the subject, *Totem and Taboo* (1912), has been called one of the most bizarre theories ever concocted, while his work *Moses and Monotheism* (1939) has been labeled "sheer rubbish" by Mircea Eliade, one of the most respected contemporary scholars in the field.

In *Totem and Taboo*, Freud linked his speculation about the Oedipus complex with the idea of totemism as the key to the origin of religion (a now discredited theory), and then he added to these theories a vague hint of Darwin that mankind originally lived, like the higher apes, in hordes, each under the control of a "father," i.e. a dominant male who had an unlimited sexual monopoly over all the females. Working with these assumptions, Freud reconstructed the origin of religion as beginning with the revolt of the sons against the father so they might gain possession of the females. They kill the father and eat his flesh—to partake thus of his power. In killing him they are acting out their childhood jealousy of the father. Their murder creates a sense of guilt, while chaos results from their rivalries over possession of the women. Out of their frustrations they band together by the help of the ordinances of totemism.

To avoid the rivalries, a taboo on incest is created: a man must marry outside his clan or family group. An animal becomes the symbol of the dead father. The prohibition against the killing of the animal is meant to prevent a repetition of the deed, while the ritual totem meals are instituted to commemorate the deed from which Freud says sprang man's sense of guilt or "original sin" and from which developed social organization, religion and moral restrictions. The memory of the father is no longer conscious, having been repressed because of the guilt aroused by his murder. The father, however, is symbolically embodied in the totem, which also serves as a symbol of the group and is normally taboo except for the sacred occasions when it is sacramentally consumed. "God," then, is nothing less than the sublimated physical father of human beings.

Critics point out many flaws in Freud's theory. It has been proved, for instance, that totemism is not the oldest, nor is it the universal, form of religion, nor did the earliest human family exhibit the traits Freud attributed to it, such as group marriage and general promiscuity. Nevertheless, Freud's view of the origin of religion gained wide currency among the intelligentsia after 1920.

Freud's approach made sympathetic and accurate study of the phenomena of religion very difficult. But his erstwhile colleague Carl Jung (1875–1961) took a more positive and fruitful approach. For Freud, religion was a neurosis. For Jung, it was precisely the lack of religion that was the cause of many neuroses. Both men agreed on the tremendous role played by the unconscious in the psychic life of the individual. But Jung eventually broke with Freud in a dispute over the nature of the unconscious. Instead of seeing it, with Freud, as merely a hidden reservoir of repressed wishes, Jung saw the unconscious as infinitely richer and more complex: a world full of impressions, symbols and images which influence our conscious minds and our dreams and which when properly interpreted can lead us to a better understanding of our psychic conflicts and promote spiritual maturity.

In addition to our individual unconscious, Jung also postulated a collective unconscious in which we all share and from which many of the most potent dream symbols or myths are derived. These symbols, or archetypes, exist in various cultures and peoples and cannot be accounted for in terms of the individual histories of those who experience them. The outstanding examples of such archetypes are the great religious symbols such as the Golden Age, Paradise and, above all, the self (i.e., wholeness, the full realization of one's selfhood). For Western man, Christ is the symbol of the self, and "redemption" means the realization of the self.

These religious symbols, according to Jung, played an important role in giving a wider meaning to one's existence beyond mere getting and spending. Without them a person might feel lost and miserable.

Jung has had a creative influence on the study of comparative religion, as is evident from the large number of scholars in this field who acknowledge their debt to him. Mircea Eliade, for example, in his book *The Quest* notes how Jung's contributions have stimulated research in the history of religion.[2]

The **psychological** approach to the study of religion, as exemplified by

2. Chicago: University of Chicago Press, 1969, p. 22.

Freud and Jung, is only one of many approaches possible. Still to consider are the **phenomenological** and the **sociological** methods of inquiry.

The ambition of the phenomenologists was to analyze the structures of the religious consciousness without attempting to explain their origin and without making judgments as to their ultimate validity. In line with the so-called father of phenomenology, Edmund Husserl (d. 1938), they practiced the method of bracketing, "whereby an object which is present to consciousness is reduced to the pure phenomenon by 'putting in brackets' or excluding from further interest those elements which do not belong to the universal essence."[3] Under this heading we would place the classic study of Rudolf Otto (d. 1937), *Das Heilige* (1917), *The Holy*, which was based on a wide knowledge of comparative religion, contemporary oriental thought and the natural sciences. Otto made an intensive study of religious experience as found in both the Christian and the non-Christian religions. He claimed that he had located the essence of religious experience in feeling, rather than in rational thought; it was, he maintained, a peculiarly human response to the overwhelming power and majesty radiant in the cosmos. He coined a term for this response—the sense of the **numinous**—and distinguished within it three separate moments: the sense of the holy, or sacred; the conviction of one's sinfulness; and the assurance of salvation. Isaiah's vision in the Temple, Paul's apparition of Christ on the road to Damascus, Muhammad's call, the theophany of the Bhagavad-Gita and many other such occurrences in the literature of mysticism testify to the universal character of the form of religious experience which Otto studied.

There is no doubt as to the reality of this phenomenon. But did Otto prove his thesis that it constitutes the essence of the religious experience? It seems not, for there are other forms of religious experience which do not fit into Otto's definition. The Buddha's, for instance, whose focus was on liberation from the impermanence of the world—nirvana—rather than on worship. Other examples, moreover, could be cited.

## THE SOCIOLOGICAL APPROACH

Finally there is the sociological approach, which considers religion in its relation to society and social patterns.

3. John Macquarrie, *Twentieth Century Religious Thought* (New York: Charles Scribner's Sons, 1981), p. 219.

A radical critique of religion played an important part in the sociological views of Karl Marx (d. 1881). Though a Jew by birth and a Christian by baptism at the age of six, he was an atheist by the age of twenty-three. In fact, his conversion to atheism antedated his conversion to communism. Hegel and Feuerbach were the two principal influences on the evolution of his thought. Hegel's dialectic of Absolute Spirit was transmuted by Marx into a dialectical materialism, while Feuerbach provided Marx with a powerful critique of religion in his work *The Essence of Christianity* (1841). This handbook for atheists posited three main arguments against the existence of God. First, the notion of God is derived from two human concepts: one's consciousness of infinity (or, as Feuerbach put it, "the consciousness of the infinite is nothing else than the consciousness of the infinity of the consciousness") plus the concept of a universal human nature. The idea of God, then, is this concept of a universal human nature which is endowed with infinity. So the attributes of God are really the attributes of the objectified nature of man. Man creates God in his own image.

Feuerbach's next argument is based on an interpretation of history. He claimed that events showed that mankind was becoming secularized and people could no longer believe in the fables of Christianity: the Bible was being replaced by reason, religion by politics and heaven by earth.

His third argument was, like the first, a psychological one: God is a product of wishful thinking. Man craves happiness, security and self-preservation but is constantly frustrated in trying to attain them. So he conjures up in his fancy a Supreme Being as the object which corresponds to these needs and wishes. (This has been called a logical fallacy by Eduard von Hartmann, who said, "It is quite true that nothing exists merely because we wish it, but it is not true that something cannot exist if we wish it.")

These arguments, however, were decisive for Marx, who made Feuerbach's critique his own. But Marx added a dimension that was completely lacking in Feuerbach, namely, the idea that religion was caused by unjust and inhuman social conditions which, in turn, religion sanctions and supports by the consolation it offers. To do away with religion, one first had to abolish the concrete social conditions that make religion necessary. Later, in *Das Kapital* (1867), Marx argued that religious and economic alienation go hand in hand and only when economic alienation was overcome and human relationships were intelligible and reasonable would the need for religion disappear.

Marx, therefore, saw no need to crusade against religion, since its demise was foreordained. But this was not the attitude of Vladimir Ilyich Lenin (d. 1924), son of a Russian school official and one of the greatest and most practical revolutionists of all times. Lenin was imbued with a deep hatred of religion, which he linked with his sufferings under the czarist regime and especially with the execution of his brother who was implicated in the murder of Czar Alexander on March 1, 1881. Lenin's disciples had to be atheists and had to fight against religion's deception of the workers. Lenin was willing to compromise with capitalism but not with religion; the regime he installed in Russia became under his successor, Stalin, the greatest persecutor of religion ever known.

As to Marx's critique of religion? Marx certainly showed—and this is his glory—the undeniable influence of socioeconomic conditions on the shape of religion. But otherwise his critique of religion is far less convincing. Marx, it seems, confused the time-conditioned expressions of religion —its dogmas, rituals, prayers, hymns and ordinances—with the essence of religion. One can admit that these dogmas, rituals, etc., reflect the dominant socioeconomic order without having to go all the way with him and say that religion is nothing else than the epiphenomenon or mirror of the socioeconomic order. As Hans Küng says, "Even if it can be proved . . . that the image of God in an ancient-Hellenistic, feudal or bourgeois society is essentially Hellenistic, feudalistic or bourgeois in character, color and imprint, it by no means follows that this image is a pure illusion, this notion of God merely a projection, this God a nonentity. Perhaps God is wholly different from all these images and each age proclaims him differently."[4] Moreover, even in the socialist states religion has not withered up, as Marx predicted. In spite of the most relentless persecution, Christianity continues to grow, rather than decline, in the Soviet Union. According to some statistics, every third Russian is said to be in one form or other a practicing Christian.[5]

Finally, Marx saw only the negative side of Christian history: the undeniable complicity of the Church at times with the forces of oppression and injustice. But he overlooked the other side: the revolutionary potential of the Gospel, which at times has generated movements of protest and liberation, as in the anti-Fascist underground during World War II or in the civil-rights movements in the United States and most recently in the Latin American struggles against fascism and imperialism.

4. *Does God Exist?* (New York: Doubleday, 1981), p. 243.
5. Ibid., p. 252.

It is interesting that today many people committed to the struggle for social justice see the possibility of a Marxism detached from its atheistic ideology. They stress the essential humanism of Marx's theory and see its atheistic component as only a passing phase. Christian Marxists, in fact, are appearing around the world. In Latin America there is a powerful movement of "Christians for socialism," while at a meeting of worker-priests of Modena in 1976 the "Internationale" was sung. Many other Christians, while reluctant to embrace Marxism—even in its more palatable democratic-socialist form—realize that the only answer to atheism is to show that belief in God can be joined with a commitment to emancipate the weary and heavily burdened. It must be proved in practice that religion doesn't have to be an opiate.

The great sociologist Max Weber (d. 1920) was also an atheist but saw the function of religion in very different terms from Marx. As "the first in practice to place sociology on a strictly scientific basis," Weber eschewed all preconceived doctrines or *a priori* syntheses.[6] He commanded an encyclopedic scholarship since unequaled by any other sociologist; and unlike Comte, Marx, Spencer and even Durkheim, Weber refused to mingle value judgments with his rigorous analyses.

Like Marx, Weber saw a close correlation between religious beliefs and social institutions. But instead of seeing religion as merely a reflection of economic relationships, he contended that at times religion helped to shape these relationships. This was the theme of his classic study *The Protestant Ethic and the Spirit of Capitalism,* which argued that Calvinism was the ethical motivating force that influenced the shape of modern capitalism. Weber noted how the otherworldly asceticism of the medieval Church was transformed by Protestantism into a this-worldly asceticism which is essential to capitalism. Like the medieval monk, the Calvinist was supposed to exercise rational self-discipline; but in contrast to the monastic ideal, he was to pursue it in the midst of the world. The medieval Church frowned on profit, but the Calvinist was taught that making a profit was one of the signs of his election, as long as the profit was put to good use. This meant putting it to work in the form of investments. Thus the Puritan was able to accumulate capital without cease.

The French sociologist and atheist Émile Durkheim (d. 1917) ranks with Max Weber as a seminal influence on the development of the sociology of religion. His most important contribution was his *Elementary*

6. Julien Freund, *The Sociology of Max Weber* (New York: Random House, 1968), p. 13.

*Forms of the Religious Life.* Its main thesis is that religion is nothing but a social phenomenon, i.e., a society's way of symbolizing its unity and the essential relationships between its members. The object of the cult was actually society itself; the god people worshiped was merely a symbol of their society, and their rites were means of reinforcing their social relationships.

Durkheim derived his theory largely from his study of totemism, which he supposed to be the most fundamental and primitive form of religion. The totem was any object—usually an animal or plant—which the people looked on as sacred. It could not be killed or eaten except on special occasions, and then the ceremony often took the form of a sacramental communion. Durkheim noted that the totem symbolized not only the clan's god but also the clan. Hence he concluded that the god of the clan had to be nothing else than the clan itself personified and represented to the imagination under the visible form of the animal or vegetable that served as the totem.

Durkheim saw religion as the permanent feature of all societies, since every society has the need to celebrate in rite and ceremony the collective sentiments and ideas that constitute its identity. But religion could no longer be taken seriously as a source of knowledge. Its explanations and interpretations of reality were prescientific and were now being superseded by science.

Durkheim's theory about the origin of religion did not win general acceptance. His totemistic approach was rejected as anthropologists showed that many primitive tribes, while possessing religion, did not practice totemism. It was also pointed out that the central Australian totemism on which Durkheim based his entire theory was not at all typical, and many of the features he regarded as characteristic of totemism are lacking in other totemic systems. In effect, Durkheim based his whole theory on a very limited amount of data and neglected other varieties of religious experience that did not harmonize with his theory. But his insistence on the social aspect of religion was a positive contribution and helped to stimulate further research on the way religious belief and practice are conditioned by social factors.

## IS RELIGION OBSOLETE?

One of the questions that concerns contemporary sociologists is whether religion is actually on the decline in the modern world. Marx thought religion was going to wither up, while Freud saw it as an illusion. Nietschze announced the "death of God." Some sociologists today agree and subscribe to the theory that society is being irreversibly secularized.

The Jesuit sociologist John Coleman sees a great need for clearly defined terms in the debate over secularization. He defines **"secular"** as referring to the area of life we can control or at least attempt to control, while the **sacred** he regards as the sphere of the mysterious, the awesome, the uncontrollable, the supremely important. **Secularism,** therefore, he defines as the denial that any such sacred sphere exists, the conviction that the universe is in no meaningful sense an expression or embodiment of purpose, the belief that it is unreasonable, other than anthropomorphically, to have toward the universe or its "ground" a relationship mediated by communication or by any other interchange of meanings—in other words, to have toward it a relationship in any sense interpersonal.[7]

Is secularism, thus defined, gaining ground in our society? Coleman reviews the vast literature on the subject and concludes that we simply can't say whether there has been a proportionate diminution of a sense of the sacred in modern society, "since no sociological study has carefully defined and measured enough of the parameters of complex social life in a comparative time perspective. Moreover, we lack any careful measure of the relative quantitative presence of the sacred and secular in earlier historical periods."[8]

Moreover, Coleman finds much else that is defective in these studies. Some of the authors use Church decline as a primary proof of secularization, without taking into account the rise of new religions and nonchurch forms of religiosity. Decline of the Church, as he says, should not be necessarily equated with decline of religion.

Others point to the declining influence of the Church on morality and political, social and economic behavior, while failing to consider the possibility of increased indirect influence of religion on individuals. Moreover the term secularization is used so loosely that it jumbles together issues

7. *Theological Studies,* 39 (December 1978), pp. 601–32.
8. Ibid., p. 602.

that should be clearly separated. Secularism is, for instance, often confused with secularity, which, unlike secularism, does not involve a denial of the sacred but merely involves the awareness that many areas of life are increasingly being brought under direct human control or manipulation.

So instead of trying to measure the degree of secularization, Coleman prefers to unpack the separate issues loaded into this term: such as the growth of pluralism, the loss of the Church's monopoly control over other institutional sectors of society, the rise of individual autonomy in religious matters, and privatization.

Coleman compares fifteen prominent sociologists' views on each of these issues and finds a good measure of agreement. According to these scholars, modern society has indeed become so pluralistic that religion today might be compared to a giant supermarket with unlimited consumer choice. It is also clear that no organized religion can any longer claim a monopoly over the individual religious impulse. People are also asserting a far greater amount of personal autonomy and freedom in their relation to the creeds and codes of the churches. It is especially clear that "Authoritarian religion based on rigid doctrinal or moral orthodoxy finds an inhospitable climate in the modern situation."[9] Finally, the majority agree that religion is becoming more privatized: people don't look to organized religion for the answers to questions of social and political morality.

But that all these trends mean that we are heading toward a more secularized society is what Coleman refuses to admit.

## GREELEY AND SECULARIZATION

Father Andrew Greeley made an interesting contribution to the debate over secularization in a study called *Religion: A Secular Theory*.[10] He contends that religious experience is widespread today—probably as widespread as it ever was. It need not have an explicit "God" content, he claims. In its primordial form it is simply a powerful propensity to hope. Moreover, this potential to be hopeful in face of the multiple outrages of existence must be grounded in hope-generating experiences. Greeley finds there is a wide variety of such experiences which refuel human hopefulness—experiences of being lifted out of oneself and becoming one with a "higher power," for instance. Such experiences have occurred to about

9. Ibid., p. 629.
10. New York: Macmillan, 1982.

one third of the American population, according to his research. Others have their power to hope refueled by less intense, more secular-type experiences: limit, or boundary, experiences, which occur when something happens that makes us realize how hemmed in we are on all sides by physiological, biological, psychological and sociological limitations and yet at the same time makes us wonder what might lie beyond the horizon of our boundaries. The limits make us aware of the gratuity, the *giftedness*, of our existence and stir up in us a sense of wonder about it all. With the wonder comes a hint of something beyond the horizon: a sense of otherness.

To experience grounds for hope, then, one does not have to undergo profound ecstatic experiences. "We need merely see a desert sunrise, the cold gleam of the sun on a frozen lake on a winter morning, a happy smile on a two-year-old, a touch of a friendly hand, the warmth of reconciliation —to both encounter our own limitations and also encounter a hint of gratuity which may go beyond those limitations."[11]

A second point Greeley makes is that this power to hope, this experience of grace, originates in the poetic, creative part of the imagination, or preconscious—which he locates somewhere between the rational and the unconscious. And it is out of this preconscious that flow the symbols, myths and metaphors that constitute the language of religion, "the strange world of meaning . . . which challenges, jars, disorients our everyday visions precisely by both showing us the limits to the everyday and projecting the limit character of the whole."[12]

The symbols *par excellence*, he says, are stories. Depending on one's religious heritage, one tends to articulate grace experiences in stories derived from that heritage. For Catholics this could mean drawing on their images of God, Jesus, Mary and Heaven, for instance, but the repertory of symbols we bring to our religious hope-generating experiences is greatly conditioned by our personal life, background and social experiences. Thus Catholics with warm and happy family relationships will tend to have warm, loving and happy images of God and Jesus. Mary, too, as a symbol might encode a "childhood experience of a mother who was warm, affectionate, devout, but also deeply involved in the family decision-making processes."[13]

God is a symbol of the "Other," which we encounter in our renewing

11. Ibid., p. 25.
12. Ibid., p. 44.
13. Ibid., p. 86.

grace experiences and limit experiences: ". . . images of otherness and symbolization of the Other vary enormously in the human condition precisely because there is such a vast range of possible experiences and of humans who experience."[14] It is not necessary to articulate one's hope-renewing experiences through images of God. Some people reject the philosophical concept of God and yet have encountered otherness and lead hope-filled lives.

14. Ibid., p. 73.

# 2

## The Question: Is God There?

The question of God's existence has haunted people from the beginning, no doubt. We have just seen how some of the great thinkers since the Enlightenment have wrestled with the problem. In our own day, the controversy over God was heated up by the appearance of Gabriel Vahanian's book *The Death of God*. His thesis was that the term "God" is no longer a meaningful factor in human concerns. The debate he opened up drew many writers into the arena. One of these was the Anglican bishop John A. T. Robinson, whose *Honest to God* called for a drastic rethinking of our understanding of God in the light of present knowledge, both sacred and secular. Three main types of atheism can be discerned among those who entered into the debate on the anti-God side: an **intellectual atheism** based on modern philosophy; a **protest atheism,** derived from Feuerbach, which insisted on the incompatibility of belief in God with human freedom and fulfillment; and a **pessimistic atheism,** which saw in the enormity of evil prevalent in the world an overwhelming argument against the existence of God. Adhering to one or other of these positions were such men as Paul van Buren, William Hamilton and Richard Rubenstein.

Just how much influence all their books had on the ordinary person is hard to say. The average American, for instance, was not converted to atheism, as a Gallup poll of 1975 shows. In fact, only 6 percent of all Americans questioned claimed to be atheists or agnostics; 94 percent believed in God and 69 percent in life after death—about the same percentages as in 1948. A similar poll in Germany showed nearly the same results.[1]

But while many pay lip service to the existence of God, it seems true that many have experienced the **death of God** insofar as traditional images of God no longer make sense for them. They feel God's absence, rather than His presence. And with this eclipse of God in their hearts has come the loss of any sense of meaning in their lives. No doubt, some of this is due to the apocalyptic events of our century: Auschwitz and Hiroshima, and the long shadows they have cast over the spiritual landscape. Images of death camps, hydrogen bombs, innocent children sprayed with napalm, the horrors of famine and disease striking down thousands of infants in poverty-stricken quarters of the globe—all this torments people and makes them question the Christian concept of an all-loving, good and merciful God. As a result, their prayers are filled with doubt and often seem empty and hypocritical. With Job they say:

> Behold I go forward, but he is not there;
>   and backward, but I cannot perceive him;
> on the left hand I seek him, but I cannot behold him;
>   I turn to the right hand, but I cannot see
>   him.[2]

One way of looking at this crisis of faith is seeing it as the final breakdown of the biblical worldview of a two-story universe. In this view, which is so deeply ingrained in all of Western religious thought, reality was divided into "earth" and "Heaven," or that part of reality one could experience and to some extent control and that part which lay beyond the senses but in some ways was more real than earth because God dwelt there with hosts of angels and directed earthly affairs: bringing good and bad weather, sickness and health, happiness and unhappiness. After being gradually undermined for several centuries by accumulating scientific knowledge, this cozy picture has all but vanished from human consciousness.

If we can't think of God, then, as some kind of absolute monarch ruling the universe from above, how should we think of Him? What meaning can we or should we give to the term "God"? If we can't speak in the old, dualistic terms, can we still speak of an ultimate reality that is somehow "beyond" that which is directly given in our experience?

1. Hans Küng, op. cit., p. 576.
2. RSV 23:8–9.

Gordon Kaufman approaches the problem from the standpoint of our experience of what he calls the ultimate limit. He notes how all of us are constantly running up against limits, which are basically of four kinds: a) external **physical** limitation caused by material objects which can restrict our activities; b) **organic** limitations we experience when we suffer illness, weakness and exhaustion; c) **personal** limitations in our dealings with others insofar as their ideas and intentions often run counter to our own; d) **normative** constraints and restrictions proceeding from our awareness of moral and aesthetic considerations such as the distinction between good and bad, beautiful and ugly. Through this experience of our own finiteness we become aware—in a rather complex process by which we generalize the immediate and particular experiences of constraints upon self into the "experience of finitude"—of an ultimate limit over against the self.

How, then, can we conceptualize this ultimate limit? If we are to do so at all, it will have to be with the aid of one or more of the actually experienced finite limiters: a physical entity in the case of physical limitations, a moral entity in the case of normative restrictions, etc. The most appropriate model to use, however, Kaufman contends, is the experience of personal limiting as known in the interaction of personal wills.

For as Kaufman says, "Though each of the limiters interprets certain dimensions of our experience significantly, none comes [so] directly to grips with our distinctive experience as persons in communities, as conscious, active, deciding, purposing beings living in a symbolical world that provides the context and the possibility for continuous communication and intercourse with others."[3]

It must be stressed that this choice of using the personal limiter as the analogical model for understanding the ultimate limit is an option of religious faith. The only experience we have is of our bare finiteness; it is a decision of faith to interpret this experience in terms of a personal limiter. "The encounter with God will involve both the 'experience' of our finitude and the faith-interpretation through which this limitedness is apprehended as owing to an active will over against us."[4]

Kaufman is not here trying to prove the existence of God. He is merely trying to show that we can use the term "God" in a meaningful way without presupposing the outdated concept of God found in the mythological two-story-universe picture sacred to Christian tradition. The con-

3. Gordon Kaufman, *God the Problem* (Cambridge, Mass.: Harvard University Press, 1972), p. 60.
4. Ibid., p. 69.

cept of the ultimate limit when interpreted personalistically points to a dynamic acting reality beyond the limit. Just as in our interaction with other persons we presuppose a reality—the active center of the self—which transcends that which we immediately perceive.

Kaufman concludes, ". . . I have attempted here to show that 'God-language' has its roots in concrete (secular) experience and that its cognitive meaningfulness can be defended, even granting the premises of 'secular man'; whether it is true or not is another question. Our analysis has brought us into a position from which we can see what would be required if the truth of this claim were to be affirmed. However, only on the ground that God had in fact revealed himself could it be claimed he exists; only if there were and is some sort of movement from beyond the Limit to us, making known to us through the medium of the Limit the reality of that which lies beyond, could we be in a position to speak of such reality at all; only if God actually 'spoke' to man could we know there is a God."[5] God as the ultimate limit, God as He is Himself, is thus profound mystery and completely beyond our grasp or comprehension.

But what about the meaning we have given to the term "God"? Both believer and unbeliever alike can agree that "God," in our culture, is a word with a rather definite meaning; it is the product of many generations. It refers to the One Who is Creator of the world, Who by His providence guides and sustains and directs all things to their intended purpose. "God" means the Lord, the One Whom we must serve and obey, our final End and Source of eternal happiness. He is also the Father Who loves His children, faithful, forgiving and at the same time absolutely just. For the believer, He is the most real of all reality, the Agent on whom all else depends. A believer finds in the symbol "God" the means of seeing life as a purposeful experience and a way of viewing the world as imbued with a personal presence. It enables one to feel at home in the world insofar as it is ruled with order and purpose. For the believer, "God is the most adequate and vivid symbol or image of ordering and orienting life."[6] On all this, believer and unbeliever should be able to agree.

But whether any reality exists that corresponds to this symbol is another question. As long as one stays on a purely metaphysical or speculative level it seems impossible that we will ever be able to answer this question with any certainty. Philosophers and theologians have argued the point for

5. Ibid., p. 71.
6. Ibid., p. 94.

centuries and no proofs have ever been adduced that satisfy everyone. God escapes our every effort to search Him out.

However, that is not the final word. In this world as it is we are not mere spectators with the luxury of pondering the question of God as neutral observers. Life forces us to act, and the way we act presupposes a certain outlook on life. We can make our decisions on the assumption that man is just an animal with no ultimate purpose in the world. Our behavior will then be shaped in a certain manner. Or we can act on some other basis or assumption. The point is that we can't avoid espousing one or another worldview that is implicit in our actions. "We have to stake ourselves, our lives and all that is dear to us, on one or another view and act and work from one day to the next in the terms it lays down for us."[7]

In this light, then, we see that God can be taken as a symbol for an understanding of life and action that is based on the assumption that our existence here has meaning and purpose. Belief in God enables us to "view the world and [ourselves] in such a way as to make action and morality ultimately (metaphysically) meaningful."[8] The question about God, then, is not primarily whether He exists, but whether the symbol of God is not the most appropriate one to anchor our life on. What other symbol is so charged with psychic energy? What other symbol—especially God conceived as absolutely loving and self-giving—is so potentially fruitful?

All of this does not mean that we are saying God is merely an imaginary construction, a convenient fiction to overcome existential despair. The commitment to God involved in this approach is a commitment to God as a reality, but verification of the belief is not based on speculative arguments but on how belief in God offers the best answer to the question, How can I find meaning in an apparently absurd world? In other words, the truth involved is a truth of life. The question we should ask, then, is, Is this symbol the most apt means of interpreting the world as we experience it, or is there another, fundamental paradigm "more adequate for grasping the world so as to enhance and deepen life"?[9]

7. Ibid., p. 104.
8. Ibid., p. 109.
9. Ibid., p. 99.

## THE CLASSIC ARGUMENTS

The Catholic Church has always insisted that natural reason can demonstrate the existence of God, and Thomas Aquinas devised five arguments to prove God's existence which have dominated all subsequent Catholic thought on the question. The first Vatican Council reiterated this tradition in asserting that God could be known from rational reflection on creation. At the Second Vatican, the bishops likewise maintained that God "provides men with constant evidence of himself in created realities."[10] However, neither council explicated the actual process by which such a natural knowledge of God is attained, though it seems to imply that some form of conceptual proofs are possible. Nevertheless few Catholic theologians today favor the kind of conceptual arguments found in the classical proofs for God's existence.

These are generally considered in four forms: the **cosmological proof,** which appeals to the principle of causality to explain the existence of motion and change in the world and then posits a first cause, since the idea of an infinite regression of causes is an absurdity; the **teleogical proof,** based on the existence of order and finality in the world, which can be explained only by supposing an infinite intelligent being capable of creating an orderly, purposeful universe; the **ontological argument,** which claims that existence is a necessary attribute of the idea of God as the most perfect and necessary being—an idea that is supposedly innate in human beings; and the **moral proof,** which claims that man's intrinsically moral and goal-oriented nature demands a goal that corresponds to his desire for the highest and ultimate good, which can only be God.

In *Does God Exist?*, Hans Küng raises some questions about these proofs. After Kant, he says, can we any longer argue from what is given empirically in the world of phenomena to "things in themselves"? Are not these arguments, rather, ingenious logical constructs, abstract and opaque, without convincing force for the average person? Proving the existence of God, moreover, seems to reduce God to just another object, like a distant star—"Is a God objectified and proved in this way still God at all?"[11]

If we simply postulate the possibility that the universe itself is the absolute, the infinite and the eternal, how can we exclude an infinite

10. "Dogmatic Constitution on Divine Revelation," 3; *Documents of Vatican II.*
11. Küng, op. cit., p. 532.

regression of causes? In dealing with the incomprehensible infinite, how can we say whether it is infinite emptiness or infinite fullness, God or nothingness? How can one justifiably argue that because we can have an idea of a perfect, necessary being that therefore such a being exists in reality?

In view of such concerns, Küng prefers to build a rational argument for the existence of God on the basis of his concept of **fundamental trust.** As he explains, it is possible for a human being to say yes or no to reality, to life. For no one can deny that reality is fundamentally ambiguous. On the one hand there is life: growth, beauty, meaning; on the other hand, death: decay, chaos and absurdity. There is no compelling reason for choosing trust over mistrust. I experience the reasonableness of trust only in the very act of trusting: ". . . in the midst of all the real menace of the nullity of being, I experience being and with it the fundamental justification of my trust."[12] Reality comes to me as a gift; it is only when I commit myself to it trustingly that I get it back filled with meaning. But trust is not a once-for-all decision; it is a task that must be constantly taken up anew. One is constantly faced with the threat of meaninglessness and anxiety.

Fundamental trust begins for a human being in the arms of his mother. Psychologists, in fact, have shown how much difference a loving mother makes for the future attitudes of the child. A child separated from his mother in infancy and left with uncaring people often suffers devastating psychical and physical consequences. The "deterioration in children is directly related to the length of the period of withdrawal of love to which the child is exposed."[13] On the other hand, the child who has a secure bond with his mother begins to explore the world and to open himself spontaneously to others and to reality. But as one matures, one's naïve trust must become the critical trust in reality of the now independent adult. Most crucial in this regard is the role of other human beings. One needs not only an "it," one needs a personal "thou"; one needs someone else to whom one can relate in a trusting way, someone who can offer, and in turn receive, love, understanding, loyalty and freedom, if one is to maintain one's sense of trust in uncertain reality as a whole.

What, then, is the connection between fundamental trust and religious faith? As the psychologist Erik H. Erikson says, there are three possibilities: a fundamental trust that comes from **religious faith,** a fundamental

12. Ibid., p. 449.
13. Ibid., p. 455.

trust **without religious faith,** and a religious faith **without fundamental trust.** But, on the whole, religious faith does help to foster and promote fundamental trust.

When all this is said, however, there still remains the question, What is the basis for fundamental trust? since reality still remains uncertain reality, more unreal than real, without evident ground or support. As Küng says, reality appears to be a riddle; founding, but itself unfounded; supporting, but itself unsupported; pointing the way, but itself without a goal. What, then, is the source of reality?

The hypothesis that God exists would solve this riddle. For if God exists, then groundless reality would not be ultimately groundless, because God would be the primal ground of all reality. Likewise, if God exists, evolving reality would not be ultimately without purpose, since God would be its goal. If God exists, we could assume "with absolutely reasonable fundamental trust that in all disunity there is ultimately a hidden unity, in all meaninglessness ultimately a hidden meaningfulness, in all worthlessness, ultimately a hidden value of reality."[14] There would also be an answer to the question of why reality appears so unreal, grounding but so ultimately groundless, so lacking in ultimate meaning, evolving but without ultimate aim. It would be because uncertain reality itself is not God, "[b]ecause the self, society, the world, cannot be identified with their primal ground, primal support and primal goal, with their primal source, primal meaning and primal value, with being itself."[15]

The same can be said for the uncertainty of my existence: if God exists, in spite of the menace of meaninglessness, my life is ultimately meaningful, because God is its ultimate meaning, and in spite of sin and failure, I can have hope, because God is my all-embracing hope.

But how do we move from the hypothesis of God to the reality of God? We first have to admit that it is possible to deny God. Atheism cannot be refuted rationally. But neither can it be rationally demonstrated. Our experience of the radical uncertainty of reality can be interpreted in a nihilistic sense, but it doesn't have to be. It is just as reasonable to affirm the existence of a primal ground, a primal support, a primal goal of that which otherwise appears grounding but groundless itself, supporting but unsupported itself. Belief or disbelief, in the final analysis, as Küng says, rests on a decision. Either way, we are faced with a risk, a venture, a leap. Basically

14. Ibid., p. 567.
15. Ibid.

it is a decision for or against reality as such. And not to choose is, in fact, a choice: one has chosen not to choose.

But it is not a matter of indifference how we choose. For to deny God is to rob fundamental trust of all justification. Uncertain reality is left without any grounding, support or ultimate meaning. Atheism "lacks not perhaps all rationality, but certainly a radical rationality, which lack, of course, it often disguises by a rationalistic but essentially irrational trust in human reason."[16] In a world without meaning, the atheist is exposed to the menace of doubt, despair and ultimate abandonment. He or she finds no answer to questions they cannot avoid: What ought I to do? Why and to whom am I ultimately responsible? Is there any point to love and sacrifice, of suffering and sin? Why am I on this earth? Why should I hope? What sustains me amid all the hollowness? How do I get the courage to face life and the courage to face death?

But to affirm God is to know why we can trust reality. It is to affirm a primal ground instead of groundlessness, a primal goal instead of aimlessness. To affirm God is by no means irrational. In the very act of affirming, I experience the reasonableness of my own reason—as the primal source and primal meaning of all reality manifests itself insofar as God is perceived as the guarantor of the rationality of human reason. Belief in God is experienced not as rational but as superrational; not as the conclusion of logic but as a relationship of trust and one that also involves relationships with our fellow human beings—for without the experience of acceptance by others, how can we experience acceptance by God? It is not a decision made once and for all, but has to be constantly risked and constantly renewed as doubts continue to assail us.

16. Ibid., p. 571.

# 3

## Changing Concepts of Revelation

Revelation is the fundamental problem in modern theology; it is at the main intersection of most of the questions we are considering. A history of the concept is virtually a history of theology, at least in modern times.

Many definitions of the term have been given, as we will see in what follows. But, in general, revelation stands for some communication by God of what we could not otherwise know about Himself, His purpose and His plan for us. It also involves an invitation by God to enter into a personal covenant with Him.

For a Christian theologian, any attempt to define the nature of revelation has to begin with the various concepts of revelation that can be gleaned from an analysis of the Old and New Testaments. There is no attempt to present a systematic theology of revelation, but we do find certain concepts of revelation. The New Testament builds on the Old Testament concept of God as One Who freely manifests His will through a history in which He intervenes in the life of His chosen people and sends messengers to them to interpret His actions on their behalf. The New Testament presents Jesus Christ as the definitive revealer, who by his words and deeds announced the good news of God's redemptive will toward all mankind. It also proclaims the role of the Holy Spirit in bringing the Church to a fuller understanding of the revelation manifest in Jesus Christ.

The Fathers of the Church did not treat of revelation systematically, but there is an implicit theology of revelation in many of their writings.

**Augustine,** the greatest of the Western Fathers, sometimes spoke of revelation as the inner light with which God illumines the soul to enable it to accept the truths contained in Scripture and the preaching of the Church. **Thomas Aquinas,** the most influential medieval genius, followed Augustine in supposing a divine interior illumination to make the mind receptive to revelation. But, unlike Augustine, he did not ordinarily refer to this illumination as revelation. Thanks to Aquinas, the concept of revelation was given a much more objective reference and indeed was equated with a body of knowledge that God has communicated to man, much of it supposedly information about God Himself but also including even many tidbits of the history of Israel and the first generation of Christians. Aquinas, in fact, distinguished between two kinds of knowledge: *natural truths,* which we could discover by the use of our unaided reason, and *revealed truths,* which were communicated to us by God. Some of the truths in the latter category could also be known by reason, but the essential truths of revelation could be known only by faith. God reveals some truths accessible to reason for the sake of our salvation and because the majority of persons would otherwise never obtain knowledge of them. As to the means God uses to communicate with people, Aquinas manifests a certain subtlety in their enumeration—including "historical events, symbolic actions, dreams, visions, ecstatic states, and purely intellectual intuitions."[1]

For Aquinas, the majority of men have no immediate access to revelation. They receive it only through the preaching of salvation.

The controversies associated with the **Reformation** pitted **Luther, Calvin** and their adherents against the Catholic theologians and the official doctrine of the Catholic Church—as defined at Trent. Both Luther and Calvin refused to identify revelation strictly with the Scriptures, although Calvin linked the two closely together, even to the point of seeing Scripture as verbally inspired. Both theologians also rejected tradition as a channel of revelation, in opposition to the Catholic teaching (later defined at Trent) that the message of the Gospel is also contained in unwritten traditions that have come down to us from the apostles. Both Protestant and Catholic theologians excessively intellectualized the concept of revelation, which they understood as almost exclusively bound up with propositions.

1. Avery Dulles, *Revelation Theology* (New York: Herder & Herder, 1969), p. 43.

## RATIONALISTS AND LIBERAL PROTESTANTS

The medieval theologians and their successors at the time of the Reformation made a distinction between truths knowable by reason and those knowable only by faith. With the arrival of the Enlightenment, in the seventeenth century, confidence in the power of human reason prompted many thinkers to deny the need for any revelation at all. The most they would concede was that God might have revealed certain truths already knowable by reason but only obscurely recognized by men because of their intellectual sloth and lack of sufficient education. The most representative of this school were the Deists and the rationalists, men like Matthew Tindal, whose book *Christianity as Old as the Creation* (1730) taught that everything worthwhile and uncorrupted in Christianity was naturally knowable and, in fact, already found in Confucius.

In the encounter with the rationalism of the Enlightenment, Catholic theologians for the most part continued to hold to the medieval concept of revelation as the supernatural and infallible communication of propositional truths. But Protestant theologians, who for various reasons were more in touch with modern culture, began to modify their doctrine and to blur the distinction between reason and faith (or revelation). The "father of modern Protestant theology," Friedrich Schleiermacher (d. 1834), was most influential in this regard. He rooted revelation in the consciousness of one's complete dependence on God, a matter much more of feeling than of intellectual perception. Christianity was simply the highest form of religion, only set off from others insofar as its founder, Jesus Christ, had a unique sense of his unity with God. In consequence, revelation, for Schleiermacher, was not embodied in doctrines and dogmas, while theology amounted only to commentary on our consciousness of God.

Schleiermacher's contemporary Georg W. F. Hegel (d. 1831), on the other hand, took a more intellectualist approach to revelation. He saw Christianity as the highest expression of the religious consciousness and regarded its dogmas as in some sense revealed. However, since these dogmas were only tentative and symbolic, they would eventually be replaced by philosophy. Hegel thus completely subordinated faith to reason.

Schleiermacher's followers were legion. Two of the most important, Albrecht Ritschl (d. 1889) and Auguste Sabatier (d. 1901), insisted, as he did, on the primacy of experience and left little room for an objective revelation that finds expression in dogmas and doctrines. For Ritschl, the only function of the Gospels is to trigger in us the same religious experience enjoyed by Jesus and his followers. For Sabatier, revelation was practically identified with prayer—with the feeling of God's presence within us. Every dogmatic expression of this feeling is merely symbolic and subject to the law of evolution. Dogmas can disappear—the eternity of hell, for instance—or change—as the concept of miracle or the Trinity—and new dogmas can appear.

## MODERNISTS AND PIUS X

The Catholic **modernists** were a small group of priests and intellectuals who made a great effort to bridge the huge gap between Catholicism and modern thought. They borrowed freely from the liberal Protestant theologians mentioned above and, like them, emphasized the primacy of experience. For **Alfred Loisy** (d. 1940), revelation was not an unchanging deposit of truths but a continuously evolving perception of our relationship to God based on religious experience. **George Tyrrell** (d. 1909), too, insisted on the experiential component of revelation while attributing only a tentative and relative value to dogmas. Equating revelation with a body of defined propositions, he thought, is to confuse revelation with theology. In his system, the authority of the Church as an interpreter of revelation is stripped of all infallibility.

The first Vatican Council issued in 1870 a document on revelation in response to numerous attacks on the traditional concept. The Council rejected the rationalist approach of Hegel and others, which allowed human reason the preeminent role in discovering divine truths. Instead, the Council upheld the concept of a supernatural revelation, which could be appropriated only by faith. At the same time, it also rejected the sentimentalist view of revelation as originating in our emotional experience of the divine. The proper object of revelation, the Council said, is the mysteries hidden in God and proposed as divinely revealed by His Church. Revelation is viewed as contained in the deposit of faith, a complex of propositions which are found in the holy books and in tradition and which express the mystery of our salvation.

It was this teaching that Pope Pius X renewed in 1907 in his condemnation of the modernists. He drew a simple and clear line between the Catholic position and the various theories of the liberal Protestants and modernists. Revelation, he said, is not the product of the evolving human consciousness or a feeling of dependence on God springing from the depths of the subconscious, but an objective collection of supernatural truths that was completed with the apostles. Against the idea that dogmas could evolve, he maintained that dogmas could not change their meaning and receive a different sense from that given them by the Church in the beginning.

The intervention of Pius X definitely settled the modernist crisis as far as the Catholic Church was concerned, but it did little to provide satisfactory answers to the questions Loisy and Tyrrell and the others were wrestling with.

One of the unfortunate legacies of the antimodernist crusade touched off by Pius X was to further isolate Catholic theologians from modern thought. For several generations, they simply continued to rehash the medieval Scholastic concept of revelation bequeathed to them by the first Vatican Council and to ignore the challenges presented by such disciplines as biblical criticism and history. Their Scholastic categories of thought seemed abstract and lifeless and failed to do justice to the tremendous depth and variety of the biblical understanding of revelation. It's not surprising, then, that a number of young Catholic theologians began to search for alternatives to the Scholastic approach and to develop a theology of revelation more in accord with the concrete realities of salvation history as proclaimed in the Bible and more open to the mystery of God's self-communication in Christ.

## REVELATION AND VATICAN II

It was these men who prepared the way for the updated Catholic concept of revelation found in the decrees of the Second Vatican Council. They broke with the static world of immutable essences of Scholastic theology and drew their inspiration from the Bible, the Fathers of the Church, and the liturgy. In their writings they moved away from the concept of revelation as primarily a deposit of immutable formulas and viewed it primarily as God revealing Himself in a series of singular, historical acts making up the history of salvation which culminates in the mystery of Jesus Christ.

The Second Vatican Council ratified this new theology of revelation in its constitution *Dei Verbum* (1965), in which it states that "revelation is realized by deeds and words having an inner unity: the deeds wrought by God in the history of salvation manifest and confirm the teaching and realities signified by the words, while the words proclaim the deeds and clarify the mystery contained in them."[2]

In the teaching of the Second Vatican Council, revelation is no longer regarded as primarily a set of doctrines but, rather, as "a person who comes to us in grace and love."[3] And the Council's view of revelation is "concrete rather than abstract, historical rather than philosophical, biblical rather than scholastic, ecumenical rather than controversial, interpersonal rather than propositional."[4] In its later pastoral constitution *Gaudium et Spes,* the Council also implicitly affirmed that revelation continues in every age.

Thus instead of viewing revelation as primarily a deposit of timeless truths, Catholic theologians began to see revelation on the model of our knowledge of other persons. This personalist approach to understanding revelation developed out of a new understanding of the way we come to know other persons. Thinkers such as Søren Kierkegaard (d. 1855) and Martin Buber (d. 1965) were most influential in this effort. They showed how getting to know another person was a unique kind of knowledge. It involves encounters in which the other person discloses something about himself, his ideas, his plans, hopes, fears and loves. One cannot compel the other person to disclose himself; he must do it freely; and one must be open to the other and trust that the disclosure is an honest and authentic self-revelation. Even though one could get to know something about the other person through other means, such as inquiries of those who know him, there is really no substitute for a personal encounter. Another point is that even though the other person discloses himself fully, much about him will always remain mysterious.

Applying this personalism to the question of how God reveals Himself to us, we find a number of analogies. The Bible tells how God, through word and act, reveals to us His plans, His nature and His love. He does so freely, and His self-disclosures occur in a history of meetings and encounters with us—especially in the history of the old and new Israel. On our part, we must be open and trusting if we are to gain a personal knowledge of Him. We might learn something about Him through study of His creation, but this would not be personal knowledge. And, as in

---

2. *Dogmatic Constitution on Divine Revelation,* 2.
3. Avery Dulles, op. cit., p. 157.
4. Ibid.

human encounters, much about Him will always remain mysterious even after He reveals Himself to us.[5]

Owen Thomas, professor at the Episcopal Theological School, Cambridge, Massachusetts, points out some important differences between the knowledge we receive in revelation and other kinds of knowledge, especially scientific knowledge. Scientific knowledge calls for an attitude of disinterestedness and neutrality, while revelation demands the opposite. In scientific knowledge, we master the subject, but revelation masters us, insofar as it leads us to submit to God. Scientific knowledge changes our understanding of the world, but revelation seeks to change us. Ordinary knowledge does not of itself lead us to community and in fact may even isolate us from others, while revelation aims to bring us into community with God and neighbor.[6]

In disclosing Himself to us, God has used history as His main vehicle. The main reason for this appears to be the fact that people reveal more about themselves in singular actions and unusual situations than in regular and uniform activity. Also, "personality is more fully revealed in dealing with persons than with things. Thus it might be expected that the most fully revealing area of God's activity will be human history."[7]

The Old Testament shows how the people of Israel saw their history as revelatory of God. It records the mighty acts of God on their behalf. Mightiest of all was their deliverance from Egypt—the foundation of their covenant and their law. God's acts of mercy and judgment are interpreted by His words, which He communicates to His people through the mouths of His prophets. In this way, God reveals Himself, His plan for Israel, His offer of salvation and His requirement of repentance and obedience. But the revelation ends on an incomplete note, a note of promise, of fulfillment. The one who would fulfill the promise is only hinted at.

In the New Testament, revelation is brought through Jesus Christ, in whom word and act are united. It is most fitting that the definitive revelation be embodied in a person, since, as one theologian remarks, ". . . a personal God can reveal himself adequately and fully only in and through the life of a person and human persons can fully understand only that which is personal."[8]

5. For an interesting treatment of this point, cf. Gordon Kaufman, *God the Problem* (Cambridge, Mass.: Harvard University Press, 1972), pp. 160f.
6. O. Thomas, *Introduction to Theology* (Cambridge, Mass.: Greeno Hadden, 1973).
7. Ibid., p. 23.
8. Ibid., p. 24.

## PROTESTANT AND CATHOLIC CONVERGENCE

Historically, Protestants and Catholics have had substantial differences, as we have seen in regard to the nature of revelation, on such connected issues as the nature of biblical inspiration, inerrancy, the role of tradition and the authority of the Church in the interpretation of Scripture.

Recently, however, there has been a gradual convergence of views on these matters, as in so many other areas of Church doctrine. One has only to compare the statement of the Second Vatican Council on divine revelation, *Dei Verbum*, with equivalent statements recently issued by the Faith and Order Commission of the World Council of Churches, to realize how much progress has been accomplished.

On the matter of the **divine inspiration** of the Scriptures, for instance, Vatican II dropped the Catholic Church's previous Scholastic explanation of it as a divine impulse affecting the intellect, will and executive faculties of the sacred writers and simply takes a functional view of inspiration in terms of the canonical books that are held to be inspired. This is not far from the view of the Louvain 1971 Faith and Order statement, which sees the authority of the Bible as manifest in its religious value for the community and then deduces inspiration as the source of that authority.

Likewise, on the question of **inerrancy**, the Second Vatican Council states, ". . . the books of Scripture must be acknowledged as teaching firmly, faithfully, and without error that truth which God wanted put into the sacred writings for the sake of our salvation."[9] This leaves room for the more liberal-minded to admit error in the Bible where this does not affect its essential message. The Louvain Faith and Order statement does not directly treat of inerrancy, but while indicating basic inerrancy it seems to allow for incidental misstatements.[10]

So while fundamentalists continue to uphold the inerrancy of the Bible in all its parts, Roman Catholic and mainline Protestant theologians allow much latitude. Oswald Loretz, a prominent Catholic theologian, speaks for many Protestant and Catholic colleagues when he argues that the Bible is true in the Hebrew sense of being reliable and faithful, but not in

9. *Dogmatic Constitution on Divine Revelation*, 11.
10. Avery Dulles, "Scripture: Recent Protestant and Catholic Views," *Theology Today* 37 (April 1980), p. 13.

the Greek, scientific sense, which demands conformity between statements and the facts they refer to.[11]

As to the question of how Scripture is related to **tradition**, this was one of the major differences between Protestant and Catholic, inasmuch as Catholics understood the Council of Trent to mean that Scripture and tradition constituted two separate sources of revelation. The Protestants, on the other hand, remained faithful to Luther and Calvin's claim that *Scripture alone* was sufficient. But Vatican II refused to affirm that there are "two sources" or that some revealed truths are found in tradition alone. At the same time, there has been a growing ecumenical consensus that the Protestant slogan *Scripture alone* is inadequate. As the Second Vatican Council put it, "It is not from Scripture alone that the Church draws her certainty about everything which has been revealed."[12] Rather, the Council sees a dynamic relation between Scripture and tradition as tradition hands on the Word of God, which is indivisibly present both in Scripture and tradition. This disposition to transcend the historic dispute was matched by the Montreal Conference on Faith and Order in 1963, which acknowledged the importance of Tradition (with a capital *T)* as the Word of God while recognizing that the particular traditions of individual churches could be in error.

Finally, in the matter of the role of Church authority in the interpretation of Scripture, Protestants and Catholics at first sight seem to differ significantly. For Catholics hold, according to the Second Vatican Council, that "an authentic teaching office plays a special role in the explanation and proclamation of the written word of God."[13] But as Avery Dulles points out, it seems doubtful that the magisterium has ever "issued an irreformable decision regarding the literal meaning of any given text," so Catholic exegetes enjoy freedom to pursue their craft in terms of their own methodology if properly deferential to official teaching, while Protestant scholars as a rule are greatly influenced by their own confessional standards and traditions.[14]

11. Ibid., p. 20.
12. *Dogmatic Constitution on Divine Revelation*, 9.
13. *Decree on Ecumenism*, 21.
14. Avery Dulles, "Scripture," *supra*, p. 26.

# 4

## Faith: Possible Today?

Faith is a multifaceted, extremely complex reality. Basic to any understanding of it is the common human experience of putting one's trust in someone. This act of faith in someone, if it is genuine, demands that we recognize the value of the other person as a "thou." It is always a response to the other person, who is perceived as inviting us to respond. It does not demand rational justification but is founded in an intuitive sense of communion with the other on a deeper level. Faith in the other person involves the desire to deepen the relationship, to know the other person better by speaking and listening in a spirit of openness and trust and love.

### BIBLICAL FAITH

The biblical understanding of faith is analogous to this common human experience. Israel is invited to say yes to God's offer of the covenant. Abraham is the great model: He "obeyed the call to set out for a country that was the inheritance given to him and his descendants, and . . . he set out without knowing where he was going."[1] And as Romans says, "Though it seemed Abraham's hope could not be fulfilled, he hoped and he believed, and through doing so he did become the father of many nations. . . ."[2]

1. JB Heb. 11:8.
2. Rom. 4:18.

Like Abraham, Israel is called to a personal relationship with God and to experience a concrete history full of joy and hope and pain and sorrow. Israel often wavers as her hopes are dashed by disaster and exile, but she is constantly called back by the prophets to renew her faith. Israel learns that faith means saying yes to God, acknowledging His goodness, wisdom, kindness and above all His fidelity to His promises.

Jesus is born into this community of faith, and he is often pictured as demanding faith from his hearers. In the stories of his healings and his exorcisms, Jesus often declares, "Your faith has saved you." In this context, we see that the faith Jesus praises is, in no small part, trust in the fact that God is indeed active in his ministry. Jesus demands faith in himself only in the sense that people are to recognize that what he says and does is the work of God. The leper, for instance, is cleansed because he approaches Jesus with a sure sentiment of faith: "If you want to, . . . you can cure me."[3] And Jesus tells the woman with the hemorrhage, ". . . your faith has restored you to health. . . ."[4] He tells his hearers they must have faith in the limitless power of God—what is impossible with man is possible with God.

It is only after the Resurrection that faith focuses on the person, the preaching and the claim of Jesus. Then the yes to God becomes a yes to Jesus. As Paul says, "If your lips confess that Jesus is Lord and if you believe in your heart that God raised him from the dead, then you will be saved."[5] This faith that persons are asked to put in God or Christ is not just an intellectual assent to a doctrine, but a vital, personal commitment of the whole person to Christ that influences all his relationships to God, to others and to the world. It means commitment also to the community of believers who worship together as well as obedience to the moral imperatives that flow from incorporation into the spirit of the community.

## CATHOLIC TRADITION

The Catholic tradition has tended to emphasize faith as a kind of knowledge, a spiritual illumination—an approach favored by many of the Fathers of the Church and also by the Scholastic theologians. Augustine, for instance, taught that the soul is blinded by the effects of sin and must

3. Mk. 1:40.
4. Mk. 5:34.
5. Rom. 10:9.

be illuminated from above. Faith, then, is a kind of mystical contemplation of God achieved through relative detachment from the world. Aquinas carried on this tradition with his frequent descriptions of faith as an inner light of the soul. For Bernard Lonergan, a twentieth-century Thomist, faith is "the knowledge born of religious love."

Closely connected with this intellectualist understanding of faith is the Catholic view which focuses on faith as assent to a determined body of doctrine, of believing whatever the Church teaches in the name of God.

## LUTHER AND CALVIN

The element of personal trust was once more emphasized by Martin Luther, who reacted consciously against the Scholastic intellectualist understanding of faith and derived from Paul's letters his doctrine of justification by faith alone. "Faith," he wrote, "is a living and unshakable confidence, a belief in the grace of God so assured that a man would die a thousand deaths for its sake."[6]

Calvin's doctrine of faith closely resembled Luther's. Calvin defined faith as "a firm and certain knowledge of God's beneficence towards us, founded upon the truth of the freely given promise in Christ both revealed to our minds and sealed upon our hearts through the Holy Spirit."[7]

This classical Protestant approach to faith remains very prominent today especially in the conservative evangelical churches and in the charismatic communities of prayer.

As Dulles says, both the Catholic and the Protestant views of faith tended to undervalue commitment—which in the eyes of contemporary theologians is the most important aspect. Thus Ian T. Ramsey holds that faith originates in disclosure experiences in which the two elements of discernment and commitment are inextricably interwoven.

Like Ramsey, Dulles would prefer that we see faith primarily as a disclosure or discernment of meaning and value coupled with a commitment to the struggle for justice. "The Church," he says, "must reconceive faith less as a set of assertions and more as a process of discernment."[8] Adopting this stance, the Church might become more adept at discernment and

6. J. Dillenberger, ed., *Martin Luther: Selections* (Garden City, N.Y.: Doubleday/Anchor Books, 1961), p. 24.
7. Quoted in A. Dulles, *The Faith That Does Justice* (New York: Paulist Press, 1971), p. 25.
8. Ibid., p. 22.

thus be able to speak out "more promptly, persuasively and unanimously on current issues such as racism, militarism, ecology and unbridled nationalism." By helping the believer to discern some meaning in the chaotic history of our times, the Church could liberate itself from the sterile intellectualism and authoritarianism which has been its curse.[9]

## LIBERATION THEOLOGY AND FAITH

One group of theologians who have taken up this approach with great enthusiasm are the proponents of liberation theology. They have consciously rejected the intellectualism and fideism of Catholic and Protestant theology. The majority of them are Latin American Catholics such as the Chilean Segundo Galileo, who notes how inadequate are the traditional categories of faith for anyone who engages in the struggle to secure social justice. "The categories of his faith . . . do not inspire or illuminate sufficiently his commitments."[10]

One of the most frequent definitions found in the writings of the theologians of liberation is faith conceived as "the **historical praxis of liberation**"—**historical** insofar as the Word of God does not come to us primarily from the Bible or the Church, but is heard in the cry of the exploited and marginalized poor. **Praxis** is a term borrowed from Karl Marx, who defined it as the conscious effort to transform social reality and make the world more human. The liberation theologians agree with Marx that any interpretation of the Gospel that does not aim at revolutionary action to overcome the alienation of the worker is itself a factor in upholding an unjust order. If we are authentically committed to the Kingdom, they say, we must join the struggle to subvert the existing social order. In the light of that **commitment**, we shall be able correctly to **discern** the present reality and determine the possibilities for the future.

The term **liberation** is preferred to the traditional term **salvation**, since the latter is tainted by its association with otherworldly concepts of religion, while **liberation** focuses attention on the process of extricating people from their condition of oppression and exploitation.

Dulles gives high marks to the theology of liberation for its faithful rendering of certain biblical themes and its accordance with the increased sense of man's responsibility for the world. For, as he says, in liberation

9. Ibid.
10. Ibid., p. 33.

theology faith is not a passive waiting on God to fulfill his promise, but an active engagement in the service of the Kingdom.

However, he says, we should not simply discard the previous intellectualist and fideist conceptions of faith in favor of the liberation concept. Rather, we should take all three theories as mutually complementary and corrective.

Moreover, Dulles expresses some reservations about liberation theology. The tendency to identify faith with **praxis**, he thinks, overlooks the fact that even sincere believers may not always practice what they believe. The theologians of liberation neglect, it seems, the psychological complexity of the act of faith, and their stress on external activity and social involvement runs the risk of minimizing the dimension of interiority in the life of faith. Dulles also questions their insistence that God speaks to us only through the poor and the oppressed. Their Marxian interpretation of the Bible would have us neglect other members of society, who are living lives of spiritual poverty and who stand just as much in need of the liberating power of the Gospel as those living in actual poverty. Finally, he thinks the advocates of liberation theology too easily equate one particular form of social organization (Marxian socialism) with the imperatives of the Gospel. The Church is rarely able to make such a sure choice between rival social systems, since both the Gospel and its tradition offer little help in this regard.

### SECULAR FAITH

There are a number of theologians today who approach the question of faith from the standpoint of the experience of many today in a culture in which the word "God" has lost all meaning. They see faith in terms of the struggle of many to find a transcendent meaning in life—in their everyday secular experience. In this context of secular experience, faith has been variously defined. One way is to see it as living in the spirit of openness to others and to life, saying yes to life in a willingness to invest one's energies —intellectual, physical and spiritual—in the people, the events and the relationships of one's life.[11] It means a constant and living quest for meaning. It is an act of fundamental trust grounded in one's experience and a creative assent to the future. Creativity—often associated only with art-

11. J. M. Powers, "Faith, Mortality, Creativity . . . ," *Theological Studies* 39 (December 1978), p. 665.

ists, writers, etc.—is actually an important part of the life of all those who struggle to shape themselves in a spiritual journey that leads to life through and beyond death. This creative assent to life, this struggle to find and affirm one's self even in the face of the negativity of human limitations—death, above all—may rightly be looked on as a gift (as expressed in traditional theology), ". . . a gift from one's life and history, a gift from those who have the patience to share this process, and in all this a gift from the One who is discovered in the depths and at the limits of one's life."[12]

Very close to this secular definition of faith is Paul Tillich's idea of faith as "the courage to be." Tillich sees this courage as a response to the three forms of anxiety that prey on the mind of every human being: the anxiety aroused by the certainty of death, the anxiety caused by feelings of emptiness and meaninglessness, and the anxiety of guilt and condemnation. Such anxiety is existential in the sense that it belongs to existence itself and is not an abnormal state of mind. In each case, one's being is threatened by nonbeing: by the threat of biological extinction, by the threat to one's spiritual life from meaninglessness and by the threat, through guilt, to one's sense of self-worth.

12. Ibid., p. 677.

# II

---

## Jesus the Christ

# 5

## The Man and the Message

Every believer knows Jesus in a way that is absolutely unique. He or she prays to Jesus as his or her Savior and Lord; meets him in the sacraments of the Church in a most intimate, grace-filled manner; receives Jesus into his or her heart as the one who gives strength to overcome sin and temptation. He or she looks to Jesus as the source of hope in eternal life and peace. Jesus is all this and more for those with faith.

### THE QUEST FOR THE HISTORICAL JESUS

However, there is another way of meeting Jesus, another way of learning about him which is not based on faith but which takes him as a historical personage and uses the ordinary methods of research to find out about him. For Jesus was indeed a real historical figure who lived and laughed and loved and worked at a certain time in a certain place. He had friends and enemies, triumphs and failures, and died in the end, like everyone else. It is this historical Jesus who concerns us here.

The historical Jesus has often been so overshadowed by the Jesus of faith that people showed little interest in the actual historical facts. It was only when some critics at the time of the Enlightenment began to question whether there ever was a real Jesus of Nazareth that a change took place. Scholars began to sift the Gospels and other sources in order to determine what was factual about Jesus as a historical person. The question they sought to answer was, What can we really know for certain about this man who supposedly rose from the dead and started a religion that is now worldwide?

As one might suspect, many theories saw the light of day. There were the extreme skeptics, who solemnly announced that Jesus of Nazareth was a total myth. There were the fundamentalists, who claimed that everything reported in the Gospels was absolute fact: Jesus really did walk on the water and drive legions of devils into a herd of pigs. And there were those who decided that while Jesus no doubt actually existed, much of what was reported about him was legend, rather than history.

This "quest for the historical Jesus" has been carried on for several centuries now, and hundreds of thousands of books and articles have been written in the attempt to sift fact from fiction in the story of Jesus. I will attempt here to give only a brief summary of the general conclusions that the majority of scholars today would accept.

### SOURCES FOR THE LIFE OF JESUS

First, when it comes to information about Jesus, we are practically limited to the Gospels. There are only a few references elsewhere in the literature of that time to Jesus and the early Christians. Several Roman authors, Suetonius (c. A.D. 120), Tacitus (c. A.D. 115) and Pliny (c. A.D. 111) make mention of Christ but tell us virtually nothing about him, while the Jewish author Josephus (d. c. A.D. 95) has a few references to him that are considered unreliable.

In using the Gospels as virtually our only source of information about Jesus, then, we must keep in mind a number of points: First, they were not written to give us a historical or biographical account of Jesus. Their primary purpose was to lead people to faith in him as Lord and Savior. As literature they really can't be easily fitted into any category and therefore are not easy to interpret. We must remember that they were most probably not composed by eyewitnesses and they certainly date much later than the events they are supposedly recounting—somewhere from thirty to seventy years later.

Second, they were originally composed from various collections of stories and sayings of Jesus that circulated in the early Christian communities in the form of sermons and catechetical material. Mark was the first one to put this material together as a "Gospel," sometime around A.D. 65. His primary purpose was not to give a chronological or biographical account of Jesus, but to give guidance to the community, to answer some of its problems and to confirm the community in its faith and its hope. The same is true of the other three authors: Matthew, Luke and John. In this sense, the Gospels were the product of the Church: the evangelists drew on the memories of Jesus preserved by the Church, and the portrait of Jesus they sketched was heavily influenced by the experience of the Church.

Third, as far as historical accuracy goes, they took a much different approach from what we would take today. They put words in the mouth of Jesus and told stories about him that were not necessarily historical but were sometimes put in mythical form—although conveying the real meaning and intent of Jesus as faith had come to perceive him. This is why we have to make a distinction between the Jesus of history and the Christ of faith.

## THE THREE LAYERS IN THE GOSPELS

If all this is so, if the Gospels are not simple history but documents of faith, how do we find the Jesus of history in them? In order to do so we must realize that there are actually three layers of tradition incorporated into the Gospels. The first layer, and the most difficult to detect, consists of the **actual words and deeds** of Jesus, which formed the historical foundation for the other two layers. The **second layer** consists of the material that belongs to the immediate post-Resurrection period, when the first generation of Christians adapted and modified Jesus' deeds and words to meet the needs of the community. The **third, and top, layer,** so to speak, is what we have today in the Gospels: the community's tradition about Jesus as edited and organized by the four evangelists. This analysis of the Gospels is the product of a great amount of New Testament scholarship over the past half century. It reflects a very broad consensus of students of the Gospels and has been endorsed by the Vatican in its document entitled *The Historical Truth of the Gospels*. It is also echoed in the Second Vatican Council's document on Revelation.

In view of this complicated picture, it should become obvious that it is no easy task to reconstruct a portrait of the actual historical Jesus. We have to do a lot of sifting and analysis in order to get down to the first layer, to Jesus himself. But it is not impossible, using today's methods of historical and critical analysis. And scholars have developed a set of criteria that enable us, with a certain amount of confidence, to retrieve authentic Jesus material.

## THE RULES OF THE QUEST

The first rule—**theological disharmony**—is based on the idea that each Gospel has a distinct theological viewpoint. Therefore material that does not agree with the author's theology is probably authentic Jesus material, which the author includes simply because its historicity is certain. An example would be passages in Mark that put the disciples in a good light, since Mark, for theological reasons, wants to show them as cowardly, full of bewilderment and wrong ideas.

The second rule—**dissimilarity**—states that words or acts attributed to Jesus that have no parallel in contemporary Judaism or primitive Christianity are most likely authentic words or acts of Jesus. An example: "Why do you call me good?"[1]—a saying that cannot be easily reconciled with the primitive Church's faith in Jesus as divine.

The third rule—**multiple attestation**—states that we have authentic Jesus material when we find the same material in independent traditions, especially if given in different forms. Thus Jesus' dealings with publicans and sinners is reported in no less than four independent literary traditions.

One applies the fourth rule—**coherence**—by building up piece by piece the historical picture of Jesus from the critically reconstructed details drawn from the first three rules. Whatever, then, is consistent with this critically reconstructed picture of Jesus may also be accepted as authentic.

The final rule starts from the fact that Jesus was executed and his message rejected. Hence we can judge as authentic words and deeds of his that **gravely offended the establishment** by challenging the conventional beliefs and practices of the time.

Using this method, scholars have been able to draw a reasonably accurate portrait of the historical Jesus which traces the main outline and basic features of his ministry, his message and his fate.

One may ask why all this is necessary. Either one believes in Jesus or one doesn't. All the history in the world won't help one to believe if one is not so disposed.

1. Mk. 10:18.

It is certainly true that historical research could never prove that God's saving act occurred in Jesus Christ. This will always be a matter of faith. But, on the other hand, our faith is based on history; it is the interpretation of a supposed historical event, namely the life and death of Jesus of Nazareth.

If history were to show that our faith interpretation is manifestly wrong —for instance, if it were to show that Jesus did not exist or that he was actually the criminal leader of a Palestinian terrorist band—then we would have to abandon our Christian faith. The critical historical method, therefore, is a necessity today, at least for those who seek an honest and intelligent faith.

## THE KINGDOM OF GOD

One point nearly every scholar would agree on today is that the key to Jesus' ministry was his message about the Kingdom of God. Almost everything he did and said as reported in the Gospels is related to this theme. Some understanding of the background of this concept is therefore essential here.

The Old Testament has many references to God's coming Kingdom, though the actual phrase "the Kingdom of God" does not occur. As used by the prophets and writers, it referred not so much to a distinct realm but, rather, to God's sovereignty over all people and therefore his claim, as king, on the obedience and loyalty of every person. But since few people actually lived in the spirit of this Kingdom, emphasis was put on its fulfillment in the future, when, as Isaiah put it:

> the wolf lives with the lamb,
> the panther lies down with
> the kid. . . .
> these will hammer their swords into ploughshares,
> their spears into sickles. . . .
> there will be no more training for war.[2]

The Kingdom of God was therefore a great symbol of hope for the people of Israel.

It was not to be the work of man but would be inaugurated by the power of God. This theme became dominant in the apocalyptic Jewish

2. Isa. 11:6; 2:4.

writings which appeared between 200 B.C. and A.D. 200. At a time when the Jewish people were again under the heel of the oppressor, these writings kept alive the age-old hope. The Book of Daniel (c. 160 B.C.), the most notable of these writings, pictured the worldly kingdoms in the form of four terrifying beasts, while the glorified people who belonged to God's Kingdom were symbolized in the form of

> (one) coming on the clouds of heaven
> . . . like a son of man. . . .
> His sovereignty is an eternal sovereignty. . . .[3]

While some thought of God's Kingdom as one that would be set up in this world, others viewed it as a transcendent, cosmic reality that would be ushered in by a total apocalypse. And growing weary of the continuing oppression, many Jews began to nurture the hope that the apocalypse would occur in the near future. This hope was the source of the zeal of the Jews who settled at Qumran, near the Dead Sea, in a semimonastic community during the second century B.C. They firmly believed that they would play a key role in the world-shattering events of the last days.

It was also in an atmosphere charged with this expectation that John the Baptist began his preaching in the desert near Qumran. John's message was brief and to the point: "The kingdom of God is at hand; repent."

Jesus' public activity coincided with John's movement, and no doubt Jesus himself was baptized by John at the Jordan. It seems likely that it was at this moment that Jesus became conscious of his own vocation even if the scene itself has been colored with legendary embellishments by the early Christian community. For all our accounts agree that at his baptism "the Spirit descended on him"—a biblical phrase denoting the call of someone to be God's messenger.

Like John, Jesus proclaimed the coming of God's Kingdom. But Jesus emphasized even more than John the imminence of the Kingdom and spoke with extreme urgency of the need to repent. Moreover, Jesus made the astounding claim that in some way the Kingdom was already present in his person, that in his ministry God was offering to men the possibility of a new relationship to Himself. This tension between the future coming of the Kingdom and its present manifestation runs through the whole teaching and ministry of Jesus and is the central paradox of the Gospels.

To drive home his message, Jesus did more than preach. He dramatized his meaning by behaving in a way that many found outrageous: consorting

3. Dan. 7:13–14.

with disreputable people: harlots and tax collectors. There is no doubt about this, for it is deeply embedded in the tradition. His reason for doing so is also clear: he wanted to show in unmistakable fashion how God offered mercy to sinners. For the experience of forgiveness was at the heart of what Jesus meant by the Kingdom. And in the parable of the Prodigal Son, Jesus conveyed this message in a touching, unforgettable story. The sinner must repent, must experience total change of heart. God, however, does not wait for him, cold and indifferent, but runs to meet him and invites him home to share in a feast of love and joy.

Jesus insisted that the time for decision, for repentance, is *now*. The Kingdom may be future, but one must choose now. The decisive element in Jesus' preaching, then, is not the expectation of the end of the world, but the challenge to decide here and now for God. One must completely change the priorities that rule one's life. Nothing must be allowed to stand in the way of the would-be disciple. "Anyone who prefers father or mother to me is not worthy of me. Anyone who prefers son or daughter to me is not worthy of me.[4]

### EXORCISMS AND MIRACLES

One of the features of Jesus' ministry that is very prominent is his exorcisms and his miracles. He often drives out devils from the possessed and not only heals the lame and the blind but performs prodigies that tax our power to believe: he walks on the water, quells hurricanes, multiplies bread and replaces the severed ear of a soldier without benefit of surgery.

There is no simple way to interpret these passages, but each incident must be related to its context. In general, we must remember what was said above about the three layers contained in the Gospels. There is no doubt that the first layer, that is, the actual words and deeds of Jesus, did undergo substantial modification as the tradition was passed on. In fact, sometimes the original episode was so modified that it is difficult to tell what actually happened. Certainly the first generation of Christians found nothing wrong with embellishing the deeds of the Master in order to express their perception of his greatness and power. There are many instances of this legend-making tendency in the case of ancient as well as

4. Mt. 10:37.

modern heroes. The stories told about Alexander the Great would be one of the best examples of this tendency.

So, what is the core of fact that is left, once you've allowed this? We must remember that the whole ancient world was filled with belief in devils and fear of devils, and sickness was linked with sin and devil possession. Since there is no reason to doubt that Jesus possessed remarkable powers of healing thanks to the force of his spiritual magnetism and to the susceptibility of persons suffering from psychosomatic illnesses, it is easy to see how his healings might often be interpreted as victory over devils.

It is most important to realize the overall significance of Jesus' miracles. They are meant to illustrate the point that God is present in a special way in the ministry of Jesus. They are dramatic signs of the power of God. Through Jesus, His chosen instrument, God is waging a tremendous war against all forms of evil, and the miracles are the most evident signs of this saving power of God. The exorcisms bring this out in a special way. For the biblical mind, Satan personified the awesome power of evil in the world and the grip it holds over humankind. The confrontation of Jesus and Satan dramatized the power of God over the power of evil and gave assurance of God's ultimate victory over all forms of evil.

The **nature** miracles are the most difficult to explain. On the face of it, they sometimes seem like arbitrary acts of a powerful magician: Jesus quells storms, walks on water, multiplies bread, and withers up a fig tree with a curse. In the light of what we have said about the complex formation of the Gospel tradition, there is obviously no need to consider these stories as literal reports of what actually happened. Various influences, no doubt, were at work in shaping the form they took: Old Testament passages, for instance, portrayed God as One Who controlled the storms and so some incident involving Jesus and his disciples caught in a storm could have been edited and reedited until the story was finally told in a way that reflected their belief in the divinity of Jesus. Likewise, the stories of Jesus multiplying the loaves and fishes might well have been influenced by the Old Testament stories of how God fed the people in the desert with manna and how Elisha fed a hundred men with twenty barley loaves. The main point, however, of these miracles as with the others is that God's healing and saving power was experienced by people through the ministry of Jesus.

Another important point to keep in mind in this connection is the way Jesus worked his miracles in response to the faith of those he healed. Those coming to him to be cured had to manifest trust in him and his

RIORDAN HIGH SCHOOL LIBRARY
175 PHELAN AVENUE
SAN FRANCISCO, CALIFORNIA 94112

message and believe that God was indeed working in his ministry. "My daughter . . . your faith has restored you to health," Jesus tells the woman suffering from a hemorrhage.[5] And Mark even says that Jesus could not work miracles if such faith was not present, as he found to be the case when he visited his home town. Jesus would not work a miracle in order to induce faith in him. He demanded a response that was genuine.

## GOD AS OUR FATHER

Who is this God of Jesus Christ? One of the passages that best reveals the unique intimacy of Jesus' relationship to God is found in Matthew:

> I bless you, Father, Lord of heaven and of earth, for hiding these things from the learned and the clever and revealing them to mere children. Yes, Father, for that is what it pleased you to do. Everything has been entrusted to me by my Father; and no one knows the Son except the Father, just as no one knows the Father except the Son and those to whom the Son chooses to reveal him.[6]

Jesus, we know, used the Aramaic term *Abba* in addressing God—a term of endearment something like our "daddy"—and a Jew would never dare use it in addressing God. In doing so, Jesus manifested his unique sense of filial relationship with God. Moreover, he taught his followers to pray in the same spirit in the simple but profound prayer that summarizes his teaching and is the perfect pattern for every Christian prayer.

Each petition of the "Our Father," when reflected on, reveals immense spiritual depths. We are to "hallow" the Father's name by giving Him the worship and obedience that are due to Him. We are to pray for the coming of His Kingdom when all will acknowledge His rule and His will. We are to ask for our daily bread so that we may perform the tasks which God gives us to do. We must forgive others, for otherwise we will not be worthy of God's forgiveness. And finally we must pray to be spared the great temptation—meaning above all persecution and trials so terrible that we might lose our faith in God and the coming of His Kingdom.

Jesus stood before his disciples as a man of prayer. He spent long periods in prayer and urged his disciples to pray often. He warned them against making a show of their piety and urged them to pray in secret as

5. Mk. 5:34.
6. Mt. 11:25–27; cf. Lk. 10:21–22.

well as in public. Above all, their prayer, like all their actions, must come from a mind and heart centered on God.

Jesus proclaimed the Kingdom of God: God was on the point of drawing near to man in a way that was unprecedented in history. "Many kings have desired to see what you see and have not seen it," he told the crowds. Unlike John the Baptist, who spoke in frightening tones of the wrath of God about to strike sinners, Jesus emphasized the joy of the new age that was dawning. He and his disciples celebrated often at meals that were so merry and full of cheer that "religious" people looked on him as a man too fond of wine and good food.

Nothing was more important in his eyes than the Kingdom, and he constantly insisted on the need for undivided loyalty to God. He knew how easy it was to set one's heart on riches, on power, on prestige. But to chase after these things was to serve mammon, rather than God. Not even family affections must be allowed to interfere with one's devotion to the Kingdom.

Jesus does not preach asceticism, however. Material things are good and can be used for the glory of God, but first place must always be given to God. There is a hierarchy of values, Jesus insists. Life and health are more important than food and clothing: "Surely life means more than food, and the body more than clothing!"[7] But even more important than life is the Kingdom of God. And until this is placed first, nothing else will be valued rightly.

The only absolute is God and His Kingdom. Even the Law—sacred and venerated, as it should be—must give place, if need be, to the demands of the Kingdom. Although, like all Jews, Jesus manifested great reverence for the Law, he did not hesitate to modify it when it stood in the way of the Kingdom.

As the eminent German biblical scholar, Ferdinand Hahn, says, "What is crucial for Jesus is not what God has done and required in the past, but his eschatological action in the present . . . this is the basis of Jesus' freedom with respect to the totality of the Old Testament and Jewish tradition . . ."[8]

The Law, moreover, no doubt, satisfied the need of human nature to

7. Mt. 6:25.
8. Ferdinand Hahn, *The Worship of the Early Church* (Philadelphia: Fortress Press, 1973), pp. 13, 17.

put some structure into one's relationship with God, some way of feeling secure in the thought that one had fulfilled one's obligations and could now go about the more important business of getting and spending. But Jesus would not go along with this legalism. He emphasized the need for a radical obedience that goes beyond all prescriptions of the Law. One who enters the Kingdom must meet each situation as it arises and be ready to give God whatever He asks of him.

Some would turn this New Law into a new legalism. "How many times must I forgive my brother?" Must I give the robber my credit cards as well as my wallet?

But Jesus illustrates the meaning of radical obedience in a passage that retains great shock value: ". . . if anyone hits you on the right cheek, offer him the other as well; if a man takes you to law and would have your tunic, let him have your cloak as well. And if anyone orders you to go one mile, go two miles with him."9

The refusal of Jesus to codify the New Law and to lay down specific commandments is nowhere better illustrated than by these three sayings. For they are practically impossible to carry out except in very limited circumstances. One could accept insult in this spirit only in a community that respected the dignity of the individual and recognized the real significance of the act. Moreover, in the world of Jesus, where men ordinarily wore only two garments, an inner one and an outer one, to hand over both would leave one naked and liable to arrest for indecent exposure.

"If we may accept the axiom that Jesus knew what he was talking about, then we must recognize that they were never meant to be taken literally. What we have here are illustrations of a principle. The illustrations are extreme, and in the one instance so much so as to approach the ridiculous; but that is deliberate. They are intended to be vivid examples of a radical demand: one should respond to the challenge of God in terms of a radically new approach to the business of living. This approach is illustrated by means of vivid examples of behavior in crisis: in reponse to grave insult, to a lawsuit and to a military impressment. Not natural pride, not a standing on one's own rights, not even a prudential acceptance is the proper response to these crises now, however much they might have been so before. In the light of the challenge of God and of the new relationship with one's fellowman, one must respond in a new way, in a way appropriate to the new situation. What the specifics of that new way are is not

9. Mt. 5:39–41.

stated. These sayings are illustrations of the necessity for a new way, rather than regulations for it. But the implication of these sayings is surely that if one approaches the crisis in this spirit, and seeks the way in terms of the reality of one's experience of God and the new relationship with one's fellowman, then that way can be found."[10]

At least it is certain that Jesus urged his followers to follow the path of nonviolence. As we become more aware of the terrible violence that has now reached a crescendo with the advent of nuclear weapons, his call takes on tremendous significance.

Jesus showed the originality of his teaching by the way he gave a new interpretation to the two great commandments of the Law. When a lawyer asked him, "Master, which is the greatest commandment of the Law?" Jesus responded by quoting from the Old Testament, "You must love the Lord your God with all your heart, with all your soul, and with all your mind. This is the greatest and the first commandment. The second resembles it: You must love your neighbor as yourself. On these two commandments hang the whole Law, and the Prophets also."[11] Linking these two commandments together, as Jesus does, and reducing the whole Law to them is without parallel in Jewish literature. The unity Jesus ascribed to them is particularly clear in Luke's account, where the words "first" and "second" have been dropped. For Jesus, love of God and man form an indissoluble unity.

Moreover, this love is not a mere sentiment but must be translated into action. Jesus himself did not merely preach love but gave himself without stint in his unwearying devotion to healing the sick, bringing peace of mind to sinners, and befriending the outcasts of society. He set no limits on the demands of love. One of his most famous parables, the story of the Good Samaritan, emphasized this point. While Jewish theologians would debate whether "neighbor" could also mean a non-Jew, Jesus took the radical approach. Not only non-Jews but even the hated Samaritans must be considered neighbors when it comes to fulfilling the demands of love. The neighbor is anyone who needs me now. The Samaritan proves to be a true neighbor to the wounded Jew by meeting the demands of love, while the priest and the Levite turn out to be much less than neighbors to their fellow Jew in need. So we must look on all our fellow human beings as neighbors if we are to carry out the true meaning of the law of love.

10. Norman Perrin, *Rediscovering the Teaching of Jesus* (New York: Harper & Row, 1967), pp. 147–48.
11. Mt. 22:36–40.

And this means even our enemies. With his command to love even enemies, Jesus is shown at his most original, insofar as he brings to expression what is only latent in the prophetic spirit of Judaism and was in danger of being lost at a time when the Jews were so oppressed by the Gentile invader. Our love is not to be conditioned by the attitude of our neighbor, but must take its cue from God Himself, Who causes His sun to rise on bad people as well as good and sheds His rain on the honest as well as the dishonest.[12] This is possible only for those who know what it means to be children of the Father and to experience his incredible, fantastically generous love. We love because he first loved us.[13] We can forgive if we dwell on the boundless mercy of the Father, Who lavishes on us His loving forgiveness.

Looking at Jesus' teaching as a whole, we note that its distinctiveness derives from the way he put the accent not on a set of rules but, rather, on the necessity of seeing the rules as a revelation of God's will. Where he thought it fit to criticize or amend the rules, he did so in order better to express the will of God.

While the Law and its norms were to be reverenced, they were good only insofar as they helped relate the whole personality to God and promote His sovereignty.

One entered the Kingdom by submitting to His rule, and this presupposed the new experience of God as Jesus revealed Him: the Father Who seeks and saves the lost. What it means to live under the sovereignty of God could not be spelled out in a list of rules; there had to be room for spontaneity and creativeness. The object was to integrate one's life and behavior with the purpose of God in the world. The rules could not be laid down in advance but must be invented in the light of the unfolding purpose of God. Jesus shows us only the direction in which we should move but does not provide us with a detailed map.[14]

12. Mt. 5:45.
13. 1 Jn. 4:10.
14. T. W. Manson, *The Sayings of Jesus* (London: SCM Press, 1949), pp. 36–37.

# 6

## Death and Resurrection

Jesus' execution by the Roman governor Pontius Pilate is reported by all four of the evangelists and is certainly a fact beyond question. The exact date of his death, however, is less easily established. It seems most likely that John's Gospel is correct in asserting that it took place on the day before the Passover feast and therefore on April 7, A.D. 30, according to our calendar.

He was executed as a political rebel, as is indicated by the inscription placed on the cross which reflected belief that he wanted to be king of the Jews.

What train of events brought Jesus to this ignominious death?

There is no doubt that Jesus met with considerable opposition in his efforts to convert his fellow Jews. He attracted huge crowds by his preaching in Galilee, and for a time it seemed that Israel would enter the Kingdom *en masse*. But it was soon apparent that the people—while struck with awe by the force of his words and the power manifest in his miracles —remained unable to comprehend his message. Even his chosen disciples balked at his intimations that he might have to suffer and die. In spite of his denials, they continued to see him as a conquering Messiah who would restore Israel to its former glory. Moreover, he had incurred the lethal hostility of the scribes and Pharisees, who were outraged by some of his remarks critical of their traditions. His refusal to accept the Law as absolute and his unprecedented claim to forgive sins convinced them that he was a blasphemer. In their eyes, Jesus arrogated an authority for himself which they reserved for God alone. Perhaps most offensive was his eating with tax collectors and sinners, which struck a blow at the very structure of Jewish society: their sense of ritual purity and moral superiority and especially its challenge to their hope that they would establish the Kingdom of God by ousting the Romans. "Jesus challenged the fundamental assumption that held the whole society together, viz. that God was on their side and that he would eventually give them—or at least the purified remnant among them—the final triumph over their enemies. Jesus indeed laid his own life on the line by such actions."[1]

This, then, is the background of his final visit to Jerusalem.

The response of the people of Galilee was most disappointing to Jesus. Besides, he had managed to antagonize Herod Antipas, the ruler of Galilee and murderer of John the Baptist. Jesus called Herod "a fox" and set off in the direction of Jerusalem. By this time he was no doubt fully aware that he stood in imminent danger of death—for the most powerful people in Galilee were already involved in plots to dispose of him. To carry his message to Jerusalem, where hostility was bound to be even stronger, was to run the extreme risk of a bloody fate. And yet the nation had to be confronted with the message of God's Kingdom in its city of destiny.

## HOW DID HE VIEW HIS DEATH?

The Gospels show, in fact, that he expected to die in Jerusalem, ". . . since," as he said, "it would not be right for a prophet to die outside Jerusalem."[2]

The important question is, Did Jesus himself think of his death as redemptive? There are a number of passages in the Gospels that interpret his death as saving and expiatory. He is pictured in the guise of the Suffering Servant so beautifully depicted in Second Isaiah:

> And yet ours were the sufferings he bore,
> ours the sorrows he carried.
> But we, we thought of him as someone punished,
> struck by God, and brought low.
> Yet he was pierced through for our faults,
> crushed for our sins.

1. Michael Cook, S.J., *The Jesus of Faith* (New York: Paulist Press, 1981), p. 63.
2. Lk. 13:33.

On him lies a punishment that brings us peace,
and through his wounds we are healed.[3]

But does this interpretation derive from Jesus himself? Some scholars say no. However, there are good reasons for believing that Jesus did see his sufferings in this light. Several texts of the Gospels, in fact, suggest it. One of these is found in Mark (10:45) in a passage where Jesus is trying to impress on his disciples that ambition for earthly power will have no place in the Kingdom, "For the Son of Man himself did not come to be served but to serve, and to give his life as a ransom for many."

The last phrase, "a ransom for many," seems to echo the text of Isaiah (53:10) which designates the Servant's death as an offering "in atonement."

Another important text is found in the passages describing the Last Supper where Jesus is quoted as saying that his blood would be poured out "for many" (Mark), "for the forgiveness of sins" (Matthew), or simply "poured out for you" (Luke). Criticism challenges the authenticity of these words on the basis that the Last Supper texts do not record the actual words of Jesus but are stylized texts derived from the liturgy of the primitive Christian community. But no one denies the facticity of the Last Supper, and it is not unreasonable to suppose that with his approaching death very much on his mind, Jesus would identify with the Suffering Servant as he offered his disciples the cup and shared bread with them.

The authenticity of these words of Jesus receive confirmation from several other considerations. First, there is no doubt that Jesus saw a connection between his death and the coming of the Kingdom, as is expressed in the essentially authentic words at the Last Supper "I shall not drink any more wine until the day I drink the new wine in the kingdom of God."[4] These words therefore imply that he saw a saving significance in his death, since the death he now sees as certain would somehow be "directly operative in the final and decisive (eschatological) action of God in bringing the Kingdom to its consummation. Exactly how remains, of course, hidden in the Father's will and, from our perspective, was only revealed in the decisive event of Jesus' death-resurrection."[5]

Second, it is certainly clear that Jesus saw his whole life as a service for others: ". . . here am I among you as one who serves!"[6] And this was not

3. Is. 53:4–5.
4. Mk. 14:25.
5. Cook, op. cit., p. 65.
6. Lk. 22:27.

merely service in the sense of acts of kindness and compassion; it went much deeper. It meant bringing people into community with God, remission of guilt. It meant a life for others and if necessary the sacrifice of one's life for others. So that even if Jesus did not explicitly speak of himself in terms of Isaiah's Suffering Servant, his whole life had that character. "There is no evidence against, but much in favor of the claim that he maintained this view even in death; in other words, that he saw his death as a representative and saving service to many."[7]

## THE LAST SUPPER

As to the actual circumstances of his death, a number of points should be remembered. First, the supper he celebrated on the evening he was taken into custody must be viewed in the light of the common meals which he was accustomed to celebrate with his disciples as signs of the coming Kingdom. It took place most probably on the eve of the Passover and followed the ritual of a festive Jewish meal.

## THE PASSION ACCOUNTS: FACT AND/OR LEGEND?

The accounts of his passion and death are more nearly history than any other parts of the Gospel. But even here we do not have neutral eyewitness accounts. Legend is intermingled with fact, and much of the material is drawn from the Old Testament to indicate that Jesus was fulfilling its prophecies. The correspondence between the Old Testament prophecies and the actual details of his passion and death could very well be contrived in order to indicate that Jesus was the fulfillment of the Old Testament. However, the overall picture is no doubt historical. In cleansing the temple, Jesus threw down the gauntlet to his enemies, who were in no little haste to pick it up. His last hours on earth brought him to the extremes of agony and despair as he was betrayed, tempted, and misunderstood and abandoned by all.

Many questions about the role of the Sanhedrin and the Jewish authorities have never been settled and probably never will: Did they hold a trial or was it only a hearing? Were there two sessions (Matthew) or only one

7. Walter Kasper, *Jesus the Christ* (New York: Paulist Press, 1977), p. 120.

(Luke)? Could the Sanhedrin pronounce and carry out a death sentence? Did they actually sentence Jesus to death?

In any case, the Sanhedrin may well have found Jesus guilty of blasphemy, inasmuch as his claim to forgive sins, coupled with the assertion of his disciples that he was God's son, implied that he himself was divine—in the eyes of a believing Jew a terrible contradiction of their sacrosanct monotheism.

There is no doubt that the Jewish leaders—high priest and elders—handed him over to the Romans, as we read in all four Gospels. There is also no doubt that Pilate would waste little time in dispatching a person suspected of messianic pretensions. It was high treason for anyone to speak about being king of the Jews in a province of the Roman Empire. The fact that Jesus refused unequivocally to deny that he was king of the Jews would have been enough to doom him, as far as Pilate was concerned.

Jesus' death, by crucifixion, must certainly be taken as historical, since his followers would never have invented so degrading a spectacle, one that provided their Jewish opponents with such a telling argument against the messiahship of Jesus. And while the evangelists differ in many of the abundant details they record about his passion, they agree as to the substance of the story. Moreover, the details of the execution accurately reflect what we know about the Roman methods of crucifixion: Jesus was nailed to a crossbeam, which was then fastened to a stake already driven into the ground, and his feet were nailed or tied with ropes to the stake.

In the throes of unendurable pain, Jesus uttered the terrifying cry, "My God, my God, why hast Thou forsaken me?"—words that could never have been invented by those who believed in his cause. He died in complete and total isolation, abandoned by all, even his *Abba*, the loving and caring Father on Whom he had staked his whole life. The Kingdom had not come. Nothing was left of the dream. Only a broken, ugly corpse to remind people of the days of glory and the message of the Kingdom.

## THE RESURRECTION—HISTORICAL OR META-HISTORICAL?

"How did a new beginning come about after such a disastrous end? How did this Jesus movement come into existence after Jesus' death . . . ? How did a community emerge in the name of a crucified man, how did that community take shape as a Christian 'Church'? . . . Why did there arise that bond to the Master which is so very different from the bonds of other movements to the personalities of their founders, as for instance of Marxists to Marx or enthusiastic Freudians to Freud?"[8]

The answer, in one word, is the **Resurrection**. This is the answer given by the New Testament, which relates how, soon after his death, Jesus' disciples proclaimed that God had raised him from the dead; that the crucified was now among the living and had sent them to proclaim this astounding message to the whole world.

What is the verdict of historical criticism as to the facticity of this supposed **Resurrection**? A better question is, What are the grounds of our faith in the Resurrection?

As always, one begins with the study of the sources. In this case we can identify two separate traditions: the *Easter kerygma*, which contains short, liturgical formulations of belief found in the early *kerygma*, or preaching of the early apostles, and the *Easter narratives*, which include the accounts of the empty tomb.

We must note at the outset that the accounts of the Resurrection present certain difficulties. First, we do not have unbiased reports, but testimonies of faith by persons already committed. Second, there is no direct evidence offered for the Resurrection, as no one claims to have been an eyewitness of the event. Third, unlike the Passion accounts, which offer a relatively clear and agreed-on sequence of events, the Resurrection accounts present no coherent sequence, and they reveal many discrepancies and inconsistencies. They do not agree on many important details, such as to *whom* Jesus first appeared, *where* this happened, *how many persons* were involved, and *when* Jesus appeared to his followers.

Moreover, the Resurrection, by its very nature, could not be a historically verifiable event, which could be placed in time and space. No TV camera, for instance, could have recorded it. As an event beyond death, it is an event outside of history and therefore more aptly termed *metahistorical*. As such, it is an object of faith, not an argument in support of faith.

One must keep this in mind as we examine the two basic kinds of sources for the Resurrection: the *kerygma* and the *narratives*.

8. Hans Küng, *On Being a Christian* (Garden City, N.Y.: Doubleday, 1976), pp. 344–45.

## THE KERYGMA

The earliest text that we have is 1 Corinthians 15:3–8, in which Paul mentions that he hands on a tradition he has received:

> Well then, in the first place, I taught you what I had been taught myself, namely that Christ died for our sins, in accordance with the scriptures; that he was buried; and that he was raised to life on the third day, in accordance with the scriptures; that he appeared first to Cephas and secondly to the Twelve. Next he appeared to more than five hundred of the brothers at the same time, most of whom are still alive, though some have died; then he appeared to James, and then to all the apostles; and last of all he appeared to me too; it was as though I was born when no one expected it.

## THE EASTER NARRATIVES: THE EMPTY TOMB

These are the stories, found in Matthew, Luke and John, that give us many picturesque details about the events supposedly surrounding the Resurrection: how the empty tomb was discovered by the women, how Jesus appeared to the disciples in the upper room, how Mary Magdalene met him and mistook him for the gardener, etc. They raise many questions of criticism, one of the most important being the question of the empty tomb.

*Was the empty tomb a reality or was it a legend?* There is divided opinion about this among exegetes. Some argue that the stories about the tomb are legendary elaborations intended only to convey a theological message, namely, the reality and corporeality of the Resurrection—in opposition to attempts at a spiritualistic interpretation. As proof, they point to the legendary character of these passages—the stylistic use of angels, the miraculous opening of the tomb, etc.

Moreover, as these scholars point out, these stories originated in their literary form only around A.D. 70, while the *kerygma*—the earliest and therefore the more trustworthy testimony to the Resurrection—found in the epistle to the Corinthians quoted above knows nothing of an empty tomb. Nor does Paul himself anywhere mention the empty tomb. Finally, there are substantial discrepancies between the accounts of the evangelists. Mark, for instance, implies, while Matthew and John (in Chapter 21) state, that the appearances take place in Galilee; but Luke and John (in Chapter 20) have them taking place in Jerusalem. Again, in Matthew and in John (Chapter 21), and perhaps by implication in Mark, the appearances indicate a risen and ascended one and are of a "more spiritual kind," whereas the appearances to the women on the way from the tomb in Matthew, the Lucan Emmaus story and the appearance to the eleven in Luke and in John 20 present a Jesus risen but not yet ascended who is manifestly corporeal, as he is touched and eats. According to Reginald Fuller, the author of one of the best critical studies on the data, even more confusion is caused by John, who implies that the ascension took place between the appearance to Mary Magdalene and the encounter with Thomas. Yet he asks Thomas to touch him. "One would expect touching to be characteristic of the preascension Christophanies, as in Luke, but John has a different view. For him Christ apparently ascends between the appearance to Mary Magdalene and the appearance to the disciples a week later."[9]

Other discrepancies include lack of agreement as to the number of women who came to the tomb: Mark and Luke have three, Matthew two, and John one; and on the number of angels: Matthew and Mark have one, while Luke and John have two. These and other differences in the accounts make it impossible to establish any coherent sequence of the events occurring in connection with the Resurrection.

For these reasons and others, many exegetes, including a majority of the Protestant critics, follow Bultmann's view that the empty tomb is a late legend. Only Roman Catholics and Protestant members of the conservative evangelical circle still uphold the historicity of the empty tomb.

However, Reginald Fuller, who incidentally is neither Roman Catholic nor conservative evangelical, favors the historicity of the empty tomb. Through redactional procedures, Fuller isolates what he considers a nucleus of actual history found in the otherwise legendary account of Mark (16:1–8), which is the basis of the empty-tomb tradition. This nucleus was "derived from a report given by Mary Magdalene to the disciples" which he locates in several verses of this chapter of Mark. This would be consistent in general with Mark's redactional procedures where we find him elsewhere drawing on pre-Marcan material.[10]

Fuller goes on to say, "If our surmise is correct, an important consequence follows. The disciples received Mary's report not as the origin and

9. *The Formation of the Resurrection Narratives* (New York: Macmillan, 1971), pp. 3–5.
10. Ibid., pp. 50–70.

cause of their Easter faith, but as a vehicle for the proclamation of the Easter faith which they already held as a result of the appearances. It is as such that the Christian historian and the community of faith can accept the report of the empty tomb today."[11]

Another strong argument in favor of the existence of the empty tomb is the fact that belief in it was based on the witness of women. Since in Jewish law women could not be used as witnesses it seems most unlikely that a story the veracity of which depended on women witnesses would have been invented.

Another argument often given in favor of the existence of the empty tomb is the difficulty of explaining how the disciples could have preached the Resurrection of Jesus in Jerusalem if the tomb was not empty. Skeptics could easily have pointed to his grave or the leaders could have explained how the body had been disposed of. But the only explanation they apparently gave was that the disciples had stolen the body (Mt. 28:11-15).

But, in any case, how important for our faith is the empty tomb? Is it important to believe that the women found the tomb empty? We must keep in mind that the empty tomb was not the origin of the Christian faith, nor can it guarantee the Christian faith. After all, it can lend itself to various explanations: somebody could have stolen the body; Jesus' death could have been only apparent; there could have been confusion as to the actual whereabouts of his grave, etc. The empty tomb of itself therefore remains ambiguous.

Even if one accepts the facticity of the empty tomb, it is clear from a close reading of the Gospels that the apostles would not have heard of it until they had already experienced the Resurrection. After the crucifixion, they fled, demoralized, to Galilee, where Christ appeared to them. It was only upon returning to Jerusalem that they would have learned of the empty tomb. As congruent with the faith they already possessed, they would then have incorporated the fact of the empty tomb into their proclamation: "He is not here, he is risen."

The historian will never know whether the women really did find the tomb empty, but that is not a matter of great importance. The point is that the disciples found the story useful to indicate the nature of the Resurrection: that the Resurrection appearances were not merely manifestations of Christ's human spirit as surviving death, as when the medium of Endor conjured up the spirit of Samuel, but, rather, the eschatological

11. Ibid., p. 70.

reversal of death, which was the content of apocalyptic hope. The stories of the empty tomb, in fact, can still serve to teach us that the Resurrection was not about the resuscitation of a corpse, but about Jesus' entry into a new form of existence.

## THE OTHER EASTER STORIES

A number of passages in Matthew, Luke and John relate some beautiful stories about Jesus and his disciples after the Resurrection. They tell how he walked with two of them along the road to Emmaus and broke bread with them before disappearing; how he called to some of them who were in a boat on the Lake of Galilee, and when they had come to shore took breakfast with them; how he challenged Thomas, who was skeptical, to touch his wounds, and so on. Modern criticism does not see these stories as literal history, but more in the category of theological discourse. Thus, in the Johannine narrative, Mary Magdalene is pictured clinging to the one she had mistaken for the gardener. The believer, John is telling us, must not cling to the earthly Jesus as a figure of the past, but recognize that in his transformed existence he continues his work in the present in the community. Again, in his beautiful depiction of the repentant Peter receiving Christ's charge to feed his flock, John is telling us that office in the new community does not depend on personal merit, but on grace alone—yet it also requires personal dedication and commitment.

## RECENT INTERPRETATIONS

In the past decade, quite a number of diverse interpretations of the Resurrection have been offered by exegetes who question the traditional explanation, based on the empty tomb (which emphasizes a corporeal Resurrection) and the appearances to the disciples. Xavier Léon-Dufour, for example, prefers to speak of some kind of spiritual experience of the disciples, while Edward Schillebeeckx defines it as an experience of conversion based on their realization of God's continuing offer of forgiveness through Jesus.

A young German Catholic exegete, Rudolf Pesch, has offered another interpretation which has created much interest. He agrees with those who deny the historicity both of the empty tomb and the stories of Jesus' appearances, but he does not postulate some radically new experience of the disciples after Jesus' death. For him, what happened to the disciples after the Resurrection was simply in continuity with the incipient faith they had in Jesus as the prophetic Messiah while he was still alive. There was no need for some extraordinary experience after his death to convince them of his Resurrection. Rather, it would be most likely that Jesus foresaw his violent death and prepared his disciples so that their faith in him could survive and encompass the trauma of his death. "They could then have interpreted the permanent salvific significance of the crucified Jesus —his mission, martyrdom, and eschatologically final authority—by the proclamation of his Resurrection, an expression of faith which takes account of Jesus' death and is distinguished from mere continuation of Jesus' message by its reference to Jesus' person."[12]

Pesch's view has by no means gained a consensus among exegetes. A number of them reject one of his key assertions, namely, that the expression used to describe Christ's appearance to Peter, *ophthe Kepha* ("he was seen by Peter"), should not be taken literally, but is an Old Testament formula used to legitimate a supposed revelation and the witness mentioned as its recipient. The passage, then, Pesch argues, only testifies to the Resurrection by naming the decisive witness to it, Peter, but provides no historical basis for asserting an actual appearance of Christ to Peter.

Pesch's critics, on the other hand, claim that the *ophthe* formula is more than a legitimation formula, and they stress the need for a new divine initiative after Jesus' shattering death—a radically new experience that would revive the collapsed faith of the disciples. Even Pesch's teacher at Freiburg, Anton Vögtle, while favorable to Pesch's stress on the importance of the disciples' experience with the historical Jesus, finds it likely that the disciples were restored in their faith by some new experience after the Crucifixion.

# 7

# Christ the God Incarnate—
# Myth or Mystery?

One of the main debates going on in the Christian Church has to do with Christology; that is, the part of theology that focuses on questions relating to the meaning of Jesus Christ. This is especially true in the Roman Catholic Church, in which many studies on Christology have recently appeared by such authors as Karl Rahner, Walter Kasper, Edward Schillebeeckx and Hans Küng—the latter two daring enough to be the object of a special Vatican inquiry.

The basic questions that Christology attempts to answer have always been the same: Was Jesus Christ truly God? Was he also human? If so, how could divinity and humanity be combined in one person?

The classic answer to these questions was given at the Council of Chalcedon, in A.D. 451, which was the most important council held during the early centuries of the Church. It stated in essence that Jesus Christ was both fully human and fully divine, both natures being joined in one person, without confusion, division or separation.

### CHALCEDON: REJECTED OR REINTERPRETED?

Many objections to the definition of Chalcedon have been voiced over the course of time. Recently a group of English theologians made a broad, frontal attack on Chalcedon in *The Myth of God Incarnate*. Among the reasons they gave for rejecting the doctrine of Chalcedon: the definition embodies cultural and philosophical concepts that are not meaningful for us; it was shaped largely by political maneuvering among the major sees of early Christendom and the emperors; its concept of a preexistent divine Redeemer is a mythical notion borrowed from sources outside the Gospels; in practice, the doctrine of the Incarnation has caused Christians to devalue the meaning of Jesus' truly human struggles and suffering; and finally, in a world more conscious of the value of all the great religions, Chalcedon smugly attributes exclusive saving power to Jesus Christ—overlooking the possibility that God's disclosures have taken a variety of forms.[1]

The general position of the Roman Catholic Church, however, as well as of many other churches, has been to uphold the perennial truth of the Chalcedon formula. Nevertheless, within Roman Catholic theological circles there have been a number of attempts recently to *reinterpret* the doctrine of Chalcedon. Karl Rahner gave special impetus to this effort in an article commemorating Chalcedon's fifteen-hundredth anniversary when he asserted that a dogmatic definition represents not only an end but also a beginning. The very fact that it is true, Rahner insisted, means that it will be the beginning of a new development of doctrine—a beginning for new questions and deeper insights—and he referred to the self-transcendence of all formulas: "They must constantly be rethought, not because they are false, but because they are true. They remain alive insofar as they are elucidated."[2]

Since then, numerous Catholic theologians have put forward new interpretations of Chalcedon, including, of course, Rahner himself, who has devoted much of his energy to this task. For these theologians, the Chalcedonian formula remains the permanently valid expression of the main Christian mystery of faith. As Rahner puts it: the hypostatic union which the Council of Chalcedon affirms "is the expression of the unsurpassable unity of God and the human in Jesus, as well as the necessary moment intrinsic to the divine self-communication of the Father made to all of us who are not Jesus."[3] So God's offer to us of Himself is embodied in Jesus in a way that is definitive and unsurpassable. Insofar as the human reality of Jesus stands for the offer of God Himself, then we can say this

1. John Hick, ed., *The Myth of God Incarnate*, (Philadelphia: Westminster Press, 1977).
2. Quoted in Walter Kasper, *Jesus the Christ* (New York: Paulist Press, 1977), p. 17.
3. Quoted by Brian McDermott, "Roman Catholic Christology: Two Recurring Themes," *Theological Studies* 41 (June 1980), p. 345.

human reality belongs absolutely to God, and this is what we mean by the hypostatic union.

Before considering some of these modern reinterpretations of Chalcedon, it might be well first to look at the scriptural and historical background of the question.

## THE DIVINITY OF CHRIST AS ATTESTED IN THE NEW TESTAMENT

To understand why Chalcedon affirmed the union of the divine and human in Christ as a unity of person, we have to analyze the New Testament assertions on this point. First, we must note that explicit testimony to Jesus as God is found in only a few comparatively late passages of the New Testament—most notably in the Johannine writings, where we read in the first chapter of John's Gospel, "The Word was God," and in Chapter 20, Thomas calls Jesus "My Lord and my God." But these Johannine writings merely make explicit what is already implicit in the other writings of the New Testament. There the conception of Jesus as a divine being is brought out in a great variety of ways: he forgives sins as only the Father can do; he feeds the people in a "desert place"; he rules the sea as the Lord does in the Psalms; he raises the dead to life as only the Father can; he promulgates a New Law and establishes a new covenant.

So it was on this New Testament foundation of belief in Jesus as both human and divine that theologians began their speculations and developed their science of Christ, or Christology.

We should note that already in the New Testament we find various Christologies of considerable diversity. Some show predominantly Judaistic, while others predominantly Hellenistic, traits. However, they all manifest essential agreement, inasmuch as they all assert the transcendence of Jesus and his central role in God's plan.

Basic to all subsequent development of the Church's doctrine about Christ was belief in one God, the Father and Creator of all things. This was to be the absolute starting point of all speculation and the safeguard against all polytheistic and dualistic theories. The problem for theology was how to integrate this monotheism with the New Testament data implying the divinity of Christ. Specifically and in their simplest form, these were the convictions that God had revealed Himself in Jesus, the

Messiah, raising him from the dead and through him making salvation available to all.

Much debate was necessary before this presence of God in Jesus Christ was clarified in a way that did justice to all the texts of the New Testament and before Jesus' unity with God was fully explicated. And as one author says, "We will find that the Church grasped the totality of the picture of Christ more in a kind of spiritual intuition than in words and formulas. For this reason expressions could vary even to the point of formulas which apparently contradicted each other."[4]

The oldest attempt to express God's presence in Jesus Christ, it seems, was the understanding of Jesus as the bearer of God's Spirit—derived from the statement of Paul in Romans (RSV 1:3f.): Jesus Christ, "who was descended from David according to the flesh and designated Son of God in power according to the Spirit of holiness by his resurrection from the dead." In Paul's thought, this conception did not exclude the preexistence of Jesus as Son of God, as is evident from Romans 8:3: "God has sent his Son . . ." although later the heresy called Adoptionism took up this concept of the divine Spirit dwelling in Jesus in a sense that excluded the preexistence of Jesus as the Son of God: Jesus, according to his humanity, was the Son of God only by adoption; Jesus was not a divine person, but only a man filled with the Spirit of God.


## THE ORIGINS OF THE LOGOS CHRISTOLOGY

More successful than this Spirit Christology was the one known as the Logos Christology, which was elaborated by such men as Tertullian, Origen and Novatian and viewed Jesus as the Word, or Wisdom, who participated with the Father in the creation as well as in the redemption of the world. The term Logos was found already in John's "And the Word [Logos] became flesh" and also in the Book of Proverbs (8:22–31), with its reference to a personified Wisdom distinct from the Father and begotten by Him as His firstborn and instrument of creation.

The concept of the Logos was also a prominent concept in the prevailing Neoplatonic philosophy, and the danger was that the Christian faith might be corrupted by such contact. This danger was made real by the Alexandrian priest Arius, who was a devotee of Neoplatonism. Neopla-

4. A. Grillmeier, S.J., *Christ in Christian Tradition* (New York: Sheed & Ward, 1965), p. 40.

tonic theology saw God as ineffable, unbegotten, without origin, and unchangeable. Arius therefore had to wrestle with the problem of how to relate this unoriginated, unchangeable being to the world of time and change. His solution was to posit the Logos as mediator between the Creator and creation, a mediator who was the first and noblest creature but created out of nothing, changeable and fallible and made Son of God only after moral probation. Against this hellenization of the Gospel, the bishops at Nicaea took a decisive stand, declaring, "we believe . . . in one Lord Jesus Christ, the Son of God, the only-begotten generated from the Father, that is, from the being *[ousia]* of the Father, God from God, light from light, true God from true God, begotten, not made, one in being *[homoousios]* with the Father, through whom all things were made, those in heaven and those on earth. For us men and for our salvation, He came down, and became flesh, and was made man."[5]

Some scholars, following the lead of the German patrologist Adolph von Harnack, charged Nicaea with thus hellenizing the Gospels. The Church, however, could not avoid entering into debate with the dominant philosophy of the time and was compelled to translate the Christian message into the language of the time in order to answer the questions being raised. And in fact, as Walter Kasper points out, the term *homoousios* did not superimpose the Greek concept of essence on the biblical idea of God, but simply meant that the Son is by nature divine and "on the same plane of being as the Father, so that anyone who encounters him, encounters the Father himself."[6]

The Council of Nicaea definitively settled the question of Christ's absolute divinity but left unsettled the question of how his divinity was related to his humanity. The orthodox theologians all agreed on the unity of divinity and humanity in Christ but had difficulty explaining the nature of this unity. The specific problem they faced was how to maintain the unity while, at the same time, safeguarding the distinction between the humanity and the divinity.

The West made important contributions to the solution of the problem with Irenaeus (d. c. 200) and his insistence on the necessary union of the Godhead and humanity in Christ in order that, united with his humanity, we might be likewise joined to his divinity, and Tertullian (d. c. 230), with

5. *The Christian Faith in the Doctrinal Documents of the Catholic Church* J. Neuner, S.J., and J. Dupuis, S.J., eds., (Westminster, Md.: Christian Classics, 1975), p. 6.
6. Walter Kasper, op. cit., pp. 176–78.

his two "states" and two "substances" of Christ, which are not mixed but are united in the one person of the God-man.

In the East, where theological speculation was rampant, basically two types of approaches competed for favor: the **Logos-sarx** (Word-flesh) type of Christology favored by the Alexandrian School, which viewed the incarnation as the union of the Word with human "flesh"—a theory that owed much to the Platonic idea of man as a body inhabited by a soul that was really alien from it. The other type was the **Logos-anthropos** (Word-man) Christology, favored by the school of Antioch, which insisted on the full and integral humanity of the God-man.

The leader of the Alexandrian school, Cyril (d. 444), emphasized the role of the **Logos,** which in his view penetrated the humanity of Christ as the fire penetrates a charcoal yet leaves it a distinct identity. Cyril's rival, Nestorius (d. c. 451), the patriarch of Antioch, in line with other great theologians of that school such as Theodore of Mopsuestia (d. 428), insisted on the complete humanity of Jesus and dwelt at length on his human experiences, weakness, ignorance and suffering.

Each side saw the danger in the other side's position. In the eyes of Nestorius, Cyril was guilty of commingling the two natures in a way that turned Jesus into a monster who was only half human, while, for Cyril, Nestorius divided Christ into two distinct persons—a Jesus united only morally with the Word and therefore incapable of being the life-giving instrument of our divinization.

For Nestorius, the union of the two natures was accomplished through what he called the *prosopon* of union; i.e., the actual historical figure of the Gospels so that the incarnate Lord remained indivisibly one in *prosopon* but twofold in nature. In line with his insistence on the separateness and distinctness of the two natures, he was loath to allow a complete exchange of subjects and predicates in speech about the God-man—as in some of the expressions favored by the Alexandrians, such as God suffered and died on the cross or Jesus created the world. In particular, he took exception to a very popular expression, "Mother of God," in reference to Mary, and this earned him the enmity of the pious, who were accustomed to honoring her with this title.

Nestorius' rival, Cyril, the patriarch of Alexandria, accused Nestorius of heresy and, with Pope Celestine on his side, demanded that Nestorius subscribe to a statement that Cyril had drawn up: the *Twelve Anathemas,* which embodied the Alexandrian theology in absolutely uncompromising terms. The Council of Ephesus (431) was called to settle the feud and led to the deposition of Nestorius by a coalition of Cyril's and the pope's followers. But it failed to heal the breach between the Alexandrians and the Antiochenes, who were led by John, the powerful bishop of Antioch. Each side condemned the other and departed for home.

However, after two years of struggle they reached an agreement in the *Symbol of Union*, in which, in spite of various concessions, Cyril was satisfied to find his main point reaffirmed, namely, the identity of the subject of the God-man with the eternal Word so that one could say God Himself meets us in Jesus Christ. Another important conclusion was also drawn: Jesus was to be worshiped in both his humanity and his divinity in one single act of worship, so that, as Walter Kasper says, "Even today a Christology will have to prove its orthodoxy by the fact that it not only regards Jesus as a model of true humanity and as the first and most perfect of many brethren, but as Lord (Kyrios) to whom divine dignity and divine worship are due."[7]

There were still diehards, however, who refused to accept the agreement. Led by Dioscorus, Cyril's successor, they managed to hold another council at Ephesus in 449 (known since as the Robber Synod), which, under the brutal domination of Dioscorus, repealed the Symbol of Union and refused to consider Pope Leo's *Tome*.

But thanks to a political reversal (the Emperor Theodosius suffered a fatal fall from his horse and his successor favored Leo's position), the Council of Chalcedon condemned Dioscorus and drew up a definition based largely on Leo's *Tome*.

The importance of Leo's contribution was not in the originality of his ideas but in the masterly way he set forth the Christology of the Western Church. His clear distinction between nature and person provided the key to the solution and is faithfully reflected in the definition issued by the Council:

> We confess one and the same Christ, Son, Lord Only-begotten, made known in two natures (which exist) without confusion, without change, without division, without separation; the difference of the natures having been in no wise taken away by reason of the union, but rather the properties of each being preserved, and (both) concurring into one Person *(prosopon)* and one *hypostasis.*[8]

7. Ibid., p. 236.
8. Trans. in R. V. Sellers, *The Council of Chalcedon* (London: S.P.C.K., 1961), p. 211.

Objections, as we stated above, have been made to Chalcedon by some theologians, the most obvious and frequent one being that by translating the statements of the Gospel into Greek philosophical terms it exchanged the biblical, concrete and historically vivid personage of the man from Galilee for a set of bloodless and abstract formulas. But the defenders of Chalcedon insist that the Church was forced to cast her message in these terms in order to safeguard essential truths. Thus, in answer to those who said that Jesus was just an inspired man like the prophets, the Church had to make it clear that he really was of one substance with the Father. And to those who tried to prove that he was actually God masquerading as a man (the tendency of the extreme Alexandrian monophysites), the Church had to declare that he was also fully human. While to those who claimed his union with God was only a moral one, it had to insist that it was a personal, or hypostatic, union.

### CHALCEDON REINTERPRETED

Among Roman Catholics, one of the centers of the new Christology was at the University of Nÿmegen, in the Netherlands, where the Augustinian Ausfried Hulsbosch declared that the Church should no longer speak of a union of divine and human in a preexisting person. His colleague Piet Schoonenberg agreed. Schoonenberg has been in the forefront of the controversies aroused by the new interpretations of Chalcedon. Schoonenberg, like the Antiochenes of the fourth and fifth centuries, is most concerned to safeguard the full humanity of Christ, and he insists that the human person of Christ was not merged in a divine person. For, as he says, if Jesus is to be fully human, then he must have everything that is essential to being human and therefore human personhood above all. To deny him human personhood would be to deny that he was human. So Schoonenberg argues it is God's Word that becomes a human person.

Schoonenberg therefore rejects the traditional notion of the divine in Jesus as a preexistent person who came down to unite with the human nature of Jesus. As far as a preexistent Trinity goes, Schoonenberg says we can be agnostics, since we do not know the Trinity outside its revelation, and this revelation occurs in the Word, which is flesh, and in the Spirit, which is poured out. So the only Trinity we know is the God who becomes triune through the process of history. Schoonenberg, in *The Christ*, reiterated his agnosticism about whether the Word originates only in becoming flesh.

Rahner also has tried to avoid such terms as preexistent Son; he insists that Jesus' being God is rather a special way of being man and so communicates the meaning of God in a way that is qualitatively new and different. Or, as Hulsbosch puts it, Jesus is not man plus God, but a particular divine way of being man.

The idea of a preexistent Son who becomes incarnate as a man is also rejected by Hans Küng, the most widely read and controversial of Catholic theologians today. In his book *On Being a Christian,* he found the idea of the Incarnation of the Son of God a stumbling block for modern man. The concept of Incarnation was not even part of the original message of the Gospel, he maintains, but achieved prominence only through its emphasis in the Gospel of John. Thanks to the success of John's Christology, there was a shift of emphasis from death and Resurrection to eternal preexistence and Incarnation: the man Jesus of Nazareth overshadowed by the Son of God. Küng finds the concept of Incarnation no longer intelligible, for, as he says, "We can no longer accept the mythical ideas . . . about a being descended from God existing before time and beyond this world in a heavenly state; a 'story of gods,' in which two (or even three) divine beings are involved is not for us."[9]

For Küng, then, the concepts of preexistence (as well as divine sonship) and Incarnation mean no more nor less than that the uniqueness, underivability and unsurpassability of the call, offer and claim, made known in and with Jesus, is ultimately from God and therefore absolutely reliable.

The bishops of Germany found Küng's Christology disturbing, and in view of its wide audience, potentially a danger to the faith. Cardinal Josef Höffner demanded that Küng give a clear answer to the question, "Is Jesus the preexisting eternal son of God, one in being with the Father?" Since Küng would give no unqualified yes to this question, the bishops issued a formal warning which declared that the book created a distressing insecurity of faith and failed to explain how its Christology could be reconciled with the creeds of the Church.

The debate over the dogma of Chalcedon warmed up to such an extent during the '70s that *Time* magazine devoted an article to the controversy in its February 27, 1978, issue. It pointed out how far some Catholic scholars had moved away from the dogma of Chalcedon and quoted a

9. Garden City, N.Y.: Doubleday, 1976, pp. 439–46.

French Dominican, Jacques Pohier, who said, ". . . at the limit it is an absurdity to say God makes himself into man. God cannot be anything other than God." They also noted a declaration of the Congregation for the Doctrine of the Faith which, in 1972, defined as an error the belief that God was only present in Christ to the highest degree.

One of the most resolute and at the same time most scholarly defenders of Chalcedon is Walter Kasper, for whom the dogma of Chalcedon constitutes an extremely precise version of what, according to the New Testament, we encounter in Jesus' history and what befell him: namely, that in Jesus Christ, God himself has entered into human history and meets us there in a fully and completely human way.

One Catholic theologian who bypassed the whole debate over Chalcedon is Edward Schillebeeckx, whose first volume of a projected several-volume study, *Jesus: An Experiment in Christology*, appeared in English in 1979. Rather than start with Chalcedon, Schillebeeckx believes that one must now start "from below"; that is, with a historical study of the public ministry, death and Resurrection of Jesus—a reflection on the historical phenomenon of Jesus of Nazareth. His work stands out from all similar Catholic Christologies by his extremely critical exegesis of the New Testament and by his strikingly original interpretation of the evidence.

Schillebeeckx faces one of the major dilemmas of Christology: if one sees the Resurrection as the decisive event which engendered the faith of the apostles and inspired their formulas exalting his unique status, this accords only minor significance to the events of his life and ministry; on the other hand, if one seeks to establish the real meaning of Jesus on the basis of his actual historical life and ministry—the quest for the historical Jesus—then the portrait one draws does not seem to validate the absolute dogmatic claims and titles that the early Church attributed to him. But, for his part, Schillebeeckx seeks to show that the features of Jesus' life and teaching do justify the later, Christological claims made for him.

What was there then in the life and teaching of Jesus which would have enabled his friends and followers even *before the Resurrection* to grasp his unique significance? Schillebeeckx asserts, on the basis of New Testament documentation, that it was Jesus' claim to be *the prophet*, i.e., the eschatological prophet, who, according to the Old Testament, would come as the special agent of God to announce the rapidly approaching rule of God. For Schillebeeckx, this claim of Jesus provides the key to his most characteristic activities: his teaching, delivered with prophetic authority; his miracles, which fulfill the prophecies of Isaiah; and also his martyrdom, for the prophet of the End Time was destined to suffer and die. It would also explain why he had to die. When he challenged the authorities with his claim to be the final prophet, they had only two alternatives: either to accept him as divinely authorized or to condemn him to death as an impostor. (Many, of course, chose the second alternative, but there were others who understood him in terms of the first.)

But, then, how did their faith move from belief in Jesus as the prophet to Jesus the Christ? This, it seems, is where Schillebeeckx breaks new ground. He indicates that a Jewish tradition well known to Jesus' contemporaries and based on certain texts of the Old Testament (including Deutero- and Trito-Isaiah, Exodus, and the Book of Wisdom) indicated that the eschatological prophet would come as the anointed revealer of the divine Wisdom, would suffer, die, be exalted and have an unparalleled intimacy with the Father. This tradition, then, formed the bridge between the self-understanding of Jesus as eschatological prophet and the proclamation of him as the Christ. Moreover, his unique *"Abba"* experience would justify the assertion of his divinity.

Thus Schillebeeckx provides a model for Christology based on a fresh reading of the Synoptic Gospels. In so doing, he notes that he is breaking with the long tradition of the Church which, since the second century, has based its Christology not on the Synoptic Gospel but on John.

## HOW ARE WE SAVED BY JESUS CHRIST?

There is a very close connection between Christology and soteriology; i.e., the part of theology that deals with the relation of Christ to our salvation—often referred to as the work of Christ or the doctrine of the atonement. The Church has never given a dogmatic definition of the atonement with the same precision as in the question of Christ's person. We have today, in fact, quite a number of approaches to the question, which fall under several headings: existentialist, liberation theology, process theology and neo-Catholic theology.

The existentialists lean heavily on Bultmann, who, in line with his program of stripping away the myths hidden in the Gospel, discards the traditional substitutionary theory whereby Christ was supposed to have suffered for us vicariously, in favor of a view of the cross as a revelation that brings us the possibility of freedom from bondage to the Law and sin.

The cross and Resurrection in this view are symbols, rather than causes, of salvation. In the preached word of the cross, we encounter the possibility of freedom and are challenged to decide whether we will accept the fact that we are accepted.

For another existentialist, Paul Tillich, salvation means overcoming the estrangement between God and man in a process of man becoming whole. The "Fall" was not a historical event, but it is a condition of being finite and separated from the ground of one's being. Salvation involves acceptance of and renewal by the New Being, which occurs through the power of creative transformation revealed in Jesus as well as in other charismatic personalities.

The weak points of existential soteriology are its substitution of religious experience for the authority of the Bible, its "abysmal neglect of the doctrine of the church,"[10] and its excessive skepticism as regards the historical Jesus.

Another form of soteriology finding much favor today is liberation theology, which confines its image of salvation to the possibilities within this world. It looks not to the *eschaton*, but to the here and now, insofar as it aims to transform the social structures of oppression. Much of its inspiration comes from a Marxian social analysis coupled with a reading of the Bible that finds revelation in the acts of God liberating the poor and the oppressed, beginning with the Exodus event, which it looks on as the model of historical salvation. Jesus came as the herald of the Kingdom of God to inaugurate a new social order of justice and freedom. The presence of God is discerned in all events of liberation and revolution. Saving faith is actualized only insofar as one shares in the struggle for greater freedom and justice. Donald Bloesch finds the main weakness of liberation soteriology in its reduction of the Gospel to ethics—entailing a new form of Pelagian justification by works or social involvement. It also leaves little room for prayer and worship and too readily overlooks the dangers of egalitarian socialism.[11]

Process theology is another option that focuses exclusively on salvation as something that occurs in the here and now insofar as human beings achieve the maximum degree of self-fulfillment. In this view, God and the world are mutually dependent, and so God, too, is enriched when human

10. Donald Bloesch, "Soteriology in Contemporary Christian Thought," *Interpretation* 35 (April 1981), p. 137.
11. Ibid., p. 138.

beings realize their full potential for happiness, self-realization and creativity. As the direct heirs of the scientific and revolutionary worldview of the Enlightenment, the process theologians see man's ultimate goal as attaining mastery over nature. Here again a major weakness is its discontinuity with the tradition.

Hans Küng is more concerned than the above authors with staying in touch with the Catholic tradition, and he sketches a brief history of the Church's efforts to answer the question of how Jesus' repulsive, ignominious death could be a salvific event. What does it mean to say Jesus died for us? Paul tried to answer this question mainly by using five metaphors: redemption, justification, reconciliation, victory and sacrifice. Since then, each age has tended to favor one or other of these metaphors to convey its meaning in terms of its own peculiar cultural situation.[12]

The metaphor of redemption was taken as a literal truth by Anselm, bishop of Canterbury (d. 1109), in constructing his theory of satisfaction, which was granted quasi-official status. According to this theory, man, by sin, had offended the infinite honor of God and incurred a guilt that was infinite. Appropriate satisfaction could be rendered only by the infinitely valuable death of the God-man, for no expiation on the part of finite man could possibly atone for his infinite guilt.

This theory represented the culmination of juridical tendencies in Western theology traceable as far back as Tertullian. Incorporated into Aquinas' synthesis, it became the standard Catholic as well as Protestant doctrine of redemption. Küng notes the defects of this theory: it presupposes a literal reading of the Genesis story of Adam and Eve and the first sin, which we no longer share; it is a legalistic interpretation of sinful man's restoration to friendship with God, which minimizes the importance of grace, mercy and love; and it isolates Jesus' death on the cross from his message and life and resurrection.

Küng would also abandon the concept of sacrifice as a term that leads to unfortunate connotations of God as sadistic in demanding the blood of His Son in order to appease His wrath. As he says, the concept of expiatory sacrifice does not have all that importance in the New Testament itself and was intended only as a metaphor until it was taken up by the comparatively late Epistle to the Hebrews and turned into an elaborate theory. Moreover, its use is problematic today, when people have no experience of cultic sacrifice. "If it is used," Küng says, "it is to be understood

12. *On Being a Christian*, pp. 419–28.

in a personal sense as 'offering, self-offering' and not with reference only to Jesus' death but to his whole way of life."[13]

As a better way of expressing what the New Testament means when it says "Jesus died for us" or for "our sake," Küng prefers the concept of representation—a concept also used by Walter Kasper in his study.[14]

## RECENT DOCUMENT OF THE BIBLICAL COMMISSION

An extensive document on Christology was published in 1984 by the Pontifical Biblical Commission, a group of twenty biblical scholars from across the world appointed by the Pope.

It offers a scholarly critique of the eleven most important types of Christology that have appeared in the twentieth century, including those by Jewish historians, the Bultmannian Existentialists, the salvation history school, the anthropological school [sic], (e.g., Teilhard de Chardin, Rahner, Küng, Schillebeeckx), the Barthians and liberation theology. The document points out the benefits as well as the risks involved in each approach.

As a model of a sound Catholic Christology the authors sketch a Christology which they base on a reading of Jewish history which interprets it as the history of a great hope founded on the expectation of God's kingdom, which would bring salvation to all human beings and radically change the human situation.

God prepared His people, the commission points out, for the coming of this kingdom by a variety of mediators: the priest, the prophet, the king, the sage. Each of them in a certain way prefigures Christ. He is also prefigured by those mysterious figures of prophecy—the Son of Man and the Servant of the Lord.

When the fullness of time came Christ appeared. In his person the promised kingdom of God was now present and at work. And "all the titles, all the roles and mediatory modes related to salvation in Scripture [were] . . . assumed and united in the person of Jesus" though they have to be interpreted in an entirely new way.

The document constitutes a most valuable contribution to the current dialogue on this crucial question.

13. Ibid., p. 426.
14. See Appendix.

# III

---

## The Church

# 8

## The Church Today

There are many people today, especially among the young, who want to believe in Jesus but are negative about the Church. Movies, TV and radio bring before them a Jesus whom they admire: a man of peace, compassionate to the suffering and a friend of the poor and the oppressed; a hero willing to lay down his life for the cause dearest to his heart and able to triumph beyond the grave by inspiring millions with faith and hope in God. But when it comes to the institution that calls itself his Church, it is a different matter. Many see it as just another big organization, preoccupied with power and the desire to control people's lives. They find its structures too hierarchical and its officials too concerned with doctrine and not enough with the actual demands of life today. They feel unmoved by its appeal to authority, since they recognize authority only in persons whose talents and leadership ability they admire. They detest its tendency to issue ipse-dixit prohibitions and interfere with their private lives and personal habits. They often find its liturgies and sermons boring and even depressing.

There is no doubt some truth in these complaints. And it raises the question: Can one have Jesus without the Church? Is there an essential connection between Jesus and the Church? Did Jesus himself found the Church?

Many divergent opinions exist among scholars regarding the origin of the Church, but one can find agreement at least on the following items:

1. Jesus himself did not intend to start a new religious community distinct from Israel—or even a distinct community *within* Israel.

2. His intention was actually to renew Israel itself and prepare it for the inbreak of the Kingdom. The Twelve he chose were merely to symbolize the twelve tribes that stood at the origin of Israel.

3. The earliest community did not see themselves as a distinct community separate from Israel, but as God's End-Time people, destined to gather all Israel together in faith in Christ and his message.

4. It was only when Israel refused to believe in Christ that the early community began the process of defining its identity as the new Israel, separate from the old.

5. Since this consciousness of being a new community developed only gradually, the origin of the Church cannot be pinpointed in time.[1]

As Gerhard Lohfink shows, it is Luke who gives the clearest picture of how the Church proceeded out of Israel, in a historical process involving a number of steps. It was rooted in the Israel of the Old Testament, which contained many just who were open to the Spirit. John the Baptist opened the period of decision when Israel was called to accept the Spirit. The next step occurred when Jesus came to gather the people together as a salvation community called and led by God. The Twelve symbolized this new Israel. And though Jesus' mission ended in disaster, his death was not the end, but, as the Resurrection shows, it ushered in the final phase of Israel's history under the rule of the Spirit. On Pentecost, the community of believers was baptized by the Spirit and realized its mission to be the true Israel, the Israel of the Spirit. Luke began to use the term "Church" only at this point, when it was clear that the Church and Israel were the same. Israel's true destiny is realized when the Gentiles are brought into the community of God's people, as prophesied by Amos:

> That day I will re-erect the tottering hut of David,
> make good the gaps in it, restore its ruins
> and rebuild it as it was in the days of old,
> so that they can conquer the remnant of Edom
> and all the nations that belonged to me.
> It is Yahweh who speaks, and he will carry this out.[2]

1. Gerhard Lohfink, "Did Jesus Found a Church?" *Theology Digest* 30:3 (Fall 1982), pp. 231–35.
2. 9:11–12.

Did Jesus, then, establish the Church? We can see that, according to Luke, the answer is no if we mean an organized society existing alongside Israel. "But if by 'Church' we mean a *gathered* Israel, then we may speak of a Church founded *through* Jesus."[3] In other words, Jesus' role was decisive in the process which led to the Church.

Sometimes Matthew 16:18 ("You are Peter and on this rock I will build my Church") is used to indicate that Jesus established the Church at a definite point in time. But note that Jesus says, "I *will* build"—in other words, from our perspective here—sometime after the Resurrection the Church will be firmly founded on Peter. So Matthew, too, had an idea of the founding of the Church as a *process*.[4]

## VATICAN II ON THE CHURCH

The Second Vatican Council issued a dogmatic constitution on the Church *(Lumen Gentium)*, which gathered together the fruits of much scholarly study and theological inquiry since the beginning of our century. In this treatise, the bishops see a foreshadowing of the Church in the history of Israel. According to the bishops, the Church is inaugurated by Christ's redemptive act of obedience which culminates in the sacrifice of Calvary. As celebrated on the altar, this sacrifice carries on the work of redemption and forms the believers into one body in Christ.

The Church is also a creation of the Spirit, who lives in the Church and guides it to the fullness of truth and unites its members in a unity of fellowship and service, bestowing on it various gifts that enable it to carry out its mission.

The Risen Christ inaugurated the Church by pouring out on his disciples the Spirit promised by the Father and endowing the Church with the same mission he had: to proclaim and establish the Kingdom of God. And in fact, "She becomes on earth the initial budding forth of that kingdom . . . as she strains toward the consummation of the kingdom."[5]

To set forth the spiritual nature of the Church, the bishops draw on many of the images used in Scripture to describe the Church: the sheepfold led and nourished by the Good Shepherd, a vineyard, a field, the

3. Gerhard Lohfink, op. cit., p. 234.
4. Ibid., p. 235.
5. *Dogmatic Constitution on the Church (Lumen Gentium)*, 5.

edifice of God whose foundation is the apostles, the holy temple, the New Jerusalem, the spouse of Christ, the mystical body of Christ.

The mystical body of Christ is built up by the Spirit, who distributes His various gifts to the members for the welfare of the Church and animates the body with love so that all are taken up into the mysteries of his life while they are united with Christ in his sufferings.

The bishops give pride of place to the image of the Church as "the people of God." A whole chapter, in fact, is devoted to exploring the ramifications of this analogy. They note how God chose the race of Israel as a people and prepared them, in a long and often painful history, for the new covenant which Jesus came to establish in his blood. Those who believe in Christ were thus constituted as the new people of God, a messianic people created not by the works of the flesh, but by water and the Holy Spirit and established as a sure seed of unity, hope and salvation for the whole human race and destined to extend to all regions of the earth and share in the history of mankind. Those who belong to it constitute a holy priesthood offering spiritual sacrifices and, above all, joining in the offering of the Eucharist. They also exercise their priesthood by receiving the sacraments, by acts of prayer and thanksgiving and by living a holy life full of good works and self-denial.

Though made up of people from all the nations, there is, the document says, but one people of God. From each of the various nations, the Church takes to herself whoever are good and noble and uses them for the glory of God.

Though all members share in its spiritual riches, not all have the same functions. There is an inner structure of the people of God which corresponds to the diversity of duties necessary for its well-being. Over this whole structured assembly of charity the chair of Peter presides as the guarantor of its unity.

The Council recognized all those Christians who dwell outside the boundaries but share in many of the blessings of the Gospel, including faith in God and in Jesus Christ as Savior, and who are consecrated by baptism and receive other sacraments, including the Holy Eucharist. They, too, receive the gifts and graces of the Holy Spirit and by him are in some real way joined with "us."

The Council also turned its eyes to the great multitude of those who do not know the Gospel of Christ or his Church, "yet sincerely seek God and moved by grace strive by their deeds to do His will as it is known to them through the dictates of conscience."[6] God will certainly save them as well as those who have not yet reached an explicit knowledge of Himself but strive to lead a good life thanks to His grace.

One of the most notable studies of the Church since the Council is *Models of the Church* by Avery Dulles, S.J., who points out that many images and models have been used in Scripture and theology to illuminate the mystery of the Church. Six of them have proven peculiarly helpful: the Church as institution, as mystical body, as sacrament, as people of God, as herald and as servant.

Among Catholics the Church as *institution* has held a preeminent place until very recently. It defines the Church primarily in terms of its visible structures and the rights and powers of its officers. The Church as *mystical body* and as the *people of God* have become popular lately. They emphasize the fellowship the members enjoy with one another and with Christ. The theme of the Church as *sacrament* recurs in many key passages of the Second Vatican Council; it views the Church as signifying in a concrete historical form the redeeming love of God for all humanity. The model of *herald* focuses on the Church as the proclaimer of the Word and on our faith as a response to the proclamation. Those Protestant theologians, such as Karl Barth, who put exclusive emphasis on this model see the Church not as a stable reality but as an event that occurs only when the Word is actually being proclaimed. Finally, the model of the Church as *servant* would have the Church in its relations with the world act no longer as a domineering teacher but rather as a humble partner respectful of the independence of the secular world's independence, appreciative of its achievements and anxious to share in the struggle of all those seeking to build a more just and peaceful society.

As Dulles says, each model ". . . brings with it its own favorite set of images, its own rhetoric, its own values, certitudes, commitments, and priorities . . . [even its] particular set of preferred problems."[7] Each has its own weaknesses also, and they should be used so as to complement, interpenetrate and qualify each other.

6. Ibid., 35.
7. *Models of the Church* (Garden City, N.Y.: Doubleday/Image Books, 1978), p. 35.

# 9

# The Question of Authority

The Church today faces an unprecedented crisis in its authority. So much of the turmoil in the Church has to do with this fundamental issue. On all sides, one sees the authority of the Church under fire. Rome itself is no longer given the same automatic deference that once was so characteristic of the Catholic spirit. Rome's decree banning contraception was largely ignored and even openly challenged by many priests and laymen. Its refusal to admit the ordination of women was taken by the liberals as only an interim report. Hans Küng has carried on a running battle with the Curia, and in spite of his decertification by the Pope is considered a hero by many Catholic theologians.

The result of all this has been a searching investigation of the nature of ecclesiastical authority by many theologians and scholars in the past several decades; there are many studies available for anyone interested in pursuing the topic.

## JESUS' UNIQUE AUTHORITY

There is no doubt that his contemporaries attributed to Jesus a unique kind of authority. As we read in the Gospel of Mark, "The people were spellbound by his teaching because he taught with authority, and not like the scribes." (NAB Mk. 1:22). He not only interpreted the Law but did so with absolute authority. In the same spirit, he dared to forgive sins and performed healings and exorcisms. So manifest was his claim to a unique authority that on occasion he was challenged to justify his attitude: "What authority have you for acting like this Or who gave you authority to do these things?"[1] The New Testament authors in general see his authority as central to his ministry.

After his death and Resurrection, his authority is seen in a new light. He is now enthroned at God's right hand and, as the Lord, rules with authority. Full authority is given to him both in heaven and on earth, as we read in Matthew. And in Philippians: ". . . all beings in the heavens, on earth and in the underworld, should bend the knee at the name of Jesus . . ."[2] for "God has appointed him to judge everyone, alive or dead."[3]

## BASIS OF THE AUTHORITY OF THE CHURCH: THE HOLY SPIRIT

In what sense, then, does the Church share in this authority of Jesus? Unless we take a very conservative view of scriptural exegesis, we must admit that Jesus gave no detailed instructions regarding the authority of the Church. However, from the very beginning, the Church conceived its authority as a gift of the Holy Spirit. As the Second Vatican Council put it: "The Spirit guides the Church into the fullness of truth and gives her a unity of fellowship and service."[4] The Spirit recalls to mind the words of Jesus and enables his followers to confess him before the world. It is the Spirit that forms the Church into a worshiping community by joining his followers to his dying and rising[5] and by enabling them to pray as they ought,[6] and the love that is poured forth into their hearts and binds them together is a gift of the Spirit.[7] It is through this action of the Spirit that the authority of Jesus is operative in the Church.

It was the Holy Spirit in the belief of the first Christians that enabled them to remember and record faithfully the teachings of Jesus. His Gospel was transmitted by the help of the Holy Spirit at first in many forms both

1. JB Mk. 11:28.
2. Phil. 2:10.
3. Acts 10:42.
4. *Dogmatic Constitution on the Church (Lumen Gentium)*, 4.
5. *See* I Cor. 12:13.
6. Rom. 8:26.
7. Rom. 5:5.

oral and written and eventually given permanent and normative authority in the books of the New Testament. It is to these documents that the Church has bound itself and to which it turns to find the inspiration for its life and mission. All authority in the Church ultimately must be grounded in these books if the Church is to be led into all truth. In the always difficult task of interpreting the Scriptures, it is shared commitment and belief that is most important in reaching a consensus as to the meaning of the Gospel and how it is to be obeyed. "It is by reference to this common faith that each person tests the truth of his own belief."[8]

## HOW THE CHURCH'S AUTHORITY STRUCTURE DEVELOPED

The interior guidance of the Holy Spirit is the basis of the Church's unity. But, like all organizations made up of human beings, the Church also needs some kind of visible authority, an external structure that enables the members to grow together and build up a community of faith, of love and of worship. The New Testament Church shows remarkable variety in the structures of authority originally devised by the local communities. The Jerusalem Church from the very beginning, it seems, enjoyed a system of control by elders and deacons patterned after Jewish usage. In the Pauline communities, on the other hand, much more room was given to the free play of the Spirit, with little attention at first to a fixed system with rules and regulations and prohibitions. The Spirit bestows his gifts generously on the community and each member has a contribution to make in proportion to the faith given to him. There are no fixed offices or any attempt to establish rank, but only the recognition that certain gifts are of more value than others to the community. Paul singles out prophecy and teaching as most important, after apostleship itself.

Likewise in the Johannine communities the only authority, in the view of contemporary scholars such as Raymond Brown, is the Paraclete, who is given to all believers without exception.[9]

As to Matthew, some theologians claim that his Gospel points to an unstructured system of prophets and teachers, with no apparent awareness of the presbyteral system of elders, but exegetes such as Rudolf Schnack-

8. Anglican-Roman Catholic International Commission, *The Final Report* (London: S.P.C.K., 1982), p. 52.
9. Raymond Brown, *The Community of the Beloved Disciple: The Life, Loves and Hates of an Individual Church in New Testament Times* (New York: Paulist Press, 1979).

enburg argue that the community rule (Mt. 18:1–20) points to the existence of an established institution for salvation which is confirmed by the power given to Peter (16:18–20). This itself implies that there is an authority in the Church, conferred by God and ordered to salvation, "which according to the evangelist's conception can hardly repose in the community as such but is rather made over to certain persons."[10]

Whichever of these opposing views is correct, it is nevertheless true that the fully structured model of Church order characteristic of Roman Catholicism becomes clearly apparent only in the pastoral epistles (1 and 2 Timothy and Titus). Several distinct grades of authority and responsibility are manifest. At its head is the apostle Paul, directly appointed by God as herald and teacher (1 Tim. 2:7; 2 Tim. 1:11), and under him his personal delegates, Timothy and Titus, who are charged with overseeing church order at Ephesus and Crete. Coming after them are the local officials commissioned by them according to Paul's instructions. The general body of the faithful are to be guided by their pastors following a well-defined ethical teaching. It is a model of church order based on a firm exercise of authority with little room left for the unpredictable impulses of the Holy Spirit. The task of the minister par excellence is to hand on the deposit of faith, with no mention made of reinterpreting the tradition. All questions are already settled. Entry upon the ministry is through a ritual act of ordination, with laying on of hands and prayer.

Until the Second Vatican Council, the Roman Catholic Church always appealed to this model of the pastoral epistles as legitimating its claim to divine authority. Stress was laid on the Church's hierarchic structure, the unbroken succession of its episcopate, the doctrine of papal infallibility in its solemn magisterium. The errors of the various Protestant churches with different conceptions of church authority were pointed out.

Opponents of the Catholic system often attacked the pastoral model of Church authority by comparing it with the charismatic, fraternal and nonhierarchic church order found in Paul's early epistles, reflecting the Spirit-filled communities he organized at Thessalonika and Corinth and in Galatia. In this view, these communities represented Paul's genuine ecclesiology, while the pastoral epistles were written by some anonymous presbyter who attached Paul's name to them in order to sanction a church order that deviated enormously from the model favored by Paul.

Some Catholic theologians recently have also taken this view. Jesus,

10. Rudolf Schnackenburg, *The Church in the New Testament* (New York: Herder & Herder, 1965), p. 74.

they say, exercised a totally spontaneous authority and warned his disciples against any kind of attempt to dominate others. They were to live together in a fraternal spirit, aiming only to be of service to one another. Paul, too, they say, always struggled against any formal dominance by one believer over another. In Paul's communities there were to be no formal ministries, but each believer was called to exercise his or her special charism for the benefit of the whole community.

## THE RENEWED CATHOLIC THEOLOGY OF AUTHORITY

Other Catholic theologians of moderate persuasion, however, find some truth in this approach but try to combine it with traditional Catholic concerns in a balanced ecclesiology that gives due weight to both the pastorals and the early Pauline epistles. Doctrinal unity and ministerial succession, yes, but also Christian fraternity, equality of all, recognition of the charisms freely bestowed by the Holy Spirit on the multitude of believers. Ministerial authority? Yes, but only in order to serve the underlying reality, which is a people endowed with many gifts and graces by the Holy Spirit.

It is this renewed ecclesiology which may be discerned in the documents of the Second Vatican Council.

In its teaching, the Council reiterates the traditional view of the hierarchical authority of the bishops, who, it says, "have succeeded to the place of the apostles as shepherds of the Church" and as a college with its head the Roman pontiff "is the subject of supreme and full power over the universal Church." However, it states that this power must be used "only for the edification of the flock in truth and holiness remembering that he who is greater should become as the lesser and he who is the more distinguished, as the servant."[11]

It also emphasizes the role of the Holy Spirit in the Church, who distributes special graces among the faithful of every rank. These gifts should be received with thanksgiving, for they are "exceedingly suitable and useful for the needs of the Church."[12]

11. *Dogmatic Constitution on the Church (Lumen Gentium)*, 22, 27.
12. Ibid., 12.

## PROTESTANT-CATHOLIC DIALOGUES ON AUTHORITY

The nature of the Church's authority has been one of the main issues discussed by Protestant and Catholic theologians in the recent dialogues. As with other questions, remarkable agreement has been reached. In its *Agreed Statement on Authority in the Church* (Venice, 1976), the Anglican-Roman Catholic International Commission reached a consensus on authority in the Church and, in particular, on the principles of primacy which the participants claim are of fundamental importance.

What is the basis for authority in the Church? they ask. As the report states, it is the influence of Christ on the members of his community, who are enabled so to live that his authority will be mediated through them.

Special gifts are given by the Holy Spirit to certain members for the benefit of the Church. The exercise of ministerial authority is one of these, and it belongs primarily to the bishop, who is responsible for preserving and promoting the integrity of the community in order to further the Church's response to the lordship of Christ. The other ordained ministers share in this ministerial authority, which is intrinsic to the Church's structure.

But all the members of the community share in discovering God's will for His Church in the midst of cultural changes and a variety of situations. Both ordained and nonordained must test each other's insights in a process of discernment and response so that the Gospel might be pastorally applied under the impulse of the Holy Spirit and the authority of the Lord Jesus Christ.

The aim of all authority in the Church is to promote a fellowship of loving service in the truth of Christ.

The basic reality of the Church is found in the local community, where the Eucharist, the effective sign of community, is celebrated. As a communion, however, the local church cannot stay closed in upon itself, but seeks fuller communion with the other churches. It sees in the other churches a reflection of its own identity and a source of mutual inspiration and support.

It is the task of the bishop to make the local community aware of the universal communion of which it is a part. He expresses this unity of his church with the others—a fact symbolized by the participation of several bishops in his ordination.

Ever since the Council of Jerusalem (Acts 15), the local communities have felt the need to maintain ties with the other communities by coming together in meetings. Such meetings may be either regional or worldwide. The decisions taken at these councils are to be considered binding upon the participant churches.

Historically, the bishop of a more prominent see also exercised a ministry of oversight to the other bishops of the region, a form of service carried out in coresponsibility with them. The purpose of this ministry is to promote right teaching, holiness of life, brotherly unity, and the Church's mission to the world. This spirit of active, mutual assistance and concern is indispensable to the Church's witness to Christ.

## CREATIVE DISSENT

One of the major manifestations of the crisis of authority in the Church today involves the tension between the theologians and the hierarchy. Since the end of the Second Vatican Council, it has become evident that considerable disagreement often exists between the teaching of certain theologians and the official teaching of the Church. By appealing to the Council, some theologians claimed a degree of freedom that would have been unthinkable but a few years before. They enunciated new interpretations of dogma in books and articles that attracted the attention of the public and often aroused considerable controversy within the Church. When Rome stepped up its investigations of some of the liberal theologians, fourteen hundred of them signed a petition demanding new procedures by the Congregation of the Faith to safeguard their rights.

One of the leading conservatives, Kenneth Baker, charges that open defiance of the magisterium is now the rule, rather than the exception, and he names as examples Hans Küng, Charles Curran, Avery Dulles, Stephen Kelleher, Anthony Kosnick, Andrew Greeley, John Giles Milhaven, John Dedek and Richard McCormick—just to scratch the surface!

Hans Küng is certainly the most celebrated of the dissenters. His skirmishes with the Curia were given wide coverage in the press. And when he was finally decertified as a Catholic theologian, on December 18, 1980, a cry of outrage could be heard around the world. Fr. Andrew Greeley scored the action of the Congregation as a terrible black mark on the Church's image. Other theologians, around the world, raised an uproar against the decision, seeing it as a forecast of a conservative swing in the Church.

The Küng case was spectacular but only one of many such affairs over the past fifteen years. The basic issue involved, the relation of theologians to the authority of the magisterium, has caused much ink to flow. To date, there is still much tension in the Church over this very tangled question.

As historians point out, one of the reasons for the current upheaval is the fact that, for centuries, Catholic theologians were held on a very short leash. They were not supposed to do creative thinking but merely to defend the teaching of the hierarchy. The definition of papal infallibility helped Rome gain even tighter control of the theologians. And Pope Pius XII was only reiterating a long-standing rule when, in his encyclical *Humani Generis*, of 1950, he insisted that once the Roman pontiff has taken a position on a controverted point of theology, it is no longer optional.

In this model of Church authority, the authoritative decrees of popes and bishops were accorded a kind of quasi infallibility because of the special grace of office the hierarchy claimed. All teaching was tightly controlled by the bishops, who were themselves closely watched by the Curia. Dissent was held to a minimum.

This system was clearly undermined by the events surrounding the Second Vatican Council. The Council itself did not directly strike at the authoritarian model. It reiterated, in fact, the obligation to assent to ordinary, noninfallible teaching of the Roman pontiff, with no mention of the right to dissent.

But indirectly the Council undermined the foundations of the authoritarian model. In a number of decrees, the positions of the Roman magisterium were reversed. In biblical studies, for instance, the Council accepted the critical approach and so laid to rest a number of antiquated opinions of the Biblical Commission. In regard to Protestant-Catholic relations, it "corrected" the views found in previous papal encyclicals forbidding Catholics to participate in the ecumenical movement. The Council called for complete religious freedom and thus disavowed the previous papal commitment to some form of union of Church and state with certain restrictions on nonconformists. Finally it took a positive view of secular progress and so terminated a long series of papal denunciations of modern civilization.

These developments vindicated such theologians as Yves Congar, Karl

Rahner and John Courtney Murray, who had been punished by the Roman Curia for advocating the very ideas now officially embraced by the Council. This obviously put the Roman magisterium in a bad light, as some of its most crucial preconciliar policies were disavowed. The lesson was clear: dissent could play a vital role in the Church. "Heresy" today might be official teaching tomorrow!

Thanks to these developments and to the general climate of opinion, which favored the freedom of the individual, dissent became a major problem for the hierarchy in the postconciliar Church. There were no easy answers, for while the Council laid down the duty of Catholics to give assent to the ordinary teaching of the magisterium, it also opened the door wide for dissent by advocating collegiality, religious freedom, modernization, cultural pluralism and dialogue.

The clash between dissenting theologians and bishops sometimes became strident, and in the case of Küng attracted enormous attention from the secular press.

It is becoming increasingly clear that it is no easy task to set the limits of orthodoxy in the Church today. One of the great shifts that occurred at the Council was to a more historically conscious way of viewing dogma. Until Vatican II, the general feeling in the Church was that its dogmatic formulas were unchangeable: such concepts as transubstantiation, infallibility, original sin and sanctifying grace were regarded as perfect expressions of the truths contained in the Scriptures and definitive formulations that would be valid until the end of time. Theologians who dared to suggest otherwise were given a severe warning by Pope Pius XII in *Humani Generis*. But the Council gave a great impetus to the concept of historicity, i.e., the view that dogmas are historically conditioned formulas and need to be reformulated when new cultural conditions arise which render the previous formulas unintelligible or at least obscure. This idea was given further amplification in the Vatican's decree of 1973 *Mysterium Ecclesiae*.

In order to fulfill this task of reformulating past doctrines, the bishops are much dependent on the theologians, whose primary function is to provide the means for a better understanding of the doctrine and to search for a language that can relate that truth more clearly to contemporary concerns. Such an enterprise is full of risk and will sometimes lead a theologian to take positions that conflict with official doctrine.

Such dissent, our history shows, may be creative. On the other hand, not all dissent is beneficial. There are obviously limits to reinterpreting

Catholic dogma. Wild speculations are of little value to the community of faith and may even needlessly disturb the less well informed.

Over the past decade, some valuable lessons have been learned: (1) the importance of dialogue between theologians and bishops; (2) the importance of securing a consensus on an issue in the Church before any attempt is made to conclude discussion; (3) a willingness to live with much disagreement in the Church, which is the price of freedom; (4) the need for those in authority to persuade by argument, rather than trying to impose their opinions by judicial pressures; (5) the recognition by Catholics that if one feels compelled to dissent from noninfallible teaching, one should do so only reluctantly and after thorough reflection and study, all the while maintaining proper respect and support for the pastoral magisterium.

There is also the realization that, if worse comes to worst, and finally, as a last resort, authority feels obliged to step in, then certain safeguards are necessary to protect the human rights of the theologian. The procedures used by the Congregation for the Doctrine of the Faith have been much criticized on this score, and some recommendations have been made that should surely be accepted. For instance, the authorities should consult with theologians who represent the whole of Catholic theology and not just one school. Another point well taken is that intervention by authority might begin at the local level—a rule that respects cultural pluralism and the varied experience of people today.

# 10

## The Church in Dialogue

Pope John Paul II journeyed to Great Britain in 1982 for a historic six-day visit. As the first pope ever to set foot on British soil, he entered Britain amid much concern about possible violent protests from hard-core antipapal forces. Only a few such minor incidents occurred, however, during the pope's visits to London, Coventry, Liverpool, Manchester, York, Edinburgh, Glasgow and Cardiff. The highlight of the trip was the gathering at the cathedral of Canterbury, where the pope embraced the Most Reverend Robert Runcie, Archbishop of Canterbury, and prayed at an ecumenical service with Anglican, Greek Orthodox and Methodist prelates for "the day of full restoration of unity in faith and love."

An even more encouraging event occurred recently in Vancouver, British Columbia, in September 1983, when the World Council of Churches accepted its Faith and Order Commission's report entitled *Baptism, Eucharist and Ministry.*

Those who think progress toward unity, nevertheless, is slow must keep in mind that the cold war between Protestants and Catholics has lasted more than four hundred years.

Rome officially committed itself to the ecumenical movement only during the Second Vatican Council. But its beginnings can be traced back at least to the World Mission Conference of Edinburgh, in 1910, which in turn came out of various Protestant missionary movements. Organizers of the conference were motivated by the desire to achieve collaboration of the various churches in the mission fields, where the disunity and rivalry of the Christians made progress difficult.

Doctrinal differences between the churches presented problems and made the hoped-for collaboration difficult. In order to get around this obstacle, many churchmen felt that it would be best to concentrate on peace and social-justice issues. This idea found expression in the World Conference for Life and Work, which met at Stockholm in 1925 as the first expressly ecumenical conference. It was carried forward through various working groups centered, from 1930 on, in Geneva.

At the same time, there was "recognition" that questions of doctrine were of vital importance and could not be permanently ignored. Hence another committee was organized to explore the possibilities of greater unity on the level of doctrine. This led to the first World Conference for Faith and Order, at Lausanne on August 3, 1927, with 385 men and 9 women representing 108 ecclesial communities.

However, not until 1948 were the two movements—Life and Work and Faith and Order—combined to constitute the World Council of Churches, made up of 147 churches represented by 351 delegates from 47 countries. The members officially proclaimed their faith in Our Lord Jesus Christ, God and Savior. They also stated they had no intention of constituting a "superchurch" or in any way infringing on the autonomy of the member churches. Much latitude was allowed for doctrinal differences, even (as was stated later, in 1950) allowing that not every church must see the other member churches as churches in the full meaning of the word. This admission enabled the Orthodox churches to enter the World Council, and by 1961 most of them had joined—including the churches of Russia, Bulgaria, Romania and Poland.

The Catholic Church officially held aloof until the Second Vatican Council. Catholics were forbidden to take part in congresses for unity without the permission of the Holy See, while Pope Pius XI, in his encyclical *Mortalium animos,* of January 6, 1928, was sharply critical of the ecumenical movement, which he saw as lacking a solid scholarly base and too willing to water down the essentials of the Christian faith. Nevertheless a number of Catholics, especially in Germany and France, continued to work for the cause of Christian unity, including the heroic Max Joseph Metzger, who brought German Catholics and Protestants together in prayer meetings until he was seized and executed by the Nazis, in 1944.

Further impetus was given to Catholic participation in the ecumenical movement by the Archbishop of Paderborn, Lorenz Jaeger (d. 1975), who encouraged Catholic theologians to meet with Lutheran theologians to discuss doctrinal issues. In 1952, the International Conference for Ecumenical Questions was formed, with important assistance from Jan Willebrands, a Dutch professor. Pope John XXIII drew on its experience when he established the Secretariat for Promoting Christian Unity, in 1960, headed by Cardinal Augustin Bea (d. 1968). In 1962 it achieved official status as a conciliar commission and was able to play a key role in elaborating the Decree on Ecumenism of the Second Vatican Council.

At the outset, the decree notes the tremendous yearning of Christians divided among themselves that "there may be one visible Church of God, a Church truly universal and sent forth to the whole world" for the salvation of the world. It rehearses in a noncritical manner the biblical data testifying to Christ's founding of the Church, and it records in brief the checkered history of the Church and the scandal of the schisms and divisions that have torn away at its unity. It also acknowledges the Roman Church's share in the breakdown of unity.

The program it lays out for promoting unity among Christians consists of a number of well-thought-out practical measures. First, Catholics are exhorted to dedicate themselves to the work of their own spiritual renewal, because we serve the cause of Christian unity most effectively when we strive to live in the spirit of the Gospel. Then it recommends frequent public and private prayer for unity, and it encourages Catholics to join in prayer for unity with their separated brethren and even allows that at times this might mean engaging in public worship together. It also insists on the need to promote greater understanding between the churches by honest and open exchanges or dialogues in which the participants, in an atmosphere of good will and lively charity, might discuss their differences.

Catholics must also, it says, make every effort to correct whatever is deficient in their own formulations of doctrine in order not to cause unnecessary obstacles to the restoration of unity. In this regard it reminds us that not all official doctrines enjoy the same degree of importance: there is a "hierarchy of truths," since they vary in their relationship to the foundation of the Christian faith. Finally, the Council urged Catholics to join with their fellow Christians in working on social problems such as the alleviation of poverty and other forms of injustice so that by working together on such projects Christians might learn to take the first steps toward fuller unity.

In dealing with the delicate issue of the ecclesial status of other churches, the Council abandoned Rome's previously simple and unqualified way of asserting its claim to be the only true Church of Christ. While refusing to recognize their ecclesial reality in an unqualified way, since they "have not preserved the genuine and total reality of the Eucharistic mystery," the Council nevertheless recognized that the Protestant churches participate in the mystery of Christ's true Church to a great degree, since they possess so many of its essential elements, including true faith in Jesus as Lord and Savior, recognition of the authority of Scripture, and the sacrament of baptism.

The decree urged dialogue especially on the true meaning of the Lord's Supper, the other sacraments, and the Church's worship and ministry.

Almost immediately after the Council, steps were taken both on the national and international levels to implement this revolutionary decree. Many official conversations have since taken place between Roman Catholic bishops and theologians and representatives of the various Protestant and Anglican churches.

To mention but some of the most notable, there were the Lutheran-Catholic Dialogue in the United States, begun in 1965, on such topics as "the Nicene Creed," "Baptism," "the Eucharist as Sacrifice," "Eucharist and Ministry," and "Papal Primacy and the Universal Church"; the Presbyterian-Reformed-Roman Catholic Consultation, which published a statement, *The Unity We Seek* (1977); and the United Methodist-Roman Catholic Dialogue/U.S.A., which issued a *Report on Holiness and Spirituality of the Ordained Ministry* (1976).

Roman Catholic-Anglican dialogues on the national and international levels also produced several important statements: *Ministry and Ordination* (1973); *Authority in the Church* (1976); a *Final Report* dealing with the theology of marriage and its application to mixed marriages, in 1975; and *Authority in the Church II* (1982).

On all the issues mentioned, there have been considerable advances, as theologians have been able to reach a degree of consensus that was previously considered impossible.


## THE LIMA STATEMENT

One of the most promising signs of ecumenical progress, as we noted, is the acceptance, in 1983, by the World Council of Churches of a document on baptism, Eucharist and ministry. Adopted by its Faith and Order Commission at Lima the previous year, it is notable for a number of reasons. First, it represents the work of some 120 theologians and church leaders from all parts of the world, including Roman Catholics and Orthodox as well as Protestants. Second, it provides a very fine synthesis of many previous dialogues which reflect the remarkable agreement already achieved.

One of the Roman Catholic theologians saw the text as a major contribution to the discussions now going on between the churches and a great challenge to Rome, since Rome finds itself confronted for the first time with a document representing a consensus of all the major denominations. And an Orthodox theologian noted how it addressed many of the Orthodox concerns in a way unimaginable only a few years ago.

In dealing with the question of baptism and the controversy over infant baptism (which some of the churches regard as unscriptural), it notes that both infant baptism and believers' baptism "embody God's own initiative in Christ and express a response of faith made within the believing community."

The Eucharist, it describes under five categories: as thanksgiving to the Father, as memorial of Christ, as invocation of the Spirit, as communion of the faithful, and finally as meal of the Kingdom of God.

As to the real presence of Christ in the Eucharist, it affirms it in a very definite way in its description of this presence as real, living, active and unique.

It asks the question, In what sense may the Eucharist be called a sacrifice? Historically, Roman Catholics, in opposition to Protestants, have insisted that it is a propitiatory sacrifice. But, in agreement with the previous dialogues of Roman Catholics with Anglican, Orthodox, Lutheran, Presbyterian and Reformed churches, the Lima statement simply affirms the sacrificial nature of the Eucharist. It then asks whether the other Christian churches should not review their reasons for accepting or rejecting the notion of the Eucharist as a propitiatory sacrifice. The text also urges every church to give the Eucharist a central place in its life, to celebrate it at least every Sunday and to encourage its members to receive frequently. Secondary matters such as whether and how to reserve the elements after the celebration, it leaves to the discretion of each church.

We may also note that while the statements of all the major dialogues on the Eucharist confess the real and true presence of the Lord, they shy away, as the Lima statement does, from using the term "transubstantiation" to describe the change that takes place in the bread and wine, although the Lima statement admits that the term does serve a purpose in confessing and preserving the "mystery character of the eucharistic presence."

On the closely connected issue of the **ministry**—perhaps the most intensely debated issue among Christians—we find a similar harmony of the Lima statement with those generated in previous dialogues. The Lima text sets the ordained ministry in the context of the service of the whole people of God, while the threefold ministry of bishop, presbyter and deacon it sees as an "expression of the unity we seek and also as a means for achieving it." Those churches that maintain this form of the ministry, it says, should seek ways of realizing its potential more fully for the most effective witness of the Church, while those with a different structure might consider adopting the ancient threefold pattern for its sign value.

One of the main obstacles to further agreement on the nature of the Christian ministry has been the Roman Catholic insistence that for a valid ministry one must be ordained by a bishop who was himself linked by imposition of hands with the historic episcopacy, supposedly stretching back to the apostles. As we can see from above, the Lima statement, as well as other statements, have attempted to cut this Gordian knot by situating valid ministry in a broader context. Apostolic succession is not simply identified with the historical chain of bishops, but is declared to depend also on fidelity to the Gospel and conformity of life and word to the teaching of the apostles. Insofar as the Church is apostolic in this sense, they consider its ministry valid. But the Roman Catholic Church still officially holds that, through the rupture of the sixteenth century, the Protestants lost contact with the historic chain of bishops, thus losing the fullness of the sign of apostolic succession. However, some Catholic theologians have accepted the broader interpretation of apostolic succession, which does not ascribe exclusive value to episcopal ordination. This is true, for instance, of the German Catholic theologians who joined their Protestant colleagues of the University Ecumenical Institutes in a *Memorandum* which maintains that the unbroken sequence of imposed hands was only a help in safeguarding the apostolic tradition and merely a good sign of the continuity and unity of the Church. Ordination itself is only the customary way of being commissioned for service to the Church. It is merely the recognition of a call already given by the community or the Holy Spirit and gives one a participation in the mystery of Christ. Catholic and Protestant churches, therefore, the statement says, ought to recognize each other's ministries.

The same conclusion has been reached in other major dialogues: the

Catholic-Presbyterian/Reformed, the Anglican-Roman Catholic International Commission, and the Lutheran-Roman Catholic (USA); it is also the position taken in the Lima statement, which asks the churches with the apostolic succession to "recognize both the apostolic content of the ordained ministry" which exists in nonsuccession churches and "the existence in these churches of a ministry of *episcope* (oversight) in various forms." Conversely, nonsuccession churches are asked to "recognize that the continuity with the church of the apostles finds profound expression in the successive laying on of hands by bishops and that, though they may not lack the continuity of the apostolic tradition, this sign will strengthen and deepen that continuity."[1]

The Lima statement also recognizes that the ordination of women in some churches raises obstacles to the mutual recognition of ministries, but such obstacles, it says, "should not be regarded as a substantive hindrance for further efforts toward mutual recognition. The Spirit may well speak to one church through the insights of another."[2]

The mutual recognition of ministries is related to a very practical question raised by the ecumenical movement: how far should Protestants and Catholics go in sharing each other's sacraments? Until the Council, such sharing was ruled out for Catholics. But with the growing convergence of Protestant and Catholic theologians in matters of faith and the realization that the major churches basically share the same belief in the Eucharist, the question of intercommunion has become a much debated topic.

In its *Ecumenical Directory*, of 1967, and its special *Instruction*, of 1972, Rome laid down certain conditions to be fulfilled in admitting other Christians to a Catholic Eucharist. The most obvious is agreement with the Catholic Eucharistic faith. The others include a serious spiritual need to receive communion and the inability to have recourse to their own minister for a prolonged period, and they must ask for it of their own accord. But it made no provision for a Catholic to receive at a Protestant Eucharist.

Some bishops have been very flexible in interpreting the Vatican instructions to the point of ordinarily allowing the non-Catholic partner at a nuptial Mass or a non-Catholic at a funeral Mass to receive Communion. Bishop Elchinger of Strasbourg ruffled some curial feathers when he also

1. Avery Dulles, "Toward a Christian Consensus: The Lima Meeting," *America*, February 10, 1982, p. 127.
2. Ibid., p. 127.

allowed the Catholic partner on certain conditions to receive at a Protestant Eucharist, since the refusal of reciprocity is truly felt to be humiliating, irritating and intolerable.[3]

Few church officials regard Bishop Elchinger's solution as an apt one, but none would deny the seriousness of the problem he addressed. Interchurch families are very numerous, and they are the ones who suffer the most from church disunity; they are also the ones most inclined to take church law into their own hands, since they often wish to bring their children up in both churches, receiving Holy Communion in each.

3. "Reports and Documentation," *Lutheran World* 22 (1975), p. 151.

# 11

# The Pope—
# Monarch or Minister?

The thorniest of all the questions facing Protestant and Catholic theologians in dialogue today concerns the role of the pope. As Paul VI said himself, the pope is the chief obstacle to unity today.

The most detailed study of the question in the United States has been conducted by a team of Lutheran and Roman Catholic scholars for the dialogue sponsored by the U.S. National Committee of the Lutheran World Federation and the Catholic Bishops' Commission for Ecumenical and Interreligious Affairs.

These scholars have issued three very important studies as the fruit of their research: *Peter in the New Testament* (1973), *Papal Primacy and the Universal Church* (1974) and *Teaching Authority and Infallibility in the Church* (1978).

A summary of the findings contained in these studies will permit us to see how much progress has been made in reaching a consensus on papal authority.

Since the pope claims a primacy over the universal Church in virtue of being the successor of St. Peter, the first step deemed necessary by the participants in the dialogue was to examine the actual role of Peter as indicated by the New Testament.

As far as the actual historical career of Simon Peter goes, the study acknowledges the difficulty of sifting out of the Gospels what role Peter actually played in the ministry of Jesus, as distinct from the role attributed to him by the Church after the Resurrection. "For instance, it is difficult to know whether Simon really was a spokesman for the intimate companions of Jesus during his lifetime or whether the instances of such spokesmanship in the Gospels are the reflection of his later role as the spokesman for the Twelve in the Jerusalem Church."[1]

As to his role in the early Church, again it is not too clear what function he performed. It does seem probable that he became known as **Cephas** because Jesus himself gave him this name. Also he was certainly the most prominent of the Twelve in Jerusalem—probably because he was the first to have an appearance of the Risen Jesus. But his special authority over the other Twelve is not clearly attested. Rather, he is pictured as consulting with the apostles and even being sent by them.[2]

However, this is not the whole story. We must also consider the **symbolic** role that Peter played in the Church. A number of images clustered around his memory, some of them no doubt based on his actual historical career, while others were no doubt idealizations.

Tracing this trajectory of images, we find Peter remembered as the great Christian fisherman, based, it seems likely, on his career as the most prominent missionary among the Twelve and the fact that he was a fisherman. He is also portrayed as the model shepherd, or pastor. Associated with this image of pastoral authority is the power of the keys of the Kingdom and of binding and loosing. Closely connected with his image as shepherd is that of Peter the Christian martyr, who like Jesus lays down his life for his sheep. Here again there is, no doubt, a historical basis insofar as evidence indicates Peter was martyred at Rome in the 60s.

Another image portrays Peter as the receiver of a special revelation— founded probably on the tradition that Peter was the first to see the Lord after the Resurrection. And this closely relates to his image as the confessor of the true Christian faith—the basis in history being his actual confession of Jesus as the Messiah during Jesus' ministry. Hence Peter would be recognized as the rock on which the Church is founded and as such the guardian of the faith against false teaching. Finally the dark side is also remembered in the image of Peter as a weak and sinful man who has to be rebuked by Jesus as "Satan" and eventually even betrays him, only to be forgiven by the Risen Jesus.

In the light of all this it is evident, as these scholars say, that we cannot assess the importance of Peter for later church history simply by evaluat-

1. Raymond Brown, Karl Donfried and John Reumann, eds., *Peter in the New Testament* (Minneapolis, Minn.: Augsburg Publishing House, 1973), p. 159.
2. Acts 8:14.

ing his actual historical role in the ministry of Jesus. We must also take into account this trajectory of images found not only in the New Testament but even going beyond into the early centuries of the Church's history. But how far this trajectory of images is rooted in the historical Peter is an important question which they do not feel ready to answer at this point. Another question they leave open: to what extent does this trajectory reflect God's providence and will and how far is it due to historical accident?

The images of Peter, then, it was felt, must be based on the historical memory that as the first to receive the revelation of the Resurrection he played the key role in the founding of the Church and in strengthening his brethren: as a great missionary who fed the sheep of Christ, as a great pastor who cared for the universal Church and as one the rest of the Church looked up to because of his special relationship with Jesus during the public ministry.

So the next question logically was whether there was need for such a Petrine ministry today, that is, one person charged with safeguarding and promoting the Church's unity. Of course the Catholic answer was obvious, but the Lutherans also could see the value of such a ministry, other things being equal.

But who should fill such an office? The Lutherans were willing to admit that the bishop of Rome had the best claim to such a ministry in the light of the papacy's unparalleled record in the cause of Church unity in the past. And they might be willing to accept the pope as head of a reunited Church if the papacy could be restructured to meet the needs of Christians today.

But could the papacy be restructured? Here the historians on both sides had a field day in trying to synthesize the enormous data of papal history. The various periods of papal history were reviewed which showed the enormous variations in the exercise of papal authority in the past and how much the accidents of history contributed to making the office (as defined by Vatican I) one that confers full, supreme, immediate and ordinary jurisdiction on the pope and endows him with that infallibility with which Christ wished to endow his Church.

## ORIGIN OF PAPAL PRIMACY

As was recognized by both sides, the actual association of a Petrine ministry exclusively with the bishop of Rome was the result of a very gradual and complex development. For a long time, Catholics held a rather simple view: Jesus himself conferred primacy in the Church on Peter (three texts were most frequently cited in favor of this view: Matthew 16:17-19, Luke 22:32, and John 21:15-17), and Peter passed this primacy on to the bishop of Rome as his successor. But today Scripture scholars of all faiths read these texts to mean only that Jesus conferred a certain preeminence on Peter among the apostles but did not directly establish the papacy as a continuing office in the Church.

How, then, did the bishop of Rome come to be recognized as the successor of Peter in a universal primacy over the Church?

There is no solid historical evidence that the bishop of Rome even claimed such a primacy until about the middle of the third century.

The Lutheran and Catholic scholars agreed that the question of papal primacy cannot be treated in terms of proof passages from Scripture or as a matter of church law, but "must be seen in the light of many factors—biblical, social, political, theological—which have contributed to the development of the theology, structure, and function of the modern papacy."[3]

Two parallel lines of development, they claim, tended to enhance the role of the bishop of Rome among the churches of the time. There was first the continuing development of images of Peter originating with the apostolic communities. In addition, there was the importance of Rome as a political, cultural and religious center and focus of unity in the contest with heresy. Other images of Peter were added to the biblical trajectory of images: Peter was reverenced as missionary preacher, great visionary, destroyer of heretics, receiver of the new law, gatekeeper of heaven, helmsman of the ship of the Church, coteacher with Paul, comartyr with Paul in Rome.

At the same time, the bishop of Rome gained increasing prominence because of the position and prestige of Rome as the capital of the empire and a great cultural mecca. It was also a very wealthy church, noted for its

3. Paul Empie and T. Austin Murphy, eds., *Papal Primacy and the Universal Church* (Minneapolis, Minn.: Augsburg Publishing House, 1974), p. 16.

munificent charity. And its willingness to be of assistance to other churches around the world considerably enhanced its influence.

Moreover, in the contest with heresies, especially Gnosticism, episcopal sees of apostolic foundation were regarded as especially helpful gauges of orthodoxy. Already in the second century, Irenaeus pointed to Rome as an unquestioned channel of pure apostolic doctrine, since it was founded by the blessed apostles Peter and Paul. All churches should agree with it, he maintained.

And in fact, Rome intervened more and more frequently in the lives of distant churches, took sides in theological controversies, was consulted by bishops on many doctrinal and disciplinary matters, and sent its legates to attend Church councils near and far.

During the fourth and fifth centuries, the papacy made continuous headway in advancing its claims to a primacy over the whole Church. It seems true that the Council of Nicaea (A.D. 325) was unaware of the doctrine of papal supremacy. Yet, as the historian T. Jalland notes, the Church had hardly accustomed itself to "speak in the language of jurisdiction whether papal or otherwise, and that in consequence the crucial question which see possessed its plenitude did not arise . . . It is clear," he goes on to say, "that the Church was moving in the direction of providing herself with the machinery for corporate action as an oecumenical society on an equal footing with an oecumenical State."[4] And as a matter of fact, we see the bishops of Rome defining their role as chief shepherds of the flock of Christ with growing consistency and precision. Pope Damasus (366–84), at a council in 382, seems to have claimed formally the possession of a primacy over all the churches in virtue not of conciliar decisions but of the Lord's promise to St. Peter. Pope Siricius (384–99) goes a step farther: He not only hears appeals but even takes the initiative. In his letters—which for the first time are now called *decretals* —he implicitly claims the right to make decisions, with universal application in matters both doctrinal and disciplinary.

With Leo I, we come to the apex of this development. Drawing on the rich heritage of papal experience and claims, he formulated a doctrine of papal primacy that was to decisively influence the later course of the papacy. The correlation between the bishop of the Roman church and images of Peter which were already suggested by his predecessors now becomes fully explicit. According to Leo, Peter was "the Rock" on which

4. *The Church and the Papacy* (London: S.P.C.K., 1944), pp. 205–6.

the Lord built his Church; his successors, the popes, were merely his temporary and mystical personifications. The Petrine function vested in the bishop of Rome was nothing less than the care for all the churches. In virtue of his office, the pope had the plenitude of power over the universal Church: he was its supreme ruler, its supreme teacher and its supreme judge.

The subsequent development of the papacy manifests both positive and negative features. Despite periods of decline and decay, Rome was able to magnify its authority by the leadership it gave in many areas of medieval life. As the chief sponsor of the missionary work among the Germanic barbarians, it was able to secure its dominance over the various kingdoms carved out of the Roman Empire. In the revival of the eleventh century, the dynamic Gregory VII gave great momentum to the movement toward papal supremacy over both Church and state. Under such popes as Innocent III, the papacy was construed as a monarchy along the lines of the secular models of the day. This development reached its zenith with the advent of Pope Boniface VIII, whose bull *Unam Sanctam* claimed papal dominion—both spiritual and temporal—over the whole earth.

Theologians of the time were not slow to justify the advance of papal power by many arguments drawn from Scripture, tradition and philosophy. The mendicant orders, in particular, proved to be able allies of the Roman popes in their struggle to vindicate their claim to absolute authority over the Church. Their pyramidal view of authority was reinforced by the increasingly dominant scholastic theology.

In the later Middle Ages, the papal canonists who saw power concentrated in the pope and descending from him to the rest of the Church were opposed by the conciliarists, who saw power ascending from the body to the head. The conciliarists were defeated, however, at the Council of Florence, which set forth a doctrine of papal primacy in terms similar to those of Vatican I.

The split between Catholics and Protestants in the sixteenth century actually increased the authority of the papacy within Catholicism. As skilled and dedicated leaders of the Catholic Counter-Reformation, the popes gained an increase of power and prestige. Then, after a century of decline in the eighteenth century, the papacy emerged as a strong force for order and stability as Europe rocked under successive waves of revolution and terrorism. Many factors contributed to the victory of the ultramontane papacy under Pope Pius IX (1846–78) at the first Vatican Council (1869–70). Chief among them was the feeling among Catholics that only a strong, centralized papacy would enable the Church to survive in a period when hostile liberals everywhere were undermining the Church's authority. The first Vatican Council responded to the menace of liberalism by exalting the authority of the pope in unprecedented fashion. As successor of Peter, it declared, he was endowed with a jurisdiction that was "full," "supreme" and "ordinary," as well as "immediate," and his solemn magisterial pronouncements on matters of faith and morals were declared to be of themselves irreformable.

The Second Vatican Council, in a totally different political and social climate, struggled to modify the absolutism of the first-Vatican-Council papacy by placing the bishop of Rome within the college of bishops—as its head, indeed—but nevertheless morally bound to share his responsibility with the other bishops, who, as a college, are likewise "the subject of supreme and full power over the universal Church."[5]

Reviewing this complex history, both Lutheran and Catholic participants in the dialogue agreed that a study of the papacy's development shows how much the office was shaped by the accidents of history and therefore underscores the possibility that the office could be further modified to meet the needs of the Church more effectively.

What chance is there, then, that Protestants might recognize the pope as the head of a reunited Church? There seems to be a new willingness to look objectively at this possibility. In a symposium published in 1976, theologians of seven denominations expressed their opinions on this matter. The only one who clearly rejected the idea was a Baptist, C. B. Hastings, who claimed that it would do violence to the Baptist idea of local church authority and autonomy.

According to the Lutheran theologians, ". . . the one thing necessary is that papal primacy be so structured and interpreted that it clearly serve the gospel and the unity of the church of Christ, and that its exercise of power not subvert Christian freedom."[6]

But they admit that there would be great difficulty in limiting church structures by the prior claims of the Gospel, unity and Christian freedom. One suggestion made is to devise structures that "would protect the legitimate traditions of the Lutheran communities and respect their spiritual heritage" and would "recognize the self-government of Lutheran churches

5. *Dogmatic Constitution on the Church*, 22.
6. Paul Empie and T. Austin Murphy, eds., op. cit., p. 21.

within a communion" as sister churches.[7] In such a case the pope's juris-
dictional power would be limited to Roman Catholics while, at the same
time, he served as "a kind of symbolic head of the larger communion of
sister churches, exercising such powers as they would be prepared to invest
in him."[8]

Various imaginative suggestions have been made for implementing such
an idea. The member churches might be given a voice in the election of
the pope. A bicameral assembly might be set up, with only one chamber
composed exclusively of Roman Catholics. There could be provision for
secretariats that would represent the concerns of the sister churches.

Even apart from the steps necessary to achieve a greater degree of
organizational unity, the pope might make an even greater effort to speak
and act as the moral leader of many Christians who are not Roman Catholics. To free him for this task, much of the administrative work of the
papacy could be shifted to others.

7. Ibid., p. 23.
8. Avery Dulles, *The Resilient Church* (Garden City, N.Y.: Doubleday, 1977), p. 130.

# 12

# Infallibility Revisited

This is no doubt the most difficult question facing those who hope to adapt the papal office to the needs of an ecumenical church. And here again the participants in the Lutheran-Roman Catholic dialogue showed a willingness to take a fresh look in the hope of somehow breaking out of the impasse caused by four centuries of sterile controversy.

In their *Common Statement*, these theologians find certain "premonitions" of the doctrine of infallibility in the early history of the Church. There is specifically concern with the faithful transmission of the Gospel, which the participants see as first embodied in creedal, liturgical and catechetical form and later incorporated in the written Gospels, which thenceforth served as normative for faith.

When did Rome assume a role of leadership in matters of doctrine? The report sees the first big step taken in this direction when the reliable transmission of apostolic teaching was linked to episcopal sees regarded as founded by apostles. Among these sees, Rome very early acquired special status for the various reasons we have cited above. And by the middle of the third century, Rome seems to have assumed special responsibility for preserving and interpreting the faith of "antiquity." Some Roman emperors included the faith of the bishop of Rome in the official norm of orthodoxy, while the popes began to make the claim that Rome had never erred in matters of doctrine.

This conviction that the Roman Church was singularly gifted in preserving the Church from error continued through the Middle Ages and found expression in such documents as the Pseudo-Isidorian Decretals, the statements of popes and theologians, and the collections of canon law. There were challenges to the idea, of course, from various quarters, and it was pointed out that individual popes such as Liberius, Vigilius and Honorius had fallen into error, and canon law itself admitted the possibility of a pope deviating from the faith. Yet the axiom the "Roman Church has never erred" survived.

Rome extended its power as court of last appeal to cover decisions in matters of faith as well. This was restated in the era of the Gregorian Reform in terms of immunity from further appeal. Soon afterward, Thomas Aquinas could describe the pope as the one to whose sole authority it belonged to produce a new version of the creed and whose judgment in matters of faith must be followed because he represented the universal Church, which "cannot err."[1]

The actual use of the term "infallibility" surfaced only in the thirteenth century, in connection with the dispute over poverty in the Franciscan Order. Advocates of papal infallibility wanted to prevent later popes from revising papal decisions having to do with the practice of poverty by the Franciscans. But it was a theologian of the fourteenth century, Guido Terreni, who first explicitly referred to the "infallible truth of the teaching of the Roman pontiff in matters of faith."

After their review of the history of the doctrine of infallibility, the theologians attempt to spell out their present position. As their brief comparison shows, Catholics tend to emphasize the importance of institutional structures in preserving the faith: specifically the definitions of faith made by councils or by the bishop of Rome alone. Lutherans, having had to improvise structures during the Reformation, have always taken a much more relative view of their authority. They have always stressed the intrinsic power of God's Word to maintain itself in reliance on the promise of God given in Jesus Christ. Church structures are necessary, but they can be deceptive as guides and they are always in danger of being regarded as ends, rather than as means. Still, the Lutherans are willing to recognize the present shortcomings of their structures for carrying on teaching and mission in a worldwide ministry.

Theologians on both sides were happy to note what they called the

1. *Quodlibetales* 9, question 7, article 16.

convergences on a number of issues related to infallibility. Above all, both sides confessed to belief in the primacy of the Gospel. While Catholics manifest renewed appreciation of the privileged authority of Scripture, Lutherans recognize the importance of tradition, now understood as the total process in which the Gospel, indeed Scripture itself, is transmitted. Liturgies, creeds and confessions are highly valued by them as embodiments of tradition.

Both sides also paid tribute to the necessity of reformulating Christian doctrine in order to meet the challenges of changing cultures and mentalities so as to present the one message intelligibly to specific audiences in reference to their particular problems.

There was also recognition of the need for ministries and structures charged with teaching Christian doctrine and also preserving it from error. Among these ministries, one would appropriately place a "Ministry in the universal Church" which would include "responsibility for overseeing both the Church's proclamation and, where necessary, the reformulation of doctrine in fidelity to the Scriptures."[2]

The Lutherans admitted that in the meantime they need an office that will enable them to speak with a unified voice on crucial doctrinal issues. But the Lutherans also thought the papal office was insufficiently protected against abuses. Both sides admitted the need to create structures that promote fuller participation of the whole Church in the formulation of doctrine. The laity, clergy, theologians and bishops have each a special role to play, and there is need in each case for structures to promote this.

In the light of the above, the participants in the dialogue raised some questions about current practices of both churches. Specifically, they wondered whether Lutherans and Catholics should not consult with each other in framing doctrinal and social ethical statements.

The Catholic theologians, for their part, in order to clear away all misconceptions, stressed several points about the Catholic dogma of papal infallibility that are often overlooked. One, Catholic doctrine is rooted in the New Testament teaching about the Holy Spirit guiding the Church to faithfully proclaim the message. Second, the primary subject of infallibility is the total Church, and Vatican I ascribed to the pope no other infallibility than that with which Christ wished to endow his Church. Third, when Vatican I stated that the decrees of the pope were *irreformable* even *without the consent of the Church*, this should not be taken to exclude the

2. Paul Empie, T. Austin Murphy, and Joseph A. Burgess, eds., *Teaching Authority and Infallibility in the Church* (Minneapolis, Minn.: Augsburg Publishing House, 1978), p. 31.

need of *reception* by the whole Church as a necessary sign of an infallible doctrine. The phrase *without the consent of the Church* was aimed at the Gallicans, who insisted that a papal definition had to be accepted in a juridical act in order to be valid. In fact, as Vatican II pointed out, the assent of the Church can never be wanting to an authentic definition "on account of the activity of that same Spirit, whereby the whole flock of Christ is preserved and progresses in unity of faith."[3] Finally, as recent Catholic statements have made clear, one should not take the term "irreformable" to mean that papal definitions cannot be changed or improved upon. Actually all definitions of faith are historically conditioned and are subject to revision (as is admitted in the Vatican decree of 1973 *Mysterium Ecclesiae*). Moreover, insofar as officials of the Church are not immune from the universal taint of sin, a dogmatic statement may be ambiguous, untimely, overbearing, offensive or otherwise deficient.

One of the big questions that always arises in any discussion of papal infallibility is about the actual concrete cases of its exercise. In other words, which papal statements are supposed to be infallible? The Catholic theologians in the dialogue took a minimalist position, finding that only two papal pronouncements in history could be qualified as infallible: the dogmas of the **Immaculate Conception** (1854) and of the **Assumption of the Blessed Virgin** (1950). They disallowed a number of papal decrees that are sometimes listed as infallible: canonizations of saints, the condemnation of Jansenism and Modernism, the bull *Exsurge* (1520), condemning Luther, as well as condemnations of various moral errors including Pope Paul VI's ukase against contraception.

As far as is concerned belief in the above-mentioned dogmas—the Immaculate Conception and the Assumption, as well as papal infallibility—the Catholic participants in the dialogue acknowledge the possibility that one might in good faith be unable to believe in these dogmas and yet be completely committed to Christ's Church.

One consequence of the clarifications of the doctrine of infallibility was the admission by the Lutherans that they could no longer simply repeat their traditional objections to the doctrine. During the course of the dialogue they began to realize that, as they said, "Catholics also wish to place their ultimate reliance not in the teaching of popes, councils, or the Church but in God's promises in Jesus Christ."[4] In fact, thanks to the agreement on both sides about the absolute primacy of the Gospel, they

3. *Dogmatic Constitution on the Church*, 25.
4. *Teaching Authority and Infallibility in the Church*, p. 64.

found it difficult to pinpoint exactly where or how they differed from each other on infallibility. Also, the Lutherans came to realize how vital it is for the churches to speak, when occasion demands, with one voice in the world and therefore how beneficial it would be for the Lutherans to have a ministry or magisterium that could articulate the doctrinal concerns of Lutherans around the globe.

It is interesting to compare the conclusions reached in this dialogue with the report of a similar one: the Anglican-Roman Catholic International Commission. Their report, issued at Windsor, Ontario, in September 1981, shows remarkable agreement with the Lutheran-Catholic statements. It, too, acknowledges the desirability of a universal primacy in a reunited Church and thinks it would be appropriate for the bishop of Rome to hold such an office, other things being equal.

But would they allow infallibility to the head of a reunited Church? The Anglicans also find great difficulty with this notion. While there might be occasions when the head of the Church would have to make decisive judgments in matters of faith—"to recall and emphasize some important truth; to expound the faith more lucidly; to expose error; to draw out implications not sufficiently recognized, and to show how Christian truth applies to contemporary issues"—but should these interventions ever be considered infallible? As they put it, "If the definition proposed for assent were not manifestly a legitimate interpretation of biblical faith and in line with orthodox tradition, Anglicans would think it a duty to reserve the reception of the definition for study and discussion."[5] The Marian dogmas they cite as an example for these raise special problems, since they seem insufficiently supported by Scripture.

On the other hand, the Anglican theologians admit that the question of reception is inherently difficult. But, somehow or other, they feel the assent of the faithful must be included in order to make a definition truly binding.

## RESPONSE OF THE ROMAN CONGREGATION

While the Vatican did not give a direct reply to the American Lutheran-Catholic dialogue, it did respond to the somewhat equivalent views

5. Anglican-Roman Catholic International Commission, *The Final Report* (London: S.P.C.K., 1982) p. 64.

of the Anglican-Roman Catholic International Commission (ARCIC). The statement by Joseph Cardinal Ratzinger, the head of the Congregation for the Doctrine of the Faith, was rather discouraging for ecumenists. It declared that the report "does not yet constitute a substantial and explicit agreement on some essential element of Catholic faith."[6] In disagreement with the report, the Sacred Congregation, for instance, claims that Jesus did institute the papal primacy of jurisdiction and personally conferred it on Peter. The Sacred Congregation also found its treatment of infallibility and the Marian dogmas inadequate. According to the Roman Congregation, the authority of the Church's teaching cannot depend ultimately on its reception by the faithful. For "[t]he task of authentically interpreting the word of God, whether written or handed on, has been entrusted exclusively to the living teaching office of the church, whose authority is exercised in the name of Jesus Christ . . . it draws from this one deposit of faith everything which it presents for belief as divinely revealed."[7]

As one critic said, the theology of the Roman Curia, so well represented in this response, makes any chance of further progress toward unity very chancy indeed.

## CATHOLIC DEBATE OVER INFALLIBILITY

But in spite of the hard-line views of the Sacred Congregation, Catholic theologians have continued to take up "hot potatoes." The subject of papal infallibility, in particular, has aroused much controversy, stimulated as it was to a great degree by the publication of *Humanae Vitae,* in 1968. There were some minor skirmishes over this issue in the late sixties, but it was Hans Küng who caused a full-scale battle to erupt when he issued his book *Infallible?* in 1971. Küng found the papal claim to infallibility one of the main obstacles to Church renewal and set out to show that it was

6. *Origins* (Washington, D.C.: National Catholic Documentary Service, Vol. 11 May 6, 1982), p. 756.
7. Ibid.

indefensible on scriptural, philosophical, historical and theological grounds.[9]

Opponents of Küng found many flaws in his arguments. He was accused of biblicist presuppositions, which prevented him seemingly from admitting the possibility of postapostolic doctrinal development. His list of papal errors and mistakes was judged irrelevant. He was also accused of attacking a straw man: an ultramontane exaggerated version of papal infallibility which was found only in outmoded pre-Vatican II theology manuals. His attack on "infallible propositions" was judged to miss the point, since Vatican I did not speak of "infallible propositions," but "irreformable definitions." Inasmuch as the former expression is philosophical and theological and the latter juridical, Küng's questioning of the former did not affect the latter.

## KÜNG GETS HELP FROM HISTORIANS

The debate nevertheless focused much attention on a doctrine that for many Christians—Catholic as well as Protestant—seemed out of harmony with the more historically conscious Church of Vatican II. And Küng's objections suddenly took on greater cogency when several historical studies appeared that seemed to buttress his position. The first was Brian Tierney's *Origins of Papal Infallibility, 1150–1350*, which appeared in 1972.[10] Tierney's work struck directly at one of the main arguments used by defenders of papal infallibility, namely the theory of development. According to this theory, the dogma was merely latent in the New Testament and took many centuries to emerge into the full consciousness of the Church. The theory assumes a set of stages along the way as the embryonic doctrine began to take on more visibility and precision.

Tierney's study, if proved correct, would completely undermine this theory, since he claims that the doctrine of infallibility appeared very suddenly in the thirteenth century, when it was invented by a few dissident Franciscans in connection with the question of evangelical poverty. The inventors of the doctrine, according to Tierney, had just succeeded in getting a papal decree (1279) espousing their rigorous views of Christ's teaching on poverty, and by getting the decree accepted as "infallible" they could make sure that no pope in the future could rescind it.

9. Garden City, N.Y.: Doubleday.
10. Leiden: Brill.

Another formidable historical attack on the doctrine of infallibility, from another Roman Catholic, a German priest in this case, was *How the Pope Became Infallible*, which appeared in Europe in 1977, the work of August Hasler.[11] The author, working in the Vatican archives, gathered an enormous amount of material from a host of sources in support of his central thesis that the first Vatican Council, which gave us the definition of papal infallibility, was not a free council and therefore its dogma was invalid.

According to Hasler, Pope Pius IX used every trick in the book to muscle the dogma through the Council: he limited the freedom of speech of the bishops, handpicked the members of the commissions and the conciliar president, exerted every imaginable form of pressure on the bishops—moral, psychological, church-political—including inserting propaganda in the Vatican newspaper, harassment of his opponents by the papal police, threats of withdrawal of financial help, etc. As Hasler documents the story, the Pope was so extremely and passionately devoted to the cause of securing his own infallibility that at times he lost control of himself in bouts of hysteria while confronting opposition bishops—berating them so savagely that several fell sick as a result.

Bishop Dupanloup, a leader of the opposition, judged the Pope extremely hypocritical and stupid, endowed with violent willpower and with a predilection for magnificence and display. Bishop Maret called the Pope false and a liar, in the presence of many witnesses.

The Pope himself repeatedly intervened in the Council at crucial moments and so manipulated the proceedings that the bishops opposed to infallibility registered their dismay by leaving Rome before the final ballot. The ultimate scandal of the whole affair, however, Hasler claims, was the way the Curia managed to cover up the ugly facts by allowing only censored versions of the Council's history to be printed.

## CHIRICO'S VERSION OF INFALLIBILITY

The totally negative approach of Tierney, Küng, Hasler, etc., does not seem a promising one. For one thing, as George Lindbeck says, you can't disprove a doctrine such as this simply by historical arguments. Moreover, many Catholic theologians—as historically conscious as can be—believe

11. Garden City, N.Y.: Doubleday, 1981.

that what is needed is a reinterpretation of the doctrine of infallibility that would do justice to history as well as to the Catholic sense of historical continuity. One of the most promising attempts is Peter Chirico's, whose book *Infallibility: The Crossroads of Doctrine* appeared in 1977.[12] Chirico examines the doctrine of infallibility in light of "the generic processes by which modern men at different levels of development and in different cultures come to definitive understanding of the faith."[13] He relates infallibility to the possibility we have as human beings of arriving at **universal meanings**. Were it not for this possibility, he claims, we would not be able to communicate with each other or understand people in the past.

In the case of Jesus Christ and his message, there are certain universal meanings that the Christian community grasps only slowly and by degrees. These are meanings that have an intrinsic relationship to and are somehow derived from the Church's experience of Christ. These meanings emerge from the whole life of the Church in a process involving a range of activities including decisions made in the light of faith, moral activities carried out, understanding and conceptualization and articulation, liturgical expression, and decisions of leadership. These meanings can be grasped infallibly thanks to their universality. They include, above all, those aspects of Christ's humanity which can be understood in universal terms and can therefore be the subject of dogmatic formulations.

According to Chirico's theory, a Christian meaning becomes universal when it exists, at least implicitly, in most Christians. "It then becomes possible for Church authorities to articulate it explicitly." But only when universal meanings exist implicitly at the level of the universal Church can the pope proclaim them explicitly. And Chirico emphasized the inseparability of the pope from the Church. It is true the definition of Vatican I stated that the "definitions of the Roman Pontiff are irreformable because of their very nature and not because of the consent of the Church." But, as Chirico explains it, this simply means that there is no legal form of consultation or voting that the pope must follow in order to arrive at the condition of infallibility. Nevertheless, the pope has to achieve certain personal conditions of being that of themselves render him infallible—processes that may involve consulting bishops, reading the past documents of the magisterium, dialoguing with theologians, interrogating the mind of the faithful, meditating and reflecting on his own past experiences in a spirit of prayer and meditation on the Scriptures. One cannot say that all

12. Kansas City: Sheed, Andrews & McMeel, Inc.
13. Ibid., p. xvii.

or any particular one of these steps is absolutely necessary. "What is absolutely necessary is that he should actually achieve universal understanding on the basis of his experience."[14]

It has been pointed out how Chirico has made an important contribution to our understanding of infallibility: he puts infallibility in a positive light instead of viewing it as mere immunity from error; doctrinal statements are interpreted in the light of their resurrectional significance, rather than by simple juridical norms; while, by putting the emphasis on "dogmatic meanings," Chirico avoids the hassle over the possibility of "infallible statements" which has bedeviled the recent debate.

### DULLES' "MODERATE INFALLIBILISM"

However, the position on papal infallibility which seems to have the best chance of uniting the exigencies of the Reformation and of *Romanitas* is moderate infallibilism, according to George Lindbeck, a Lutheran scholar. Avery Dulles agrees and makes a good case for it in one of his recent studies.[15] As a starting point, Dulles points to the need to have an office in the Church charged with protecting the Gospel from corruption —that it makes sense to believe that the holder of such an office would be graced by God to assert the truth of the Gospel in a decisive and obligatory manner when error threatened to pervert its truth. Dulles then tries to meet the objections of those haunted by the specter of a pope imposing his own arbitrary opinions on the members of the Church in the guise of infallible dogmas.

He shows how a fundamentalistic understanding of infallibility is no longer necessary in the light of the principles laid down in *Mysterium Ecclesiae* (1973). According to this Vatican document, two things have to be kept in mind when one deals with dogmatic pronouncements: the transcendence of divine revelation and the historicity of human formulations. As to the first, we must realize that all dogmatic formulations are only human attempts to express truths that by their nature outstrip the power of speech to capture the mystery of being.

As to the second, *Mysterium Ecclesiae* acknowledges the historical conditioning that affects all statements of faith. Thus dogmatic statements can be limited in a number of ways: first of all by their presuppositions

14. Ibid., pp. 224–25.
15. *A Church to Believe In* (New York: Crossroad, 1982), p. 145.

such as the "context of faith or human knowledge"; next by their concerns—that is, the kind of questions they were attempting to answer; then by their thought categories—that is, "the changeable conceptions of a given epoch"; and finally by the available vocabulary.

Examined in the light of these criteria, we can see how inadequate Vatican I's definition of infallibility appears to be. Many of its presuppositions, for instance, we no longer share, including such ideas as the adequacy of human propositions for communicating divine truths, and hence its lack of tolerance for pluralism in formulating these truths; the belief that the Christian Church was fully and adequately present in Roman Catholicism and therefore allowing no dimension of "ecumenicity," which today requires that Christians of all churches be heard when any doctrinal question is to be decided; finally the assumption that the faith is a collection of divinely guaranteed propositions, so that a mistake about one of these would supposedly entail the destruction of faith itself.

Another point is important: Vatican I declared that the pope, under certain conditions, enjoyed the same infallibility that the Lord bestowed on his Church, but did not deal with the more basic question of what infallibility means or to what extent the Church enjoys it. Much scope is left, therefore, for interpreting what is really involved when one attributes infallibility to the pope.

As noted above, dogmas are influenced by the changeable conceptions and vocabulary of given historical periods. This is certainly true of the definition of papal infallibility which bears the imprint of the world views of the bishops at Vatican I. For the most part, their understanding of reality tended to be static and unhistorical as compared with our more dynamic and historically conscious approach. This needs to be taken into account when we endeavor to interpret their key terms, such as **ex cathedra**, "irreformable," "definition" and "infallibility."

In the light of these considerations, therefore, Dulles maintains that we need to restate the dogma of papal infallibility in a way more consonant with our own thought forms, in order "to convey more clearly to a new generation what the older expressions really intended."[16] Perhaps we should even drop the term "infallibility," although he thinks it can be salvaged.

Moreover, he thinks the dogma of papal infallibility as well as the two Marian dogmas (the Immaculate Conception and the Assumption) are

16. Ibid.

too unclear in their meaning and too marginal in importance to be imposed, as they presently are, under penalty of excommunication. Acceptance of them, therefore, should not be made a condition of reunion with other Christians.

A reinterpretation of infallibility along these lines would provide a nonauthoritarian form of authority for the Church—an authority with which one might disagree but which at the same time one would take seriously in a listening spirit. It would mean admitting the possibility of error in the Church's teaching but at the same time acknowledging limits to disagreement. One might have to oppose certain teachings of the Church, but it would be in the spirit of "loyal opposition." As Karl Rahner understands it, infallibility means assuming the truth of what the magisterium teaches but then subjecting the teaching to a most rigorous scrutiny —using all the tools of Scriptural criticism, history, philosophy, etc., in order to "separate the propositionally specifiable affirmations from the conceptual or symbolic framework in which they are embedded . . . thus helping to determine the range of possible interpretations, including many new ones to which they are susceptible in new situations and contexts . . . church dogmas are thus genuinely relativized while yet retaining a propositionally identifiable continuity . . . [they exclude] certain options permanently yet still [leave] freedom in searching for new answers to new questions . . ."17

17. Quoted in George Lindbeck, "The Reformation and the Infallibility Debate," in *Teaching Authority and Infallibility in the Church* (Minneapolis, Minn.: Augsburg Publishing House, 1978), p. 115–16.

# 13

## Images of Mary

One of my treasured memories is connected with my stay in Rome as a student. I was able to be present on November 1, 1950, in St. Peter's Square when Pope Pius XII defined the dogma of the Assumption of the Blessed Virgin Mary. It was an unforgettable experience. Thousands of people were streaming into the square when I arrived there, at dawn, and Bernini's enormous bowl was almost filled up. In spite of the crowd, I managed to find a spot not too far from the great white papal throne. Many hours later, after I had waited under the hot sun while being jostled by the huge throng, I was rewarded with a clear view of the papal procession as the pope took his place on the dais and proclaimed the dogma. "Mary," he said, "having completed the course of her earthly life, was assumed body and soul into heavenly glory." Though none of us in the square were aware of it at the time, the definition marked the end of an era of Marian theology and piety.

### DEVOTION TO MARY IN THE EARLY CHURCH

Devotion to Mary, as far as the historical record goes, appears very early in the Church, and by the middle of the fourth century was very strong especially in the East, where the feast of the purification was kept in Jerusalem on February 14. It was in the East that legends of Mary were first related and hymns were composed, where churches to her honor were first built and her feast was introduced, and where images of her were crafted. It was above all in the East that we find Mary first celebrated as "Mother of God," nowhere with more enthusiasm than in Alexandria. But the image of the perfect, immaculate Virgin did not yet gain full consent. Even Athanasius found flaws in her, and though in general the Fathers of the fourth century lost no opportunity to praise her, Chrysostom, on the other hand, accused her of unbelief and vainglory.

In the West, devotion to Mary advanced more slowly. It was Ambrose (d. 397), who gave Western Mariology its decisive direction. For Ambrose, Mary's perfect physical and moral purity was necessitated by her divine motherhood, for, he says, Christ would not have chosen for his mother a woman defiled by the seed of man.[1] Ambrose also affirmed her intimate relationship with the Church—a theme likewise developed by his disciple Augustine. Jerome defended her perpetual virginity with such power and erudition that it could no longer be challenged.

Both East and West rejoiced to see her divine motherhood officially defined at the Council of Ephesus in 431.

From this point on, the Eastern and Western streams of devotion separated. In the East, feasts multiplied and devotion became ever more fervent, while in the West devotion was more restrained, especially in Rome. Only in Gaul do we find her bodily assumption affirmed, while there are no references to her exemption from sin.

## MEDIEVAL DEVOTION

By the ninth century, however, we find that Greek influence has begun to exert considerable influence on Western Mariology. Greek influence is very apparent in the hymn *Ave Maris Stella,* the most popular of all Marian hymns, and the image of the Star of the Sea becomes a favorite theme. An anonymous Greek homily on the Assumption, dating from the tenth century and diffused throughout the West, contained all the principal features of Byzantine Mariology: Mary, radiant with a more than celestial purity and superior to the seraphim, has removed the curse of death transmitted from Eve. Uncorrupted by the birth of her Son, she was also immune to the corruption of death, since Christ, her Son, has taken

1. Hilda Graef, *Mary: A History of Doctrine and Devotion* (Sheed, 1963, 1965), Vol. 1, p. 88.

her to himself. She is glorified as the ark of salvation, the bridge and ladder by which we ascend to heaven. Christ promises to make her the "propitiation for sins." Whatever is said about the Virgin may be possible, for she is a mystery beyond human reason. One should not analyze this mystery but simply approach it in a spirit of profound faith.

During the twelfth century, new influences begin to bear on Mariology: Scholasticism, the Crusades, feudalism and the concept of courtly love. Anselm (d. 1109), the father of Scholasticism, who exerted tremendous influence on Mariology, insisted on her share in the redemption—basing his opinion on a strict parallelism between her divine motherhood and the fatherhood of God. His disciple, Eadmer (d. 1124), produced the first detailed exposition of the doctrine of the Immaculate Conception. He links her freedom from original sin not only to her dignity as mother of the Redeemer but also to her position as mistress and empress of the whole universe. The doctrine of the Assumption, which until then found little favor in the West, now begins its triumphal march. As with the Immaculate Conception, the chief argument given at the time was its fittingness.

The most popular of all Marian prayers, the *Hail Mary*, which appeared circa 600 in the East, now appeared in a shorter version in the West and was used in prayer for the success of the Crusades. The most influential preacher of the twelfth century, Bernard of Clairvaux (d. 1153), enunciated the principle, often quoted by later popes, "God willed us to have everything through Mary."

The Virgin Mary has often been seen as an antierotic symbol and antisexual image, but there is, in fact, a certain amount of material in popular medieval Marian literature which emphasizes the sensuous and even the erotic. A contemporary of Bernard of Clairvaux, Philip of Harvengt, dwelt on the sensuous aspect of Mary's love of Jesus: "He enjoys their mutual embraces as much as she, when he, kissing her, reposes most sweetly between her breasts." Another author of the time gave free play to his imagination in describing her physical charm, which for him embodied the ideal of a German medieval maiden: he extols her beautiful blond hair framing her blue eyes and aquiline nose while her red, moderately full lips, parted in a smile, reveal perfect white teeth.

The doctrine of Mary's Immaculate Conception was very slow to win general acceptance. Augustine's teaching on the matter, for instance, was not clear, but it seems that he did not hold the doctrine. Pope Leo the Great upheld the traditional teaching of the Latin Church that Mary was not exempt from the universal guilt of mankind. As we mentioned above, it is only when we come to Anselm's disciple, Eadmer, that we find a detailed defense of the doctrine. But many powerful voices were raised against the introduction of the feast of the Immaculate Conception, which was beginning to spread throughout the West. Most of the great Schoolmen, including Aquinas and Bonaventure, followed Peter Lombard's view that since Mary was conceived in the ordinary way she could not have been exempt from original sin. It was John Duns Scotus (d. 1308) who took a fresh approach to the question and taught that Mary was preserved from all stain of original sin in virtue of the anticipated merits of Christ. The crux of his argument was in viewing original sin as a privation, instead of linking it with concupiscence, as in the prevailing Augustinian view. God, therefore, could have infused grace into her soul from the very first instant. Enthusiastically taken up by his fellow Franciscans, Scotus' teaching gradually conquered all opponents, and in 1476 Sixtus IV approved the feast of the Immaculate Conception.

## THE REFORMATION AND MARY

When we approach the period of the Reformation, the general symptoms of spiritual decline are manifest: the hair-splitting verbal subtleties of the Scholastics, for instance; the decadence of monastic life; and the sad state of the mendicant orders. Devotion to Mary also reflects this trend, as it often degenerated into superstition. This is quite evident in the sermons of Bernardino of Siena (d. 1444), one of the most popular Franciscan preachers of the day and later canonized. In a shocking example, Bernardino says, "O the unthinkable power of the Virgin Mother . . . one Hebrew woman invaded the house of the eternal king; one girl, I do not know by what caresses, pledges or violence, seduced, deceived and, if I may say so, wounded and enraptured the divine heart." And Bernardino even attempts to prove that in some respects she is superior to God himself: "God," he says, "could only generate God . . . but the Virgin made him finite, mortal, poor . . ."[2] Mary actually did more for God than God did for man, he dares to say. If at this level such excesses could occur, one is not surprised at the absurdities that became the common coin of Marianists and led inevitably to the Protestant reaction.

2. Ibid., p. 317.

The Reformers, though extremely critical of much of the current Catholic doctrine and practice, did not jettison the entire Marian tradition. Luther and Calvin both defended her perpetual virginity and the dignity of her divine motherhood. Luther, in fact, retained much more of the tradition than Calvin, who was more consistent in including Mary in his dogma of man's absolute impotence in the work of salvation. So where Luther still allowed for Mary's power of interceding for us, Calvin completely rejected it. And though Luther insisted on her emptiness and lowliness, he seems to have kept a real affection for the little maiden "whose faith he deeply admired and whose grace he never doubted."[3]

Devotion to Mary became a crucial issue in the bitter polemics of the Counter-Reformation. Protestants gradually abandoned it almost completely, while Catholics carried on the medieval tradition. The Rosary, which dates from A.D. 1100, became particularly popular and was ardently promoted by the Jesuit Peter Canisius (d. 1597).

## EXCESSES OF COUNTER-REFORMATION MARIOLOGY

The Catholic tendency to go to excess in venerating Mary, which was always present in the Middle Ages, remained strong in post-Reformation times. One can find abundant examples in Hilda Graef's history. We find it, for instance, in one of the most popular treatises: Louis-Marie Grignion de Montfort's (d. 1716) *True Devotion to the Blessed Virgin*. "The greatness of her power," he writes, "which she exercises even over God himself, is incomprehensible."[4] In some way, he says elsewhere, the devil fears her more than God himself. The true devotee of Mary will totally consecrate himself to her, never dare to approach Christ except through her and even in the sacred reception of Holy Communion allow only Mary to speak to Jesus for him. In more or less the same vein should be placed the *Glories of Mary*, of Alphonsus Liguori (d. 1787). The most popular of all books on the subject, it gathers up countless legends and incredible miracle stories to buttress the author's main contention, that all graces given by God pass through Mary, who as our merciful advocate is able to restrain the avenging arm of her angry Son.

The opposite trend, however, gained the ascendancy as the spirit of the Enlightenment penetrated deeply into the Church. Judged by the canons

3. Ibid., Vol. 2, p. 10.
4. Ibid., p. 59.

of rationalism, devotion to Mary appeared to be a medieval relic. The Hail Mary was dropped and the Rosary abandoned. Her feasts were reduced to a minimum and her shrines forsaken.

After the devastation inflicted by the French Revolution, the Church experienced a remarkable revival during the nineteenth century, as rationalism was succeeded by the powerful romantic movement, with its cultivation of mystical and emotional states of mind. In harmony with this mood, devotion to Mary took on a new life and was given a strong endorsement by the popes and also by a series of remarkable apparitions.

Outstanding in his devotion to Mary was Pope Pius IX (d. 1878), who spent a thirty-two-year pontificate battling against the rising tide of liberalism and counted on Mary to lead the Church to victory. His definition of the Immaculate Conception, in 1854, can be seen as a gesture of defiance to liberals both within and without the Church as well as to Protestants, who were deeply offended by the dogma.

## APPARITIONS OF MARY

In addition to the papal definition, a series of apparitions also contributed to her cause. At Paris, in the rue du Bac, in 1830, Zoé Labouré, a simple peasant girl, before entering the novitiate of the Daughters of Charity, claimed that Mary visited her and instructed her to spread devotion to a medal engraved with the words "O Mary, conceived without sin, pray for us who have recourse to you." In 1846 at La Salette, in France, two young illiterate children claimed they were visited by a woman, wearing a long white dress and bathed in radiant light, hovering above the ground, who told them to warn people to turn away from their sins.

In 1858, four years after the definition of the Immaculate Conception, Bernadette Soubirous (d. 1879), the teenage daughter of a poor miller, claimed to have had a number of visions in a nearby grotto of a pretty young girl with a rosary over her arm who told her, "I am the Immaculate Conception."

Shrines were erected at the scene of the apparitions, and pilgrims by the hundreds of thousands flocked to Lourdes, where the Church of the Immaculate Conception was finished over the grotto in 1872. Miracles began to multiply at Lourdes, and in 1884 a medical bureau was established to investigate them. Bernadette herself was canonized in 1933, and the centenary of her apparitions was celebrated with great fervor in 1958.

In our own century there has been no lack of purported apparitions. One scholar has counted thirty, involving three hundred individual visions in Western Europe between 1930 and 1950 alone, all claimed by children.

The one at Cova da Iria, near Fátima, in Portugal, in 1917 had the most spectacular results. Three illiterate children, Lucia dos Santos, and her cousins Francisco and Jacinta Martos claimed that while tending sheep they were frightened by a flash of lightning and began running away in terror until reassured by a pretty little lady hovering over a tree nearby. She conversed with them and promised to return on the thirteenth of every month—for six months until October 13, when she would tell them who she was and what she wanted. Word spread; crowds gathered. The anticlericals, who were powerful at the time, were enraged, and the local administrator, Arturo de Oliveira Santos, had the children imprisoned and terrified them with threats of boiling them in oil. But they refused to change their story. As month succeeded month and vision succeeded vision, suspense built as people awaited the climactic miracle promised by the Virgin for October 13. When the great day finally dawned, some seventy thousand highly excited people gathered at Cova weeping and praying in a heavy rain. Lucia claimed the Lady appeared and told her she was the Lady of the Rosary and informed her that the war was ending that day. (It actually ended thirteen months later). Then the rain stopped, and at Lucia's cry, "Look at the sun!" many in the crowd looked and saw, as they claimed, the sun dive and dance around the sky while emitting multicolored rays.

It might be noted that while officially approved by the Church, the apparitions mentioned above are not obligatory matters of belief for Catholics. Approval by the Church does not guarantee their historical truth or authenticity but only means that sufficient evidence has been adduced to allow for the veneration of the Blessed Mother at the site of the supposed apparition. Some observers, in fact, favor a psychological explanation of these phenomena. They point out the curious resemblance of many details of the purported visions to prior experiences of the children involved. They also note the puerile nature of some of the remarks attributed to the Virgin. In addition, child psychologists claim that children and adolescents have considerable eidetic gifts, being able to visualize as outside themselves objects they have consciously or subconsciously conjured up in their imaginations. One psychologist, for instance, in a test of six boys found they could be conditioned to believe they actually saw and heard a battle of medieval warriors above a tree.[5]

The popes of the twentieth century continued to promote devotion to Mary, and Pope Pius XII climaxed this effort by solemnly defining the Assumption. "It is to be a dogma revealed by God," he said, "that the Immaculate Mother of God, Mary ever Virgin, when the course of her earthly life was finished, was taken up body and soul into the glory of heaven." The solemn definition was followed four years later by the proclamation of a Marian year to celebrate the centenary of the definition of the Immaculate Conception. Pius XII also established the feast of her queenship and exhorted the bishops to encourage devotion to Mary.

## VATICAN II'S VIEW OF MARY

The Second Vatican Council, eleven years later, opened up a new chapter in the history of Catholic Mariology. The new approach they took can be summarized in several points. First, after much debate the bishops decided not to issue a separate treatise on Mary but to include its statement on Mary as simply one chapter in its general *Dogmatic Constitution on the Church, Lumen Gentium.* The implication here is significant. It indicated that the bishops wanted to emphasize the fact that in spite of her unique prerogatives Mary was still to be regarded as a fellow member of the Church and not as some kind of semidivine being exalted above the Church, all impressions to the contrary caused by misguided piety notwithstanding. Second, one notes a strong biblical emphasis in the Council's text on Mary, an emphasis duly acclaimed by Protestant observers at the Council. This priority given to Scripture enabled the bishops to produce a very sober treatise unmarred by the excesses that sometimes are found even in official documents on Mary.

What was the sum and substance of the Council's Marian doctrine? Mary, the Council says, must be venerated above all the saints because of her sublime dignity as mother of God and mother of the Redeemer. At the same time, she is to be honored as mother of the Church insofar as she cooperated "out of love so that there might be born in the Church the faithful, who are members of Christ their Head."[6] Mary's role in our

5. Ibid., p. 145.
6. *Dogmatic Constitution on the Church,* 53.

salvation was already foreshadowed in certain Old Testament texts such as the one that promised victory over the serpent, in the third chapter of Genesis, and the one in Isaiah that spoke of a virgin bringing forth a son named Emmanuel.[7] Mary, indeed, is the new Eve, who by total faith and obedience and complete devotion to the person and work of her Son untied the knot bound by the first Eve's disobedience. Mary was entirely holy, and free, from the first instant of her conception, from all stain of sin.

According to the Council, "the maternity of Mary in the order of grace began with the consent which she gave in faith at the Annunciation and which she sustained without wavering beneath the cross."[8] At every point in her Son's life, Mary stood at his side cooperating in an utterly singular way with his work of restoring supernatural life to souls. And in the same way, taken up to heaven, she continues this saving role by her manifold acts of intercession for us. This mediation of Mary in no way infringes on the dignity and efficacy of Christ, the unique Mediator, for it is merely the most notable example of the way God enables his creatures to share in his Son's saving work of redemption.

She is an example of motherhood in an eminent and singular fashion. She is also an example of holy virginity, since she brought forth God's Son —not knowing man but overshadowed by the Holy Spirit. She is, in fact, a model of all the virtues and in a certain way incarnates the essence of the Gospel, since, contemplating her, we enter more fully into the supreme mystery of the Incarnation. Through meditation on Mary the Church progresses in faith, hope and charity and becomes itself a mother, bringing forth to a new and immortal life children who are conceived in the Holy Spirit and born of God.

The Council warmly recommends devotion to the Blessed Mother of God, which it says has always existed in the Church and which need in no way detract from our adoration of the Son, for the two forms of prayer are on totally different levels.

In fact, devotion to the Mother of God serves the cause of Jesus by helping to make him rightly known, loved and glorified and all his commands to be observed.

Finally, while exhorting the faithful to maintain the traditional practices and exercises of devotion, it cautioned theologians and preachers to avoid the two extremes of exaggeration and reductionism. True devotion,

7. Ibid., 55.
8. Ibid., 62.

it reminds us, "consists neither in fruitless and passing emotion, nor in a certain vain credulity."[9]

While Protestant and Catholic theologians have moved slowly in exploring the ramifications of the Council's new approach to Mary, the impact of the Council on Marian devotion and theology within the Church has been tremendous. Devotion to Mary declined precipitously as old forms of piety disappeared with little replacement. Rosaries and scapulars were discarded, statues of Mary were removed from many parish churches, old hymns faded from memory, and May Day celebrations disappeared.

Marian theology, too, has been much affected by the critical attitude engendered by the Council. Interest has shifted from such topics as the priesthood of Mary or Mary as Co-Redemptrix to topics involving the scriptural and historical foundations of Mariology. The ecumenical movement also has had a profound influence on the direction of Marian studies, as Catholic and Protestant scholars have engaged in dialogue on the role of Mary from the standpoints of their respective traditions.

### THE LUTHERAN-CATHOLIC DIALOGUE

One of the most important of the dialogues was carried on by Lutheran and Catholic theologians in the United States from 1975 to 1976 and might be characterized as a quest for the historical Mary.

The scholars subjected the Marian passages in the New Testament to the same critical analysis used in evaluating the Jesus material. *Three layers of tradition* were presupposed. As in the case of Jesus, it proved no easy task to uncover the bottom, or *first, layer,* consisting of the actual words and deeds of Mary.

As we pointed out above in the chapter on Jesus, the *second layer,* or pre-Gospel tradition, is the product of the first generation of Christians, who, according to their various situations and concerns, selected the original deeds and sayings and adapted and modified them in line with their theological viewpoints. The *third layer* is the material as we actually have it in the New Testament. It is the product of the individual evangelist, who selected, combined and rethought the pre-Gospel tradition in order to shape a narrative that reflected his theology.

9. Ibid., 67.

As the Lutheran and Catholic scholars point out, it is much more difficult to discover the actual, historical Mary than the historical Jesus, because Mary is mentioned only a few times during the ministry of Jesus. Moreover, there is still a tendency to confuse the *second layer* with the *first layer* and hence to think that once we have identified the pre-Gospel tradition we have reached history. But we must keep the three layers distinct—not out of a negative or skeptical spirit—but in order to respect the nature of the Gospels as works of faith which were written not to give us historical information but to bring out the religious meaning of the Christ event.

What, then, do the Gospels tell us about Mary?

The infancy narratives (first two chapters of Matthew and Luke), the scholars agreed, contained the most detail about Mary. However, it is very difficult to determine how much of this is "first-layer" history. As they point out, we can hardly suppose that the narratives are based on eyewitness accounts—for a number of reasons. First, there is no indication that Mary and Joseph supplied such information. Secondly, a number of items found in the infancy narratives are difficult to reconcile with information in the Gospel accounts of Jesus' ministry. The infancy narratives, for instance, picture the baptist as a relative of Jesus, while in the fourth Gospel, John says of Jesus, "I myself did not know him."

The third point: Matthew and Luke seem to contradict each other. How, for instance, can one reconcile Luke's account of the peaceful return from Bethlehem of Joseph and Mary with Matthew's story of a flight for their lives from Bethlehem to Egypt or Matthew's indication that Mary and Joseph were natives of Bethlehem with Luke's that they were natives of Nazareth and went to Bethlehem only because of a census?

## A DIVERSITY OF IMAGES OF MARY

The dialogic scholars also bring out the diversity of images of Mary contained in the Gospels, a diversity that constitutes a serious problem in any attempt to reach agreement on a theology of Mary satisfactory to both Protestants and Catholics. Protestants favor an image of Mary that they base mainly on Mark's Gospel, while Catholics draw their image of Mary mainly from Luke's Gospel.

Specifically, Protestants focus on Mark 3:20–35, which they interpret in a way that puts Mary in a rather disedifying light. In this passage, Jesus

and his disciples are in a house near the Sea of Galilee and a huge crowd
has gathered around the house, preventing anyone inside from leaving to
get food. His family *(including Mary)*, hearing about this, come to take
charge of him, believing that he is out of his mind. (They reject the more
benign interpretation, which would have his family going out of the house
—where they are already gathered with Jesus' other disciples—in order to
keep the crowd from harming Jesus.) When they send word for him to
come out, Jesus in reply looks at those seated around him in a circle and
says, "Here are my mother and my brothers. Anyone who does the will of
God, that person is my brother and sister and mother."[10] In effect, according to the typical Protestant interpretation, Jesus draws a sharp contrast between his natural family and those open to the will of God, who
form his eschatological family. Thus, according to this interpretation,
Mary was not one of Jesus' original disciples. Mark, in this view, does not
exclude the possibility that at some point she became one, but he gives no
indication that this ever took place.

Catholics have traditionally, however, focused on Luke, who opens his
Gospel with a paean to Mary. She is addressed by the angel as one highly
favored by the Lord. She is told that she will be the mother of the Messiah. His birth will come about through the power of the Holy Spirit, who
will overshadow her. She is described as the perfectly obedient handmaid
of the Lord, whose response to the angel's words is "Let what you have
said be done to me."[11] She is greeted by Elizabeth as blessed among
women. And Mary, in turn, praises God in the marvelous canticle the
Magnificat.

As the dialogicians point out by putting the Magnificat on the lips of
Mary, Luke associates her with the defense of the poor and lowly—a
theme that is prominent in his version of salvation history. Mary is
thereby given an important role in that history, "a representative role that
will continue from the infancy narrative into the ministry of Jesus and
finally into the early church."[12]

The rest of Luke's infancy narrative—the birth of Jesus, the homage of
the shepherds, the presentation in the Temple—continues to show Mary
as a devout and obedient servant of God, one who meditates on "all these
things" as she continues to grow in understanding of the divine plan

10. Mk. 3:34–35.
11. Lk. 1:38.
12. R. Brown, K. P. Donfried, J. Fitzmeyer and J. Reumann, eds. *Mary in the New Testament* (Philadelphia: Fortress Press, 1978), p. 143.

centered in her Son and yet at times fails to understand, as in the Temple when Jesus rebukes her: "Did you not know that I must be busy with my Father's affairs?"[13]

Outside of the infancy narratives, Luke refers to Mary in only two other passages. The first of these is parallel with the passage of Mark (3:20–35) just discussed, which shows Jesus inside with his disciples and Mary and his brothers outside. Unlike Mark, however, Luke does not seem to point up the contrast between his spiritual family inside and his biological family outside, but in fact speaks favorably, it seems, of them as "those who hear the word of God and put it into practice."[14]

The other scene is at the beginning of Acts, where, consistent with a picture of the mother and brother as fruitful disciples, he places them alongside the eleven and the women. Thus, in Luke's view, Mary was the first to hear the Gospel, even before Jesus' birth; during the ministry she was praised as one of those who hear the word of God and do it; and after the death, Resurrection and ascension, she is shown as remaining faithful in the midst of the community as they all wait for the coming of the Holy Spirit.

## JOHN'S VIEW OF MARY

As the participants in the dialogue noted, John's Gospel is somewhat ambiguous on Mary's role, although Catholics tend to see him as basically in agreement with Luke. In the passage describing the wedding feast of Cana, John shows Mary as having only a very limited understanding of Jesus. When the wine runs out, she informs Jesus of the fact, with the implication that he should take care of the matter. But she receives the response, "Woman, why turn to me? My hour has not come yet."[15] The use of the term "woman" seems to indicate that Jesus puts little value on physical motherhood in itself, while the rest of the phrase indicates the failure of Mary to realize that the work that the Father has given Jesus has precedence over the claims and interests of his natural family. This would be in line with the passage of Mark discussed above (3:20–35), where Jesus seems to contrast the claims of his physical family with his spiritual one. However, as the report of the Lutheran-Catholic dialogue points out, we

13. Lk. 2:49.
14. Lk. 8:21.
15. Jn. 2:4.

should not exaggerate the negative light here thrown on Mary, for the fact that Jesus finally does supply the wine "makes it virtually impossible to maintain that the scene contains a harsh polemic against his Mother."[16]

In sum, in the first part of his Gospel, John is closer to Mark than to Luke in his reading of Mary's role. While John puts her in a more favorable light at Cana than Mark does at Capernaum, they both show Jesus rejecting any special claim she might have on him in virtue of her physical motherhood. Unlike Mark, however, John brings Mary back into the narrative at the end—in a most positive way—when he places her at the foot of the cross with the beloved disciple. The symbolism here is clear: Jesus gives his mother a spiritual role as mother of the disciple par excellence. They represent symbolically his new spiritual family, based on discipleship. And Mary, as the mother of the beloved disciple, becomes herself a model of belief and discipleship. The dialogue concludes, "We did see in John's own symbolic treatment of Jesus' Mother an opening made for the process of further Marian symbolizing within the Church."

Reviewing this conflicting evidence about Mary in the New Testament, the Protestant scholar Wolfhart Pannenberg claims that it shows how little we really know about the historical Mary. Her chief significance, he holds, is symbolic. Raymond Brown, S.S., tends to agree. Brown sees a definite line of development in the New Testament extending from Mark's rather ambiguous portrait of Mary through Matthew's assertion of the virginal birth to Luke's view of her as the first Christian disciple and to John, who assigns her a symbolic role in his new family as the mother of the most beloved disciple. Mary's discipleship is thus seen as the key to all the later developments of Marian doctrine and devotion.

In the effort to find some common ground today, both sides need to clarify their positions. Catholics could acknowledge that the Marian doctrines, in particular the Immaculate Conception and the Assumption, are not explicitly found in the New Testament but at the same time legitimately argue that they are in line with the New Testament view of Mary as the first disciple. Thus the Immaculate Conception would mean that while every human being, through faith and baptism, is freed from sin

16. *Mary in the New Testament*, p. 193.

through the grace of Christ, Mary, as the first disciple of Christ, was given this grace even before she was conceived.

Protestants, on the other hand, while not willing to accept the Marian doctrines, might be ready to admit that these doctrines are not opposed to the total Scriptural witness to Mary.

Moreover, as Christians become more aware of the wonderful unity in diversity among the various Christian churches, Protestants might be willing to admit that veneration of Mary is deeply rooted in the Christian tradition and is a practice of piety with great spiritual potential. At the same time, Catholics could profit from Protestant criticisms of some forms of Marian devotion. Thus Gottfried Bachl, who is generally positive regarding Catholic veneration of Mary, has also noted some problems. As he points out, Mary in Catholic devotion took over the Holy Spirit's function of mediating grace. Moreover, the virginity of Mary, which in the New Testament testified to the new creation, was later used to foster an anti-erotic view of life and a taboo of sex. Stress also was placed on Mary's passivity, and this was held up as a model for Catholic women.[17]

## THE VIRGIN BIRTH

One of the issues that has recently stirred up much controversy in the Catholic Church is the question of the virginal conception of Jesus; that is, whether he was conceived by Mary without the intervention of any male. It is sometimes inaccurately referred to as the "virgin birth," which can also mean Mary's virginity in the act of giving birth itself (that is, with no tearing of the hymen). Until a few years ago it would have been unthinkable to raise this issue in the Catholic Church. But the big shift in attitude toward Mary occasioned by the Council encouraged some theologians to take a new look at this question, using their newly adopted tools of historical and literary criticism.

This theological speculation first came to the notice of the average Catholic when the Dutch Catechism appeared, in 1966, and was castigated by Rome for its ambiguity about the "virgin birth." A commission of cardinals appointed by the pope ordered the Dutch bishops to issue a revised edition of the Catechism clearly teaching the virginal conception of Jesus, but they refused. A compromise was finally reached when the

17. Bachl, "Veneration of the Mother of Jesus," *Theology Digest* 26 (spring 1978), pp. 54–56.

bishops agreed to add an appendix containing the Vatican's instruction reiterating the traditional doctrine of the virgin birth.

Since then, there has been much debate among Catholic theologians as to whether Catholic faith demands belief in the virgin birth as a biological fact or as only a symbolic concept.

We should note first that explicit testimony to the virgin birth is found only in the infancy narratives of Matthew and Luke. Matthew states it more clearly than Luke. As Matthew puts it, "His mother Mary was betrothed to Joseph; but before they came to live together she was found to be with child through the Holy Spirit . . . she has conceived what is in her by the Holy Spirit."[18] Compare this with Luke: "Mary said to the angel, 'But how can this come about, since I am a virgin?' 'The Holy Spirit will come upon you,' the angel answered 'and the power of the Most High will cover you with its shadow. And so the child will be holy and will be called Son of God.' "[19]

There are no other explicit references to the virgin birth in the Scriptures. Some try to find implicit references to it in certain passages of Paul, in the Gospel of Mark and in John's Gospel, but probably the majority of scholars would agree with Raymond Brown that the evidence lacks compelling force.[20] Of course, as Brown also points out, the silence of Paul, Mark and John does not mean necessarily that they did not know of the virginal conception. It's simply impossible to know how widespread belief in the virginal conception was in New Testament times.

Since doubts first arose about the historicity of the virgin birth, various theories have been proposed to explain the origin of the concept. One of the most common explanations is to trace it to the influence of pagan traditions, in which there are many examples of such a belief, e.g., the virginal conception of the Buddha, Alexander, Augustus, etc. But the parallels are not persuasive, as they consistently involve gross sexual misconduct involving a divine male impregnating a woman through some form of physical penetration.

Jewish parallels are not very convincing either. One often cited is the famous passage of Isaiah 7:14:

> The Lord himself, therefore,
> will give you a sign.
> It is this: the maiden is with child

18. Mt. 1:18, 20.
19. Lk. 1:34–35.
20. *The Birth of the Messiah* (Garden City, N.Y.: Doubleday, 1977), p. 525ff.

and will soon give birth to a son
whom she will call Immanuel.

Matthew himself quotes this, not from the Hebrew but from the Greek Septuagint: "The virgin will conceive . . ." But there is no need to construe the Greek text to refer to a virgin birth. It could merely mean that a maiden now a virgin would conceive once she was married. So it is unlikely that Matthew first came to the idea of the virginal conception of Jesus by reflecting on this passage. However, if he was already convinced Jesus was virginally conceived, then he could have colored the passage with a new interpretation.

Another hypothesis would trace the tradition to Mary herself. But this explanation faces the difficulty that the memory surfaced only in the later writings (Matthew and Luke). Why was it apparently so late in appearing in the Christian records? and why is Mary depicted in a number of passages as not understanding who Jesus was? Certainly she communicated no profound Christological understanding to his followers, who came to understand only after the Resurrection and, indeed, at first seem to have proclaimed that Jesus had become Messiah, Lord, or Son of God through the *Resurrection*, never mentioning the virginal conception."[21] Its absence in Paul is the most puzzling of all, since he covered all the important themes of early Church belief.

An explanation favored by many is based on the likelihood that it was widely known that Jesus was born noticeably early after Joseph and Mary came to live together. Rather than attribute this to illegitimacy (which his enemies might have done) "Matthew, convinced of the sinlessness of Jesus, may have believed that freedom from sin had to reach to his origins as well, and may thus have emerged with the idea of a virginal conception."[22] The weight of this argument is somewhat increased if we add to it the possible influence of a creedal affirmation that Jesus was begotten Son of God through the Holy Spirit.

But, for many Catholics, the most compelling argument in favor of the physical reality of the virgin birth is the consistent and universal teaching of the Church—from at least A.D. 200 to our times. But does the confession "born of the Virgin Mary" in the creed intend to make a statement about biology or to highlight the unique relationship of Jesus to God—his eternal sonship?

21. Ibid., p. 526.
22. *Mary in the New Testament*, pp. 94–95.

Ultimately, as the scholars in the Lutheran-Catholic dialogue concluded, one's attitude toward church tradition would probably be the decisive force in determining whether one views the virginal conception as a *theologoumenon* or a literal fact.

Certainly it is important to keep in mind, as Hans Küng points out, that the virgin birth does not belong to the core of the Gospel. Neither Jesus' divine sonship nor God's fatherhood is dependent on the virgin birth. Nevertheless the virgin birth, apart from its historical or biological veracity, is a meaningful symbol: that with the coming of Jesus, God has made a new beginning. Karl Barth, who upheld its historicity, saw the virgin birth as necessary to underline the mysterious character of the Incarnation and as a sign of the divine initiative in the work of our redemption. The virgin birth "means that God Himself—acting directly in His own and not in human fashion—stands at the beginning of this human existence . . . it is the denial, not of man in the presence of God, but of any power, attribute or capacity in him for God."[23]

The opposite point of view within Protestantism is represented by such theologians as Emil Brunner, Paul Tillich and Rudolf Bultmann, who for various reasons reject the historicity of Mary's virginal conception. Brunner sees the assertion of the virginal conception as due to the needs of dogma. There was the need for a sign and a biological miracle to announce the birth, the need for escaping the transmission of original sin in human generation, the needs of a false puritanism in matters of sex. Since we have outgrown these needs, Brunner argues, there is no reason why we should not accept that Christ's full humanity demands his procreation in the normal way.

For Bultmann the virginal conception is rooted in the mythical worldview characteristic of the New Testament. For him the virgin birth was a myth introduced by Hellenistic Christianity to indicate that Jesus' origin and meaning transcended both history and nature.

Tillich finds only a subjective value in the dogma and in Mariology in general. As a symbolic representation of God, man and their relation, the Virgin Mary may or may not have revelatory significance, depending on your point of view. For most Protestants, Tillich claims, the Virgin Mother, Mary, reveals nothing and is as meaningless as Apollo. This is consistent with his general understanding of revelation, which, he contends, comes to man through many channels, none of which in themselves

23. *Church Dogmatics* (New York: Charles Scribner's Sons, 1956), Vol. IV, 1, p. 207, and Vol. I, 2, p. 188.

convey absolute truth. The Bible itself is filled with symbol, myth and legend and is indifferent to history. Any attempt to find immutable truth in creeds and dogmas is pursuit of idols. "Man must reject his greatest temptation to think he can know absolutely God or truth."[24]

24. Quoted in Thomas O'Meara, *Mary in Protestant and Catholic Theology* (New York: Sheed & Ward, 1966), p. 239.

# 14

## The Saints

Has anyone heard the litany of the saints recently? Like so many cherished Catholic traditions, devotion to the saints has all but disappeared in many parts of Catholic Christendom. Along with indulgences, Friday abstinence, novenas to the sorrowful mother and first Fridays, prayer to the saints has lost its charm. Statues of Francis and Dominic, of Ignatius and Mary Magdalene, of the Little Flower and Maria Goretti have been relegated to the basement and the attic, where they stand gazing vacantly on the discarded and dusty remains of ornate altars and discolored confessional screens.

Is this eclipse of the saints only temporary? Have we impoverished ourselves a little spiritually by neglecting a devotion that has existed almost from the very beginning of the Church? Will there be a renaissance of piety toward the saints—albeit in new forms and with a better understanding of their true significance for the life of the Church? These are questions that naturally occur to anyone who studies the history of devotion to the saints.

It's well to recall that the bishops at the Second Vatican Council did not give much attention to the role of the saints. In their *Dogmatic Constitution on the Church, Lumen Gentium,* they simply reiterated the traditional teaching, which encourages the faithful to rely on the intercession of the saints in heaven, to love them and honor them and make use of their power and help in obtaining benefits from God through His Son,

Jesus Christ, our Lord. By reason of the mystical bond that joins all members of God's Church, both living and dead, we share in their merits. The bishops remind us also that, as images of Christ, the saints vividly manifest God's presence, show us a sign of His Kingdom and draw us to greater holiness. At the same time, aware of the charge that devotion to the saints detracts from the worship due God alone, the bishops caution the faithful to avoid all excess and to honor them more by the intensity of active love than by multiplying external practices.

Scripture itself does not dwell at any length on devotion to the saints. As with other Catholic traditions, one finds only the seed of what later developed into an elaborate theology. But a basis for devotion to the saints is found in St. Paul's confidence in the prayers of the living: "Pray," he says, "that I may escape the unbelievers in Judaea, and that the aid I carry to Jerusalem may be accepted by the saints."[1] While further support for the doctrine is found in the understanding of the Church as Christ's mystical body, so that, as St. Paul says, "You then are the body of Christ. Every one of you is a member of it . . . If one part hurts, all the parts are hurt with it; if one part is given special honor, all the parts enjoy it."[2] The members of Christ's mystical body depend upon the head for their entire life and activity and enjoy a vital union among themselves. There is also the passage of Ephesians (2:20) which relates the Church on earth to the Church in Heaven as a holy temple founded on the apostles and prophets, with Christ Jesus as the capstone. Finally, the Epistle to the Hebrews speaks of the "cloud of witnesses" that surround those who are still wayfarers.

## ORIGIN OF DEVOTION

Devotion to the saints is first manifest in the cult rendered to the martyrs. Recall that from the very beginning the Church faced violent opposition, and its first martyr, Stephen, was stoned only a few years after the Resurrection, while tradition records that both Peter and Paul were executed for preaching the Gospel. Wave after wave of persecution continued to buffet the Church, and many thousands of Christians were condemned to suffer excruciating torments at the hands of their executioners. Their fellow Christians were bound to be impressed and inspired

1. Rm. 15:31.
2. 1 Cor. 12:26–27.

by their example of courage and faith and to remember with gratitude their glorious triumph. For them, the martyrs were the perfect Christians, marvelous imitators of Christ and the apostles, pure and immaculate spirits. They lavished praise on them and held their memory in highest honor. Many accounts we have of their deaths were written by eyewitnesses who themselves aspired to join their ranks. To die a violent death for Christ was the ambition of many a noble soul in the early Church, and there are numerous records of martyrs facing the rack, the sword and the wild beast in a state of exultation and joy at being allowed to shed their blood for Christ. Often we read how the martyr was in such ecstasy that he seemingly felt no pain. Eusebius' *Church History,* for instance, tells how a Phrygian martyr named Alexander was so absorbed in prayer that he endured the most ferocious torments without uttering a word. The famous African martyr Perpetua was in such ecstasy that she felt nothing while being tossed on the horns of a wild bull.

Even before their final agony, the martyrs were venerated by the Church while locked in prison. One of the official duties of priests and deacons was to visit the martyrs and comfort them by celebrating the Eucharist with them and ministering to their needs. Other visitors would bring gifts and shower affection on them, kissing their chains and showing them every mark of esteem and admiration.

All of this, however, was only a foretaste of the devotion poured out on them once they were dead. It was common in the ancient world for relatives of a deceased person to gather at his tomb, especially on the anniversary of his birth, bringing flowers and perfumes and sharing a meal in his memory. The same custom no doubt inspired the Christians to gather at the tomb of a martyr to celebrate the Eucharist—but on the anniversary of his death, rather than of his birth. And instead of only a restricted circle of friends and relatives, the whole community would congregate.

Each local church kept its list of these anniversaries, which constitute our first martyrologies.

As long as they lived under the shadow of persecution, the Christians kept their celebrations at the tombs restrained and discreet. With the advent of freedom and the new era ushered in by Constantine, however, they could give full vent to their enthusiasm for the martyrs. Huge basilicas were built over or near their tombs, and immense crowds swarmed around their altars. Their feast days were celebrated with brilliant and splendid liturgies.

The bodies of the martyrs were shown great reverence, and their relics were gathered and preserved for future veneration. This practice is mentioned for the first time in the "Martyrdom of Polycarp." There we read: "We collected the bones that were more precious to us than costly gems and more valuable than gold, and we buried them in a suitable place. There, as far as possible, one will gather in joy and gladness if the Lord will let us celebrate the anniversary day of his martyrdom."[3]

At first the body of the martyr was treated with religious awe, and those who built churches over the relics took great care not to disturb the resting place of the saint. But eventually a change in attitude took place and the practice began of moving the body to satisfy some political or religious purpose. This practice began among the Greeks, and the first recorded translation of the body of a martyr took place at Antioch in the middle of the fourth century at the behest of the ruler, Gallus. Henceforth the idea caught on and the saints began to travel. Constantinople proved especially greedy; the emperors had many holy corpses brought to rest in its churches in ceremonies of great pomp and solemnity.

It took only one step more to begin the practice of dividing up the corpse and scattering the relics around the Christian world. This would lead unfortunately to various abuses as the relic itself became an object of a distinct cult. This "translation of relics" eventually led to the practice of requiring a relic of a saint to be placed on every altar where Mass was to be celebrated. And in fact until very recently no priest would celebrate Mass on an altar lacking an altar stone holding relics of a saint.

At first, devotion to the martyrs was restricted to praise and imitation, but already by the third century we find belief in the efficacy of their intercession.

The martyrs were venerated as inspiring models, heroic Christians who imitated Christ even to sharing in his sacrificial death. They were held up as examples to inspire others with the courage to face persecution and death. They were admired for their ability to withstand the terror of suffering and death for the sake of a spiritual ideal.

They were also regarded as spirits endowed with supernatural power, who would work miracles for those who invoked their names or venerated their relics. They could heal the blind and the crippled, change the heart of the sinner and even work prodigies of nature. The faithful saw them as channels of the same awesome power so manifest in the ministry of Jesus

3. "Martyrdom of Polycarp." In Herbert Musurillo, ed., *The Acts of the Christian Martyrs* (New York: Oxford University Press, 1972), p. 18.

and the apostles. (This belief in the power of holy persons to work prodigies was likewise found among the pagan worshipers of gods and heroes.) History shows that people became increasingly fascinated with the power of the martyrs as miracle workers, so that their role as models was greatly deemphasized.

## THE CONFESSORS

An important development occurred with the arrival of the Constantinian era of peace. Persecution ceased and martyrdom became a rarity, but the need for heroes persisted. Attention now shifted to those Christians who led lives of extraordinary asceticism and penance. People realized that one could suffer a slow martyrdom by practicing extraordinary austerities: leading a life of perfect chastity, depriving oneself of food and sleep, wearing a hair shirt, scourging oneself, etc. This type of martyrdom was the special province of the monks and solitaries who now began to people the deserts and the mountains. A technical name was given to them to distinguish them from the actual martyrs. They were called the "confessors." In his most influential *Life of St. Anthony* (A.D. 356), St. Athanasius recounted in fantastic detail the fastings, hardships, devotion to solitude and demonic temptations of his hero and made it plain that Anthony's life easily rivaled the heroism of the martyrs: "There in his cell Anthony was daily a martyr to conscience in the sufferings he endured for the faith. He practiced a much more intense asceticism, for he fasted constantly and wore a garment of skin, the inner lining of which was hair."[4]

But a problem immediately presented itself: A martyr could rather easily be identified, since the circumstances of his death were a matter of public knowledge, as a rule. But how could one evaluate the claim of a confessor to authentic sanctity? While some reliance could be put on witnesses who vouched for their extraordinary ascetic practices, there was still the possibility of human error. A far more convincing criterion was the confessor's ability to perform miracles, not only during his lifetime but after his death. And from the sixth century on, this criterion became the sine qua non for establishing a confessor's right to a cult. Hagiographical literature of the patristic era shows how a typical saint's life had to com-

4. Lawrence Cunningham, *The Meaning of the Saints* (New York: Harper & Row, 1980), p. 17.

bine a strong ascetic element and a testimony to his miraculous powers, with the latter increasingly predominant.

The emphasis on the miracle-working power of the saint at the expense of his more accessible qualities of character is very evident from this time on. Lawrence Cunningham, in his recent study *The Meaning of the Saints*, shows how evident this tendency is in the earliest and most influential lives of the saints. *The Life of Saint Martin of Tours* (c. A.D. 403) by Sulpicius Severus, was a model for all subsequent hagiographies of the West for the next millennium. It offers such an unrelieved catalog of miracles, prodigies and healings that one easily overlooks the true significance of Martin as not only the founder of Gallic monasticism but also the greatest missionary to rural France.[5]

This emphasis on the miraculous was so strong in the Middle Ages that the role of the saints as models of the Christian life was completely overshadowed by their quality as repositories of power—power that flowed above all from their relics. One may surely speculate on how closely related this attitude was to the belief in the ancient world that sacred power emanated from certain persons or objects, so that pagan gods and heroes were worshiped above all as channels of sacred power.

The social value and role of relics in the Middle Ages indeed can scarcely be overestimated. They were used in the taking of oaths, as magnets to draw masses of pilgrims to shrines and monasteries, and as a source of civic pride.

This emphasis on the miraculous rooted in the cult of the martyrs and confessors is still found in the canonization process. Ordinarily several miracles are still demanded before Rome will canonize a proposed saint. The only exception is the case of a martyr whose martyrdom can be exactly and historically determined. According to canon law, at least two miracles are required before a person can be beatified (which allows him or her to be venerated in a particular region or in a particular religious order) and then two more indicative of the intercessory power of the saint are demanded before final canonization. The miracles themselves are scrutinized by experts and generally involve a cure of some organic disease that cannot be explained by natural powers.

5. Ibid., p. 19.

## SEPARATING FACT FROM FICTION

Our knowledge of the lives of the saints comes from a tremendous variety of sources—written tradition including annals, chronicles, biographies, as well as unwritten sources including monuments and various pictorial records. Among the most important are the lists which individual churches kept of their martyrs and confessors and which are recorded in the *kalendaria* and *martyrologia*. As one might suspect, knowing the human propensity to distort and exaggerate—especially where hero worship is involved—this mass of documents is a hodgepodge of fraud and legend mingled with fact.

The effort to separate fact from fiction in this mountain of material has been going on since the seventeenth century and the rise of historical criticism. No single group has done more in this effort than the Bollandists, a remarkable community of Jesuit scholars founded in the seventeenth century whose sole purpose is to produce lives of the saints based on a critical study of authentic sources. In spite of trials and difficulties, disruptions caused by wars and revolutions, persecutions from obscurantists in the Church and upheaval in the Jesuit Order itself, the Bollandists have persevered in their mission. The first two volumes of their *Acta Sanctorum (Lives of the Saints)* saw the light of day at Antwerp in 1643.

The Bollandists have numbered among them some of the giants of historical scholarship; the first and greatest of these was Daniel Van Papebroch (d. 1714), who in his fifty-four years of labor set the incredibly high standards that have ever since guided their work. Papebroch combed the archives and libraries of Europe for material dealing with the lives of the saints and thus began the immense collection of documents that constitute the Bollandist library. Papebroch was no skeptic, but as David Knowles says, ". . . he had no mercy for what he proved false by legitimate criticism, and he did not hold that a historical or critical argument could never be more than a probable one, or that a false or superstitious tradition, however venerable or harmless, should be allowed to pass as authentic."[6] Papeboch did not escape attacks from people in the Church who then as today are frightened by historical criticism and are loath to abandon cherished legends. The history of the Bollandists, in fact, gives

6. David Knowles, *Great Historical Enterprises* (London: Thomas Nelson, 1963), p. 15.

comfort to those who believe that truth in the long run can triumph over the forces of intellectual sloth and timidity.

One of the most distinguished in the long line of Bollandists was Hippolyte Delehaye (d. 1941). In his work *The Legends of the Saints: An Introduction to Hagiography* (translation of *Les Légendes Hagiographiques,* 1905), Delehaye ranged over the enormous treasure of the lives of the saints and was able to disentangle the complex of factors by which historical truth becomes corrupted in the popular mind and imagination.

As Delehaye explains, some medieval writers did not really pretend to write history; they merely intended to serve up some pleasant, lively story that would drive home a moral lesson, and they would borrow or invent some such story. The day might come, however, when people will have forgotten that this life of the saint was a mere pious fiction. A cult of the fictional saint might even develop, and so the calendar of the Church's saints would acquire another weird addition. One of the most famous instances of this transformation is no doubt the story of St. Christopher—of the ubiquitous medal picturing him as a giant with staff in hand carrying a child on his shoulder. Christopher, it seems, was an otherwise unknown martyr of Asia Minor who died possibly under the persecution of Diocletian. Medieval authors, however, built on this slim foundation the story of a cannibalistic monster who upon being converted to Christ became a ferryman and hermit. One day a child appeared at the stream, and when Christopher hoisted him to his shoulder to carry him across, he nearly buckled under his crushing weight. He subsequently was favored with a revelation that showed him the child was Christ himself, burdened with the sins of the whole world.

Even more curious is the entry of the Buddha into the medieval calendar of saints, under the name Josaphat. The story of the Buddha was carried by crusaders or merchants from the East and was changed into the life of Saint Josaphat, no doubt a medieval corruption of *bodhisattva,* an attribute of a future Buddha.

In 1968, the Vatican abolished the feast of St. Philomena, to the consternation of her devotees. Her legend actually dated only from the nineteenth century, when relics from the cemetery of Priscilla were misconstrued to be the relics of a martyr. A glass vial thought to have originally contained the blood of a martyr was found in the catacomb near some bones with an inscription which read, *LUMENA—PAXTE-FI.* This inscription was mistranslated to read: "Philomena—Peace be with you."

And an elaborate biography of the supposed saint was concocted out of thin air. But archaeologists were able to prove to the satisfaction of the Vatican that the word "lumena" did not refer to a person but was most likely just a conventional expression such as "beloved one" found in many ordinary tombs while the vial also was a commonplace object found around the tombs.

## CANONIZATION BY THE PEOPLE

The Church only slowly refined the process whereby a person was recognized as a saint and as such entitled to the veneration of the faithful. For many centuries, the making of a saint was a very democratic affair. Before any official proclamation, the cult of a saint first depended on popular acclaim.

How did people come to believe that so and so was deserving of saintly honors? First, there had to be evidence of supernatural power, above all in its most compelling form: the ability to work miracles. The saints sent rain, healed the sick and even raised the dead. The saints manifested their power also in other ways; some received Christ's stigmata on their bodies. Some radiated a celestial light or were lifted off the ground as they prayed, like Thomas Aquinas, whose brethren saw him rise two feet above the ground absorbed in prayer.

Asceticism was another sign of God's special favor. Every community had its holy ascetic, who in the popular mind helped to expiate the sins of his more earthbound fellow citizens. The ascetic endured long fasts and went for days without sleep, and when forced by nature to rest took only the hard ground for his bed. Above all, the saint was admired for his chastity. Renunciation of sex was an absolute necessity in the popular estimation of sanctity. The lives of the medieval saints are filled with accounts of their successful struggles to subdue the flesh—often under extreme provocation. Thomas Aquinas, for instance, had managed to keep his sexual impulses under control until the day his mother sent a beautiful wanton into his room in order to seduce him. As she began to entice him by her lascivious gestures, he felt for the first time the full force of his lower nature and only saved his virtue by violently thrusting her out of his room. Later, in a dream, he beheld two angels, who tied a girdle around his waist as a pledge that God would grant him perpetual virginity. From then on, we are told, Thomas abhorred the sight of women and avoided their conversation.

As a recent sociological study of the saints indicates, the greater number of medieval saints preserved their virginity. Prince Casimir of Poland was directed to take a bride but refused, intending to dedicate himself to chastity and a life of penance. When he fell ill, the doctors prescribed sexual intercourse as a remedy, and his parents cooperated by having a beautiful virgin placed in his bed. But he refused to embrace her, vowing to preserve his innocence even to death. And die he did—not long after![7]

Among the great number of stories exalting the heroic chastity of the saints, few are as graphic as the case of William, bishop of St. Brieuc, who it seems was so handsome that he spent much of his time fending off the assaults of scheming women. When he died and was being prepared for burial, it was found that his penis was as undeveloped as a child's.[8]

Another prerequisite for a saint in the medieval mind was a reputation for good works. The saint labored in charity for the needy and the sick, practicing the gospel of love to a heroic degree.

Study also shows that another important factor in gaining popular acclaim was a position of power. The medieval roster of saints contains a disproportionate number of princes, bishops, abbots and abbesses who often wielded great power in the affairs of state. At first sight this seems to contradict the emphasis of the Gospel on humility and meekness. But, for the medieval mind, the virtue of humility could be most dramatically displayed by a prince or bishop who exercised his great power in imitation of Christ's gentleness and compassion.


## PAPAL CANONIZATION

For a long time, the Church limited its intervention merely to ratifying the popular choice of a saint. The usual practice in the early Middle Ages was for the bishop merely to proclaim the person a saint after investigation showed that he was worthy of the esteem already bestowed on him by the public. Recourse was sometimes had to the pope, but only to add greater solemnity to the proclamation. The first such papal canonization on record was that of a Saint Uldaricus in 973, during the reign of Pope Bene-

7. D. Weinstein and R. Bell, *Saints and Society* (Chicago: University of Chicago Press, 1982), p. 29.
8. Ibid., p. 74.

dict VI. However, as papal power over the Church was asserted with increasing success from Pope Gregory VII's reign (1073–85), it became more and more common for the bishops to ask the popes to proclaim the saints and order the *translatio* of their relics, which was usually done with great pomp and ceremony accompanied by the expected miracles. In 1234, as papal power neared its apex, Pope Gregory IX reserved the right of canonization to the papacy alone. While popular piety continued to discover many local saints, the popes during the thirteenth and fourteenth centuries were very restrained in proclaiming saints—limiting their canonizations mainly to members of the mendicant orders or to certain persons of high rank. In fact, papal canonizations amounted to only about one in ten of the widely recognized saints of the thirteenth century.

Canonizations, in fact, present a convenient index of the fluctuations of papal power. During the Babylonian Captivity, with the popes absent from Rome, canonizations were rare—only eight during the whole of the fourteenth century. And in the following century there were only sixteen.[9]

During the period of the Counter-Reformation, as the popes once more assumed leadership over the Church, they succeeded in getting complete control over the cult of saints as part of a general effort to unify and centralize the Church. The haphazard medieval approach to selecting saints promoted a fragmentation of loyalties, practices and beliefs. Under papal guidance, the saints would now serve as symbols of unification. The decrees of Urban VIII in 1642 gave the papacy absolute control in the selection of saints.

The scholarly future Pope Benedict XIV produced a definitive treatise on canonization in his *De Servorum Dei Beatificatione et Beatorum Canonizatione*, in four huge folio volumes, in 1734. With some modifications, its procedure is still basic. Three requirements were laid down: all candidates must manifest doctrinal purity, heroic virtue and miraculous intercession after death.

The first concern, doctrinal purity, seemed obvious: the Church could not allow a heretic to receive its official honors. The second condition, heroic virtue, was supposed to be a sure sign that the candidate was an instrument of God and not of the devil. An agent of Satan might work miracles, but a person who practiced heroic virtue could not be in league with the devil. The third requirement, miraculous intercession after death,

9. Ibid., pp. 168–69.

was important because while others might work a miracle on earth, only a saint could intercede in heaven on behalf of the faithful.

## IS CANONIZATION IRRELEVANT TODAY?

The whole canonization process has been called into question lately. Its emphasis on the miraculous, for instance, appears medieval. Critics also point out how the bureaucracy tends to produce saints that reflect its own clerical mind-set, with little appeal to the average Catholic. A simple glance at the present calendar of saints, in fact, shows how thoroughly the clergy have monopolized it. A saint, one might conclude, is any notably pious European who founded a religious order in the post-Reformation period. Recent canonizations underscore the advantage. In the period 1965–75 there were sixty-two persons canonized. Forty of these were martyrs—priests, religious and lay folk—from the Elizabethan period in England. Individuals canonized numbered twenty-two, of whom eight were women founders of religious orders and the rest were men founders, with the exception of an archbishop. Not a single lay person!

The theology implied is the two-story model of the Church (supposedly laid aside at Vatican II), which considered the religious state of life superior to the lay state inasmuch as the one who professed religious vows was supposed to pursue "perfection," while the ordinary Christian merely sought salvation.

The obvious antisexual prejudice found in the calendar is another limitation. The great preference for virginal and unmarried saints is today certainly offensive to the great mass of Christians who no longer share this medieval worldview. All the bizarre stories reflecting the medieval obsession with sexual purity do not commend the calendar to a modern Christian.

Finally there is the test of doctrinal orthodoxy. According to present rules, no one can be admitted to the calendar of the saints whose orthodoxy does not measure up to the strict standards of official Catholic belief. In practice this has served to eliminate some notable candidates who have been eminent examples of Christian life and pioneers in adapting Catholic tradition to a new age but whose expressions of belief were sometimes open to misinterpretation. Think, for instance, of the obstacles in the way of Teilhard de Chardin's canonization.

And what about men and women of heroic sanctity outside the Roman communion? People like Dietrich Bonhoeffer or, going back further, John Wesley or even Martin Luther. Their example and influence has been of tremendous value to the Church. They were not only models of Christian holiness but leaders who revealed new ways of living the Gospel. In popular esteem they are recognized as saints, but their chance of being canonized is slight indeed. And yet the Second Vatican Council recognized the fact that heroic sanctity does exist outside the visible bounds of the Roman Church.

One may indeed argue (as Lawrence Cunningham does) that canonization has become largely irrelevant. The assumptions governing it no longer are operable for the great majority of Christians. People are no longer inclined to veneration of the saints in the sense of rendering them prayerful homage. Decline in this kind of devotion is too obvious to need proof.

On the other hand, however, it is also obvious that people still need "saints": men and women whose lives are inspiring examples of Christian commitment and signs of God's grace in the world. One has only to note the number of outstanding figures who have been canonized by popular opinion: Pope John XXIII, Martin Luther King, Jr., Thomas Merton, etc. The Church obviously needs such heroes, courageous spirits who not only witness to the vitality of the Christian tradition but provide models for new ways of living it.

On this last point, Karl Rahner is worth quoting:

> They are the initiators and the creative models of the holiness which happens to be right for, and is the task of, their particular age. They create a new style; they prove that a certain form of life and activity is a really genuine possibility; they show experimentally that one can be a Christian even in "this way"; they make a certain type of person believable as a Christian type . . . Their death is . . . the seal put on their task of being creative models, a task which they had in their lifetime, and their living on means that the example they have given remains in the Church as a permanent form.[10]

10. Quoted in Lawrence Cunningham, op. cit., p. 76.

# IV

---

## Liturgy and Sacraments

# 15

# Liturgy—Sacrament of Christ

Of all the changes enacted by the Second Vatican Council, probably nothing was more startling to the average Catholic than those affecting the liturgy. Overnight the Mass was transformed. An age-old ritual had decreed that the priest stand facing a remote altar with his back to the people while he murmured in incantatory Latin the sacred words of the Mass. But now the altar was brought forward and the priest stood behind it facing the congregation. Instead of whispering the prayers in Latin, he now read them aloud in the language of the people. Many of the old rites and ceremonies were discarded. Previously the faithful were taught to observe a prayerful demeanor and attitude, hardly noticing their neighbor, but now they were asked to turn and greet him with a "sign of peace."

Catholics were thus rather brusquely drawn into a period of liturgical renewal.

Since then, many other changes have occurred in the liturgy. One may now receive communion in the hand. Laymen may now help the priest in distributing communion. It is possible for a layman occasionally to preach, and women are now admitted to the sanctuary as lectors at Mass and as ministers of Holy Communion. The confessional has all but disappeared, as those who still seek the sacrament of penance often make use of the new form, which allows priest and penitent to face each other in a private room, rather than behind the screen in a dark box.

## WORSHIP   UNIVERSAL

The Christian liturgy is but a specific manifestation of a universal human phenomenon. Worship, as Rudolf Otto showed in his book *The Holy*, is a peculiarly human response to the overwhelming power and majesty radiant in the cosmos.

No civilization has yet been discovered without its religion, its peculiar sense of the sacred hidden at the very heart of reality.

Primitive people, as anthropologists point out, regarded all the main events of life as to a great extent beyond human control, wrapped in mystery and to that extent revelations of the sacred. Through various rites, they connected these events with a higher power on whom they felt dependent. Birth, marriage and, above all, death were surrounded by a complex of ceremonies that inspired awe and evoked the spirit of worship.

Primitive worship was emphatically communal, and this was perhaps best expressed in the sacred meal shared by the whole community. It regularly reminded people of the sacredness of life, one's connectedness with the community, and the community's dependence on the divine, however that was conceived. The ritual action by which the primitive person related to this hidden but very real reality was extraordinary in its exuberance. Unlike modern industrialized citizens, primitive people felt no need to justify their actions by rational arguments. They threw themselves totally into the ritual, with gestures, song and dance, in their attempt to enter into the mystery.

Intimately related to the ritual was the myth, or story that explained in dramatic and usually fictional terms the origins of human life or of the community. As J. D. Crichton says, "The events had taken place in a kind of timeless time and since they 'explained' how the community came to be, it was vital to keep in touch with them if the community was to retain its cohesion." It was necessary therefore to reenact the myth annually in ritual fashion, making the past event present so that the community could establish contact with it and be renewed.[1]

Worship, then, is deeply rooted in human nature itself. One might as well ask why people eat and drink, work and play, as ask why they pray and worship. As someone has said, to worship is

1. Cheslyn Jones, Geoffrey Wainwright and Edw. Yarnold, S.J., eds., *The Study of Liturgy* (New York: Oxford University Press, 1978), p. 7.

to quicken the conscience by the holiness of God,
to feed the mind with the truth of God,
to purge the imagination by the beauty of God,
to open the heart to the love of God,
to devote the will to the purpose of God.[2]

## BASIS OF CHRISTIAN WORSHIP

Christian worship has its own distinctive character, given to it by the set of beliefs on which it is based. Christian worship is understood primarily as a *response*. God takes the initiative and we open our hearts to Him in return. God shows His love for people by His great acts: creation of the world, followed by the whole history by which He gradually revealed Himself, culminating in the definitive revelation of Himself given in the life, death and Resurrection of His Son, Jesus Christ. The whole record manifests the continual willingness of God to offer His love to His children, to make them His people and bind them to Himself by a covenant that is the expression of His love. Abraham is singled out because he responds in faith to God's offer to make him the father of many peoples. God seals His covenant with Abraham, and the great figures of the Old Testament who follow him show the same faith in God's promises. Through faith in God's fidelity, Moses is able to lead his people to freedom and bind them by a covenant to the God Who saves. In times of spiritual crisis, prophets arise to rekindle the lukewarm faith of the people. Finally, one comes whose response of faith is total and absolute. "[w]ith him it was always Yes . . . That is why it is 'through him' that we answer Amen to the praise of God."[3]

It is this pattern of God's call and our response in faith which is the heart of all Christian worship. When we worship, we respond to God's call by praise, thanksgiving and supplication.

This Word of God is transmitted to us through the Scriptures, which are the heart of all Christian worship. Its basic message is always the same: God offers Himself to us and invites us to respond in faith, to commit ourselves completely to Himself. By uniting self with Christ, the believer is enabled to offer fitting praise and adoration to God. Christ is the High

2. William Temple, quoted in Franklin M. Segler, *Christian Worship* (Nashville, Tenn.: Broadman Press, 1967), p. 4.
3. 2 Cor. 1:19–20.

Priest, who, through his one and only perfect sacrifice on the cross, reconciles us with the Father.[4] Through him we all have access to the Father.[5] From earliest times, Christians prayed to the Father through Christ the Mediator. As Colossians puts it, "And whatever you do, in word or deed, do everything in the name of the Lord Jesus, giving thanks to God the Father through him."[6] "As the first of a new humanity Jesus offers the Father the worship that is due to him and so precedes mankind on the way back to the Father."[7]

As Pope Pius XII said in his encyclical *Mediator Dei*, "Along with the Church, therefore, her Divine Founder is present at every liturgical function: Christ is present at the august sacrifice of the altar both in the person of his minister and above all under the eucharistic species. He is present in the other sacraments, infusing into them the power which makes them ready instruments of sanctification. He is present, finally, in the prayer of praise and petition we direct to God, as it is written: 'Where there are two or three meet in my name I shall be there with them.' "[8]

The Church in the liturgy not only prays through Christ to the Father but also makes Christ himself an object of its praise and adoration. The New Testament shows that, from the beginning, Christians rendered worship to Christ as well as to the Father. This is clear from the liturgical hymns to Christ found throughout the various epistles. Most noteworthy is the great song found in Colossians (1:15–16):

> He is the image of the unseen God
> and the first-born of all creation,
> for in him were created
> all things in heaven and on earth:
> everything visible and everything invisible.

Throughout the celebration of the Eucharist, prayers of adoration are directed to Christ, notably in the *Kyrie eleison* (Lord, have mercy), the *Gloria,* the *Benedictus* and the *Agnus Dei.*

4. Heb. 9:25–28; 10:11–15.
5. Ibid.
6. Col. 3:17.
7. A. Verheul, *Introduction to the Liturgy* (Collegeville, Minn.: Liturgical Press, 1968), p. 40.
8. Mt. 18:20.

## THE ROLE OF THE HOLY SPIRIT

It is also important to understand the role of the Holy Spirit in the liturgy. The New Testament lays great stress on the work of the Holy Spirit in the *salvific* events it records. Mary conceives the God-man through the power of the Holy Spirit. Jesus is anointed by the Holy Spirit for his prophetic mission. He utters his prayer to the Father under the inspiration of the Holy Spirit and promises to send the Holy Spirit on his disciples. He fulfills the promise on the morning of his Resurrection when he bids them, "Receive the Holy Spirit."[9] And Pentecost symbolizes in spectacular fashion how the Son continues to pour out the Holy Spirit upon his Church. Under the inspiration of the Spirit, members of the Church proclaim the glory of God, speak in tongues and prophesy.[10]

All this makes it obvious why the Church in its worship is completely dependent on the Holy Spirit. Through the presence of the Spirit in us by baptism, we share in the nature of the Son: "Everyone moved by the Spirit is a son of God."[11] And it is through the Spirit that we have access to the Father. "The Spirit too comes to help us in our weakness. For when we cannot choose words in order to pray properly, the Spirit himself expresses our plea in a way that could never be put into words . . ."[12] Hence Paul calls the infant Christian community of Corinth a temple of God's Spirit.

For this reason, the Church in its liturgy calls on the Father to send the Holy Spirit. It counts on the Holy Spirit to release the desire for praise and prayer, to create in the minds and hearts of the congregation an awareness of God.

## LITURGY AS SACRAMENT

Another aspect of the Christian liturgy deserving our attention is its sacramental character. It speaks to our senses as well as to our mind, not only to our ears but also to our eyes, our nose and our mouth. It uses not

9. Jn. 20:22.
10. 1 Cor. 14:1–25.
11. Rom. 8:14.
12. Rom. 8:26.

only words but actions, gestures and symbols. In Christ the Word became flesh. In the liturgy, the word becomes water, wine, bread and oil. By entering into the material world in the person of Christ, God sanctified all matter and made it an apt vehicle to communicate his spiritual life.

The symbols chosen by Christ and his Church to open the mind and heart to divine reality were not arbitrarily chosen. Its basic symbols— water, oil, bread, wine—were naturally suggestive of and harmonious with the spiritual effect intended: water to signify the spiritual washing away of sin, oil, a symbol of healing, bread and wine of nourishment.

Some of the Church's symbols were borrowed from existing religious rites but then transposed in meaning. The Eucharist, for instance, is based on a Jewish religious ritual meal taken in a spirit of thanksgiving for Yahweh's benefits.

The tendency of religious symbols to lose their original suggestive power as time passes and formalism creeps in or culture changes is a well-known fact. Hence liturgical renewal demands that we restore the sign value to symbols that have lost their original force. We need a real washing at baptism, bread that looks and really tastes like bread, etc.

## LITURGY AS THE EPIPHANY OF THE CHURCH

The *Constitution on the Sacred Liturgy,* of the Second Vatican Council, teaches that the Church "reveals itself most clearly" in the celebration of the liturgy "when a full complement of God's holy people, united in prayer and in a common liturgical service (especially the Eucharist) exercise a thorough and active participation at the very altar where the bishop presides in the company of his priest and other assistants."[13] The same constitution also says, "The liturgy is the summit toward which the activity of the Church is directed; at the same time it is the foundation from which all her power flows. For the goal of apostolic works is that all who are made sons of God by faith and baptism should come together to praise God in the midst of His church, to take part in her sacrifice, and to eat the Lord's supper."[14]

We are often reminded today by theologians that Christ is the sacrament of God, i.e., that God's redeeming love took historical and visible form in the person of the man from Nazareth. The Church, on the other

13. *Constitution on the Sacred Liturgy,* 41.
14. Ibid., 10.

hand, may be seen as the sacrament of Christ, signifying in historical and visible form the redeeming grace of Christ. "It signifies that grace as relevantly given to men of every age, race, kind and condition."[15]

It is important, then, that the Church manifest this grace of Christ in a visible way. And this is done most tangibly and vividly in the Eucharist, where Christ is present in his own congregation as the crucified and resurrected Savior. The Church most fully appears as a sign of Christ when its members are united around the altar in a spirit of faith and love to celebrate what God has done for them in Jesus Christ.

Thus, as the Second Vatican Council reminds us, "The Liturgy is . . . the outstanding means by which the faithful can express in their lives, and manifest to others, the mystery of Christ and the real nature of the true Church."[16] The liturgy, then, may rightly be called the *epiphany* of the Church: in the liturgy, the Church becomes visible. It is or should be where we most intensely experience the reality of the Church.

Obviously, if what we have said so far is true, then those present at the liturgy must actively participate in it. The liturgy must be the action of the whole community not only in theory, but in reality. Hence the bishops at the Second Vatican Council insisted that those present at the mystery of faith "should not be there as strangers or silent spectators; on the contrary, through an adequate understanding of the rites and prayers they should take part in the sacred action conscious of what they are doing, with devotion and full collaboration."[17]

For this reason, all liturgical rites are designed for the participation of the community. Through the rites, the kiss, the handshake, they relate to each other and also to the community. A true community demands interaction between its members, a face-to-face relationship, and, in the Christian community, a sharing of persons bound together by faith and love. Through their experience of worship, the members should deepen their commitment to each other and to the community.

## VATICAN II'S REFORM

An era of reform of the liturgy was opened up by the Second Vatican Council when it passed its *Constitution on the Sacred Liturgy*, in 1963.

15. Avery Dulles, *Model of the Church* (Garden City, N.Y.: Image Books, 1974), p. 72.
16. *Constitution on the Sacred Liturgy*, 2.
17. Ibid., 48.

The general objectives were to make the liturgy more *simple*, more *participatory*, more *intelligible* and more *dynamic*. The rites were simplified by eliminating repetitions, bows, kisses, signs of the cross and genuflections, and other elements that did little to enhance the liturgy. Much emphasis was placed on making it participatory by assigning many responses to the people and above all by putting the liturgy in the vernacular so that they could understand what was being said. The bishops also made the liturgy more intelligible by rearranging it so that the intrinsic nature and purpose of its several parts as well as their connection was made more evident. To this end, they clearly marked off the liturgy of the word from the sacrificial part by a differentiation of space: the liturgy of the word was to be conducted at the ambo and chair, while the sacrifice was to take place at the altar.

Finally they restored a dynamic quality to the liturgy by making provisions for further change and adaptation. History shows that during the first fifteen centuries the liturgy was subject to a constant process of change provoked by cultural and social forces. It was the Council of Trent which froze it and cut it off from further renewal and adaptation. But the bishops at the Second Vatican Council lifted the restrictions of Trent and once again opened the liturgy to adaptation. In Article 37 of the *Constitution on the Sacred Liturgy*, the bishops rejected the concept of rigid uniformity, and in Article 38 they allowed for "legitimate variations and adaptations to different groups, regions and peoples," leaving it, in Article 40, to the bishop of each region to determine "which elements from the traditions and genius of individual peoples might appropriately be admitted into divine worship."

The bishops left the implementation of the principles and decrees concerning the liturgy to the pope, just as the Council of Trent did. In 1964, Pope Paul VI created a commission to aid him in carrying out this task. Popularly known as the Consilium, this commission was headed by Cardinal Lercaro, with Father Annibale Bugnini as its secretary. It was supposed to work with two other curial bodies charged with overseeing the implementation of the *Constitution on the Sacred Liturgy*, the Congregation of Rites and the Congregation for Divine Worship.

For six years, the liturgy was in a great state of ferment. There was much confusion, and since 1970 it is evident that Rome's main concern has been to hold the line and discourage further experimentation and innovation. The trend away from a rubrical and legislative understanding of the liturgy has been checked, and Rome once more seems preoccupied with the proper execution of prescribed rites. And in spite of the Council, which gave the bishop authority to permit legitimate variations and adaptations, the responsibility of the bishops in matters liturgical has once more been narrowed down in practice to simply securing obedience to the directives of the Holy See. This attitude seems unfortunate to many observers, since it threatens to bring liturgical renewal to a halt.

# 16

## Sacraments—
## Christ's Love Made Visible

One of the hallmarks of Catholic worship is its extensive use of sacraments —those ritual and symbolic actions that are often celebrated with great solemnity. The celebrant, richly attired in antique vesture, uses water, wine, oil, bread, etc., as he acts in the person of Christ. For Catholics, the seven sacraments are as precious as the Gospel, and indeed are the Gospel put in bodily language.

The bishops at Vatican II stated very succinctly the meaning of the sacraments. "The purpose," they said, "of the sacraments is to sanctify men, to build up the body of Christ, and finally, to give worship to God. Because they are signs, they also instruct. They not only presuppose faith, but by words and objects they also nourish, strengthen, and express it."[1]

The bishops also recognized the need for a revision of the sacramental rites in order to make them more intelligible to the faithful. Accordingly they set up guidelines for the revision of the sacraments, and as a result many changes were introduced in sacramental practice in the years following the Council. How successful these have been in deepening the sacramental consciousness of the faithful is a moot question. But at least the changes have helped to scotch the impression of some people that the sacraments are magic. They have also restored the social character of these privileged symbols as acts of the whole community.

1. *Constitution on the Sacred Liturgy,* 59.

## THE HUMAN NEED OF RITUAL

Since sacraments are fundamentally ritual behavior, it might help our understanding of sacraments to inquire first of all into the role of ritual in ordinary life.

For many people, the word "ritual" has negative connotations suggesting formalism and lack of authenticity. But a different view has come to prominence through recent investigations in psychology and anthropology. The importance of ritual in the formation of individual personality and social life has been underscored in the writings of such authors as Erik Erikson. This psychologist believes that our need for ritual is derived from our experience in infancy. Ritual interplay between mother and infant—especially the morning greeting ritual, when she calls the infant by name and attends to its physical needs—is most significant. This ritualized interaction between mother and infant, according to Erikson, addresses not only the physical needs of the infant but also his emotional needs, especially the need for mutual recognition and affirmation. Once having experienced this face-to-face recognition, the infant will have a constant hunger for it, which must be satisfied in some ritual form.

This experience of face-to-face recognition is carried over into religious ritual as the sense of a hallowed presence, or the **numinous**. As Erikson puts it:

> We vaguely recognize the numinous as an indispensable aspect of periodic religious observances, where the believer, by appropriate gestures, confesses his dependence and his childlike faith and seeks, by appropriate offerings, to secure a sense of being lifted up into the very bosom of the supernatural which in the visible form of an image may graciously respond, with the faint smile of an inclined face. The result is a sense of separateness transcended, and yet also of distinctiveness confirmed.[2]

Common to both of these rituals—the "greeting" ritual of infancy and the adult religious rituals—is the reconciliation of opposites, which takes place in four ways. First, in both rituals the mutuality of recognition occurs between two unequals: infant vis-à-vis mother and human vis-à-vis the divine. Next, the mutuality of recognition manifests both a highly personal as well as a communal aspect. Each infant-mother relationship is

2. *The Religious Situation* (Boston: Beacon Press, 1968), pp. 714–15

unique, yet follows a stereotyped pattern, just as each worshiper's experience is unique though its ritual form is common to all. Again, the repetitive character of the ritual does not preclude spontaneity: the infant smiles and laughs each time his mother greets him. The worshiper repeatedly experiences God's love in new ways within the same ritual. Finally, ritualization provides a means of coping with ambivalence. The mother can be perceived as both a loving and a threatening presence; God can be felt as both loving and fear-inspiring. "Ritualized affirmation therefore becomes indispensable as a periodic experience."[3]

Erikson's conclusions have been confirmed and amplified by anthropologists, who see ritualization as humankind's way of dealing with the spiritual polarities they experience: the conflicting forces impinging on our existence: life-death, meaning-absurdity, good-evil, sacred-profane, etc. These must somehow be integrated if we are to achieve wholeness, unity. According to the anthropologists, ritualization provides a means of holding these opposing but related experiences together.

In this connection, Bernard Bro sees ritual as the means of integrating the three most significant polarities we experience: actual self vis-à-vis ideal self, self vis-à-vis the other person and self vis-à-vis the world. As he sees it, the ideal self is always, in fact, unattainable. Every realization of our ideal self will always be partial. And so, to achieve wholeness we must somehow relativize the ideal self. Through ritual—in this case, the sacraments—we relativize our ideal self by sharing in the power of another: ". . . the sacraments offer us a chance to cooperate completely in our own fulfillment while demanding that we distinctively relativize our self-image."[4] We also experience opposition from the other person, since the total self of the other will always remain beyond our grasp, always fundamentally a mystery. Ritual allows us to respect this difference and yet achieve a positive relationship with the other—attaining communion without domination.

Finally, in our relation with the world we experience it both as our familiar home and at the same time as strange and even harsh. Ritual enables us to commune with this world symbolically to interpret it and give it meaning.

In sum, ritual can help us to move beyond our experiences of negativity, limitation and alienation and find positive meaning.[5]

3. Cf. George S. Worgul, *From Magic to Metaphor* (Paulist Press, 1980), pp. 53–56.
4. Ibid., p. 65.
5. Ibid., p. 67.

As George Worgul points out, in the light of these findings ritual is not something peripheral to human life but is at the very basis of what it means to be human: "It opens the possibility for an individual or community to resolve the experience of fragmentation and bi-polar oppositions which define human existence. It neutralizes the negative power of the ideal self, others, and the world and transforms it into an occasion for growth and maturation."[6]

Anthropologists and sociologists also have made some contribution to a better understanding of the human dimension of the sacraments. As they point out, through the repetitiveness of ritual, one achieves a certain intimacy with the original, charter event from which the community traces its origin and identity. The ritual must often be repeated because of what B. Brinkman calls "unfinished business," that is, our failure to fully achieve the element or values which the community or individual stands for. Thus, "[i]n the reenactment of the charter event, the opportunity is offered for 'catching up' with and beginning to embrace again the fullness aimed at but yet to be completely attained."[7]

## SACRAMENTS IN THE NEW TESTAMENT?

The foundation of sacramental theology is found in the New Testament.

If we analyze the New Testament, we find definite evidence of the use of sacraments in the first Christian communities. The early Christians did not limit themselves to cultic activities, for they insisted that their faith should affect the whole of life. But they shared with their fellow Jews a belief that God could manifest his favor by means of material signs. They did not impose circumcision on their converts, but they did continue the washing of baptism, which formed a part of the ceremony of admission of a Gentile proselyte to the Jewish religion. They also took meals together in a spirit of great joy, sharing the bread and wine in memory of Jesus' last supper with them.

They did not call these rites *sacraments* (a term that was applied only much later), but that is certainly what they were: ritual actions symbolic of invisible spiritual realities. They were outward signs of genuine spiritual experiences: those who were baptized felt a change of heart, felt closer to

6. Ibid.
7. Ibid., p. 83.

God, felt release from guilt and uplifted by the Spirit; when they took part in the Eucharist, they felt united with Christ and one another in a unique spiritual communion. At the same time, they saw these experiences as the work of the Holy Spirit.

This consciousness of the Holy Spirit working in their midst is brought out most clearly in the description of Pentecost found in the second chapter of the Acts of the Apostles. On that day, while gathered in one room, the disciples were dumfounded by what they heard and saw: a noise that sounded like a powerful wind, an apparition of tongues of fire while they all began to speak to the crowd that gathered in a medley of foreign languages. Nor were they any longer disheartened and fearful. They began boldly to proclaim the Gospel of Jesus Christ. Surely such an occurrence could not be explained in simple human terms. It could only be the work of God Himself: His Holy Spirit.

Moreover, they found that by laying hands on their converts they could give the Holy Spirit to them as well. When Saul, their persecutor, converted to Christ, he sought out Ananias, in Damascus. Ananias laid hands on him, and Saul was filled with the Holy Spirit and became Paul, the indomitable apostle. Peter and John laid hands on the Samaritans, and they received the Holy Spirit. This imposition of hands was certainly a sacramental action, for it symbolized something unseen, a spiritual reality: the "pouring forth" of the Holy Spirit upon the person. At the same time, it had visible effects in the transformation of the person's behavior.

From the very beginning, Christians sought to deepen their understanding of these ritual actions, which played such a central role in their faith. To help in this effort, they drew on various sources: primarily the words and actions of Jesus himself as well as the Old Testament and their own spiritual experience.

## EARLY THEOLOGY OF THE SACRAMENTS

The African theologian Tertullian (d. c. 220) was the first to use the Latin term *sacramentum* in a Christian sense. Familiar with the Roman use of the term to describe the oath a newly initiated soldier took to the emperor, he applied it by analogy to baptism as the initiation rite by which the Christian pledged his life to Christ. Then, by extension, it was gradually applied to the other ritual actions of the Church. For a long time, *sacramentum* was used very broadly to cover a great many rites and ceremonies common to the Church's liturgy. And as we shall see, it was narrowed down only in the Middle Ages to designate the seven most important rites.

An important point to be noted here is that from the very beginning, theologians saw a close correspondence between the outward rites and the inward, spiritual effect. They were not just symbols; they were effective symbols. They actually caused what they signified, i.e., insofar as God Himself used them to produce their spiritual effects. They were not therefore human inventions, but revelations of God. Nor were they optional; they were necessary means of salvation. This was something they not merely believed on the strength of Scripture but found verified in their own experience.

In addition to Scripture and experience, the Fathers of the Church found another valuable tool in elaborating a theology of the sacraments. This was Greek philosophy—especially Neo-Platonism, which put much emphasis on spiritual realities.

It was through the use of this philosophy that one of the most important developments in sacramental theology occurred. This was the idea that some sacraments imprinted an indelible seal, or character, on the soul.

The basis for this theory is found in the various passages of Scripture which speak of God marking his people with a seal, as in Second Corinthians, where Paul speaks of God marking the followers of Christ with the seal of the Spirit.[8] There are also passages that refer to the Christian as receiving the image of God through the work of the Spirit. So, for Paul, becoming filled with the Spirit means to bear the image of God by becoming conformed to the image of His Son.[9] Eventually through philosophical reflection the conviction grew that the seal was not just a metaphor, but actually a metaphysical reality. The actual practice of the Church lent support to the theory, since a person could be baptized or ordained only once—as though the person baptized or ordained was stamped spiritually with a seal, or image, that could never be lost.

The theory of the seal played a key role in resolving the controversy over rebaptism and reordination, which plagued the ancient Church for several centuries. On one side were ranged the Donatists, a large body of African Christians, followers of Donatus, the bishop of Carthage who refused to accept the ruling of the Council of Arles, in 314, that decreed

8. 2 Cor. 1:22.
9. 2 Cor. 3:18.

that baptism by apostates was valid. On the other side were ranged the majority of African Christians, who claimed they were following traditional Catholic practice in refusing to rebaptize converted apostates and heretics. The schism was deep and lasting. Eventually, rival bishops representing both sides occupied the major sees.

## AUGUSTINE'S THEOLOGY OF THE SEAL

Augustine was thrown into the controversy when, after a long, painful religious quest, he was baptized by Ambrose of Milan, returned to his native Africa, was ordained and shortly after chosen to head the diocese of Hippo, in 395, to prevent it from coming under Donatist control. He devoted a number of his voluminous writings to the debate with the Donatists, and this led him to carry the doctrines of the Church, the sacraments and sacramental grace to a level not reached by any of his predecessors and thereby to exert a lasting influence on all subsequent Western theology.

In providing a solution to the controversy, Augustine took as his starting point the undeniable fact that traditional Catholic practice did not sanction the rebaptism and reordination of apostates and heretics. The reason for this, Augustine asserted, was that in every sacrament there are three components: first, the rite, or visible ceremony; second, the interior seal conferred by this rite; and finally, the grace of God that the seal was supposed to communicate. When one was baptized or ordained, one would receive the seal, but not necessarily the grace, which depended on the willingness of the recipient to cooperate with the grace. Hence, persons who were baptized could still sin, could continue to embrace heresy, etc., but if they repented or disavowed their heresy, they would not have to be rebaptized, because they retained the indelible seal which caused grace.

Augustine also insisted that the seal was conferred even if the minister himself was sinful or heretical, since the rite owed its efficacy and its meaning not to the minister but to Christ himself, who instituted the rite. The meaning of the rite remained the same whether the minister was a saint or a sinner.

An important era of sacramental theology came to a close with the death of Augustine. The succeeding centuries were not favorable to the development of theology—marked as they were by barbarian invasions, the downfall of the Roman Empire and the general eclipse of culture and learning.

Sacramental practice, however, continued to manifest the diversity and development characteristic of an earlier period. Confirmation was separated from baptism. The Eucharistic liturgy was enshrined in a dead language and became a sacred spectacle. Penance lost its public character and became private confession. The marriage ceremony came to be understood as a sacramental rite. Ordination to the priesthood was broken down into a series of separate steps. The anointing of the sick became extreme unction—the final anointing of the dying.

Besides these seven ritual acts, there were many others performed by the Church, such as veneration of relics, use of holy water, visiting sacred shrines, etc. And for many centuries there was no general agreement as to how many of them should be called sacraments. Augustine's understanding of a sacrament, for instance, was very broad and included the Lord's Prayer, the Easter liturgy, the sign of the cross, the baptismal font itself and penitential ashes.

## MEDIEVAL SACRAMENTAL THEOLOGY

With the revival of theology in the twelfth century, an attempt was made to specify the actual number of sacraments. Some theologians found as many as thirty, while the more conservative narrowed them down to as few as five. Peter Lombard (d. 1160), whose *Book of Sentences* served as the standard textbook for many centuries, enumerated seven sacraments, which he distinguished from the sacramentals, insofar as the former he considered causes as well as signs of grace, while the sacramentals he considered only signs of grace. Thanks in part to the enormous success of the book, Peter's enumeration stuck, and found its way into the official documents of the Church.[10]

Sacramental theology took some big steps forward after Peter Lombard. Building on Augustine's theology of the spiritual character or image conferred on the soul by the sacramental rite, the theologians were able to distinguish between the *sacramentum,* or outward ceremony, the *sacramentum et res,* or interior change or character (seal) produced by the *sacramentum,* and the *res tantum,* or the spiritual benefit or grace flowing

10. Joseph Martos, *Doors to the Sacred* (Garden City, N.Y.: Doubleday, 1981), pp. 31–71. A very good account of this whole history.

from the *sacramentum et res*. Aquinas interpreted these distinctions in terms of Aristotelian philosophy. According to Aquinas, the *sacramentum et res*, or interior character, was a supernatural power which, for instance, enabled the recipient of baptism to conform his life to Christ, the recipient of confirmation to publicly witness to the faith, the recipient of ordination to devote his life to the sacramental ministry of the Church.

Aristotle's influence on medieval theology was tremendous. In the area of sacramental theology it can be seen in the adoption of many of his terms to explain the operation of the sacraments. In his analysis of reality, for instance, Aristotle distinguished between *matter*, or sheer potency in nature, and *form*, or that which actualizes the potency and makes it what it is. This distinction was borrowed to distinguish between the external, sensible elements of the sacrament (the matter or potency) and the meaning (form) given to these elements by the words and intention of the minister. Aquinas also used Aristotle's concept of instrumental cause to explain how the sacraments produced their effects: God used them to communicate his grace to mankind.

Another concept of far-reaching importance was developed at this time: *ex opere operato*, literally meaning "by the work having been worked." As applied to the sacraments it meant that as long as the ritual was validly performed (the correct material gestures with prescribed words pronounced by a proper minister with the proper intention), the sacramental reality would be conferred on a recipient who had the intention of receiving it.

Thanks to Aquinas' insistence on the causal nature of the sacraments, much emphasis was placed on their correct performance. The canon lawyers busied themselves with discovering the minimum standards necessary if the sacraments were to be spiritually effective. Thus they held that the sacrament was conferred *ex opere operato* whether or not the minister was himself in a state of sin or whether or not the recipient was spiritually disposed to cooperate with the grace contained in the sacrament.

It's important to remember that, according to the theologians, a validly performed sacrament had two effects: the *sacramentum et res*, or sacramental reality (such as the indelible character conferred by baptism, confirmation and holy orders, the body and blood of Christ, etc.), and the *res tantum*, or sacramental grace.

Accordingly if the ritual was validly performed, the recipient, it was believed, would automatically, as it were, receive the sacramental reality (the *sacramentum et res)*, though he might not receive the sacramental grace (the *res tantum)* if sin kept him from being open to it.

The period after the death of Aquinas (d. 1274) saw a gradual decline in theology as the Thomists engaged in largely sterile controversy with the Scotists, the followers of the Franciscan genius John Duns Scotus (d. 1308). Both schools were scorned by the Nominalists, who radically opposed the basic philosophical principles of both Thomists and Scotists, espousing, as they (the Nominalists) did, the theory that one could not know things in their essences.

In the area of sacramental theology the decline was evident in an extremely abstract and dry approach to the sacraments. They were treated as "spiritual realities in the soul that were neither experienced nor known except in virtue of the sacramental rites . . . the grace they caused was an unexperienced entity, given to those whose souls were properly disposed, yet hidden and unknown except by faith."[11]

Aquinas and the great masters of the thirteenth century had drawn upon their own experience as well as upon scriptural and philosophical sources in elaborating their theology of the sacraments. But now sacramental theology lost its contact with lived experience as theologians merely repeated the ideas of the great masters. Into this vacuum of real thought, canon lawyers stepped in and established their dominance. Legalism and hairsplitting became the order of the day as the canonists debated such questions as how dirty the water could be and still be proper matter for baptism, or what parts of the canon a priest could omit and still say a valid Mass. Preoccupation with the sacraments as causes led to the neglect of their power as symbols, and the "minimalists' rules for the valid administration of the sacraments, instead of being the barest acceptable standards, tended to become the norm."[12]

All of this could foster the impression that the sacraments were really magic. *Ex opere operato* was the key phrase. No matter how uninspiring the liturgy, no matter how distracted the participants, the sacraments conferred grace automatically—at least that was how the ordinary folk perceived it. The words of baptism were pronounced, and original sin was washed away. The priest, often with no one in attendance, mumbled the sacred words in a whisper, and bread and wine became the body and blood of Christ.

11. Ibid., p. 92.
12. Ibid., p. 90.

## LUTHER AND CALVIN

The Protestant Reformation was, on its spiritual side, to some extent a protest against this mechanical approach to the mysterious working of God's grace.

Catholics claimed that the primary effect of the sacraments was an interior transformation, the sacramental reality *(sacramentum et res),* which was a metaphysical reality, not directly perceptible by experience. This led them to devalue the experiential side of the sacraments. The Reformers, for their part, emphasized the need for an experience of God's grace as an essential element in the reception of a sacrament. For Luther, the decisive element in the sacrament was always the word of promise—a promise accompanied by a sign instituted by God. The promise was the forgiveness of sins, a promise that was evident only in the case of baptism and the Lord's Supper; hence, he restricted the number of sacraments to these two.

Since a sacrament communicates the divine promise of acceptance, Luther said, it must be grasped and accepted in a personal act of faith, as in the case of any offer from one person to another. Thus he lamented the carelessness with which the sacrament of baptism was so often administered and received—in part because the participants did not understand the Latin rite—and so he began baptizing in German to excite the faith and devotion of those involved.

Luther took the medieval doctrine of *ex opere operato* to mean that grace was communicated regardless of the spiritual disposition of the recipient and even in the absence of real conversion of heart. He declared, "It is heresy to hold that the sacraments . . . give grace to those who place no obstacle in the way."[13]

For Calvin, too, the purpose of the sacraments was to express the promises in such a tangible way that we become as certain of them as though they were before our very eyes.[14] Like Luther, he found the doctrine of *ex opere operato* the reason for the quasi-magical and mechanistic use of the sacraments in the Roman Church. He therefore laid stress on the importance of the faith of the recipient and on the role of the sacraments as part

13. Quoted in Paul Althaus, *The Theology of Martin Luther* (Philadelphia: Fortress Press, 1966), p. 348.
14. William Niesel, *The Theology of Calvin* (Philadelphia: Westminster Press, 1956), p. 214.

of a personal dialogue between the believer and God. And he held that the administration of the sacrament must always be accompanied by a preaching and proclaiming of the Word. "Nothing . . . can be more preposterous than to convert the Supper into a dumb action. This is done under the tyranny of the Pope . . ."[15]

Other reformers were even more radical in their rejection of the medieval Catholic sacramental system. Ulrich Zwingli (d. 1531), the Swiss Reformer, denied any spiritual efficacy at all to the sacraments. They were merely social signs which were used by Christians to witness to their faith. They did not confer grace and were not necessary for salvation.

The Protestant churches, therefore, in fact, manifest a great variety in their doctrine on the sacraments, although most of them have retained at least baptism and the Lord's Supper, though some of them have followed the Anabaptists in rejecting infant baptism. But the need for sacraments is so deeply rooted in human nature that they have elevated other rites and actions of their liturgies to near-sacramental status.

## TRENT'S DECREES ON THE SACRAMENTS

The Council of Trent was the Catholic Church's belated response to the Protestant Reformers. It took the popes more than two decades to assemble the bishops after Luther first raised his cry, and then it took the Council of Trent eighteen years (1545–63) to complete its work. But when it was finished, even critics had to admit the job was well done. Trent ranged over the issues raised by the Protestants and defined the Catholic position in such clear and trenchant language that thenceforth everyone knew exactly where the Catholic Church stood. For the next four centuries, the authority of the Council of Trent was virtually unchallengeable within the Catholic Church.

More than half of its doctrinal decrees dealt with the sacraments, although Trent did not set out to expound a complete doctrine on the sacraments. Its main concern was to address the issues raised by the Reformers. In so doing, the bishops showed little desire to be conciliatory. For the most part, they simply reasserted the medieval Church's understanding of the sacraments. The number of the sacraments, they declared, were seven—no more and no less—although not all of the same dignity or

15. John Calvin, *Institutes of the Christian Religion* (Grand Rapids, Mich.: Eerdmans, 1957), IV, 7, 39.

necessity. No allusion at all was made to the complex history behind the gradual recognition of this number of sacraments.

Christ, they asserted, instituted all seven of them. And again there was no discussion of the complex problem of scriptural exegesis involved in this assertion.

As early as 1520, in his *Babylonian Captivity of the Church* and in his *Disputations*, Luther had discarded the scholastic theology of the sacraments. There he defined a sacrament as a sign instituted by God signifying a promise of forgiveness of sins which became efficacious only through faith. They were signs requiring faith and only operative through faith. Their power completely depended on faith. The mere performance of the rite was of no value. So much for *ex opere operato!*

Unfortunately, Trent did not fairly report Luther's teaching on the sacraments, since they neglected to use his later, more mature writings. Unfortunately also, they merely took a polemical stance in condemning what they believed were the errors of the Protestants without setting forth a positive theology of the Catholic sacramental system. Most unfortunately—over much opposition—they simply reiterated the medieval expression *ex opere operato* instead of using the more ecumenical language *ex virtute Christi* or *"ex actione Christi,"* which Aquinas actually preferred in his later writings. The result was to strengthen the Catholic tendency toward a mechanical view of the sacraments.

Trent also upheld the scholastic teaching as to the indelible character imprinted on the soul by baptism, confirmation and holy orders. And against Luther they downplayed the importance of the minister's intention—insisting only on the need for the minister to conform his intention to that of the Church. But the validity of the sacrament, Trent said, could not be affected by the possibly sinful state of the minister.

On the other hand, to rebut the charge of magic, the bishops at Trent noted that the measure of the grace received is essentially dependent on the faith of the recipient, as one opens oneself to the sacramental grace infused in one's soul.

In addition to its decrees on the sacraments in general, Trent also treated the sacraments individually, recapitulating medieval doctrine pertaining to them.

During the next four centuries, sacramental doctrine and sacramental practice among Protestants continued to manifest a wide variety as each Church was able to interpret the ambiguous statements of the Bible in accordance with its basic standpoint. Quakers, for instance, abandoned sacraments altogether. Catholics, on the other hand, were now tightly controlled by Rome, which imposed the Roman Missal and the Roman Ritual, as reformed by Trent, on all the dioceses. Little room was left for change, and so the sacramental rites of the Catholic Church remained amazingly uniform throughout the world. Sacramental theology also remained basically static—confined for the most part to refining subtleties bequeathed to theologians by the medieval Scholastics—including such topics as the nature of the character bestowed by the sacraments, the type of causality they involved, or the precise manner of their institution by Christ.

## RENEWAL OF CATHOLIC SACRAMENTOLOGY

The twentieth century opened up a new chapter in the history of sacramental theology and sacramental practice. The renewal of the Church instituted by the Second Vatican Council involved especially a renewal of the sacramental life of the Church. In its *Constitution on the Sacred Liturgy*, the Council urged the pastors of the Church to lead the people to a full and active participation in the rites of the Church and committed them to make the rites more intelligible and more inspiring so as to eliminate any suggestion of mechanicism or magic in their performance. In fact, this vision of sacramental renewal stands right at the heart of the whole Church renewal program envisaged by the Council.

Behind this effort stood a theological renewal, which can be traced to the work of a number of northern European scholars who in the 1930s and 1940s broke out of the world of Tridentine Scholasticism and took a fresh view of many questions. Unlike the typical Catholic theologian of the time, these men were thoroughly acquainted with contemporary philosophical thought and were deeply influenced by historical and biblical criticism. As a result they were aware of the extremely complex history of the sacraments and the variety of forms they had assumed over the centuries. They were especially aware of the fact that modern sacramental practices could not be found simply as such in the Church of the New Testament. Their studies enabled them to break with the mechanistic and legalistic theology of the sacraments inherited from Trent.

One of the most influential representatives of this new school is Edward Schillebeeckx, who broke new ground in sacramental theology with his book *Christ the Sacrament of the Encounter with God*, first published in

1960. The key word here is *encounter,* for Schillebeeckx sees all religion as in some way a personal encounter with God. And basic to his thesis is the idea that Jesus as a man incarnated the redeeming love of God in human form. His actions, then, were manifestations of God's love for man and in themselves therefore possess a divine saving power and thus cause grace. This is especially true of those actions that most clearly reveal God's saving power: Christ's miracles and the great mysteries of his life: his Passion, death and Resurrection. Thus Jesus may rightly be called the primordial sacrament—the visible manifestation or revelation of the divine grace of redemption. And so "personally to be approached by the man Jesus was for his contemporaries, an invitation to a personal encounter with the life-giving God, because personally that man was the Son of God. Human encounter with Jesus is therefore the sacrament of the encounter with God . . . Jesus' redeeming acts are therefore a 'sign and cause of grace.' "[16]

But how are we today to encounter the glorified Lord? For Schillebeeckx the answer is clear: just as contemporaries of Jesus could encounter God in the historical, tangible, concrete person of Jesus, so today we can encounter Jesus in the historical, tangible reality of his body, the Church, and in the historical, visible and tangible sacraments, which are the embodiment of his heavenly saving actions.

As the history of religion shows, humanity needs sacraments—symbolic actions and material things that are much more powerful than mere words to communicate a sense of the mystery of existence. Christ conveyed the love of God through his whole bodily presence—laying hands on the sick, anointing and washing the feet of his disciples, offering his body for his disciples, handing them bread and wine. Since he was God, there is an eternal dimension to his earthly acts. As Schillebeeckx says, "Since the sacrifice of the cross and all the mysteries of the life of Christ are personal acts of God, they are eternally actual and enduring. God the Son is therefore present in these human acts in a manner that transcends time."[17]

"What Christ alone did," Schillebeeckx says, "in the objective redemption, although in our name and in the place of us all, he does now in the sacraments."[18] The saving activity of Jesus, which was visible during his earthly life, is now sacramentalized, rendered visible through the official

16. *Christ the Sacrament of the Encounter with God* (New York: Sheed & Ward, 1963), pp. 15–16.
17. Ibid., 35.
18. Ibid., 67.

actions of his body, the Church. The sacraments therefore are primarily and fundamentally personal acts of Christ himself that reach and involve us through his Church. They make possible a reciprocal human encounter with Christ. For it is in the Church's sacraments that Christ wants to make the expression of his saving love visible within the sphere of our earthly life and earthly world.

Surely it is most human, as Schillebeeckx says, to show our love for someone not only by words but also by acts and gestures. The flowers I send to a friend render my love visible in a certain way. Christ's love, too, is rendered visible for us in the sacraments.

But did Christ himself institute them? Familiar with the complex history of the sacraments, Schillebeeckx did not try to argue that Christ instituted all of them directly. As the primordial sacrament of Christ, the Church could legitimately designate some of its most sacred acts as sacraments of Christ in a special way. Moreover history shows that they have changed very much in their outward form in the course of history.

Schillebeeckx also answered the charge that Catholic belief in the *ex opere operato* working of the sacraments derogated from God's sovereign freedom and led to a mechanical view of the working of the sacraments. As he pointed out, the doctrine merely means that the sacrament is a perceptible sign of God's exceeding generosity, while it also presupposes a more than merely human origin of the Church. In making present the saving mystery of Christ, it manifests the gratuitous offer of grace. Or, as Rahner says, *ex opere operato* tells us that God's offer of grace to us in the sacrament is absolutely unconditional and certain, but does not do away with the freedom of the individual, who may respond with either a yes or no.

(It is interesting to note here how *ex opere operato* is patient of an ecumenical interpretation, as Lutheran theologian Arthur Piepkorn points out, for "a properly administered sacrament is always and unfailingly a divine offer of grace. This fact is utterly independent of the faith of the recipient. But the offer becomes effective, the communication of grace takes place only when there is a right *motus,* that is faith in the proffer of grace, in the user's heart."[19])

One of the questions often asked about the Catholic sacraments is why seven—no more, no less—as Trent put it? There are indeed many other

19. Arthur C. Piepkorn, "Baptismal Doctrine in the Churches." In Paul C. Empie and T. Austin Murphy, eds., *Lutherans and Catholics in Dialogue I–III* (Minneapolis, Minn.: Augsburg Publishing House, 1966), p. 49.

signs of God's grace, but these seven are privileged inasmuch as they are the principal gestures of the Church as a community. In fact, these seven constitute the Church as community and serve to unify and identify the diverse communities that make up the universal Church. As Juan Segundo says, "They have the disadvantage of entailing a certain routineness and a basic a-temporality if they are taken in isolation from a creative community that keeps fashioning new signs, but still they serve to instruct, question, and commit the Church in its totality. They bring the solidarity of a common quest to people who are living through different and even radically opposed situations and challenges. They ensure that each individual base community in the Church will not escape into an over facile and uncritical unanimity in its response to a specific urgency."[20]

## A MORE HUMAN VIEW

Previously, theologians both Catholic and Protestant emphasized the transcendent aspect of the sacraments as efficacious signs of the mysterious working of God in the human heart. Today, many Catholic theologians and educators tend to focus on the human aspect of the sacraments as celebrations of what is most meaningful and precious in human experience. The sacraments are viewed as festive rites that celebrate the love of God as experienced and related to our own story. For we need to step back, as Tad Guzie says, and see what is happening in our lives—in a setting that dramatizes and makes it visible. "In the sacramental moment, we take a breather from our story-making in order to frame and see better the stories we are living."[21]

"Festivity should not be understood only as a time of joy and laughter. Death needs to be celebrated and that is why there are funeral rites. Mourning is a form of festivity which enables us to absorb the experience of death so that we can go on with life. Sickness is a profound experience that needs to be owned, and that is why there is a sacrament of the sick. Reconciliation after a rupture is often a long and painful process, but like sickness it is an experience that calls for a festive act."[22]

20. *The Sacraments Today* (Maryknoll, N.Y.: Orbis Books, 1974), pp. 59–60.
21. *The Book of Sacramental Basics* (Glen Rock, N.J.: Paulist Press, 1981), pp. 20–21.
22. Ibid., p. 21.

# 17

# The Sacraments of Initiation

The charge, often heard, that the sacraments were ecclesiastical magic, contained some semblance of truth when infant baptism was involved. Water was poured on the head of an infant crying and screaming and (Catholics were taught to believe) the stain of original sin was washed off its soul. Administered by a priest using Latin formulas, the whole ceremony conveyed the impression of the occult and the mysterious. Moreover, the Church's insistence that the child be baptized as soon as possible after birth added to the atmosphere of superstition and magic surrounding the sacrament. It is interesting to note that, as late as 1958, the Holy Office insisted so strongly on the immediate administration of baptism after birth (as in canon 770) that Catholic hospitals began to install baptismal fonts in their chapels so that the infants born there could be immediately baptized, rather than in the parents' parish church. As Aidan Kavanagh points out, had the Second Vatican Council not been summoned the following year, it is possible that this development would have spread, "lending a pronounced clinical character to baptism." Canon 746 had already mandated intrauterine baptism in cases of necessity.[1]

But while the general attitude before the Council was complacent, there were those who questioned the prevailing discipline. This was particularly true in the French Church. Thanks to the criticism of baptismal practices raised by some scholars, an effort was made in the Latin Quarter

1. Kavanagh, *The Shape of Baptism: The Rite of Christian Initiation* (New York: Pueblo Pub., 1978), p. 98.

of Paris in 1957 to experiment with adult baptism as the norm. There was first a brief catechumenate during Lent with instruction centered on the theme of water: in the creation, the Flood and the crossing of the Red Sea; then baptism was administered by immersion and was joined with confirmation and completed by the Eucharist.

## ORIGIN OF BAPTISM

Purification rituals were commonplace in the Jewish religion, but the immediate ancestor of Christian baptism is no doubt found in the baptismal rite practiced by John at the Jordan and which the Gospels portray as the beginning of the movement launched by Jesus. John may have derived his baptism from the practice of Jewish proselyte baptism, but the evidence for this is not very clear. More probable is the view that John took over the practice from the Qumran community (the community of the Dead Sea Scrolls) and combined it with the prophetic idea of the need for an eschatological cleansing before the End. John's baptism therefore symbolized the cleansing of the faithful remnant in expectation of the "baptism" of Spirit and fire which would occur in the Messianic age.

Christian baptism as we find it after Pentecost still has much in common with John's baptism. It is performed with water and involves repentance, but it is now done in the name of Jesus with the belief that it bestows the Spirit. Like John's, it still looks forward to the final redemption, but unlike John's, it represents the fulfillment of Israel's hope.

What is new, then, in Christian baptism is that it imparts the Spirit.

How did this change occur? It was the baptism of Jesus himself that made the new rite possible. This was the "great event which changed Johannine into Christian baptism."[2] In the accounts of Jesus' baptism in the Synoptic Gospels, we read that after his baptism the Spirit of God descended upon him, and a voice from heaven proclaimed him to be God's beloved Son. The meaning is clear: as the promised Messiah, Jesus is anointed with God's Spirit, which possesses him entirely, indicating a permanent condition of unity with the Father—a fact symbolized perfectly by the imagery of the dove that descends from heaven. In the Gospel of Mark, he is proclaimed Son in terms that suggest he would carry out the role of Second Isaiah's servant of Yahweh, who would, through his

2. Geoffrey Lampe, *The Seal of the Spirit* (New York: Longmans, Green, 1951), p. 33.

suffering, atone for the sins of many. The baptism of Jesus, then, symbolized the new relationship that would be established between God and man through his saving work. When he had fulfilled that work, his followers were baptized to show their response in faith to his work of reconciliation prefigured in his baptism. It also accomplished union with Christ, because it brought one into the Church, which is his resurrected body.

It is clear, therefore, that practice of baptism was not based on a direct command of Jesus but on the memory of John's baptism and above all of Jesus' baptism. And there is little reason to doubt the testimony of the Acts of the Apostles that the rite of baptism was practiced in the Church from its earliest days. This is clear from Acts 2:38. "You must repent," Peter answered "and every one of you must be baptized in the name of Jesus Christ for the forgiveness of your sins, and you will receive the gift of the Holy Spirit."

As the passage shows, the author of Acts associates three meanings with baptism: first, it conveys forgiveness of sins; second, it is performed in the name of Jesus Christ; and third, it bestows the gift of the Spirit.


## NEW TESTAMENT THEOLOGIES OF BAPTISM

The most important theology of baptism is Paul's. He took it from the Hellenistic missionary communities and "corrected it at decisive points to coincide with his cross-centered Christology and his eschatological reservation (the 'not yet')."[3]

Paul, for instance, stressed the connection of baptism with the crucifixion of Christ, against those who believed that through baptism we escape the necessity of the cross. Baptism, Paul says, commits us to a constant struggle with sin so that "we might be slaves to sin no longer." Baptism means a life marked by the cross: ". . . always, wherever we may be, we carry with us in our body the death of Jesus, so that the life of Jesus, too, may always be seen in our body."[4]

Some of the Corinthians believed that baptism had already given them a share in the Resurrection, so that they were now free from mundane moral duties. But, as Paul reminded them, baptism meant obedient

3. Reginald Fuller, "Christian Initiation in the New Testament," in *Made, Not Born* (Murphy Center for Liturgical Research, Notre Dame, Ind.: University of Notre Dame Press, 1976), p. 18.
4. 2 Cor. 4:10.

commitment to the lordship of Jesus. It guarantees salvation no more than the "sacraments" of the Old Law did—for many of the Israelites who were baptized in the Red Sea and ate the manna in the desert still ended up as renegades and, in putting God to the test, were destroyed.

One of the questions often debated by scholars is whether Paul was influenced in his theology of baptism by the mystery religions, such as Cybele's, which were so popular at that time and taught that one could share in the fate of the cult deity by participating in certain mysterious rites. Certain New Testament passages, it is true, do reflect this influence ("You have been buried with him, when you were baptized; and by baptism, too, you have been raised up with him. . .).''[5] But Paul himself, as distinct from the author of the Deutero-Pauline epistles, betrays little of such influence and in fact strove to distance himself from such interpretations. He took pains to correct Hellenistic theology where the influence of the mystery religions distorted the essential Christian message. Dying with Christ, for instance, was for Paul much more than simply sharing the fate of a cult deity. It was the beginning of a moral process of dying to sin and of walking in the newness of life.


## DEVELOPMENT OF THE BAPTISMAL RITUAL

We have few records to guide us here during the first several centuries of the Church. As in other respects, the early Church was pluralistic in its liturgy. One of the earliest accounts of baptism in the Roman tradition is found in Justin Martyr's *First Apology* (c. A.D. 150). The converts, he says, "are led to a place where there is water . . . [and] are then washed in the water in the name of the Father . . . of Jesus Christ and of the Holy Spirit," and it tells how they are then led back to the assembled brethren, where they share in the Eucharist.[6]

More detailed accounts are found in Tertullian's *On Baptism* (c. 200), and the *Apostolic Tradition* (c. 215), probably of Saint Hippolytus.

According to the *Apostolic Tradition*, the period of instruction called the catechumenate normally lasted three years; it emphasized moral development, rather than just intellectual training. The lessons were given in a setting of prayer and worship. In the final phase of preparation, the catechumen was examined in the presence of the whole community, it seems,

5. Col. 2:12.
6. Quoted in Aidan Kavanagh, op. cit., p. 43.

whose main concern was how well the catechumen was beginning to live his or her faith. At these Lenten scrutinies the catechumen prayed and was prayed for and also exorcised. On Holy Saturday the elect were assembled by the bishop to undergo an exorcism, during which they renounced Satan and recited the creed, which they had memorized. This was followed by the vigil service of Easter.

The actual baptism began when the baptismal party arrived at the place of baptism, where the bishop prayed over the water. Those chosen then disrobed, loosening their hair and removing all jewelry, lest any "go down into the water having any alien object with them." Then, after another exorcism, the candidate stepped down naked into the water, where a presbyter in the font laid his hand on the candidate and asked whether he or she believed—first in the Father, then in the Son, and finally in the Holy Spirit.

After each question the candidate answered, "I believe," and was immersed in the water by the assisting deacon. Coming out of the water then, the candidate, while still wet and naked, was anointed with the oil of thanksgiving and was then dried and dressed. When all were baptized, they were presented to the assembly, and the bishop laid his hand upon them and invoked the grace of the Holy Spirit upon them. He then anointed each on the forehead as he touched his or her head, saying, "I anoint thee with holy oil in God the Father Almighty and Christ Jesus and the Holy Ghost." Whereupon he greeted them and gave them the kiss of peace. "Thenceforth," says Hippolytus, "they shall pray together with all the people. But they shall not previously pray with the faithful before they have undergone these things."[7]

## CONFIRMATION BECOMES A SEPARATE SACRAMENT

The emergence of confirmation as a distinct sacrament in the Western church was a very slow process, covering a span of some eight hundred years—if we take as our starting point the structure of the Roman initiation rite as described in documents of the sixth century and as our terminal point the fully developed theology of confirmation as a separate sacrament found in the work of Thomas Aquinas (d. 1274).

As Nathan Mitchell points out, the original initiation rite, consisting of

7. Ibid., pp. 61–64.

the water bath, anointing and the reception of the Eucharist, was split eventually into three parts, so that the neophyte, after being baptized with water, might have to wait years before being anointed by the bishop in a separate ceremony—now called confirmation—and also might have to wait years before being admitted to the Eucharist.

As he also says, ". . . the most obvious problem is also the one most difficult to resolve satisfactorily: why does the West eventually elect to maintain the episcopal presidency of a portion of the initiation rite, viz., the laying on of hands and consignation with chrism, at the expense of the very unity of the rite itself?"[8]

No doubt, the growing practice of baptizing infants had much to do with this, but it is interesting to note that the Christian East took a different course, maintaining the unity of the total initiation rite so that even infants were baptized, confirmed and communicated in a single rite.

As noted above, in the baptismal rite described by Hippolytus there were two anointings, one performed by the priest (or presbyter) at the font and the other by the bishop in the midst of the assembly, but both in the course of a single ceremony. However, as the Church expanded from the cities into the countryside, diverse arrangements prevailed. In some places, as in Spain, Gaul and northern Italy, the priest, it seems, performed the second anointing in place of the bishop, who could no longer conveniently preside at every baptism. Rome, however, tried to maintain Christian initiation as a single ritual under the presidency of the bishop. And when Charlemagne (d. 814) unified much of Western Europe and joined forces with the pope, he attempted to impose the Roman usage to some extent on his vast empire. According to his reform, adults were to be baptized by the priest on Easter and receive a final anointing by the bishop a week later, on the octave of Easter.

The impact of Charlemagne's reform on subsequent theology was enormous. The theologian Rabanus Maurus (d. 856), meditating on this newly imposed separate anointing by the bishop, provided a justification for it that had great repercussions. According to Maurus, while the anointing by the priest effected the descent of the Spirit and the consecration of the Christian, the anointing by the bishop conferred the fullness of the Spirit in sanctity, knowledge and power.[9]

Mitchell insists on the complexity of the evolution of confirmation into a separate sacrament and notes that while the reform of Charlemagne was

---

8. "Dissolution of the Rite of Christian Initiation." In *Made, Not Born*, p. 52.
9. Ibid., p. 56.

very important, ". . . episcopal confirmation was not an unwelcome bastard that appeared suddenly to embarrass the Christian pedigree. There were signals and symptoms of its eventual appearance much earlier in western liturgical history."[10] Certainly social, political and even economic factors all played a role.

Some scholars have tried to argue that confirmation as a separate sacrament is found in the New Testament. They normally cite three passages from Acts to support their case: First, Acts 8:4–17, which tells how when the apostles in Jerusalem heard that the Samaritans had accepted the word of God and were baptized, they sent them Peter and John, who prayed and laid hands on them, whereupon they received the Holy Spirit. But this passage merely testifies to the organic growth of the Church from its source community, in Jerusalem, where the Spirit was first given.

Likewise, Acts 10:44 is often cited, which tells how Peter spoke to Cornelius the Roman centurion and his family, and the Holy Spirit came down on all of them and they were baptized. But the point of the passage, again, is not to indicate a separate sacrament, but to emphasize that the mission of the Church is not only to the Jews but to all people.

Finally, Acts 19:1–7 tells how after Paul baptized some disciples of John the Baptist at Ephesus, he laid hands on them, and the Holy Spirit came down on them. But the real point here is only to show that baptism in the name of Jesus confers the Holy Spirit.

As Geoffrey Lampe shows in his study *The Seal of the Spirit*, at the beginning baptism in water was the sole rite; there was no special sacrament of "Spirit-baptism" in the earliest days of the Church. Baptism in water was sufficient to confer the seal of the Spirit, which was the inward mark, or stamp, of the indwelling Spirit of God received by the convert, who, justified by faith in Christ through baptism, sacramentally participated in his death and Resurrection.[11] Anointing with chrism and the solemn imposition of hands was added later, and the invention of a new sacrament, confirmation, emerged from the "confusion which beset patristic thought on Baptism, sealing, and the gift of the Spirit from the late second century onwards."[12]

At the Reformation, all the Protestant churches rejected confirmation as a sacrament on the grounds that it was unscriptural, but some of them

10. Ibid.
11. Ibid., p. 307.
12. Ibid., p. 301.

retained parts of it as a ceremony for adults who were baptized in infancy and who were ready to reaffirm their faith and accept with full consciousness the obligations of baptism.

Given this historical background indicating how slowly confirmation emerged as a separate sacrament, it is interesting to watch Thomas Aquinas deal with the problems he faced in trying to work out a theology of confirmation—trying to prove that Christ instituted the sacrament, but able to find no solid evidence that Jesus or the apostles had used chrism in conferring the Spirit. To get around this formidable obstacle, he made use of the distinction between *res* and *sacramentum,* between the interior grace conferred and the external sign. Christ, he said, simply conferred the *res* on the apostles, without the external sign.

Perhaps the weakest link in his argument was his attempt to find historical precedent for an episcopal rite of confirmation. In doing so, he used a collection of spurious material called the Isidorian, or False, Decretals—ninth-century forgeries he thought were actual records of the early Church. Thus he derived some of his most important ideas, such as confirmation effecting a "fullness" of grace and a grace for "strengthening" from the bogus "Letter to the Spanish Bishops," supposedly written by Miltiades, an early-fourth-century pope. To differentiate the spiritual effects of baptism and confirmation, Aquinas appealed to an analogy of the human passage from childhood to adulthood, baptism corresponding to spiritual childhood, confirmation to spiritual maturity.

## INFANT BAPTISM

The legitimacy of infant baptism was an issue first raised during the Reformation by the Anabaptists, who received their name (rebaptizers) from their practice of baptizing only adult believers. But, outside of the Anabaptist tradition, there was little concern with the problem of infant baptism among either Catholics or Protestants until our times.

Recently, however, the question of infant baptism has aroused much controversy. In the 1940s, Karl Barth rejected the general practice of infant baptism and claimed that the practice was unknown in the early Church. Another eminent New Testament scholar, Oscar Cullmann, called Barth's manifesto "the most serious challenge to infant Baptism which has ever been offered," but then proceeded to argue against him on historical grounds.[13] Other scholars joined in the debate without either side producing conclusive arguments for its case.

The Catholic Church, hearkening to its long tradition favoring infant baptism, has continued to mandate the practice.

What does history really say? As we indicated above, the data of the New Testament can be interpreted either negatively or positively on the question. It is only when we reach the second century that we find specific evidence of infant baptism. But it was still by no means a universal practice. In fact, a variety of approaches can be found in the historical records of the third and fourth centuries: there were those, like the convert Emperor Constantine (d. 337), who delayed their baptism until the approach of death in the belief that it would wash them clean of all their sins and also enable them to escape the rigorous penances imposed by the sacrament of penance at the time. There were also those who delayed their children's baptism until after their adolescent passions subsided, when they were believed less likely to succumb to temptation. On the other hand, with infant mortality rates extremely high, there were a growing number of parents who wanted their children baptized immediately after birth, lest they die uncleansed.

Augustine lent the weight of his great authority to this practice. In debate with a British monk, Pelagius, who challenged the widespread practice of infant baptism, Augustine worked out a theory to explain why the Church insisted on infant baptism. The sin of Adam, he argued, was transmitted to all his descendants through the act of procreation, and the stain of this sin could be removed only by baptism. And he did not shrink from drawing his logical conclusion: those who died without baptism would all be damned.

In any case, within a hundred years after Augustine, infant baptism became the norm, possibly due in part to the barbarian invasions, which gave an impetus to anything that might promote the solidarity of social groups. The effects on the ritual of baptism were enormous. The catechumenate disappeared, and a ceremony spanning several weeks was telescoped into an hour or less. And when the monks set out to convert the barbarians of northern Europe, it was this stripped-down version of baptism—the only one they knew—which they spread through the land. Moreover, they administered it in Latin—a language few of their converts spoke.

13. *Baptism in the New Testament* (Philadelphia: Westminster Press, 1950), p. 8.

For a long time, the custom was observed of having the infant baptized on Holy Saturday, but in view of the high risk of the infant's dying in the interim, some bishops began to encourage the parents not to wait for the annual baptism, at Easter. But it was not until the Council of Florence (1438–45) that the custom was given the force of law and parents were obliged to have the infant baptized shortly after birth. The ceremony was now witnessed by only sponsors and relatives, while immersion was replaced by pouring the water on the head of the child. The practice of giving the child Communion immediately after baptism was retained, however, and this only disappeared gradually—in line with the trend that saw lay persons in general seldom receive Communion.

As we have pointed out, infant baptism has remained the norm in the Catholic Church and in most Protestant churches until our own time. Questioning of the practice has become common only in the past several decades, and until the Second Vatican Council was largely confined to the Protestants. With the renewal inspired by the Council, however, Catholics, too, have lately begun to debate the issue.

Those Catholics who question the practice of infant baptism point out how often the parents are influenced by spurious motives: it's a hallowed custom and a matter of family tradition; it provides the occasion for a family party or village fiesta; it is superstitiously regarded as a means of warding off physical or spiritual evils; it is a way of procuring a useful document which eliminates later legal or ecclesiastical problems; it is done to please the grandparents, etc. Whereas in the early Church, instruction in the faith had to precede baptism, today it is supposed normally to follow it, but given the weak faith or lack of faith of so many parents, this assumption has little validity. The instruction given is hardly more than a veneer.

Theologically, the grounds for insisting on infant baptism no longer seem valid. Scriptural study no longer supports the necessity of infant baptism, while historical studies show that in the early Church, adult baptism was the norm and was performed with no sense of urgency. Often the catechumen had to wait years before being baptized.

Moreover, the practice of making infant baptism the norm has helped to create the situation of a Church composed formally of a large, inert mass of nominal Christians who have little understanding of what it means to be a member of a Christian community. It definitely diminishes the credibility of the Church's claim to be, in the words of Vatican II, "a sacrament or sign of intimate union with God and of the unity of all mankind."[14]

As a result of such probing, pastors are becoming more and more reluctant to automatically administer baptism to the children of parents whose motives appear questionable.

The question of how to make infant baptism more meaningful preoccupies many observers. One obvious solution is to provide catechetical programs not only for children but for the parents as well. Many dioceses are presently making a great effort to institute such programs.

Another remedy proposed is the formation of genuine communities of Christians, so that the significance of baptism as incorporation into a community of believers would be enhanced. As it stands now, the present parish is often too large to convey to its members any sense of real community. There is definitely a need for smaller communities to help the member feel part of the Church.

An even more radical solution has been proposed, which would involve delaying the baptism of children until after they had first passed through a catechumenate and were prepared to make a responsible decision to choose membership in the Church.

But, as Ralph Keifer says, the real problem "is not infant baptism but that baptism makes no discernible difference in the lives of so many people." However, he questions whether the present attempt to formulate "standards" for admission are the answer either. In the New Testament, the main requirement seems to be hospitality! Christians are constantly exhorted to care for one another. This is the true concern—not how much catechism they know. From this perspective, in admitting neophytes to our community what we should be concerned about is how committed they are to building up the community. As he says, ". . . the baptismal creed . . . is not so much a statement of belief as the voicing of a stance. To say that one believes in God the Father, maker of heaven and earth, is to say that one believes in one's own goodness and that of others and that one has hope for the destiny of the human race. To say one believes in the Holy Spirit is to commit oneself to living in active dialogue with a community which claims discipleship with Jesus and community in the Holy Spirit. Anyone who agrees to live by virtue of hospitality and to worship in the household of the faith has agreed to these affirmations."[15]

14. *Dogmatic Constitution on the Church*, 1.
15. *Blessed and Broken* (Wilmington, Del.: Michael Glazier, 1982), p. 91.

A large amount of agreement about the nature and effects of baptism has been reached in the dialogues instituted between Catholics and Protestants at the behest of the Second Vatican Council. The Lutheran-Catholic Dialogue on Baptism, held in 1965, came to the conclusion that the two faiths were in substantial agreement in their doctrine of baptism. Even more impressive, as we already have noted, is the agreement on baptism reached at the meeting in Lima in 1982 of the Faith and Order Commission of the World Council of Churches, which gathered some 120 theologians and church leaders from a wide variety of churches, Orthodox, Roman Catholic and Protestant. Their statement on baptism noted that "the difference between infant baptism and believer's baptism becomes less sharp when it is recognized that both forms of baptism embody God's own initiative in Christ and express a response of faith made within the believing community."[16] But the relation between baptism and confirmation (or Chrismation) was left as an unresolved difference between the churches.

## VATICAN II's REVISIONS

The revision of the Mass, imposed by the Second Vatican Council and inaugurated shortly after the Council, startled the average Catholic and shook many out of their lethargy. But it is no exaggeration to say that the most radical reform of ritual in the Church was yet to come. This was the revision of the initiation rites of baptism and confirmation, which was carried out between 1969 and 1973. In that short time, a thousand years of liturgical history was erased, and a huge leap was taken back into the early Church.

An advance warning of the coming revolution was given when the new order for the baptism of little children was issued, in 1969. It aimed to restore the close link between the community and baptism, as it emphasized the solidarity of all the members in Christ and the close connection between baptism and the paschal mystery of Christ's death and Resurrection. But it is the new order for the Christian initiation of adults, of January 6, 1972, which represents the most dramatic chapter in the liturgical revolution wrought by the Council.

If the intent of this ritual is realized, baptism will no longer normally be

16. Quoted in *America,* February 20, 1982, p. 127.

a marginal event in the life of the average parish. It will be one of the main events of the year, involving pastor, people and neophytes in intense encounters spread over a year or more—demonstrating and symbolizing the radical nature of the decision to commit oneself to Jesus Christ.

The main feature of the initiation rite for adults is the restoration of the ancient catechumenate, according to which a prospective convert is prepared for baptism in a series of stages designed to test his or her commitment to the Lord. The initial stage, the precatechumenate, is aimed at those who evince some interest in the faith and is supposed to be a time when those sympathetic to the faith are given a friendly welcome and encouraged to get acquainted with members of the community and the basic tenets of the Church.

When and if the sympathetic inquirer decides to seek baptism, he/she then applies for admission to the catechumenate. Upon acceptance, the candidate is given a sponsor, who assumes a supportive role in guiding the individual through the whole process. The ritual of admission includes a formula of adherence to the Church, the tracing of the cross on the forehead and the sense organs, and the imposition of hands.

During this stage, the catechumen receives instruction from competent members of the community and to some extent shares in the prayer and worship, though not in the Eucharist. The aim is not merely the communication of knowledge, but to help the individual grow in the faith by living it and celebrating it in a liturgical mode. After a certain period of time, which can vary greatly from place to place, the candidate is examined, and if found ready is advanced to the final stage.

This occurs ideally during Lent. It opens with the actual rite of election on the First Sunday of Lent, when the candidates are presented to the community, are formally examined together with their sponsors, and a formal declaration of their election is made. On the Third, Fourth and Fifth Sundays of Lent, the "scrutinies" are held at Mass, when special prayers are said and special blessings are pronounced over the candidates asking God to strengthen them and heal them. Later, at a special session, a copy of the creed and the Lord's Prayer is given to each to learn.

Finally, on Holy Saturday (preferably) the sacrament of baptism is administered to the candidates in a ceremony that may be performed in two separate sessions. The first includes a reading of the Gospel, a brief homily, the recitation by the elect of the profession of faith, the rite of opening the ears and mouth (Ephphetha), and the choice of a Christian name as well as an anointing with the oil of catechumens—if this is retained by the episcopal conference of that region.

The actual baptism ordinarily takes place during the Easter Vigil, after the blessing of water, when in the presence of the community the candidate renounces Satan and professes his faith and then is baptized by either immersion or the pouring of water. He is then confirmed and receives the Eucharist with the rest of the congregation.

The newly baptized members of the community are supposed to receive special attention and help from the community during the weeks immediately following their baptism. During this period of the "mystagogy," the neophytes are encouraged to sit in a special place in the Church and take part in the Mass with their godparents as they begin their life of witness and service in the community.

As we have indicated, confirmation is still separated from baptism in the case of children, but this is questioned by some. As our historical study shows, confirmation was always a part of the initiation rite in the early Church and was separated from baptism only for various political and sociological reasons. And in fact, the Orthodox Church has always kept the two united.

The question therefore may rightly be asked: "If age is a serious obstacle to receiving confirmation why then is age not a serious obstacle to receiving baptism?"[17]

As Ralph Keifer says, postponing confirmation to a later age and interpreting it as a sacrament of commitment or maturity undermines the understanding of it as an action of God as well as of man. "Man's commitment is not the measure of God's grace." Perhaps a better alternative would be to enroll children as catechumens and defer full initiation to a later age. At any rate, as Keifer says, "The present practice is a theological and pastoral anomaly. It separates the gift of the Spirit from entry into the body of the risen Lord, violates a sacramental continuum and leads to the notion that there are degrees of membership in the Church among the baptized."[18]

17. Aidan Kavanagh, "Christian Initiation of Adults: the Rites." In *Made, Not Born*, p. 128.
18. Ibid., p. 141.

# 18

## Eucharist

There have been various attempts in the history of theology to deny that Jesus himself really instituted the Eucharist. The radical Protestants, for instance, derived it from the primitive Church's understanding of itself. According to this theory, the Lord's Supper originated when the disciples, after the Resurrection, felt the need to gather and celebrate a meal together in memory of the many meals they had enjoyed with Jesus during his lifetime. Their experience of fellowship at this memorial meal helped them see themselves as the body of Christ sharing in a new covenant sealed by his blood. They expressed this self-awareness through the words they pronounced over the bread and the wine. The later, materialistic interpretation of Jesus' presence in the bread and the wine came about only through the influence of Hellenistic thought patterns.

It is true that we cannot simply take the Gospel accounts of the Last Supper as unadulterated history—for the reasons enunciated in Chapter 5, in discussing the three-layer structure of the Gospels. And in fact, the two separate traditions we have of the Last Supper (the Pauline-Lucan tradition—Lk. 22:20a parallel 1 Cor. 11:25; and the Marcan tradition—Mk. 14:24 parallel Mt. 26:27–28) are by agreement of most scholars liturgical formulae current in the early Church.

However, they were not pure inventions but were based on what actually happened. For it is surely beyond dispute that Jesus celebrated a farewell meal with his disciples and surely beyond dispute that he would have been conscious of his certainly approaching death, and surely he would have said something to interpret his death in such a way that his disciples would not fall into despair.

And in fact our surmise is confirmed by a passage in the accounts of the Last Supper that most scholars see as definitely derived from the earliest core of tradition, namely, the words "I tell you, I shall not drink wine until the kingdom of God comes" (Lk. 22:15–18; see 1 Cor. 11:26) or, as given in Mark, "I tell you solemnly, I shall not drink any more wine until the day I drink the new wine in the kingdom of God" (14:25).

As Edward Schillebeeckx says, the hard core of historical fact contained in these passages is the explicitly uttered conviction of Jesus that this is to be the last cup he will drink with his disciples while on earth. So although even the words about drinking it new in the Kingdom may be secondary, what is certainly historical is that Jesus, even when facing death, continues to offer his disciples (as he has so many times) the (last) cup: "This shows Jesus' unshaken assurance of salvation, so that the addition of the 'until' clause in Mark and Luke, albeit secondary, is simply a way of making explicit the concrete situation."[1] Death therefore, Jesus says, is powerless to obstruct the coming rule of God which he has proclaimed. Moreover, in spite of his approaching death, by passing the cup to the disciples Jesus continues—as he did through the meals they celebrated—to offer them a saving fellowship with himself. "The link suggested here . . . is more one between fellowship with Jesus in the present and the saving, eschatological fellowship with him, which is to come. In other words, the coming of God's rule remains linked to fellowship with Jesus of Nazareth."[2]

As Robert Jenson says, "Recollection of the Last Supper probably played a role in the origin of the Supper mostly as interpretation of the renewed celebration of fellowship."[3] So, to reconstruct the process of the early Church's interpretation: There was first only the meal of joy, celebrated in remembrance and fulfillment of the eschatological promises made by Jesus at his Last Supper and before. "Then interpretation of these meals by the cross-theology created the Supper as we know it; and the liturgical formulation of this interpretation created the two 'This is . . .' sayings. Since all the canonical phrases interpreting the bread and cup cannot simultaneously be attributed to Jesus at the Last Supper, some of them must have arisen in some such process; perhaps, then, all of them."[4]

1. *Jesus: An Experiment in Christology* (New York: Seabury Press, 1979), p. 309.
2. Ibid., p. 310.
3. *Visible Words* (Philadelphia: Fortress Press, 1978), p. 64.
4. Ibid., p. 65.

Another important factor in creating the Eucharist was no doubt the fact that some of the experiences of the Risen Jesus occurred at the common meals of the newly revived fellowship of Jesus' followers. As we read in Acts 2:46, these meals were also celebrated in a spirit of eschatological joy in anticipation of the fulfillment of Christ's promise that he would come again. The Aramaic phrase *maranatha* (Come Lord Jesus) captures this spirit of anticipation and joy.

Both Paul and Luke, in their passages describing the Last Supper, have the words "Do this." By these words the Church is given definite instructions to repeat what Jesus did at the Last Supper. But what did he do? Essentially he gave thanks over the bread and the cup and shared them with his disciples.

There has been much discussion as to whether the Last Supper was a Jewish Passover meal. Whether it was or not is not too important. What he undoubtedly did do was observe the ritual common to every Jewish meal, namely the breaking of the bread at the beginning and the rite of thanksgiving over the cup of wine at the end.

Taking the first cup, therefore, he no doubt uttered the traditional blessing which pointed toward the Messianic banquet, when God's people would enjoy the fulfillment of God's promises, made through the lips of the prophets. This is alluded to in the words "I tell you, I shall not drink wine until the kingdom of God comes."

At the breaking of the bread, Jesus would have repeated the traditional blessing *(berakah,* in Hebrew) of the bread:

> "Blessed be thou, JHWH, King of the universe, who bringest forth bread from the earth."[5]

At the end of the meal, when he took the cup, he would have pronounced the three customary blessings:

> Blessed are you, Lord our God, King of the universe, you who feed the whole world with goodness, with grace and with mercy.

> We thank you, Lord our God, for giving us as our inheritance a desirable, good and ample land.

5. Louis Bouyer, *The Eucharist* (Notre Dame, Ind.: University of Notre Dame Press, 1968), p. 102.

Have mercy, Lord our God, on Israel, your people, and on Jerusalem, your city, and on Zion, dwelling place of your glory, and on your altar and on your temple. Blessed are you, O Lord, who build up Jerusalem.[6]

In these prayers, as we can see, God is praised for His goodness as Creator, as experienced in the meal, and also praised for His saving acts in the history of Israel. So the praise of God is also a remembering of His acts. While the remembering of His past acts must look forward to His future and final acts. So every Thanksgiving or Eucharist must have three essential parts: "doxology, recitation of saving history, and eschatological invocation."[7]

The sharing of the bread and the cup gives each participant a share in the fellowship with all present and with the God to Whom the thanksgiving is made.

Thus, what must be kept clear is that when we respond to the command to "do this," "it is the rite with bread and cup, just described, that is mandated"; that is, "to share bread and drink together from one cup in fellowship in the praise of God."[8]

Also, as stated in Paul and Luke, "Do this for my remembrance" or "as a memorial of me." As we noted, thanksgiving in the biblical sense is always a remembering of God's acts, and in this case we give thanks by remembering what God has done for us in Jesus.

Our Eucharist, as we can see, is derived from the ordinary Jewish table ritual of grace before and after meals. And in fact the Christian Eucharist continued to develop within the forms of the Jewish *berakah*. The first formulas of the Christian Eucharist are but these Jewish formulas with certain words added. This is clearly illustrated by the earliest example we have in the *Didache* (c. A.D. 120), in which a Hebrew prayer with only a few new words is given as the Eucharistic prayer of the congregation.

It is also evident that, from the very beginning, the Church understood these words to mean that Jesus Christ was truly present in the assembly when the Eucharist was celebrated. In his First Epistle to the Corinthians, Paul teaches that by eating the bread and drinking the cup, Christians are united in an intimate fellowship, because the Eucharist is Jesus' body and blood: "and so anyone who eats the bread or drinks without recognizing the Body is eating and drinking unworthily towards the body and blood of

6. Ibid., pp. 102–3.
7. Ibid.
8. Robert W. Jenson, *Visible Words* (Philadelphia: Fortress Press, 1978), p. 69.

the Lord . . . because a person who eats and drinks without recognizing the Body is eating and drinking his own condemnation"[9]—two verses that at least imply the doctrine of the real presence.

A closely related passage witnessing to the Church's belief in Christ's real presence is 1 Corinthians 10:16, where Paul says, "The blessing-cup that we bless is a communion with the blood of Christ, and the bread that we break is a communion with the body of Christ." Some have tried to argue that Paul here does not mean communion with the physical body of Christ, but a spiritual union with the Christian community, which Paul elsewhere calls the body of Christ. But this interpretation overlooks the next verse, where Paul states, ". . . we form a single body because we all have a share in this one loaf."[10] In other words, we are the body of Christ precisely because we share in the bread of the Eucharist (the one loaf). Here the bread must mean more than a mere symbol of Christ, for how could a mere "symbol" establish a unity which is completely real?

Another powerful indication of the primitive Church's belief in the real presence of Christ in the Eucharist is the passage of John's Gospel:

> "I tell you most solemnly,
> if you do not eat the flesh of the Son of Man
> and drink his blood,
> you will not have life in you.
> Anyone who does eat my flesh and drink my blood
> has eternal life,
> and I shall raise him up on the last day.
> For my flesh is real food
> and my blood is real drink.
> He who eats my flesh and drinks my blood
> lives in me
> and I live in him."[11]

John also points out that it is the ascension which makes the sending of the Spirit possible and hence also our sacramental meal. "For the element which really mediates life there is not the flesh as such but the accompanying Spirit, by which the Godhead in Jesus is meant."[12]

9. 1 Cor. 11:27, 29.
10. 1 Cor. 10:17.
11. Jn. 6:53–56.
12. Johannes Betz, "Eucharist." In *Sacramentum Mundi* (New York: Herder & Herder, 1968), Vol. 2, p. 261.

### THE EARLIEST MASS

Two thousand years separate our Mass from the Last Supper, and while the essence of the Mass has remained unchanged—namely, the sacramental words uttered over bread and wine followed by the eating and drinking of the consecrated gifts—its external form has undergone many changes.

It is clear that the Christian Eucharist was based on the Last Supper, at which Jesus blessed the bread and distributed it, then partook of the meal and finally uttered a solemn blessing over the last cup of wine. No doubt this order was followed at first by his disciples at the Eucharists they celebrated after his Resurrection. But a transposition soon occurred when the blessing of the bread was joined with the blessing over the wine at the end of the meal, as is already indicated in Mark's Gospel, written circa A.D. 65.

However, for some time, a regular meal was taken before the double blessing, as we can see from Paul's complaints about the way the Eucharist was celebrated at Corinth: ". . . when you hold these meetings, it is not the Lord's Supper that you are eating, since when the time comes to eat, everyone is in such a hurry to start his own supper that one person goes hungry while another is getting drunk."[13]

The persistence of such disorders, as well as the difficulty of accommodating the increasing number of converts, led to a separation of the Eucharist from the communal meal. And instead of it being held on Saturday evening, it was now transferred to Sunday morning. Since such a rite would ordinarily be very brief, consisting of the two blessings and the consumption of the bread and wine, it was found appropriate to join it with a service of the Word, which was modeled on the Sabbath liturgy of the synagogue.

The early Christians were very familiar, of course, with the synagogue liturgy. Paul, for instance, when visiting a city often began his evangelizing by preaching at the regular service of the local synagogue.

The synagogue service began with a greeting and reflection, followed by a reading from the Torah (the Law), a hymn and reflection. A second reading was taken from the Prophets. A sermon came next to relate the

13. 1 Cor. 11:20–21.

readings to present concerns, and the service concluded with a prayer, blessing and dismissal.

This basic structure is clearly evident in the earliest description we have of the Mass, which dates from A.D. 150 and comes from Justin Martyr (d. c. 165), a convert professor of philosophy:

> And on the day named after the sun, all who live in city or countryside assemble, and the memoirs of the apostles or writings of the prophets are read for as long as time allows. When the lector has finished, the president addresses us, admonishing us and exhorting us to imitate the splendid things we have heard. Then we stand and pray, and, as we said earlier, when we have finished praying, bread, wine, and water are brought up. The president offers prayer of thanksgiving, according to his ability, and the people give their assent with an "Amen!" Next, the gifts over which the thanksgiving has been spoken are distributed, and each one shares in them, while they are also sent via the deacons to the absent brethren.
>
> The wealthy who are willing make contributions, each as he pleases, and the collection is deposited with the president, who aids orphans and widows, those who are in want because of sickness or other cause, those in prison, and visiting strangers; in short, he takes care of all in need.
>
> The reason why we assemble on Sunday is that it is the first day: the day on which God . . . created the world, and the day on which Jesus Christ our Savior rose from the dead . . .[14]

This format—readings, sermon, prayer, offering of gifts, thanksgiving, Communion—was no doubt common to most congregations in the Western Church by the second century and has remained the basic structure of our Mass.

Jewish influence is also very strong on the oldest liturgical text of the Mass that we have, which is taken from the *Apostolic Tradition*, of Hippolytus (d. c. 236), a Roman theologian. In its basic structure it is similar to the Jewish *berakah*, which is not surprising, since it was no doubt used by Jesus himself at the Last Supper. This canon has exerted profound influence on all subsequent eucharistic prayers and has been rewritten as the Second Eucharistic Prayer, of the recently revised Roman liturgy:

> *Bishop:* The Lord be with you.
> *Congregation:* And with thy spirit.
> *Bishop:* Hearts up.
> *Congregation:* We have [lifted] them to the Lord.

14. A. Hanggi and I. Pahl, eds. *Apologia* 1, 67, in *Prex Eucharistica: Textus e variis Liturgiis antiquioribus selecti*—Spicilegium Friburgense 12, Fribourg, 1968.

*Bishop:* Let us give thanks to the Lord.

*Congregation:* It is meet and right.

*Bishop:* We thank Thee, God, through Thy beloved Servant Jesus Christ, whom in the last times Thou hast sent us as Savior and Redeemer and Messenger of Thy counsel, the Logos who comes from Thee, through whom Thou hast made all things, whom Thou wast pleased to send from heaven into the womb of the virgin and in her body he became flesh and was shown forth as Thy Son, born of the Holy Spirit and the virgin to fulfill Thy will and prepare Thee a holy people, he stretched out his hands, when he suffered, that he might release from suffering those who have believed on Thee.

And when he delivered himself to a voluntary passion, to loose death and to break asunder the bands of the devil and to trample hell and to enlighten the righteous and to set up the boundary stone and to manifest the resurrection, he took a loaf, gave thanks, and spake, "Take, eat, this is my body which is given for you." Likewise also the cup and said, "This is my blood which is poured out for you. As often as you do this, you make my commemoration."

Remembering therefore his death and resurrection, we offer to Thee the loaf and the cup and give thanks to Thee that Thou hast counted us worthy to stand before Thee and to do Thee priestly service.

And we beseech Thee, that Thou send down Thy holy Spirit upon this offering of the church. Unite it and grant to all the saints who partake of it to their fulfilling with holy Spirit, to their strengthening of faith in truth, that we may praise and glorify Thee through Thy Servant Jesus Christ, through whom to Thee be glory and honor in Thy holy Church now and ever. Amen.[15]

Many other features of our liturgy were borrowed from the Jewish liturgy, including such formulas as "The Lord be with you"; "Peace be with you, and with your spirit"; "Let us pray"; "Amen"; "Alleluia," as well as even some of the furniture of the synagogue such as the presidential chair.

## THE EVOLVING FORMAT OF THE EUCHARIST

At first the celebrant had considerable liberty in improvising prayers, including even the solemn eucharistic canon. There was, however, a strong tendency to uniformity, and in spite of the widely scattered locations of the Christian communities, their liturgies remained remarkably similar. Justin's picture of a second-century Mass, just cited, no doubt

15. Hippolytus, *Church Order* 31, 11:21., in F. X. Funk, ed. *Cambridge Ancient History* XII, 11 (New York: Cambridge University Press, 1956), pp. 524–25.

reflected the liturgy of many churches around the Mediterranean, for he was widely traveled. Various factors accounted for this high degree of unity: The desire to remain faithful to the common faith as delivered in tradition was certainly the strongest. There was also the centralizing role played by the major cities in relation to the hinterland. Another factor was the collegial system of authority, whereby bishops made it a point to keep in close contact with each other.

Within this general framework of agreement, however, in each region of the empire there developed liturgies with their own peculiar rites. In this way, a number of liturgical families arose centered around the major cities of the empire. Without attempting an exhaustive enumeration, we will mention here the most important. In the East: 1) the Alexandrian liturgy of St. Mark along with the Coptic liturgies of St. Cyril, St. Basil and St. Gregory; 2) in Antioch and its region, the liturgy of St. James, the liturgy of West Syria and the liturgy of East Syria; 3) the Byzantine liturgy, centered in Constantinople, sometimes referred to as the liturgy of St. John Chrysostom. In the West: 1) the Romano-African liturgy, stemming from Rome and North Africa; 2) a variety of non-Roman Latin liturgies of the Gallic type: the Spanish (Mozarabic), Gallican, Milanese and Celtic.

The conversion of Constantine had a great impact on the development of the liturgy. Huge churches had to be built to contain the numbers of people now assembled for the services. A corresponding elaboration of the liturgy took place as elements of the imperial court ceremonial were introduced. Much of the pomp and splendor of the medieval Mass was derived from this period. Special vestments, lights, incense, genuflections and episcopal insignia came into use. Thanks to Constantine, the bishop was accorded a status equal to the highest civil dignitaries. He was allowed to wear a distinctive headgear, move about in a special type of sandals and sit on a throne. The bishop of Rome, as the near equal of the Emperor, could even exercise the right to have people genuflect to him and kiss his foot.

There was a growing tendency during the fourth century to insist on the awesome nature of the Mass and its transcendent wonder. Cyril of Jerusalem, for instance, in his catechetical lectures (c. 350), refers several times to the "fearful presence" upon the holy table and instructs communicants on how to receive the host reverently in their hands—with left hand supporting right. The denial of Christ's divinity by the Arians, no doubt, led the orthodox to thus emphasize Christ's divine majesty and to exaggerate his distance from mankind.

The feeling of the mystical and the unworldly was especially strengthened in the East, where by the end of the fourth century it became customary to screen off the holy table by curtains. But the first iconostasis, a screen with three doors, decorated with figures of angels and prophets, was erected in Justinian's Santa Sophia (consecrated in 538), in Constantinople, and subsequently adopted in all Greek churches.

The liturgy of Rome was characterized by greater sobriety and restraint. It was originally celebrated in Greek, a sign that many of the early Christians in Rome were from the Greek-speaking provinces or, like many Romans, spoke Greek as a second tongue.

The earliest copy of a Latin eucharistic prayer we have is found in the works of St. Ambrose of Milan (d. 397); it later formed the core of the medieval Latin Mass. In contrast to the Eastern theology, which stressed the invocation of the Holy Spirit as the decisive moment of consecration, when the bread and wine are transformed, Ambrose focuses on the Lord's words of institution as effecting the change.

The formation of the liturgical calendar began with the special significance accorded to Sunday as the day of Christ's Resurrection and hence as the day Christians ordinarily gathered for their weekly liturgy. But it did not become a public day of rest until the fourth century, when Constantine forbade all official litigation on that day.

Easter was celebrated very early—by the beginning of the second century. But its date was calculated differently in the East and in the West. At Rome it was observed on the Sunday after the Jewish Passover, but in Asia, it immediately followed the fourteenth of the Jewish month of Nisan, the beginning of the Passover. Pope Victor (d. 198) tried to make the Asians conform to Western usage but failed. However, the Roman custom finally prevailed everywhere.

Pentecost and Epiphany were the next feasts added to the calendar; the latter, on January 6, coincided with pagan festivals celebrating the birth of the new year. Christmas originated only in the fourth century, when Constantine joined it with a pagan feast celebrating the birthday of the sun, on December 25.

The period of forty days of penance preceding Easter, known as Lent, began as a time of preparation for candidates seeking baptism. The entire Christian community participated in the exercises, which included daily celebration of the Eucharist. Out of this developed the practice of more frequent celebration of the Eucharist throughout the year instead of only on Sundays.

Very little was added to the Roman calendar for several centuries. Then, in the sixth century, it was thought appropriate to have a season of preparation before Christmas also, and so the season of Advent was added to the calendar. Thus the idea of making the liturgical year reflect the life of Our Lord came about very gradually. It was only in the early Middle Ages, however, that feasts honoring Our Lady and the martyrs and saints began to proliferate.

The prayers for use at the Eucharist were eventually collected in books called "sacramentaries," the most important being those of Leo the Great (d. 461), Gelasius (d. 496) and Gregory the Great, popes who, though much concerned with the liturgy, had little to do with their actual compilation.

## THE MEDIEVAL MASS

Roman liturgical creativity virtually ceased by the seventh century. The next outburst occurred in the realm of the Franks under Pepin (d. 768) and his son, Charlemagne (d. 814). The Franks, converted at the time of Clovis (d. 511), had a liturgy of their own, but Pepin and Charlemagne sealed an alliance with the pope and wanted to bring their Church into a closer relationship with Rome. Much enamored of Rome and things Roman, they decided to impose the Roman liturgy on their people. Liturgical books were brought across the Alps and distributed to the clergy to copy and put in use.

The Franco-German clergy in turn went to work on this liturgy in a creative spirit and freely adapted it to their own needs and culture. They added many prayers which were much more emotional and imaginative in content than the cold, abstract Roman collects, and they also enriched it with some spectacular and impressive ceremonies, such as the Palm Sunday procession and many of the most beautiful Easter Vigil rites.

By a strange turn of events, this Roman liturgy as revised and enhanced by the Franks was eventually brought back to Rome to replace the ancient Roman liturgy. This occurred when Rome, in the tenth century, fell prey to the terrible disorder and chaos as civilization in Europe once more began to crumble. The papacy itself became the slave of local Roman factions, and the most unworthy popes imaginable sat enthroned on the chair of Peter. As they performed their liturgical duties carelessly or not at all, the clergy and people lost interest in the liturgy and even allowed their liturgical books to disintegrate.

This decay was arrested when the revival of culture began under the aegis of the German Ottonian emperors. Otto I had himself crowned in Rome in 962, and he and his successors took an active interest in reforming the Roman Church. One of their main concerns was the dilapidated state of the liturgy, and they charged their own, German clergy with the work of its reform. Otto's clergy made use of the liturgy they brought with them, that is, the hybrid Franco-Roman liturgy. It was this liturgy which the reformed popes, beginning with Gregory VII (d. 1085), gradually imposed on the whole Latin Church.

The period between Gregory VII and the Council of Trent, in the sixteenth century, has been called a time of "dissolution, elaboration, reinterpretation and misinterpretation."[16] For a variety of reasons, almost all sense of community participation in the Mass was lost. The language barrier was a formidable obstacle, since few people could understand Latin. In addition, acts once performed by the people, such as the offertory procession, were dropped, and most people communicated only rarely if at all. The Mass became exclusively the priest's business, with the people reduced to the role of spectators. They stood at a distance, separated from him by a heavy railing, which emphasized the sacredness of the sanctuary. No longer did the priest consecrate ordinary bread. Now the bread was unleavened and prepared in coin-like form. If (unlikely event) they did receive Communion, they were not allowed to take the wafer in their hands, standing as they once did; now they had to kneel and receive it on the tongue, while the chalice was denied them.

The transcendental, awesome and mysterious nature of the Mass was allowed to blot out almost completely the original spirit of a community meal. It was something that happened at the altar, it was the "epiphany of God." It was something you watched. The various actions of the priest were no longer intelligible in this context, so they were given mystical and allegorical significance. The Mass became a kind of pageant representing the life, death and sufferings of Christ. The "Gloria" was sung to remind one of the angels announcing the birth of Christ. Then came the reading of the Gospel—the tale of his public life and preaching. This was followed by the silent prayers of the priest, who signified Christ praying in the

16. Theodore Klauser, *A Short History of the Western Liturgy* (New York: Oxford University Press, 1979), p. 94.

garden of Gethsemane. When he stretched out his arms, he represented Christ suffering on the cross. Five times he made the sign of the cross over the chalice and host in order to signify the five wounds. When he knelt, it was to signify Christ's death, and when he stood up again, it was to signify his Resurrection.

The main object of the layman in coming to Mass was to see the consecrated wafer, and for many, the climax came when the priest elevated it after the Consecration. A warning bell was rung beforehand to alert the faithful, many of whom would wander around town, going from church to church just to be present at the elevation. Sometimes they would pay the priest a special stipend just to hold the host up higher and for a longer time, and some even engaged in lawsuits in order to get the best place for viewing the host. This attitude gave rise to various devotions that focused on the host. The entire town would come out on such feasts as Corpus Christi, in June, when the priest would carry the host through the town encased in a glittering gold monstrance.

One of the main questions medieval theologians raised in regard to the Eucharist had to do with the real presence of the Lord. Precisely, they inquired "whether the actual, historical body of Christ was present in the Eucharist, or whether bread and wine were only its symbol with which some power of God was associated," as was already held by the monk Ratramnus of Corbie (d. 868).[17] Berengar of Tours reiterated the views of Ratramnus in his work *De Sacra Coena,* in which he denied the possibility of material change in the elements and refused to admit that the body of Christ came down from heaven and was carnally present on the altar. His opponents, led by Lanfranc (later, archbishop of Canterbury), insisted that through the Consecration the bread and wine are miraculously changed into the substance of the body and blood of Christ, with nothing remaining of the bread and wine except their appearances. To describe this change, they used the term "substantial conversion." Later the term "transubstantiation" was preferred and was made official at the Lateran Council of 1215, when belief in transubstantiation was made *de fide.* Aristotle's distinction between substance and accidents was utilized to show the possibility of such a change.

While all agreed that the Mass was a sacrifice, they could not agree on what constituted the sacrificial character of the Mass. Some saw the sacri-

17. Josef A. Jungmann, S.J., *The Mass* (Collegeville, Minn.: The Liturgical Press, 1976), p. 70.

fice in the breaking of the host and the Communion, when the body of Christ was ground with teeth, and blood was poured into the mouths of the faithful. For others, the Consecration was the decisive moment. Aquinas was the first to hold that the sufferings of Christ was the actual sacrifice and the Mass a sacrifice insofar as it re-presented Christ's sacrifice on Calvary. He was the first to bring out clearly the idea that the separate consecration of the two species represented the separation of Christ's body and blood in his Passion.

## THE REFORMATION

Speculation led to some dangerous conclusions. The subtle medieval doctor, John Duns Scotus elaborated a theory on the fruits of the Mass which held that the priest could apply them to individuals who regularly paid a stipend to receive these special benefits. This encouraged the major abuse associated with the medieval Mass: the multiplication of private Masses (Masses said without a congregation) by stipend-hungry priests who hawked Masses and made excessive promises as to their benefits. People were led to expect all manner of favors: they would not be struck blind, a relative's soul would be released from purgatory, they would not die a sudden death, etc. Some priests would offer many Masses on a single day.

It is the widespread existence of such abuses that helps one to understand the Reformation. Luther and Calvin denounced the traffic in Masses and excoriated the priest proletariat who made their living selling Masses.

One of their main concerns was to restore a sense of community participation in the Lord's Supper. They made it understandable by translating it into the language of the people, emphasizing participation by the whole community, who were taught to sing stirring new hymns. The sermon—a much neglected part of the Mass because of the poorly educated and theologically illiterate priests—was made a central part of the service.

The theological issues raised by the Reformers have continued to divide Catholics and Protestants down to our times. They rejected transubstantiation and the belief in the Mass as a propitiatory sacrifice. For Luther, propitiatory sacrifice meant the Mass was viewed as a good work of man, rather than as a free gift of God. He wrote:

As the greatest of all abominations I regard the Mass when it is preached or sold as a sacrifice or good work . . . Although I have been a great, grievous, despicable sinner, and wasted my youth in a thoughtless and damnable manner, yet my greatest sins were that I was so holy a monk, and so horribly angered, tortured and plagued my dear Lord with so many Masses for more than fifteen years.[18]

He saw belief in the propitiatory character of the Mass as the cause of many abuses such as the commerce in Masses. For Luther, the Mass communicated Christ's assurance that our sins have been forgiven. We can do nothing but accept this promise in faith, and since one can have faith only for oneself, the Mass cannot be offered for others, whether living or dead.

The Council of Trent later flatly rejected this view:

If anyone says that the sacrifice of the Mass is merely an offering of praise and thanksgiving, or that it is a simple commemoration of the sacrifice accomplished on the cross, but not a propitiatory sacrifice or that it benefits only those who communicate; and that it should not be offered for the living and the dead, for sins, punishments, satisfaction and other necessities, *anathema sit.*[19]

While the Reformers, for the most part, agreed in rejecting the doctrine of the Mass as a sacrifice, they could not reach agreement on the question of the real presence of Christ in the Eucharist. Luther and the Swiss Reformer Zwingli (d. 1531) met in a colloquy at Marburg in 1529 and sharply disagreed, with much banging of fists on the table. Zwingli asserted a mere memorial presence of Jesus in the sharing of the bread and wine, while Luther held to his bodily and objective presence. Later, Calvin drew closer to Luther than to Zwingli on this issue in asserting that the bread and wine are instruments by which Our Lord Jesus Christ himself distributes to us his body and blood. Unlike Luther's view, Christ was not localized in the bread and wine, but, on the other hand, the Eucharist was not a mere psychological aid to grasping spiritual reality, but the means by which God accomplished his promise. The presence of Christ in the Eucharist was an objectively real presence. This doctrine became the standard dogma of non-Lutheran Protestantism. The Council of Trent in response reiterated the Catholic dogma of transubstantiation.

18. "Confession Concerning Christ's Supper." In *Luther's Works* (Philadelphia: Fortress Press, 1961), XXXV, pp. 370–71.
19. J. Neuner, S.J. and J. Dupuis, S.J., eds. *The Christian Faith in the Doctrinal Documents of the Catholic Church* (Westminster, Md.: Christian Classics, Inc., 1975), p. 405.

## PROTESTANT LITURGIES

The main Protestant eucharistic liturgies which emerged from the Reformation can be classified into two main types, insofar as they were based on the Lutheran or Calvinist understanding of the real presence. Luther devised his German Mass for the people of Wittenberg in 1525, and it became the model for subsequent Lutheran liturgies. Calvin took as his model the liturgy developed at Strassburg by Martin Bucer and made it the chief service of the churches stemming from his theology and known as the Reformed churches. As Calvinism became the international form of Protestantism, its liturgy greatly influenced the liturgies of the various national churches that stemmed from the Reformation. It was the dominant influence, for example, on Thomas Cranmer's *The Second Book of Common Prayer* (1552), which became the definitive Anglican liturgy. As James Hastings Nichols asserts, "On the determinative issues of the Lord's Supper the *Book of Common Prayer* finds its closest kin in Bucer and Calvin rather than in Lutheran or Roman services."[20]

In addition to the Protestants committed to a liturgical form of worship, others appeared who favored a nonliturgical, or free, form of worship. A strong factor in the spread of these informal, or free, liturgies were the Congregationalists, the left wing of the Puritans. They eschewed set forms of prayers and emphasized long readings from Scripture and even longer sermons, while confining the celebration of the Lord's Supper to once a month. The order of the service could be freely modified by the individual minister. Little trace was left of the medieval ritual.

This tradition of nonliturgical worship became especially characteristic of the Presbyterians, Congregationalists, Methodists and Baptists.

A very popular form of nonliturgical worship—held outside, in the open air—originated among Protestants at the time of the Great Awakening, in the eighteenth century. John Wesley, the founder of the Methodists, was especially fond of this form of service as a way of reaching the unchurched. The goal of the service was to inspire individuals to make a personal decision or commitment in some form or other. These revivals were especially popular on the American frontier.

Wesley himself was very devoted to the real presence of Christ in the

20. *Corporate Worship in the Reformed Tradition* (Philadelphia: Westminster Press, 1968), p. 64.

Eucharist and celebrated it or received it on an average of once every four days. His Communion services lasted sometimes several hours, so great was the number of communicants. But the Methodists, Americans in particular, did not follow their founder in this regard and, as J. Robert Nelson points out in a recent dialogue, the Methodists are still very luke-warm in their attitude towards the Eucharist. They celebrate the Eucharist only every three months or so, and the service is quite often very short, depending on the whim of the minister. The bread and wine remaining are often treated with little reverence after the ceremony—a situation by no means confined to the Methodists.[21]

All forms of Protestant worship were greatly influenced by the prevalent rationalism and secularism of the Enlightenment. In many branches of Christianity the sacramental dimension was almost completely lost. Among the Congregationalist churches of New England, a Unitarian movement arose, which rejected most of the traditional Christian doctrines and favored a liturgy that was heavily moralistic and rationalistic, with little resemblance to the traditional eucharistic worship.

It is interesting to note in passing that as James Hastings Nichols says, it is the churches that retained a strong eucharistic structure of worship who led the way in the twentieth-century effort to recover the full dimensions of Christian belief in the redemption.

The Catholic Church, of course, stood completely apart from the other Christian churches in modern times by its refusal to modify at all the medieval liturgy bequeathed to it by Trent. In 1570, Rome issued the *Missale Romanum,* which corrected the medieval abuses but kept the Mass in Latin. Under Pope Pius V (d. 1572), it was imposed on the universal Church and remained virtually unchanged until the 1960s.

## THE CATHOLIC LITURGICAL MOVEMENT AND VATICAN II

However, the determination of Roman authorities to maintain a static liturgy did not prevent a Catholic liturgical movement from springing up in the twentieth century. It was rooted in a growing sense of history and the realization that there was no "correct" liturgical model but only more or less successful attempts to relate the Gospel to transient cultural forms. Pope Pius X, though conservative himself, gave it an impetus with his

21. "Methodist Eucharistic Usage." In Leonard Swidler, ed., *Eucharist in Ecumenical Dialogue* (New York: Paulist Press, 1976), p. 88.

decrees on church music and frequent Communion. His *motu proprio* on Church music, *Tra le sollecitudini* (1903), used for the first time the liberating words "active participation of the faithful." These words inspired the Belgian Benedictine Lambert Beauduin (d. 1960) to issue his challenge at the Catholic Congress of Malines in 1909: "The people must share in the liturgy," words that marked the beginning of the Catholic liturgical movement.

The German-speaking Catholics quickly took the lead and, under such charismatic spirits as Pius Parsch, in Austria, and Romano Guardini, in Germany, the liturgical movement began to spread through the Church. Pius XII's encyclical *Mediator Dei* (1947) gave the movement official standing, and a series of papal initiatives modifying the age-old rites followed.

All of this prepared the way for the great reform of the liturgy at the Second Vatican Council. In its *Constitution on the Sacred Liturgy* (1963), the Council laid down the principles for reform. After stressing the absolute importance of the liturgy for the spiritual life of the Church, it laid down the goal of reform: "the full, conscious, and active participation . . . by all the people."[22] To achieve this it stipulated as the primary norm that "the rites should be distinguished by a noble simplicity; they should be short, clear, and unencumbered by useless repetitions; they should be within the people's power of comprehension, and normally should not require much explanation."[23] It also made provision for the use of the vernacular.

Since 1964, the papal commission for the implementation of the Council's decrees on the liturgy introduced many changes into the Mass, which radically transformed its outward character. The people were supposed to take an active role through the various responses and acclamations which were assigned to them, while they were also recruited to act as readers and to bring up the gifts at the offertory procession. Whereas the priest was previously allowed little freedom to alter the formulas of the service, he was now encouraged to improvise greetings and prayers and take various initiatives in making the ceremony more meaningful to the congregation. Much greater emphasis was placed on Scripture by the introduction of a new lectionary with a three-year cycle of Sunday readings instead of the old one-year cycle, and the priest was instructed to preach regularly on the Scriptures.

22. *Constitution on the Sacred Liturgy*, 14.
23. Ibid., 34.

## DIALOGUE ON THE EUCHARIST

Until the Second Vatican Council, Catholics regarded Protestant eucharistic worship as invalid. They were forbidden to take part in Protestant services, and few would dream of ever taking Communion from a Protestant minister.

The Council, however, dramatically changed the climate of Protestant-Catholic relationships. Catholics were encouraged to join in prayer with their separated brethren, and Catholic theologians were invited to engage in dialogue with them to acquire a better understanding of the doctrinal differences that still divide the two sides. Since then, as we have explained above, tremendous progress has been made by the theologians in achieving a consensus on many previously divisive doctrinal issues, including the central question of the Eucharist.[24]

24. Chapter 12.

# 19

## Penance

One of the most startling developments in the post-Vatican II Church has been the desertion by the faithful of the sacrament of penance. Until just a few years ago, regular confession was a must for any faithful Catholic. Long lines of penitents awaiting their turn in the darkened box was a common scene in most Catholic churches on Saturday afternoon and evening, and hearing confessions was usually the priest's most burdensome task, as he had to sit for long hours with his ear bent to the screen while people whispered their sins and peccadilloes usually in boring and monotonous fashion and then waited for him to offer some moralistic platitudes and give them absolution with a sign of the cross.

Within a few years after the end of the Council, in 1965, this chapter of Catholic piety came to an abrupt end. Almost overnight the long lines vanished, as the great majority of Catholics simply stopped using the sacrament. It was a weird development. One of the most characteristic practices of Catholicism practically disappeared overnight, with very little furor. No one publicly attacked the confessional or urged people to stay away. A silent consensus simply spread, and people abandoned this ancient and venerable means of experiencing God's forgiveness.

To those familiar with the history of penance, this desertion of the confessional is perhaps less disturbing. As they know, it has happened before. For a long period of time—roughly from the sixth to the ninth centuries—Catholics made little use of the sacrament and began to frequent it again only when it was radically revised to meet their needs.

## PENANCE IN THE EARLY CHURCH

From the very beginning, the Church had to face the problem of what to do with the sinner in its midst. Sin was certainly not invented by the Christians; human failure, human malice, human guilt and the need to find forgiveness are as old as mankind and fill the pages of world literature. Christians, however, found the remedy through faith in Jesus Christ and through incorporation into his community of disciples through baptism.

But what if the converted person fell back into serious sin in spite of his conversion and baptism? As we know from Paul's letters and other New Testament documents, this was a vexing problem. There were people in the early communities who were guilty of creating factions of quarreling and jealousy. It is obvious that the congregation of "saints" was filled with sinners. It is also obvious that the normal means of obtaining forgiveness for ordinary sins was by participation in the Eucharist. Here the baptized pleaded for forgiveness in the great prayer of Our Lord, which was recited before Communion, while the eucharistic table fellowship with the Lord and with one another was a dramatic means of experiencing healing and reconciliation with God and neighbor.

However, some sins were so scandalous and disruptive of community life as to call for the expulsion of the offender. Paul advised the Corinthians to expel the incestuous man, although the discipline was intended ultimately to effect his salvation.[1] It is also noteworthy that some means of reconciliation was available for those who had greatly offended the community.[2]

While there may have been some rigorous Christian communities that refused to readmit the expelled sinner, it seems likely that the more common practice was to readmit sinners who sincerely performed works of penance. This is the most plausible interpretation of our earliest documents on this subject: the *First Letter of Clement* (c. 96) and *The Shepherd of Hermas* (c. 140).

These first centuries were a period when the Church's structures of ministry and discipline were in a fluid state; it is obvious that the Church only gradually developed a system for dealing with its notorious sinners. Apparently, the first indication we have of a standard ritual provided for

1. 1 Cor. 5:1–5.
2. 2 Cor. 2:5–11.

the recognition of a person as an official penitent, the imposition of certain works of penance, the public support of the prayers of the faithful and eventual reconciliation with the Church. It is found in the writings of Tertullian (d. c. 230). According to Tertullian, the rite included wearing penitential clothes, fasting and tearfully expressing one's sorrow for sin before the community and begging their intercession. His account leaves some questions unanswered, such as how one became a penitent and how the process was completed. Nor does he clearly specify the role of the bishop.

Origen, a contemporary of Tertullian, discusses the question in his various writings and lists seven ways of obtaining forgiveness: baptism, martyrdom, almsgiving, forgiveness of others, conversion of sinners and great love. The seventh, and more onerous, way, he says, is penance. If one confesses one's sins to another person, one should be careful to find a spiritual person, who manifests the fruits of the Spirit and is thereby qualified to practice such a ministry. It is by no means clear that he would restrict this ministry to priests.

The Decian persecution, in the middle of the third century, precipitated a grave crisis in the Church and helped to establish the bishop's right to control over the sacrament of penance. Many Christians succumbed to threats of torture and repudiated their faith. When they later sought pardon from the Church, the community was divided over the procedure for readmitting these apostates. In some instances, certain "confessors"—those who had endured grievous tortures without denying the faith—took it upon themselves to offer pardon to those who had apostatized. Cyprian, bishop of Carthage and eventually a martyr himself (258), refused to sanction these pardons, claiming that reconciliation with the Church was a matter for the bishop to determine—a position eventually accepted by the universal Church.

Cyprian provides a picture of how penance was administered at this point. Those guilty of a grave sin (such as murder or apostasy) presented themselves to the bishop to confess their sin. They were assigned their penance (apparently in the steps mentioned by Tertullian). Upon completion of the penance, which usually took years to perform, the bishop imposed hands on them, signifying their reconciliation with the Church, and they were once more readmitted to Communion.

## PUBLIC PENANCE: FROM THE FOURTH TO THE SIXTH CENTURIES

The tendency toward a rigorous and systematic approach to penance is very pronounced by the fourth century, especially in some of the Eastern churches. Penitents were classified according to the gravity of their sins and were assigned special places in the Church; the "hearers" were allowed to stand just within the entrance hall, but only for the Scripture readings and homily; the "kneelers," inside the nave, had to maintain a posture of self-abasement, and they, too, had to leave before the Communion proper; the "bystanders" were permitted to remain for the whole Mass. The duration of the period of penance was often extremely long, and besides the humiliation of being excluded from Communion, the penitents were obligated to a life of extreme austerity: wearing coarse garments, keeping the hair cropped, abstaining from sexual relations, and curtailing other pleasures. Details would vary from province to province, but certain features were universal: penance was always public; it was never administered more than once to the same person; if a sinner relapsed he was left totally to the mercy of God.

Those penitents who completed their penance were sacramentally reconciled with the Church—on Holy Thursday, as a rule. They prostrated themselves before the bishop, who raised them up while placing his hands on them, signifying their restoration to full Communion with the Church. This act of absolution or reconciliation with the Church was the essential sacramental act and still is.

The system made extreme demands on human nature, for once enrolled in the ranks of the penitents, a person was condemned for life to an inferior status in the Church: one could never be admitted to the clerical state, and if already a cleric, one was stripped of this status; nor could a penitent hold public office or even have marital relations. Even after absolution, one had to live as a monk.

The severity of the conditions attached to public penance was such that it gradually fell into disuse. Some bishops, notably Caesarius of Arles (d. 543), even counseled their people to avoid public penance unless they were of advanced age, ill or at the point of death. They were advised to seek other means of obtaining forgiveness, such as prayer, fasting and works of mercy.

## A NEW SYSTEM EMERGES: PRIVATE PENANCE,
# 600–1200

By the year 600, the system of public penance was virtually extinct. Its extreme rigor and legalistic approach had frightened most Christians away. However, a new system was already taking shape that promised to fill the vacuum—mainly through the influence of Celtic monk-missionaries who brought this form of private penance with them to the European continent in the sixth and seventh centuries. It originated in the Irish monastic discipline whereby monks who had seriously deviated from the rule, after confessing their faults to the abbot, were expelled from the common table and common worship and were required to undergo various forms of penance before being readmitted to the exercises of the community and to the Eucharist. Eventually all the diverse forms of sin were listed with the appropriate penance in manuals, or "penitentials," which measured the amount of penance according to the gravity of the sin. In spontaneous fashion, this discipline spread throughout the Church during the seventh century. Ordinary Christians found it spiritually comforting to confess their sins to an abbot or, if not possible, a priest, who then assigned them an appropriate penance from the penitential (usually some form of fasting) and then readmitted them to the Eucharist when they had completed their penance.

The difference between this type of penance and the old, public canonical penance is striking. This new system is completely private—a spiritual transaction between confessor and penitent. Moreover, the bishop need no longer be involved, since the rite of reconciliation, consisting of an imposition of hands with prayer begging God to forgive the sinner, could be administered by the abbot or priest, and it was repeatable. The penitent could ask for it as often as he felt the need.

No doubt these features—its privacy, its accessibility and its leniency—explain its popularity with the people.

In spite of its moribund state, however, the old system of public canonical penance was not given up without much conflict. We find echoes of a battle that must also have been waged elsewhere in the records of the Third Council of Toledo, in 589, which noted with dismay that some Christians, "as many times as it pleases them to sin . . . ask a presbyter to grant them pardon," and in order to put an end to such an "abominable presumption," it commanded that penances be given according to the rite prescribed by the ancient canons. Those who relapsed into sin after being reconciled were to be treated with the severity of the ancient canons. As late as 813, bishops of France at councils in Reims, Tours and Chalon-sur-Saône called for restoration of the ancient penitential discipline and condemned the penitential books as filled with evident errors and composed by unworthy authors.

But it proved impossible to uproot the Irish system. The penitential books continued to proliferate and the new discipline to spread. "Out of the conflict," as Ladislas Orsy says, "a new balance emerged in the form of an enduring yet precarious compromise . . . public penance should be done for public and notorious wrongdoing; private penance was allowed for secret sins."[3]

But the compromise proved unsatisfactory, and gradually the Irish tariff penance with private confession and absolution granted before satisfaction replaced most other forms of reconciliation in Western Christianity.

The penitential books prescribed very severe penances, thus perpetuating the legalistic spirit of the older system. The punishment was supposed to fit the crime. Years of fasting, strokes of the lash and compulsory pilgrimages were regularly prescribed for serious sins, and in many cases the penitent had little chance to complete the penance in a lifetime. Eventually, however, a system of commutations was devised by which a penitent could substitute a shorter but even more severe penance for a longer one or even hire others to help him carry it out. Then, with the increasing tendency to reconcile the penitent prior to the performance of the penance, milder forms of penance—usually the recitation of certain prayers—came to prevail, and the penitential books faded out of the picture.

A second major change occurred as penances became easier and a new answer to the question, How do I know I am forgiven? had to be found elsewhere than in the willing performance of the severe penances. The answer was first found in contrition: sincere sorrow for sin was accepted as more valuable than satisfaction in obtaining pardon. This idea was popularized by Peter Abelard and taken up by such influential authorities as Hugh of St. Victor, Gratian and above all by Peter Lombard.

But if contrition was the essential element, the question naturally arose, then, Why is absolution by the priest necessary? Some radicals answered

3. *The Evolving Church and the Sacrament of Penance* (Denville, N.J.: Dimension Books, 1978), p. 44.

that it wasn't. But the hierarchical Church was not about to follow in this antisacramental and antisacerdotal direction. After all, confession of sins was regarded as obligatory long before theologians began to speculate about the primacy of contrition. Moreover, confessing sins to a priest was a venerable practice. Nor should one forget the factor of social control, which would be an important consideration for the medieval state Church. And so the medieval Church, at the Lateran Council of 1215, came down hard on the necessity of confession at least once a year.

The theologians, however, did not find it so easy to justify confession's necessity—but, of course, they finally managed. Peter Lombard, while exalting contrition, refused to bow to mere logic and found a way at the same time to uphold the necessity of confession. He and his disciples argued that the priest's role was to certify that the penitent was forgiven, to assign the penance and perhaps remit some of the punishment by his absolution.

Aquinas provided an even better rationale for the necessity of confession by combining the contrition of the penitent and the action of the priest "in a causal unity that produced grace, and thus made the priest logically indispensable."[4] For Thomas, the external acts of the sacrament of penance—the penitent's confession and expression of contrition—were the outward signs of interior penance or genuine contrition, which in turn was caused by the infusion of grace. The absolution of the priest operated as an instrumental cause of this infusion of grace.

The contrition necessary to obtain God's forgiveness had to be "perfect" contrition, since imperfect contrition—a sorrow for sin primarily motivated only by the fear of punishment—lacked the essential element of true love of God necessary for conversion of heart. So, for Aquinas, the specific gift of the sacrament was in transforming imperfect to perfect contrition. "This seems to be a very helpful scheme: the external activity of the sacrament is there for the purpose of disposing the penitent to true contrition, and the inner experience of contrition has as its purpose to open the penitent to the reconciling and healing grace of God."[5]

The debate of the theologians over the role of the priest found an echo in the change at the time in the formula of absolution pronounced by the priest. The traditional formula was a prayer to God to forgive (along with

4. Thomas Tentler, *Sin and Confession on the Eve of the Reformation* (Princeton, N.J.: Princeton University Press, 1977), p. 23.
5. Monika Hellwig, *Sign of Reconciliation and Conversion* (Wilmington, Del.: Michael Glazier, 1982), p. 99.

a declaration absolving the penitent from further ecclesiastical penalties). Between the years 1000 and 1200, however, this was changed to a simple declaration of absolution: "I absolve you from your sins in the name of the Father and of the Son and of the Holy Spirit."

## MEDIEVAL PRACTICE OF PENANCE

Aquinas' contribution to the theology of penance, as we have seen, was his explanation of why confession was necessary for forgiveness. It was only the priest's absolution, he held, which could apply the merits of Christ's atonement to the guilt of the sinner. And in cases where the sinner was not fully contrite, the sacrament transformed his imperfect contrition to the perfect contrition necessary.

However, for Thomas, imperfect contrition was allowable only in the case of a sinner who was mistaken about the quality of his sorrow. It would be unthinkable for a person who was consciously not fully contrite, to be forgiven. This is where Duns Scotus differed. For him, perfect contrition was something exceptional—found only in saints capable of great devotion. Attrition—a sense of sorrow at sin with the intention of not sinning again—he held sufficient for the reception of the sacrament. And so he emphasized the power of the priestly absolution in forgiving sins.

In effect, by demanding less of the penitent, Duns Scotus made confession easier and more comforting, as the sinner would be less likely to doubt that he had met the requirements. "Scotist theology firmly established the role of the priest and the benefits of absolution in bold and precise language."[6]

The necessity of confession to a priest was universally held by this time in the medieval Church. As to how often the penitent must confess, the Lateran Council laid down the obligation to confess at least once a year. But, in addition, there were other occasions when confession of sins was obligatory: if one was conscious of serious sin and in mortal peril or before receiving the Eucharist or before the performance of a solemn religious act. Also, if the sinner had a confessor available and would not have a similar opportunity within the year and his conscience insisted that he confess immediately.

6. Thomas Tentler, op. cit., p. 26.

Priests were directed to hear confessions in an open and public place (the box did not come into use until the second half of the sixteenth century) and to take special precautions when hearing the confessions of women, so as to avoid all suspicion. According to the medieval manuals for confessors, the procedure was similar to the one older Catholics are familiar with. The priest welcomed the penitent with words of encouragement and kindness, while the penitent then confessed his sins, usually in a kneeling posture. After telling all the sins he could remember, he concluded with a prayer beseeching God, Mary, the saints and the priest for their mercy. He was then given his penance: prayer, fasting, alms, etc.—and was absolved by the priest. Then, customarily, he handed the priest a coin for his trouble.

One of the duties of the confessor, as stated in the manuals, was to interrogate the penitent to make sure that he made a complete confession. The same manuals provided lists of pertinent questions that were often extremely detailed. The good confessor was supposed to strike a happy balance between being too inquisitive and not inquisitive enough. A curious example of how far some confessors might go in their questioning is found in Jean Gerson's treatise *On the Confession of Masturbation,* a fifteenth-century self-help book for confessors. The following is the kind of question he suggests to extract information from too reticent penitents: "Friend, do you remember when you were young, about ten or twelve years old, did your rod or virile member ever stand erect? . . . What then did you do, therefore, that it wouldn't stand erect?" If the penitent refused to answer, the confessor was advised to be most explicit: "Friend, didn't you touch or rub your member the way boys usually do?"[7]

The medieval Church, while very sensitive to the evils of all manner of vice and sin, was inordinately concerned about sexual sin. Its theology of marriage and sex was greatly influenced by St. Augustine, who linked sex so strictly with procreation that he held as sinful all sexual activity by married couples that was not consciously ordained to procreation. The medieval manuals for confessors show the influence of Augustine by the deep-rooted suspicion of sexual pleasure they manifest. They instructed the confessor to interrogate the penitent carefully about his motives for having intercourse with his wife (excessive pleasure was to be avoided as at least venially sinful) and whether unnatural positions were used; as defined by Albert the Great and generally accepted, the only natural position was

7. Ibid., pp. 91–92.

with the woman underneath, the use of other positions being generally condemned as sinful, though theologians differed on the gravity of the sin.

Other matters for questioning involved such things as whether the spouses had intercourse while the woman was menstruating or pregnant or whether they did so in a holy place or during the holy seasons or before receiving Communion. The experts differed on the sinfulness of these practices. Some took a lenient view, like Berthold of Freiburg, who insisted on the mutual obligation of the spouses to render the sexual debt even if it meant interrupting a church service!

> And if the married man is in church at the divine service and the other asks him to leave, he should be obedient and do her will—and he does so without sin.[8]

According to the more lax authors, one might even have intercourse with one's spouse in Church if one was forced to remain there for a long time, as in a case of emergency shelter.

## THE REFORMATION

The theology and practice of sacramental confession was one of the primary targets of Luther, Calvin and the other Reformers of the sixteenth century. Luther denied that it was instituted by Christ, but he was not absolute in his condemnation of confession; he felt it could be a source of consolation. He urged his followers to confess, and he himself often confessed. But he was totally opposed to the medieval Church's system of obligatory confession to a priest and denied the pope's right to command yearly confession. He also denied that a complete confession was necessary or even possible, and he found the lengthy interrogations of the priest intolerable.

Luther's doctrine on contrition and absolution struck at the heart of the medieval system of confession. For Luther, contrition was not focused at a particular time or on a particular sin. It was a pervasive sense of one's impotence and worthlessness before an all-just God, and it involved faith in His promise of forgiveness. The consolation one receives does not derive, as in the medieval system, from the power of the ordained priest's absolution or the completeness of the confession or the sincerity of the sorrow, but simply from being reminded of God's promise of forgiveness.

8. Ibid., p. 218.

Reiterating Abelard's position, he held that the priest merely declares this forgiveness. As a consequence, in the Lutheran confession nothing was left of the old discipline of reservations, jurisdiction, penances, indulgences and purgatory itself. A Lutheran was not to stew over making a complete confession, but simply to confess those offenses that were open, serious or troublesome and, above all, to believe in the promise of forgiveness.

Calvin attacked the same aspects of the medieval system as Luther: its legalism, its lack of scriptural basis, its obligatoriness and its claims to a monopoly of forgiveness. Like Luther, he thought it could still offer consolation to the sinner, but because of its obligatoriness and the need to precisely enumerate one's serious sins, he called the Roman form a spiritual slaughter. So confession gradually disappeared in the Protestant churches.

The Council of Trent simply reiterated the traditional doctrine of the Church on the sacrament of penance. All the main negations of the Reformers were met by vigorous reaffirmations. Trent asserted that penance was truly a sacrament instituted by Christ and necessary for the remission of serious sin; at least once a year, all serious sins must be confessed individually and specifically, including relevant circumstances; interior contrition is declared absolutely necessary for its efficacy and likewise the absolution of the priest; the satisfaction imposed by the priest is held to be an essential part. But it admitted that serious sin could be forgiven before reception of the sacrament if one was perfectly contrite and intended to receive the sacrament when possible.

As Thomas Tentler points out, it is possible to view the medieval system of penance, with Luther and Calvin, in a negative way or, with Loyola and the Council of Trent, in a very positive way. As the product of a long evolution, the system itself was extremely complex. Each side could point to certain of its features to prove its case. For the critics, it was either Pelagian and rationalistic in the way it stressed merit and human effort, or it was ritualized magic because of its stress on the power of the priest's absolution. It was also deemed legalistic by its frequent reference to jurisdiction, reservations and various restrictions. It could even be regarded as lax by its readiness to offer instant forgiveness for the most serious sins.

Thomas Tentler's judgment on the system is worth repeating:

Was Sacramental confession *"Pelagian,"* the natural product of a religion of works? The heavy emphasis on the benefits of submission to the keys indicates, rather, that special powers are necessary to supplement weak human beings precisely because they lack those Pelagian powers to achieve justifying contrition on their own. Was it then a *magical* ritual? On the contrary, it demanded the most rationalistic and conscientious effort on the part of the faithful penitent, whose purification certainly depended on his own intentions. Was it a purely *legalistic* and externalized religious ritual? For similar reason that charge ignores the obvious: because authorities on confession expected obedience in the depths of conscience, an inner guilt at transgression, and a willing acceptance of personal spiritual obligations. Was its moral and sacramental theology decadent and excessively *lax?* Such a conclusion would surely have to overlook plain facts: that it always defined moral regulations in detail, imputed guilt to sinners individually, asserted the necessity of sincere cooperation with sacramental grace, and taught in sensitive areas of human conduct a harsh moral code. Did it heedlessly create *scrupulous consciences?* One would have to ignore the explicit attempts of some of the best and most prestigious authorities to prevent and cure scruples of conscience to hold that view. Was it a *clerical tyranny?* That charge cannot make sense if we recall that priests were also subject to the guilt of conscience and restricted to this institution for its cure. Indeed, if priests could establish their separateness and superiority through regulations on sexuality, they also had to conform to sexual regulations that were much harder than those imposed on the laity. Priests did not author a conspiracy, they participated in a system.[9]
(My emphasis on certain words)

On the other hand, as Tentler points out, by selecting other evidence one could also come up with evidence on the other side and find the system indeed Pelagian and rationalistic by its insistence on human effort and merit; legalistic by reason of its whole network of canonical reservations, restrictions and jurisdictions; even lax if judged by the demands of the Gospel, and sometimes tyrannical insofar as imposed by a male celibate caste.

As we said above, the point is that the system was extremely complex, being the product of a long evolution.

We should also remember that while Luther and Calvin undoubtedly spoke for many sensitive souls who found it an intolerable burden, others, like Loyola, could testify to its great spiritual value and the comfort it gave equally sensitive souls. Moreover, the churches of the Reformation found

9. Ibid., pp. 363–64.

that doing away with it solved some problems but created others involving discipline and reconciliation.

Little development occurred in the theology or practice of the sacrament after the Council of Trent. A few changes occurred such as the installation of a screened partition between priest and penitent, which was made mandatory in 1614 to safeguard anonymity and to reduce the danger of sexual indiscretion on the part of the priest, especially in hearing the confessions of women. Also, priests guilty of soliciting sexual favors from penitents were automatically suspended from saying Mass and hearing confessions. And a priest who disclosed anything revealed to him in confession was to be excommunicated.

## VATICAN II'S REFORM

On the eve of the Second Vatican Council, Catholics remained faithful to the practice of frequent confession. But some moral theologians were already taking a new direction and preparing the way for the changes that were to come. For instance, they questioned the prevailing legalistic view of sin as simply the violation of laws and commandments. The more progressive moralists, such as Bernard Häring and Joseph Fuchs, began to think of sin more in terms of distorted personal relationships. Also, more attention was given to the motives of a person. The murkiness of all human motivation was noted and also a greater awareness of how often a person was faced with competing values in making moral decisions. Thus, in calling for a revision of the Church's ban on birth control, the Louvain theologian Louis Janssens argued that a person might have to sacrifice the biological integrity of the sexual act in order to safeguard a higher value, namely, the mutual love of the spouses.

Other factors also played a role. Thinking Catholics were becoming more aware of social injustice as the sixties spawned movements of protest and dissent. They felt guilty about sins of society we all share in, such as racism, militarism, oppression of the poor, etc. But the very private confessional did not seem the proper remedy for the feelings of collective guilt these sins engendered.

How sensitive the bishops at the Second Vatican Council were to these considerations is not clear, but, in line with their general willingness to revise the liturgy of the Church, they did call for a revision of the rites and formulas for the sacrament of penance so to "give more luminous expression to both the nature and effect of the sacrament."[10] Many of them were becoming aware of the great changes that had taken place in the past administration of the sacrament, and they felt justified in allowing further change.

The new rites for the sacrament of penance were issued by the Sacred Congregation for Divine Worship in 1973 and first became available in the United States in Advent 1975.

Three separate rites of reconciliation were provided: one for individual penitents, another for several with individual confession and absolution, and a third for several penitents with only general confession and absolution.

The rite for the individual penitent made some important changes. The dialogue between priest and penitent could now be held face to face if the penitent so desired. The priest was encouraged to be flexible and to avoid a legalistic approach. He was to begin the dialogue with a suitable biblical phrase recalling God's love and our need to turn to him with a ready heart and then to encourage the penitent to confess fully. Finally he was exhorted to give a penance that would help the penitent overcome the sin confessed.

The most innovative feature of the new Ordo is the second, or communal, rite, to be celebrated by the community in a service consisting of hymns, scriptural readings, prayers and a homily as a preparation for a general examination of conscience, individual confession of sins, and absolution.

The main criticism of this rite is directed at the insistence on individual confession and absolution, which, it is said, interrupts the flow of the service, often prolongs it in a boring way, and undermines the significance of the rite as a collective confession of sin.

The third rite does provide for general confession and general absolution but is supposed to be used only in situations in which the number of people in attendance is too large to allow for individual confession; it is to be used with the proviso that the penitent later submit his serious sin(s) privately to a confessor.

10. *Constitution on the Sacred Liturgy*, 72.

## DECLINE OF CONFESSION

One thing is clear: the renewal of the sacrament of penance has not arrested the decline in its use. As Bella English reported in the New York *Daily News* in 1981: "For centuries, confession was as much a part of a practicing Catholic's week as going to the grocery store. But today its status is shaky and its future uncertain. Only 18 percent of practicing Catholics who responded to a 1978 Gallup poll had gone to confession in the previous month."[11] Another observer, Rev. Michael Henchal, executive director of the diocesan liturgical commission in Portland, Oregon, predicted that if things kept going at the current rate, the sacrament would cease to exist in ten years.[12]

Much speculation exists about the causes of the decline. No doubt, one of the principal reasons is a changing understanding of morality. As long as Catholics could believe that sin was essentially the violation of a given code of laws and commandments, it made relatively good sense to mention the kinds of violations and their frequency. But with the greater importance attributed to motivation and the emphasis on sin as essentially a failure of love, it becomes more difficult to sort out one's sins. Luther long ago pointed out how our most radical sins escape our perception. Many Catholics today would agree with him.

Also, for a long time, sexual transgressions were in the forefront of people's minds when sin was mentioned. The Catholic confessional box, with its aura of secrecy, symbolized the embarrassment people felt in relating intimate details of their sexual life to a totally inexperienced celibate. The whole business often generated an orgy of guilt. And confession seemed to many to intensify the neurotic character of the faults they confessed and to make their repetition almost inevitable. As they became more aware of this pattern, many Catholics simply quit going.

Another factor is the prevailing confusion over what constitutes a mortal sin. With the breakdown of the authoritarian model of Church authority, Catholics find no easy way to answer this question. Polls show only too clearly how little agreement there is among Catholics as regards sin. In the realm of sexual morality especially, the revolution of the '60s has affected

11 Quoted by Edward Marciniak, "The Sacrament of Penance," *America*, July 16, 1983, p. 25.
12. Ibid.

them as much as any group. As a result, many practicing Catholics who lead otherwise exemplary Christian lives but disregard the Church's strict sexual code do not feel guilty and reject the confessional, which symbolizes for them an outdated morality and the tendency of the Church to foment guilt feelings about sex.

An interesting question arises here: how much has the new Mass contributed to the abandonment of the confessional? Every Mass starts with a confession of sin and a prayer by the priest for forgiveness. Moreover, the Mass itself, as the celebration of Christ's great act of reconciliation, is filled with prayers and phrases that speak of the forgiving power of the Lord's Supper. In its central position, the Lord's Prayer is the climactic prayer for reconciliation with the Father, while the sign of peace expresses in a powerful way one's desire for reconciliation with one's neighbor. Surely anyone who participates in the Eucharist devotedly and intelligently is bound to feel forgiven and reconciled. Hence there is bound to be a diminished sense of need for private confession.

It certainly seems true, then, as Monika Hellwig says, that people are staying away in great numbers because they do not find the sacrament meeting a spontaneously felt need. And the only way to attract them back is to find a way that meets a felt need.[13] The deep human need to which the sacrament is addressed is the need to return to the Father's house from exile, to come home to one's true place, to find liberation from fear, boredom and frustration, to find one's authentic existence behind the many masks of unreality, to find peace from restlessness, anxiety and discontent, to find a bottomless inner peace with God, with other people and all fellow creatures, with one's own dependency and limitations and with the uncertainty of the future and the certainty of death . . . Sin as sin is not directly accessible to experience, though the Bible and tradition teach us to identify it as the disorientation that leaves our lives turned away from God and therefore lacking in focus and integration. What is directly accessible to experience is the restlessness, the discontent, the fear and diffuse anxiety, the inability to live in harmony and community with others, the inability to accept our own dependency, poverty and limitations.[14]

As Ms. Hellwig says, the obvious reason why people are abandoning the confessional is its failure to meet their legitimate expectations. They want to have some experience of renewal, some feeling of being transformed, some sense of being reconciled with God and others.

13. *Sign of Reconciliation and Conversion,* p. 155.
14. Ibid., pp. 107–8.

Many who do not find this experience in the sacrament find it in other ways: in small groups where people meet in an atmosphere of prayer and openness and mutual acceptance and are willing to admit their weaknesses and need for conversion. The experience of forgiveness in such a context can be very real indeed.

Again, there are persons who have the gift of healing souls because of the trust they inspire. Their door is always open to those troubled and anxious. They have strong faith in God, they pray often and are able to communicate to others some sense of God's love and the peace He is ready to give His children. Healers such as these abound in the Church and exercise a true ministry of reconciliation without, in many cases, even being conscious of it.

For many the sacrament of penance would make sense only because it either presupposes such an experience and proclaims and celebrates it or helps to engender it.

The new rites are certainly a step in the right direction insofar as they are designed to promote true conversion and a sense of communal reconciliation. But many still have difficulty with the requirement that they confess privately all their serious sins. Church officials who insist on this requirement, no doubt, feel they have no alternative, since the Council of Trent formally defined this as essential to the sacrament.

But some theologians are not so sure. Many of them believe that the Church could dispense with this obligation and, in fact, could find radically new ways of celebrating the sacrament, ways more apt to foster true conversion and a deeper sense of Christian community. They argue that there is simply no historical justification for the claim that this obligation is by divine command. History shows that for many centuries the Church celebrated the sacrament in radically different fashion, did not demand annual confession of serious sins, and therefore could today experiment with new ways of celebrating the sacrament more attuned to present needs—perhaps in "a more penitentially oriented eucharistic rite."[15]

The bishops took up the matter again in their synod in the fall of 1983 devoted to the theme "Penance and Reconciliation in the Mission of the Church." The bishops noted the huge drop uniformly around the world in the reception of the sacrament over the previous fifteen years. Some estimated that overall decline in the number of Catholics receiving the sacrament might now be as great as 70 percent. The most frequently men-

15. James McCue, "Penance as a Separate Sacramental Sign," in *Concilium* (New York: Herder & Herder, 1971), p. 64.

tioned factors accounting for the drop were loss of a sense of sin, greater secular influences that diminish faith in God, lack of priests to man the confessionals, and confusion over the difference between mortal and venial sins.

As a remedy, some proposed greater use of the third rite, which features general confession and general absolution. But the prefect of the Congregation for the Doctrine of the Faith, Joseph Cardinal Ratzinger, turned thumbs down, citing the danger of depersonalization and collectivization of the sacrament. However, observers do not see this as a definitive response, since so many of the bishops evinced sympathy for general absolution.

## INDULGENCES

The appearance of indulgences, in the eleventh century, was closely tied in with the evolution of the sacrament of penance. The practice of granting indulgences is rooted in the belief that a penitent needed support by the prayers of the Church in the effort to pay the debt of penance. We have seen how this support was vividly demonstrated in the penitential practices of the early Church, when priests and people offered intercessory prayers for the penitent, who was banished for a time from their midst.

When penance became private, the intercession of the whole Church on the sinner's behalf took a different form: the so-called *absolutions*, which were official prayers for the remission of sin, pronounced by the bishop, in virtue of the power of the keys, on behalf of a specific penitent. The penitent in turn showed sincerity by the performance of some good work such as an offering.

The transition from the practice of granting absolutions to that of indulgences occurred when the general prayer for remission of sins became the formal remission of a strictly determined amount of ecclesiastical penance, in the belief that God would cancel the corresponding amount of punishment due to sin.[16]

The most ancient indulgences we know of date from the middle of the eleventh century and were granted in consideration of some good work such as giving alms. One of these, for instance, reduced a fast imposed as a penance from three days a week for a year to one day a week for that

16. Bernhard Poschmann, *Penance and the Anointing of the Sick* (New York: Herder & Herder, 1964), p. 215.

period. Eventually the indulgences simply spoke of so many days or so many years. And at first it was always made clear that the remission had to do simply with ecclesiastical penances, with a prayer that God would likewise see fit to remit the punishment he would otherwise inflict. But eventually there was an explicit claim that the indulgence remitted the divine punishment.

One of the earliest and most famous indulgences was granted in 1095 by Pope Urban II to crusaders who set out to recover the Holy Land. It was a plenary indulgence, insofar as the pope remitted the entire canonical penance.

Theologians took cognizance of indulgences only very gradually. Some, like Abelard, found them totally objectionable. But a theological justification was slowly worked out.

General agreement was eventually reached that indulgences remitted the punishments otherwise to be endured in purgatory. This was a big step, since previously the Church had claimed only the power to remit the penalties for sin due in this life. But now it asserted that its jurisdiction extended to the penitent's relationship to God beyond death—a relationship previously left in the hands of a merciful God. In remitting these, the Church began to use the same juridical language it had previously employed in remitting its own canonical penances.

One of the most difficult questions was how to justify the Church's claim to remit punishment due to sin, since the good work required as a substitute—often a small sum of money—was obviously not the equivalent to time spent in purgatory. To solve this problem, recourse was had to a so-called treasury of merits built up by Jesus and the saints and entrusted to the Church to dispense to those in need.

Eventually it became official doctrine that indulgences could be applied to the souls in purgatory on the supposition that as equal members of the mystical body of Christ they, too, could participate in the merits of their saintly fellow members. It was a dangerous development, however justifiable it might have been in theory, since it involved considerable ambiguity. The actual efficacy of the indulgence was sometimes described in technical Latin as *per modum suffragii*—meaning "insofar as God hears the prayers of the Church." It also minimized, of course, the aspect of personal repentance, which up to that time had always been an important part of receiving an indulgence. A door was thus opened to the unscrupulous preacher to present an indulgence as a quasi-automatic and easy means of salvation. Abuses of all sorts cropped up, as indulgences were used to replenish Church coffers and provide the funds for fighting papal wars. Finally, a peculiarly gross example of indulgence huckstering aroused the wrath of Luther and triggered his revolt against the pope.

In response to Luther, the Council of Trent did not offer a detailed defense of its doctrine on indulgences. It merely affirmed two main points: that the Church has received from Christ the power to confer indulgences and that their use confers real spiritual benefits. Recently the popes have seen fit to encourage the faithful to continue making use of them.

## INDULGENCES TODAY?

Is it possible to interpret the Church's doctrine on indulgences in a way that makes sense to a modern Catholic? The starting point, no doubt, has to be a proper understanding of the official definition of an indulgence: "a remission before God of the temporal punishment due to sins whose guilt has been forgiven," which is conceded by Church authority "from the Church's treasury of the living by means of absolution, and for the dead by means of intercession."[17] The important distinction here between the guilt of sin and the temporal punishment due may be interpreted in the light of the experiential fact that even though one's sin is forgiven, the psychological remnant left by sin in the form of habits, attitudes and inclinations to evil persist and are only dispelled by a painful period of purgation. Even though one's conversion is sincere, the disorientation of the self cannot be instantaneously corrected.

So the "temporal punishment due to sin" should not be thought of as if God implacably demands his pound of flesh. Rather, it refers to the psychic cost involved in reordering one's emotions and affections. In pursuing this total conversion, the sinner, according to Church doctrine, is well advised to undertake penances such as prayer, fasting and works of mercy. These, however, are only supposed to foster the process of discernment, so essential to conversion.

In the ancient Church, the intercessory prayers of the Church were supposed to aid the sinner in this discernment and to help him carry out the canonical penances. The efficacy of an indulgence still rests primarily on this intercessory prayer of the Church, which is intended to support

17. *Codex Juris Canonici.* Transl. in J. Neuner and H. Roos, *The Teaching of the Catholic Church* (New York: Alba House, 1967), p. 330.

the sinner as he wrestles with "the temporal punishment due to sin" on his journey to total conversion.

As Monika Hellwig says, "The granting of an indulgence simply underscores what is happening all the time, namely, that the saving grace of Christ's redemptive death and resurrection anticipates and welcomes our conversion at every step of the way, making that which is in itself impossible not only possible but a joyful task and a light burden."[18] Moreover, the indulgences are also effective insofar as the "good work" required for the obtaining of the indulgence often has a community dimension: pilgrimages and novenas, which foster a sense of solidarity with all those in the Church who are struggling against sin. Such good works therefore often prove more effective for continuing conversion than do imposed penances.

The danger, of course, is that the language used in the grant of indulgence, namely, such terms as "seven years and seven quarantines," could imply the cutting short of a time of punishment envisaged as stretching into the next life. The indulgence then might be understood as canceling the obligation of doing penance as an essential part of a continuing conversion. The consequences could be most harmful, especially in the area of social sin. Conversion here demands a constant willingness to accept one's responsibility to repair the damaged network of relationships that constitute our sinful situation. It would be most unfortunate if indulgences were used in a way that weakened one's commitment to such a conversion.

18. *Sign of Reconciliation and Conversion*, pp. 128–29.

# 20

## Anointing of the Sick

Jesus' power over sickness was one of the signs that marked him as the Messiah, in accordance with Isaiah's prophecy that when the Messiah came, the blind would see again, the lame walk, the lepers be cleansed, the deaf hear, the dead be raised to life.[1] Many incidents are given in the New Testament that show his remarkable powers of healing. Whether or not he sometimes used oil with his healing, as was quite common in the East, is not indicated, but it is reported of his disciples when Jesus sent them out to preach. Mark notes how "they cast out many devils, and anointed many sick people with oil and cured them."[2]

The epistle of James indicates that anointing of the sick was continued in the community of Jerusalem: "If one of you is ill, he should send for the elders of the church, and they must anoint him with oil in the name of the Lord and pray over him. The prayer of faith will save the sick man and the Lord will raise him up again; and if he has committed any sins, he will be forgiven."[3]

During the next centuries, the indications of a healing ministry with anointing are not very frequent, but there are a few texts that show its existence. One of the clearest of these is found in the *Apostolic Tradition*, of Hippolytus, where we find a petition "that this oil . . . may give strength to all that taste of it and health to all that use it."[4]

1 Lk. 7:22.
2. Mk. 6:13.
3. Jas. 5:14–15.
4. Quoted in Bernhard Poschmann, op. cit., p. 238.

Origen and Chrysostom commented on the Epistle of James, mentioned above, but they connect the anointing mentioned with the sacrament of penance, indicating they understood the sickness referred to as a spiritual sickness.

A different exegesis of the passage, however, is given by Pope Leo I (d. 461) in a letter to Bishop Decentius. In explaining the passage, the pope makes several points: 1. The bishop alone has the right to consecrate the oil. 2. In the absence of the bishop the priest may anoint the sick person, and this anointing is sacramental. 3. The oil may also be used by lay persons for a nonsacramental type of anointing. This text became the basis for theological discussion of the sacrament in the West.

There are many accounts in the early Middle Ages of saints and holy people who brought about miraculous cures with the use of consecrated oil. Saint Genevieve of Paris, for instance, healed many sick with oil blessed by her bishop. And another holy woman, Austrebertha, the abbess of Pavilly, is reported to have anointed a nun caught in the collapse of a building and thereby saved her life.

The evidence of the first eight centuries indicates indeed that it was regarded as a sacrament aimed primarily not at the dying, but at the sick. The emphasis, however, was not on the one who applied it, but on its blessing by the bishop. Once blessed, the oil could be applied by either a priest or a lay person. Both types are mentioned as a means of healing the sick. The Venerable Bede (d. 735), from whom we have the first complete commentary on the Epistle of James, mentions both types of anointing, though he makes forgiveness of sins dependent on confession to a priest.

Two things happened, however: the anointing was reserved to the priest, and it became a rite for the dying, rather than the sick generally.

The question occurs, How did a rite administered to the sick with a real hope for their recovery change to one exclusively reserved for those at the point of death, with little chance of recovery? The origin of this practice must be traced to the East, where it was customary to anoint those doing public penance. Then, when for the reasons mentioned above penance became almost exclusively a sacrament for the dying, they were anointed as part of the rite.

Anointing thus was looked on as part of the rites of final penance, which people shied away from receiving until practically beyond recovery, since those who received the sacrament and by chance recovered were bound by the ancient canons to severe penitential practices such as abstaining from all marital relations, etc. Thus the anointing came to be called extreme unction.

Until the ninth century, there was no prescribed ritual for the anointing. This lack was remedied by Alcuin of York, Charlemagne's outstanding scholar, who composed a rite that he attached to the Gregorian sacramentary and which in the tenth century was adopted by Rome as the official Roman rite.

The sacrament was not widely used during the Middle Ages. Since people would often wait until the very last moment before calling the priest, the sick person would often die before it was administered. Moreover, the anointing had developed into an elaborate and lengthy ceremony, often performed in church and requiring the assistance of several priests. Since it was customary to remunerate the priests, the whole affair could be quite costly, and this discouraged its use by those with little means.

When Peter Lombard compiled his list of seven sacraments, in the twelfth century, he included extreme unction among them, and eventually this became official. Speculation about the nature and effects of the sacrament occupied the great medieval Scholastics. They all agreed that oil consecrated by a bishop was the *matter*, but differed about the *form*.

Another question that caused some difficulty was in regard to the effects of the sacrament. Should physical healing be regarded as one of its fruits? If so, in what sense? Since some prayer formulas still referred to physical healing in addition to forgiveness of sins, many of the earlier Scholastics included physical healing among the effects but only insofar as the healing would be spiritually beneficial for the sick person.

But since in actual practice the sacrament was confined to people at the point of death, references to physical healing gradually disappeared from the ritual, and the later Scholastics emphasized the spiritual effects of the sacrament. Both major schools of theology, the Franciscans and the Dominicans, came to agree that the essential difference between penance and extreme unction consisted in the fact that while penance remitted serious sins, extreme unction removed any additional obstacles preventing the soul from immediate entrance to heavenly glory. And both schools recommended it only for those who were at the point of death. The Scotists, in line with their belief in the automatic effectiveness of the sacraments, recommended it only for those who were so ill they could no longer even sin.

## THE REFORMATION AND TRENT

Luther and Calvin attacked the doctrinal foundations of extreme unction. They denied that Christ instituted it and denied that James 5:14–15 referred to a sacrament for the dying. Calvin held that James referred to a special type of charismatic, miraculous healing which God granted to the primitive Church as a sign of the divine power of the Gospel, but which was no longer needed once the Church was established and the Gospel firmly rooted in the hearts of believers.

Unlike Calvin, however, Luther recommended anointing of the sick as a rite that might console and comfort the dying, but only insofar as they put their trust and confidence in God alone and not in any power residing in the rite itself.

The Council of Trent upheld the medieval view of it as a sacrament instituted by Christ, but recognized the need to correct the abuses associated with its administration. It refused, however, to canonize the Scholastic theology which saw it as exclusively a preparation for the passage of the soul into eternity. It simply stated that it was to be used for the sick— especially for those who were dangerously ill.

The centuries after the Council of Trent saw little change in the doctrine or practice of extreme unction. A few minor questions left hanging by medieval theologians were settled, such as whether it should be administered to children (by the seventeenth century it was given only to those capable of serious sin) or to those who had just died (they were to be conditionally anointed).

## THE NEW RITE

The theological ferment preceding the Second Vatican Council and paving the way for it affected the understanding of this sacrament as well as the others. Historical and biblical studies shed light on its origins and development and indicated a need for its revision, which was effected by the apostolic constitution *Sacram unctionem infirmorum* and the decree *Infirmis cum ecclesia,* both issued in 1972.

A number of important changes were made: the term "extreme unction" was dropped in favor of "anointing of the sick." This reflected the shift away from viewing it mainly as the final act of the Church assisting the soul as it enters eternity and toward seeing it as a means of strengthening and healing both body and soul.

The priest was also encouraged to confer the sacrament in a way that brings out its positive message. Often, the old rite was conferred hurriedly when the sick person was unconscious or nearly so and those present merely knelt while perhaps making a few responses. The new rite invites the sick person and those present to share fully in a service of readings and prayers while the priest counsels and assists the sick person and his or her relatives and friends, to comfort them and help them respond with faith and trust to the mystery of suffering and death.

Many modifications have been introduced in the new discipline. If necessary, the priest may consecrate the oil to be used. The sacrament may be conferred on a person before surgery if the operation is a serious one. It may also be given to the elderly infirm even if they are not dangerously ill, and provision is made for making this type of anointing a community celebration, with the congregation present as during Mass. One who is already dead is not to be anointed (unless there is some doubt about this condition). The old practice of anointing the forehead and the five organs of sense has been changed to a simple anointing of the forehead and hands, although an additional anointing may be given on some part of the body affected by the illness or disease. The oil no longer has to be olive oil but may be oil from any plant.

# 21

## Marriage—Still Forever?

When was marriage invented? A Swiss ethnologist of the nineteenth century, J. J. Bachofen, propounded a view that intrigued and fascinated many of his contemporaries. He claimed that primitive man lived in small packs totally ignorant of marriage and promiscuous as monkeys. The German socialist Friedrich Engels and the Russian revolutionary Peter Kropotkin, among others, used his theory to buttress their radical views of family and society. But when science replaced fantasy, it was found that among the hundred primitive peoples still on earth not one of them lived without some form of marriage and some form of restriction on sexual freedom. "Marriage, it appeared, was a genuine human universal, like speech and social organization."[1]

Nevertheless there are some who predict the end of marriage as an institution and as the cornerstone of society. All sorts of voices, especially from the Left, even urge its downfall. Kate Millett, a leading feminist, expects marriage to wither away once women have achieved full equality.

In view of the large number of unwedded living together and also the zooming divorce rate, it is no wonder that many think marriage is finally on the way out.

But there is another side to the picture. In spite of the present disarray and confusion, marriage is actually more widespread than ever. As Morton Hunt shows, a considerably larger percentage of our adult population was

1. Morton Hunt, "The Future of Marriage." In James E. DeBurger, ed., *Marriage Today* (Cambridge, Mass.: Schenkman Publishing Co., 1977), p. 683.

married in 1970 than was the case in 1890, and the marriage rate has been climbing steadily since 1963.

Also, we must consider the fact that alternatives to traditional monogamy do not seem all that promising: "shacking up," after all, is merely another form of marriage; it simply omits legal status. The only truly revolutionary alternative is group marriage, with many people living together, pooling their resources and sharing the tasks of housekeeping and child rearing and sometimes even sexual partners. But the latest research shows most group marriages are unstable and last only a few years.

Marriage, in fact, has proved to be a most durable and adaptable institution. Its antiquity is reflected in many of the ceremonies used in weddings today. The handing over of the bride by the father, for instance, reflects the ancient custom whereby the father was paid a price for his daughter, whom he escorted to her new home. The white gown and bridal bouquet we know were customary among the ancient Romans. The sharing of the cake derived from a ceremony of offering a wheaten cake to the Roman household gods—part of a ceremony of inducting the bride into the religion of the groom. The bride's ring symbolized for the Romans the price that at an earlier time had been paid for the bride. And carrying the bride over the threshold recalled the more primitive time when the bride was literally abducted by the groom.

### THE JEWISH AND CHRISTIAN TRADITIONS

Among the Jews, marriage was definitely a male-dominated institution. The wife was regarded as the property of the husband and had few legal rights. Adultery, for instance, was prohibited not as a breach of trust but as a violation of the husband's property rights. Polygamy was allowed, and divorce of the wife by the husband. However, the prophets struggled to elevate the moral ideal of marriage by insisting that it should be a covenant founded on faithful love of husband and wife. Hosea compared marriage to the love between Yahweh and Israel. Other passages, in the Song of Songs, Tobit and Proverbs extolled marriage as a bond uniting the couples in a love that was exclusive and permanent.

Divorce, however, remained an acceptable option and could be legally demanded only by the husband, although the wife could obtain it if the husband consented.

It was Jesus who asserted in most radical fashion the true nature of the marriage covenant. In response to those seeking to determine whether he sided with the more lenient or more severe rabbinical school—both of which permitted divorce—he repudiated both, by asserting that Moses had allowed divorce only because of their hard hearts. "But from the beginning of creation God made them male and female. This is why a man must leave father and mother, and the two become one body. They are no longer two, therefore, but one body. So then, what God has united, man must not divide."[2]

It must be noted that we find a different version of this saying in Matthew, who, it seems, modified the original teaching of Jesus as recorded in Mark and Luke. Matthew has Jesus say, ". . . the man who divorces his wife—I am not speaking of fornication—and marries another, is guilty of adultery."[3]

How do we explain this discrepancy? Jesus, it seems, took the same radical, unequivocal position on divorce as he did on many other issues—forbidding all anger, lust, use of violence, swearing, etc. The early community, however, as Matthew shows, had to modify his teaching in response to practical realities.

Paul upheld Christ's vision of indissoluble marriage as a reflection of the Creator's will: the married couple should love each other faithfully and permanently as Christ loves the Church; but he, too, allowed divorce—in the unique case in which a Christian was married to an unbeliever who made it impossible for the Christian to practice the faith.

The marriage relationship, for Paul, is unique insofar as it reflects the relationship of Christians whose love reflects Christ's love of his Church. While Genesis saw marriage as a sacred reality, this becomes fully apparent only in the marriage of Christ and his Church. Thus the relationship between husband and wife theologically is set apart from all other human relationships. Christian reflection on this would eventually justify the Church's regarding marriage as a sacrament.

There is not much else about marriage in the New Testament. For many centuries, marriage remained a purely civil and family affair and was celebrated often without any special Church blessing. The Church began to intervene with the custom of the bishop or priest blessing the newly married couple. Gradually the clergy took a more active role, such as placing the veil over the couple or joining their hands together. But there

2. Mk. 10:6–9.
3. Mt. 19:9 (see also Mt. 5:32).

was no obligatory Church ceremony connected with marriage in the West until the eleventh century. Then, as part of an effort to outlaw secret marriages, Church officials required all marriages to be solemnly blessed by a priest. It soon became customary for the spouses to hold the weddings near the church so that, after marrying, the couple could immediately seek the priest's blessing. The next step was to hold the marriage itself in the church. Eventually the Church took complete control of marriage, regulating all its aspects with a complicated network of laws.

For a long time, the Church wavered in her attitude toward divorce. The exception clause in Matthew allowed some flexibility, and at least in some places in the early Church divorce and remarriage were tolerated. In the East, legal regulation of marriage and divorce was left to the government, which in the Code of Justinian made provision for divorce. Divorced Christians were allowed to remarry in the Church even, but second marriage was not regarded as sacramental.

In the West, however, a stricter interpretation of Jesus' words eventually prevailed. The first churchman we know of to hold that no marriage could be dissolved—not even for adultery—was Ambrose. His protégé Augustine strengthened this position by developing a theology of marriage as a sacrament that he likened to baptism. According to Augustine, in both cases the sacramental character consisted of assimilating the person spiritually to Christ: in baptism, to his death and Resurrection, in marriage, to his fidelity to the Church. As with the baptismal likeness to Christ, the likeness to his fidelity inscribed in the marriage bond could not be removed by any sin. "The marriage bond is dissolved only by the death of one of the partners."[4]

It took many centuries, however, for the Church to prohibit divorce absolutely. But, by the twelfth century, the prohibition against divorce was made absolute, as Augustine's doctrine of marriage's sacramentality won universal recognition. Peter Lombard included it in his list of the seven sacraments, and theologians worked out its theology. The consent of the couple, ratified by sexual intercourse, was seen to constitute the metaphysical bond, which was unbreakable since it was a sacramental sign of the equally unbreakable union of Christ and the Church. Henceforward in the West no marriage between Catholics could be dissolved unless it could be shown that there was some defect in the marriage contract itself.

This medieval view of marriage was rejected by both Luther and Cal-

4. *On the Good of Marriage*, 24. Quoted in Joseph Martos, *Doors to the Sacred* (Garden City, N.Y.: Doubleday, 1981), p. 481.

vin, who admitted divorce in certain restricted cases. They rejected the argument based on Ephesians 5:21–33 (the mainstay of the Catholic theology of marriage as a sacrament). According to both Reformers, the great mystery mentioned here does not refer to ordinary marriage but to the spiritual marriage between Christ and his Church. Moreover, Calvin added that one can justify calling a ceremony a sacrament only if it was clearly appointed by God to confirm a promise, but the New Testament indicated no such promise for the wedding ceremony.

The Council of Trent condemned these views and reiterated the doctrine of marriage as a sacrament and reaffirmed the Church's right to regulate it—including the right to grant dispensations affecting marriage laws and the right to annul unconsummated marriages, as well as to forbid remarriage. It also struck at the practice of secret marriages by declaring that thenceforth, for a valid Christian marriage, the couple had to exchange their vows in the presence of a priest and two witnesses.

Within the Catholic Church itself in the twentieth century a great debate raged as a number of progressive theologians began to challenge the traditional legalistic understanding of marriage. According to this view, marriage was essentially a contract for the procreation and education of children, while mutual support and growth in love were considered secondary. The progressives objected to this emphasis on the legal and biological aspects and argued for a more personalist and biblical perspective.

Their thinking had a great influence on Vatican II's doctrine of marriage as contained in *Gaudium et Spes* (the pastoral constitution on *The Church in the Modern World),* in which the distinction between the primary and secondary ends was dropped and great prominence was given to the importance of love. Marriage, it says, should be an intimate partnership of life and love—a free and mutual giving of self, experienced in tenderness and action. It should be a love directed and enriched by the redemptive power of Christ and the salvific action of the Church. As a sacrament, it fortifies and consecrates the couple for their duties to each other and to the children. In this document, marriage is no longer a contract but is called a covenant. It is also called a community of love and fidelity, and children are seen as the fruit of this love.

A new order of celebrating marriage was also issued by the Sacred Congregation of Rites after the Council. It permitted Mass to be said at weddings of Catholics marrying baptized non-Catholics. It also made some provision for marriage to be celebrated at home and permitted the regional conferences of bishops to prepare rites suitable for their people.


## DIVORCE?

The Council reaffirmed the constant teaching of the Catholic Church that a sacramental marriage could not be dissolved. But many Catholics nevertheless went ahead anyway and joined the increasing number of Americans who have divorced. In fact, the divorce rate among American Catholics is now almost as high as it is for other Americans—which in the past ten years has doubled for those above twenty-five and trebled for those under that age.

Why this acceleration of marital breakdown? Most observers would attribute it, above all, to the recent and tremendous change in the relationship of the sexes. Until relatively few years ago, most marriages were based on a patriarchal structure, in which the man was superior. The wife was expected to submit in most matters to the husband. There were exceptions, of course, but even where the wife was dominant, she held sway only within the home. Outside, the man reigned supreme. Moreover, there were many social and economic factors that might keep a woman from seeking divorce.

The movement for female equality, however, has made large strides in the past few decades, and many women today will no longer accept a subordinate role. They also have a much better chance of gaining financial independence by going to work. They are no longer willing to grant the privileges men have come to view as their right. In brief, their expectations no longer match their husbands', and they find communication in this regard very difficult.

Birth control also has given the woman much greater freedom, since she no longer need be constantly pregnant. Families generally are small, and women find it possible to combine domestic responsibilities with outside jobs.

This shift has been described as a change from the *patriarchal* to the *companionship* model of marriage. Its psychological ramifications are many. The companionship model of marriage requires the couple to relate at a deeper level of their personalities. This deeper intimacy makes greater demands, and it is often the frustration of these demands that causes marital breakdown. Because of a faulty upbringing, a spouse may come to a marriage burdened with potentially crippling emotional problems, which, perhaps subconsciously, he or she expects the partner to solve. One of the most common of these is the *anxious attachment* syndrome, caused by a parent or parents who either rejected or threatened to reject or desert the child. The child often learns to cope with the intense anxiety it experiences by developing defense mechanisms such as denial, projection, rationalization, repression and suppression, which later surface in a marriage. Such a one, who is anxiously attached to the spouse, has a great need to be loved but a low tolerance of criticism and will deny responsibility, or project blame onto the partner, or (for instance) displace bad feelings about the boss by taking them out on the spouse or children, or rationalize bad behavior and refuse to admit the consequences of actions or omissions.[5]

Since a greater amount of emotional maturity is demanded by marriage today, those who marry young run a much greater risk of ending in divorce. Statistics show that the rate of divorce is at least double for those who marry under twenty.

Studies of more specific causes of divorce have disclosed many factors that tend to move couples toward divorce: premarital pregnancy, poor housing and financial conditions, disparity in educational and religious backgrounds, lack of any religious commitment, unwillingness of the husband to share in household tasks, jealousy of the other's friends, feeling of being confined on the part of the wife who gives up her job for housekeeping and children, sexual maladjustment especially since people have come to expect more from sexual relations, etc.

Since Catholics are as prone to divorce as anyone else, this confronts the Church with an enormous problem. Since present discipline forbids divorced Catholics who remarry from receiving Communion, many of them simply accept the fact and leave the Church. However, an increasing number are finding a solution by getting their previous marriages annulled.

Before the Council, the conditions for an annulment were very stringent and well defined: basically either there had to be something defective about the consent given to the marriage (such as proof of coercion) or some sexual incapacity or some other well-defined canonical impediment. However, the new emphasis of the Council on marriage as a covenant and a partnership of love enabled canonists to discover other reasons for al-

5. Jack Dominian, *Marriage, Faith and Love* (New York: Crossroad, 1982), pp. 34–42.

lowing annulments. For example, psychological immaturity that prevented one or both of the partners from being able to make the kind of commitment needed for a true "partnership of love," as well as a spiritual immaturity which prevented the person from forming a true covenant marriage.

In view of the small number of cases adjudicated relative to the large number of Catholic divorces (estimated at 10 percent in 1971), it is obvious that the tribunals would soon be swamped if all Catholics who had probable grounds for annulment submitted their cases to the tribunals. For these and other reasons, numerous critics have called for the abolition of the tribunal system. For example, Lawrence Wrenn, a former *officialis* of the archdiocese of Hartford and chairperson of the Canon Law Society committee studying the tribunal system, concluded that the system was both meaningless and dysfunctional. He argued that the Church should change its teaching on indissolubility and allow remarriage when, in the judgment of the local parish, there are good reasons for doing so.

But can the Church change its ancient tradition that a true Christian marriage can never be dissolved? Many canonists and a number of theologians say yes: the Church should allow divorce and remarriage when the previous marriage is dead.

Some argue from history. The Church, they say, did not always regard the marriage bond as indissoluble, since it did allow remarriage of the divorced in certain—admittedly restricted—instances. Some suggest that the Church merely receive those remarried after divorce back to Communion without, however, recognizing the second marriage as sacramental, since it fails to signify what a Christian marriage should: the unremittingly faithful love of God and Christ for people.

Another argument would have the Church abandon its abstract Scholastic definition of marriage in favor of a strictly phenomenological one based on what marriage actually is today. Marriage, it is claimed, is not what it used to be when the Church's canonical regulations were devised. Today it is an agreement of two people to live and grow together in an interpersonal relationship of self-giving love. When this intention ceases, therefore, it is no longer a marriage and therefore can no longer be considered a sacrament.

One of the most widely approved suggestions was for the Church to institute a two-stage approach: The first would consist merely in the exchange of vows in the presence of a minister by those committed to an indissoluble union. The second stage would be reached only when the couple had navigated the rocks and shoals and had reached a truly deep level of commitment. At this point the Church would consecrate their marriage as now truly sacramental and therefore indissoluble.

A solution often used by some priests and even urged by such prominent theologians as Bernard Häring is the internal-forum approach. They receive a divorced and remarried person back to Communion on the grounds that even though he or she cannot get an official annulment of the previous marriage, there are nevertheless good grounds for challenging the validity of the previous marriage. Therefore the person has a right to Communion.

Similar to this is the recommendation of some theologians to respect the consciences of the divorced and remarried and admit them to Communion even when the first marriage was likely a valid one but is no longer recoverable. Charles Whelan, S.J., in a similar recommendation endorsed by *America,* noted that the Church could not bless the second marriage, since it did violate Christ's teaching on indissolubility, but when the second union offered solid grounds for being a stable union, the couple should be admitted to the sacraments.[6]

Charles Curran, who is not famous for mincing his words, comes right out and says the Church simply should change its teaching on the indissolubility of marriage. He claims that the natural-law arguments (basically that indissolubility is demanded for the good of the children, the good of the spouses and the good of society) no longer hold water. Neither, he says, does the argument that Scripture forbids divorce and remarriage, for both Matthew and Paul allowed exceptions. And, he says, we have to admit that some Fathers of the Church allowed divorce and remarriage, which in some places was accepted practice. So Curran concludes that we can interpret Jesus' words in this case, as we do with other parts of the Sermon on the Mount, as a radical ideal which it is not always possible for sinful humans to attain.

What about the argument that marriage is supposed to be a sign of God's loving fidelity to his people and therefore must be a permanent commitment, since God's fidelity is permanent? Curran answers that marriage will always be an imperfect sign. Surely a marital union that is permanent but not really loving is not adequate. There are many ways in which a marriage can fall short of being an adequate symbol of God's love for his people. A breach of permanence is only one of them. A second

6. Quoted in Richard McCormick, *Notes on Moral Theology, 1965 Through 1980* (Washington, D.C.. University Press of America, Inc., 1981), p. 551.

marriage, on the other hand, could be in some ways a sign . . . of God's mercy and forgiveness.

However, in spite of all the voices calling for the Church to relinquish its adamant stand on indissolubility, observers do not see any change forthcoming in the near future. They remember Pope John Paul II's ringing affirmation of official teaching in his sermon on the Mall, in Washington, D.C., in 1979: "When the institution of marriage," he declared, "is abandoned to human selfishness or reduced to a temporary, conditional arrangement that can easily be terminated, we will stand up and affirm the indissolubility of the marriage bond."[7]

In the synod of 1980, the bishops discussed family life today. At its conclusion they voted on a number of propositions, which they submitted to the Holy Father. In one proposition, by a vote of 200 to 2 they affirmed the traditional doctrine of the indissolubility of a consummated sacramental marriage, and by a vote of 190 to 10 they refused to allow those Catholics who are divorced and remarried to receive Communion. However, they urged the Catholic community to make every effort to support those divorced and remarried and encourage them to attend Mass and share in the life of the Church so they don't feel separated from the Church. They also called for a new and more profound study of the whole question of indissolubility in order to make more visible the pastoral solicitude of the Church.

7. *Origins* (Washington, D.C.: National Catholic Documentary Service, Vol. 9 (October 18, 1979), p. 280.

# 22

# Holy Orders:
# The Meaning of Ministry Today

One of the most dramatic changes in the post-Vatican II Church involved its understanding of ministry. Until the Council, ministry was almost exclusively the province of the clergy, with the laity largely reduced to a passive role.

The Second Vatican Council did not disavow the previous theology of ministry. It continued to reserve the term "ministry" for bishops, priests and deacons. It reiterated the traditional teaching that priests are set apart by ordination, which marks them with a special character, "and are so configured to Christ the Priest that they can act in the person of Christ the Head."[1] They share in a special way in the mission of the bishops, the successors of the apostles, and to this extent share "in the authority by which Christ Himself builds up, sanctifies, and rules His Body."[2] Their primary duty is the proclamation of the Gospel of God to all. They are to preside over the Eucharist, which itself is "the source and apex of the whole work of preaching the Gospel," as "the ministers of Him who in the liturgy continually exercises His priestly office on our behalf by the action of His Spirit."[3] Bound together hierarchically with the bishop, they are to administer all the sacraments. Finally they must carry out the office of pastor by attending to the manifold duties involved in building up a genuine Christian community. In this role they must keep in mind the

1. *Decree on the Ministry and Life of Priests,* 2.
2. Ibid., 2.
3. Ibid., 5

goal, which is to educate all to Christian maturity. In meeting this responsibility, they are to consider the special needs of each group: the married,
the single, parents, youth and especially the poor.

But, at the same time, the Council gave an impetus to a broader understanding of ministry by exhorting the priest to form communities that
would be open in love and action to the wider community beyond the
Church, to build up communities made up of men and women educated
to Christian maturity, ready to recognize their gifts and employ them for
the good of the Church and the good of mankind. Moreover, the decree
struck a blow at the concept of a priestly caste system by placing the priest
in the Church as a brother among brothers called to "friendly and fraternal dealings with . . . other men."[4]

The general thrust indeed of the Council was away from the authoritarian clerical model, toward a participatory model of the Church. Thus one
of its most significant documents, *Lumen Gentium*, the constitution on
the nature of the Church, shifted the emphasis from the Church as a
pyramidal structure to the Church as the whole people of God, and laid
stress on the fundamental equality of all as regards basic vocation, dignity,
and commitment. Most important in this regard was its emphasis on the
common priesthood of the faithful, which all share by reason of baptism.

The Council thus laid the groundwork for a renewed understanding of
ministry in the Catholic Church. While it continued to reserve the word
"ministry" for clergy, it recognized the active part the laity should have in
the mission of the Church and in service to the community. Moreover,
Paul VI in his 1973 reform documents *Ministeria quaedam* and *Ad pas-
cendum* revived the ancient ministries of lector and acolyte as permanent
ministries of lay people, which opened the door to further development of
lay ministries.

The changes in the liturgy also had quite an effect on the image of
ministry. The new position given to the priest, the use of the people's
language, and the presence of other "ministers" in the sanctuary profoundly altered the Catholic's view of the priest. Consider his new position, for instance. Formerly, he mounted steps to the altar and, standing
with his back to the people, acted visibly as a mediator between an awesome deity and a prostrate people. Now he faced the people from behind a
"table" and invited them to join with him in prayer. The relationship no
longer emphasized the authority of the priest and the passivity of the lay

4. Ibid., 17.

person, but projected the image of a leader who encourages the people to engage in dialogue with God and with each other.

This impression was strengthened by the use of the vernacular. Previously the use of a special language set the priest apart and made the Scriptures seem remote in time and cut off from dialogue. God had spoken once upon a time and everything was settled. But when Scripture is heard in a fresh, contemporary idiom, it encourages people to understand the liturgy as a continuing conversation with God and to regard the priest as one who listens with them, rather than as one who delivers oracles from on high. The presence of other ministers around him in the sanctuary indicates that his ministry is no longer an exclusive one.

For these and no doubt other reasons, a tremendous shift has occurred in the Catholic understanding of ministry. Fr. John Coleman, S.J., calls it a "paradigm shift" in a recent article, in which he analyzes this shift from the standpoint of a sociologist. He points out how the term ministry has become a catch phrase among Catholic professionals so that almost everybody in the Church has or does a "ministry": there are ministries to the divorced, to gays, social ministries of advocacy, liturgical planning ministries, those to the sick and dying, etc. For Coleman this extension of the term ministry in an undefined and largely unreflective way denotes a profound change in lay-clergy relationships. "Both ordained and nonordained share ministry. The laity, far from being a residual category, now provide the generic term, ministry, for which the ordained are a mere subspecies."[5]

The language shift indicates that baptism is now seen as the basis of all the sacraments, including ordination, so that ordination must be understood in terms of baptism, rather than vice versa. A different theology of charisms is also presupposed by this new use of the term ministry. It sees the various gifts of the Spirit as freely distributed within the community, subject only to the supervision of those ordained. Office, in fact, is now viewed as subordinate, in a sense, to charism, for the priest does not create or distribute the gifts.

Another change implied by this new terminology is the emphasis it places on skills, accountability and competence. Being ordained formerly meant the achievement of instant status: people paid respect to the collar itself, with not too much scrutiny of its wearer. But now the minister, whether ordained or not, will be judged by the quality of his or her perfor-

5 "The Future of Ministry," *America*, March 28, 1981, p. 244.

mance and the amount of specialized training and experience he or she brings to his or her task.

Finally the new terminology implies a changed model of authority in the Church: a collegial, nonmonarchical structure in tension with an existing hierarchical and pyramidal one. "To speak of ministry is to evoke this whole gestalt of the priority of baptism, charism, competence and collegiality over ordination, office, status and hierarchy."[6]

No doubt, as Coleman points out, the explosion of ministries in the Church is also related to the simple fact that there simply aren't enough priests to do the job. This is a worldwide phenomenon. The Catholic clergy are still resigning in large numbers, and there is no possibility of replacing them, given the present decline in the numbers of seminarians. In country after country, as a result, the average age of the clergy has increased dramatically; in French Canada, for instance, from forty-five to fifty-four within a decade.

Coleman quotes a Dutch study that shows that on an index on which 100 would represent complete replacement by ordinations for every 100 losses due to death or resignation, the Netherlands registered 8, Belgium 15, Germany 34, France 17, Italy 50, Ireland 45, Spain 35, and Portugal 10. The same is more or less true of seminarians, who in almost every country in Europe and North America have decreased by half over the past decade.[7]

As to the United States, researchers indicate that the Catholic Church will have 50 percent fewer active clergymen by the end of the century than it has today. In 1972, there were some 22,000 seminarians, while in 1982 there were some 11,000. According to the Official Catholic Directory, there are now 58,085 religious and diocesan priests in the United States, and researchers predict there will be fewer than 25,000 by the end of this century. This decline comes at a time when the Catholic population of the United States is increasing. The 1984 Official Catholic Directory counted 51,207,579 Catholics—up 57,737 from the previous year.

The shortage of clergy is even more acute in the third-world mission countries, where roughly 50 percent of all parishes and missions lack a resident priest.

It is in this context, then, that we must view the emergence of a new understanding of ministry. Under the pressure of a shortage of priests,

6. Ibid., p. 245.
7. Ibid., pp. 246–47.

there has been a tremendous growth of new, nonordained ministries, such as catechists in Africa and leaders of base communities in Latin America. History, it seems, is forcing the Church to break away from the clerical caste mentality, with its stranglehold on ministry, in favor of a theology that looks to the natural leaders of the community to take up forms of ministry previously reserved to the ordained, celibate, male clergy.

## MINISTRY IN THE EARLY CHURCH

Recent Catholic scholarship has also contributed to the changing view of ministry. In tracing the two-thousand-year history of the ministry, scholars such as Raymond Brown, Bernard Cooke and Edward Schillebeeckx have helped to modify the simple picture so often given of the priesthood: Jesus, the catechisms taught, ordained the apostles priests at the Last Supper, and they in turn went out and eventually ordained others to succeed them, and so the chain of ordination has continued unbroken down to our time.

The trouble with this simple picture is that it is based on a rather shaky assumption: that the office of priesthood has continued basically unchanged since the time of the apostles. Actually the weight of evidence favors the view that the earliest Christian communities didn't know of an office of priesthood as such, but only various types of ministries which were only later consolidated into the office of priest. Moreover, while the Jerusalem community favored the office of presbyter or elder, the Pauline communities, according to many scholars, were led by those whose role did not come from appointment to an office but was due to spontaneous recognition of their charisms by the community.

So we really can't say who at first had the right to celebrate the Eucharist and forgive sins. The New Testament sets down no norms. In fact, as Edward Kilmartin, S.J., says, "It is highly probable that the community reckoned itself the principal celebrant and considered that the leader's function was to pronounce the Eucharistic prayers in the name of all. Thereby in principle many Christians would qualify on the basis of their Christian lives and ability to serve in this capacity."[8] This would explain such passages as one in the *Didache* (10,7) (a "catechism" dating from

8. "Eucharist in Recent Literature," *Theological Studies* 32, (March 1971), p. 270.

around A.D. 100) that tells how prophets were allowed to preside at the Eucharist.

The development of the office of the priesthood is, in fact, a very complex one. There is certainly no reason for doubting that Jesus chose the Twelve, but, as Raymond Brown points out, Jesus himself said that his purpose in doing so was that they might sit on (twelve) thrones judging the twelve tribes of Israel.[9] The symbolism is quite obvious: the renewed Israel called together by Jesus would begin with twelve men, just as the original Israel began with the twelve sons of Jacob/Israel.

As to the role of the Twelve after the Resurrection, we have little information. There is no evidence that any of them ever acted as heads of local churches (in a role analogous to our bishop). There are only passages in the New Testament in which they are shown exercising a collective policy-making authority, having been given, it seems, the power to bind and loose by Jesus himself. The first local church administrators mentioned in the New Testament are not the Twelve, but the seven Hellenist supervisors, listed in Acts 6:5, who at the behest of Peter are designated by the community and who not only supervised but also preached and taught, as we see in the case of Stephen, one of their number.[10]

The counterpart of the Hellenists was the other Jewish Christian group at Jerusalem, the Hebrews, who were designated the "presbyters," an office likely borrowed from the Jewish synagogue. James is singled out as the leading presbyter, who exercised supervision at Jerusalem. A common misconception has James succeeding Peter as head of the Church at Jerusalem, but this is based on the erroneous idea that Peter was ever the local leader of the church in Jerusalem. For, as Brown concludes, "In the mid-30s . . . it would appear that the need was recognized for local supervision of the Hebrew and Hellenist communities in Jerusalem and was met in two different ways, respectively, by James and by the seven Hellenist authorities . . . The urging of the common assembly by the Twelve which led to this development is the closest the Twelve ever come in the NT to appointing local church leaders."[11]

Nor did the apostle Paul, who founded many churches and exercised definite supervision over them ever take on the role of local church leader. Who, then, were the leaders of his communities? As Paul indicates, lead-

9. *"Episkope* and *Episkopos:* The New Testament Evidence," *Theological Studies* 41 (June 1980), pp. 323–24.
10. Acts 7.
11. Brown, op. cit., pp. 327–28.

ing the community is one of the charismatic gifts given to the members. According to Edward Schillebeeckx, whose interpretation we are mainly following here, such a gift still had no significance as *the ministry;* "it is one of the many services which all the members of the community owe to each other . . . each person cannot do everything."[12]

In fact, for Paul, prophesying and teaching were the gifts *par excellence.* The prophets and teachers, as Schillebeeckx says, seem to have been incipient leaders, but leading the community as a ministry did not yet have its full significance. Thus in the house communities, the host and his wife would play a leading role, as in the case of Philemon and his wife, Apphia.[13] Paul sometimes refers to these community leaders as "those who are over you," but it is impossible to describe precisely what these "ministers" do in their service to the community.[14]

As Philippians shows, Paul confided special authority to certain of his fellow workers—notably Timothy and Titus, whom he set over the local leaders. He sends Timothy to Philippi as "his successor" with the same authority he has. This shows a certain concern on his part for what will later be called "apostolic succession." "However, the basis of this succession is 'the community of faith' between Paul and Timothy."[15]

The question of local church leadership becomes most prominent in the last third of the century, after the death of the great apostles Peter, Paul and James, in the 60s. As we gather from the so-called Pastoral Epistles (Titus and 1 and 2 Timothy) it is a time when certain companions of Paul claim authority over the local churches in view of their special relation to Paul. Like Paul, these apostolic delegates *never acted as local church leaders,* but supervised a whole group of churches—a function that disappeared with their disappearance. (There could be no apostolic succession in this sense.)

At this point we now find local church leaders holding established offices. Leadership of the community depends primarily on official designation, rather than on the possession of a charism. But we know little about how the selection of these leaders occurred. The *Didache* indicates that the community itself could choose their leaders.[16] "There is nothing in the New Testament literature about a regular process of ordination. (And

12. *Ministry: Leadership in the Community of Jesus Christ* (New York: Crossroad, 1981), p. 9.
13. Ibid., p. 10.
14. Ibid.
15. Ibid., p. 11.
16. Raymond Brown, op. cit., p. 332.

enced in the life-style of Jesus himself. The community is bound to this apostolic norm of "discipleship of Jesus," which has to be actualized again and again in new historical circumstances. *Diakonia*—such service as concern for oppressed and suffering humanity—is one of the chief apostolic characteristics of the community of God.[20]

4. As Schillebeeckx also points out, the concept of the ministry just enunciated is clearly contained in canon 6 of the Council of Chalcedon (A.D. 451). There it was laid down emphatically that no one could be ordained in the Church unless he was called for service to a particular community. All absolute ordinations, that is, where the candidate was not asked by a particular community to be its leader, were declared null and void. This ecclesial concept of the ministry was clear and definite and remained so until medieval times.[21]

This essential connection between the ministry and leadership of the community is also brought out most clearly in the accounts of ordination in the early Church that we find in the *Apostolic Tradition*, of Hippolytus, and other texts of the time. The whole community, with its clergy, as is shown in this account, chooses its bishop. The initiative rests with the community, since the community of necessity must have a leader and therefore it has the right to choose one. And as the primary carrier of apostolicity, it interrogates the candidate to make sure of his fidelity to the apostolic faith. Then hands are laid on him by fellow bishops to indicate that his office is a gift of the Holy Spirit. Neighboring bishops are usually chosen for this role to bring out the bond between the individual communities of God and to show their willingness to engage in mutual criticism of each other's faith. The power of the Spirit is called down upon the candidate as the one whom the community has here and now chosen to be its leader.

"In this liturgy the decisive element is the gift of the power of the Spirit . . . with which Jesus himself was filled and with which he fills the church."[22] In view of its early history, therefore, Schillebeeckx holds, the so-called power of ordination and its character consists simply in appointment to lead a particular community, together with the gift of the Spirit.

Another point of interest, he maintains, is that the laying on of hands was regarded as secondary. The essential nucleus of ordination was being recognized as the leader of a particular Church community.

20. Ibid., pp. 29–37.
21. Ibid., pp. 38–48.
22. Ibid., p. 45.

5. How, then, did the medieval and Tridentine theology of the priest-hood develop—remote, as it seems to be, from Chalcedon's, which stressed the essential link between the community's leader and the community celebrating the Eucharist? Schillebeeckx traces it to a number of nontheological factors in medieval history, such as the feudal practice of the secular lords who erected churches that often did not serve actual living communities but only served as status symbols. Even more important was the radical reinterpretation of canon 6 of the Council of Chalcedon, which forbade ordinations of priests unless they were called to lead a particular community. The Third Lateran Council (1179) instead allowed priests to be ordained as long as they were assured of a proper living, whether or not they were claimed by a particular community. Another factor was the impact of the renaissance of Roman law, which detached the power of leadership from the concept of "territoriality." Also was the fact that "at a time when virtually everyone was baptized, the boundary between 'the Spirit of Christ and the spirit of the world' came to lie with the clergy. As a result the priesthood was seen more as 'a personal state of life,' a *'status,'* than as a service to the community; it was personalized and privatized. In particular, the new conceptions of law *(jus),* and thus jurisdiction, brought about a division between the power of ordination and the power of jurisdiction . . . one of the most fundamental factors which marks off the second Christian millennium from the first . . . For although the ordained man might not be assigned a Christian community, that is, legally speaking, had no *potestas jurisdictionis,* by virtue of *ordinatio* he had all priestly power in his own person."[23]

So henceforth, in contrast with the ancient Church, a priest is primarily ordained to celebrate the Eucharist, rather than to be the leader of the community. This medieval view is a narrow, legalistic version of the theology of the ancient Church, which chose the minister primarily to build up the community; he would then, obviously, be the one to preside at the Eucharist.

The Council of Trent then sanctioned this medieval view in its canons, which stressed the priest's cultic activity and said nothing about the tasks of community building by preaching and teaching. Concentration on the cultic aspects of the priesthood to the detriment of the pastoral also helped to magnify the importance of celibacy. Since priesthood is essentially defined by relation to the cult, the priest is thereby set apart from

23. Ibid., pp. 52–58.

the people, and priestly celibacy is seen as the expression of this essential separation.


## HAS SCHILLEBEECKX PROVED HIS CASE?

Considering the fact that Schillebeeckx is treating an extremely sensitive question—one with tremendous practical implications for the future of the Catholic priesthood—it is not surprising that his study has been scrutinized with exceeding care by other scholars and certainly by Rome.

The debate promises to be long-drawn-out, for it involves nothing less than reinterpretation for Catholics of virtually the whole New Testament and the whole history of the Church.

Some of the main objections posed to Schillebeeckx's thesis:

1. A number of critics reject his view of the "Twelve" as chosen by Jesus only to symbolize a new beginning for Israel. These scholars hold that the Twelve were endowed with real authority by Jesus, which they exercised in the primitive community. Hence they say Schillebeeckx is wrong in his definition of apostolicity as "awareness of the community that it is carrying on the cause of Christ," rather than seeing it as a concrete link with persons who had received a mandate from Christ.

2. His interpretation of the Johannine and Matthean communities as originally charismatic ones without a presbyteral order is considered subjective and tendentious.

3. Some Catholic scholars reject his interpretation of Acts 14:23 and 20:17–35—texts that speak of Paul and Barnabas appointing elders and admonishing them to carry out their office faithfully. As we have seen, Schillebeeckx sees these texts as merely indicating that a few early communities outside of Jerusalem accepted the presbyteral order—not that all the early communities were so structured.

4. Schillebeeckx interpreted canon 6 of the Council of Chalcedon to mean, "Only someone who has been called by a particular community [the people and its leaders] to be its pastor and leader authentically receives *ordinatio*," so that for him the essence of *ordinatio* is not the laying on of hands but "the calling and mandate of the sending of someone by a particular Christian community (the people and its leaders)."[24] Therefore, he claims ministry should be defined essentially in ecclesial terms and not

24. *Ministry*, p. 39.

as an ontological qualification of the person of the minister. But his critics maintain that the canon does not say that the candidate must be *called by* a particular community, but only that the person must be ordained *for service* to a particular community.

5. Against Schillebeeckx's contention that the premedieval church knew nothing of an indelible priestly character conferred by ordination, his critics cite evidence from those centuries that supposedly shows that there was some such idea. For example, the refusal to reordain a deposed minister when he was reinstated in his ministry. Obviously, therefore, the man when deposed had not simply become another layman—what then remained from his ordination?

6. Yves Congar addressed several questions to Schillebeeckx: "Do you not excessively diminish the role and value of the imposition of hands? Do you not replace ordination by the mandate and reception of the community? Can one define the priesthood by 'leadership' recognized or received? And where then is the sacrament—act of God—completing the human action?"[25]

7. Finally his view that all the people concelebrated with the president of the assembly has been challenged. Some evidence from the fourth century is given by his critics to show that only those ordained were regarded as actually "offering" the eucharistic sacrifice.

## CELIBACY TODAY?

The question of celibacy has come to the fore today for many reasons. Historical and theological studies have called into question some of the assumptions on which the discipline is based, while the great numbers of priests resigning on account of celibacy has also raised questions about its usefulness.

The discipline of clerical celibacy, we must recall, has existed in the Roman Church for more than fifteen hundred years. Its origins are traceable to certain Roman popes of the fourth and fifth centuries who imposed this discipline on the clergy. There is much debate about the reasons why they wanted to make celibacy obligatory for priests. Some argue that the main motive was ritual purity—which involved the notion that sexual intercourse rendered a person unworthy of approaching the altar.

25. "Bulletin d'ecclésiologie," *Revue des sciences philosophiques et religieuses* 66 (Janvier 1982), pp. 101–4.

This concept is clearly stated in one of the first examples of papal legislation on the matter, a text of Pope Siricius: "If intercourse is a defilement, it goes without saying that a priest must remain ready to perform his heavenly duty, so that he does not find himself unworthy when he must plead for the sins of others . . ."[26]

There is no doubt that a number of other factors contributed to the decision to impose celibacy on the clergy in spite of the fact that most of them were already married. There were, for instance, ascetical trends that exalted virginity and disparaged sexuality and marriage—a trend particularly evident in the success of the monastic movement, which by the fourth century was very widespread; also, there was the increasing tendency to emphasize the cultic and ritualistic aspects of the priestly ministry at the expense of the pastoral tasks such as preaching—a sacralization of the ministry that tended to encourage a separation of clergy from people and their adoption of celibacy as part of a more demanding lifestyle which would prove their "holiness"; there was also the argument that a celibate would have more liberty to devote himself undistractedly to God; finally there was also the prevailing Neo-Platonic philosophy, which was dualistic in seeing the body and its functions as somehow the enemy of the higher, or spiritual, side of man and sexual intercourse as therefore unworthy.

It is remarkable that the Church has ever since continued to keep this law on its books, although at times it has been flagrantly disregarded in practice. After each period of decline, however, there has always come a period of renewal of the discipline. One of these was the reform pushed by Pope Gregory VII (d. 1085) that culminated in the decree of the Second Lateran Council (1139) that nullified any marriage attempted by a cleric.

As one may imagine, over its long span of history the meaningfulness of this discipline has often been called into question. And until our own day the main arguments given in its defense have remained much the same as first enunciated in the fourth century, namely, the superiority of a life of continence to marriage, and the need for a priest to maintain ritual purity. This is true even of the papal statements of the twentieth century.

It is only with the Second Vatican Council that we notice a definite shift in perspective. As one can see by reading not only its statement on the priesthood but also the reports of the Theological Commission, the traditional arguments based on ritual purity and the superiority of virginity

26. Quoted by J. Komonchak, "Celibacy and Tradition," *Chicago Studies* 20 (Spring 1981), pp. 7–8.

were abandoned. Celibacy is now to be valued because it helps the priest devote himself more readily to the service of God and man and, as stated in *Lumen Gentium (On the Church)*, it is a stimulus to charity and a special source of spiritual fruitfulness in the world.[27]

In no areas of Church life was the impact of the Second Vatican Council more devastating than in its effect on the clergy. As the full implications of the *aggiornamento* began to sink in, the clergy began to show how little prepared they were either by training or experience to cope with the multitude of new options and ideas that were suddenly presented by the Council. Many of them lost their bearings and felt let down by the bishops. Some carried the spirit of freedom and openness all the way and began to question everything previously held sacred. Naturally celibacy came under severe challenge, and many priests found they could no longer put up with it. They left the priesthood in great numbers, confronting the leaders of the Church with a crisis of unparalleled proportions.

Many voices were raised calling for an end to obligatory celibacy. Pope Paul VI responded with an encyclical on priestly celibacy, which failed to quiet the protest. It was then that the bishops gathered at the second "ordinary synod," of October 1971, to deal with the "identity crisis" of the priests.

As Edward Schillebeeckx shows in his study of the synod, one of the main concerns that surfaced at the synod was the need many bishops felt —almost obsessively—for an exact definition of the "essential difference" (Vatican II) between the universal priesthood and the official priesthood. (The New Testament itself seems little concerned with drawing any clear dividing lines, according to Schillebeeckx.)

A clear division of opinion soon showed itself at the synod. In fact, polarization is a more accurate term. The problem, it seems, was that it proved impossible to give universal, uniform answers to problems that needed to be handled variously in the various local churches.

One thing was soon clear: the majority of the bishops were determined to uphold the traditional discipline. Even the ordination of married men was discountenanced, for fear of encouraging those seeking to do away with the discipline altogether. There was also the feeling that it would be bad to make such a radical change at a time when everything was already

27. *Dogmatic Constitution on the Church*, 42.

so unsettled in the Church. And many still believed that obligatory celibacy was necessary to safeguard the total availability of the priest.

It was quite obvious that most of the bishops took a very *a priori* position against any change, and some made statements that betrayed a curious disregard of the Protestant experience with married ministers. The fact that no Protestant ministers were invited to give testimony is itself indicative of the closed mentality that characterized the synod. One African bishop, who was irked by the prevailing fear of taking risks, said, "God's act of creation was also full of risks." And, he added, if they couldn't muster the courage to take risks, they should "give up celebrating the eucharist and baptizing, and tomorrow I will go and plant cabbages."[28]

Schillebeeckx sees the root cause of the inability of the bishops to deal realistically with the problem of celibacy in a mistaken interpretation of the Tridentine doctrine of **character**. The special, indelible character conferred on the priest at ordination is taken to mean that the priest is set apart from the community in a separate ontological state, as it were. His power to perform the Eucharist is seen as a kind of personal possession and constitutes the veritable **raison d'être** of his priesthood. Ordination confers on him a power he can exercise on his own even if the whole of the community is absent. So, to "be a priest" is to be a "cultic priest," one set apart from the people. Celibacy in this context appears as almost a logical necessity, given the heritage of negative views of sexuality derived from the ancient Church. It also explains the typical spirituality recommended to the priest before the Council, which held that as a mediator between God and the believers, he was defined by his relationship with the altar and should avoid too much fraternizing with the laity.

Schillebeeckx, on the other hand, in accordance with his views on the evolution of the ministry presented in this chapter, argues that this interpretation of ordination and character does not square with the actual history of the first thousand years of the Church, which saw the priesthood as one ministry among the many that make up the totality of ministries that constitute the Church. In this light, the statement of *Lumen Gentium* that the ordained priesthood is "essentially different" from the priesthood of the believing people of God, he would interpret as "the confirmation of a specific and indeed sacramental function and not as a state."[29] When presiding at the Eucharist, the priest acts as representa-

28. Edward Schillebeeckx, *Ministry*, pp., 122–23.
29. Ibid., p. 70.

tive of the whole Church in carrying out the priestly vocation of offering praise and thanksgiving to God. This does not mean that his ministry is merely an extension of the common priesthood, but that it belongs "to another realm of the gifts of the Spirit," in the words of the Anglican–Roman Catholic International Commission, which took basically the same position as Schillebeeckx on the nature of the ministerial priesthood.

The Anglican–Roman Catholic statement also called the ordained minister the "focus of leadership and unity, responsible for 'oversight' especially in keeping faithful to the apostolic faith and watching over its transmission to the Church of tomorrow."

Schillebeeckx himself thinks there are basically two arguments for abolishing the law of celibacy: First, it would mean that those ministers who chose to be celibate would be doing so in complete freedom—thus enhancing the value of celibacy as a special gift of the Holy Spirit. Second, every Christian community has a right to have presidents and to celebrate the Eucharist. But a growing number of them have been deprived of this right due to the shortage of ordained ministers. And it now appears certain that this shortage will become increasingly severe unless the law of celibacy is abrogated.

Pope Paul VI, in his encyclical on priestly celibacy, offered a number of reasons for maintaining the discipline. It conforms the priest more closely to Christ, who himself was celibate. It excites him to greater love of Christ, since he can thereby dedicate himself unselfishly to all the children of God. And it anticipates God's coming Kingdom, when love will triumph over all the limits of the flesh.

But in spite of the arguments in its favor, it is interesting that priests themselves—at least a majority of them in the United States—do not favor obligatory celibacy. Polls consistently show that a high percentage of priests are in favor of making celibacy a matter of personal choice. A majority of the laity, in the United States at least, hold the same opinion.

Many priests base their negative attitude toward obligatory celibacy on their actual experience. They simply do not feel that celibacy helps them love God or people more. And they find the loneliness a terrible trial.

Another telling argument against obligatory celibacy is the finding of a study commissioned by the American bishops that 66 percent of priests were psychologically underdeveloped, not having achieved a level of growth appropriate for their age. According to the study, celibacy acted as a hindrance to their full development, inasmuch as it prevented them from achieving any real intimacy with another human being.

## ORDINATION OF WOMEN?

Many see a close connection between the law of celibacy and the exclusion of women from the priesthood, the chief factor in each case being the previously mentioned ontological and sacerdotalist conception of the ministry, which is quite easily associated with feminine and sexual taboos.

Like the question of celibacy, the question of the ordination of women is a most critical one. Dire predictions have been made about the consequences if the Church continues its present exclusion of women from the priesthood. A "staggering" exodus of women will soon occur, according to Margaret Ellen Traxler, a founder of NCAN (National Coalition of American Nuns) unless there is a change.

The Vatican attempted to close debate on the topic by its declaration of October 15, 1976, reiterating its opposition to the ordination of women mainly on the grounds that in order to adequately represent Christ at the Eucharist the priest must be male. The maleness of Christ was not accidental, it insists, but essential to the profoundly symbolic nuptial language of Scripture, which describes God's people as the spouse of God, the divine bridegroom. Only a male priest therefore could fittingly symbolize Christ as the bridegroom come to possess in spiritual communion his bride, the Church.

Instead, however, the declaration intensified the debate, and the number of Catholics favoring the ordination of women increased from 36 percent in 1977 to 40 percent by 1979, according to a Gallup poll. It seems likely that the number in favor will continue to grow in spite of John Paul II's stand against changing the present policy.

## NEW FORMS OF COMMUNITY

Many Christian communities already lack a priest and have to resort to various makeshift arrangements in carrying out their worship. In this context, the question is frequently raised whether in the absence of a priest other recognized leaders of the community might preside at the Eucharist. Schillebeeckx would allow this, provided such leaders have received "the *ordinatio* of the church, specifically in a liturgical celebration by the community which accepts it with the laying-on of hands by leadership teams from its own and neighboring communities."[30] But he is opposed to the view that "any believer at all can preside at the eucharist even when leaders of the community ('priests') are present."[31] Such a practice, he maintains, would be in violation of the total tradition of the Church as found in the New Testament, as well as in the ancient, medieval and post-Tridentine period. But the Vatican soon made clear its rejection of Schillebeeckx's view.

Schillebeeckx, however, points out the theological conundrum now evident in the fact that in many communities that lack priests there are de facto leaders, male and female, who perform many tasks of pastoral ministry but are not allowed to preside at the Eucharist.

In many areas where priests were either lacking or unable to provide the kind of leadership sought by dynamic and progressive lay people, small groups of Catholics came together to pray and worship and sometimes to celebrate the Eucharist—if a priest could be found—in so-called underground or floating parishes. These experiments were regularized in some dioceses, where the bishops encouraged the formation of small groups within each parish who would meet regularly to pray and share Scripture insights. This happened, for instance, in the diocese of Newark, New Jersey, where the program was called RENEW and reached some 80 percent of the diocese's 252 parishes by 1979. Its success has encouraged other dioceses to try the same approach.

The movement toward alternative Catholic communities has been especially successful in Latin America, where Brazil alone already counts some forty thousand. While these small groups differ widely from one another, some being in continuity with the parish structure, while others are independent and even in conflict with it, there is no doubt that they represent a significant development, especially when we realize that change in the Church has often come from such grass-roots experiments.

One of the basic questions they raise is why so many local parishes are not able any longer to satisfy the spiritual needs of their members. Apart from the circumstances in which there simply are not enough priests to go around, we find much truth in Andrew Greeley's view that the answer is

30. Ibid., p. 139.
31. Ibid.

twofold: lack of effective pastoral leadership and lack of any theological vision of what a parish should be.[32]

Greeley insists that a parish exists to actualize the meaning of the Kingdom of God in today's urban setting by inspiring people to reflect on their experience in the light of their religious tradition, confronting current problems with a sense of the creative possibilities latent in the Gospel. One of the main problems, as he sees it, is that the pastor is still captive to a past ideology whereby he saw himself mainly as a guardian of the faith. Our slumbering parishes could come alive if the pastor could only realize the potential a parish has for dealing with the major problems facing people today: the devastating effects of constant change, the rootlessness of urban existence, the assault on human values by unbridled technocracy, and the need to integrate the vast amount of facts poured out on us by the sciences!

The model of authority, however, still current in many parishes, is the order-giving one (to use Greeley's term), even though it is proving less and less effective. In today's parish, the truly effective leader is the one who knows how to raise the right questions, challenge people to respond to them, and provide the kind of inspiration that leads them in a Christian direction.

How far the Church can and will move in the direction of greater democracy in its decision-making process is a crucial question. There can be little doubt that much revision of structures is still necessary if the Church is to remain credible to intelligent Catholics. Historical studies have made it clear that Church order from the very beginning has been an evolving thing and that one should not dogmatize very readily about which features of the present Church order are divinely ordained and which are relative and therefore changeable. Legitimate questions are being raised, such as why people should not elect their bishops and pastors (as was the practice in the early centuries of the Church) and why we should not have fixed terms of office for the bishop and even for the pope. However, even some more liberal theologians think that complete democratization of the Church is not possible if, as our theology holds, officials receive their power from Christ himself. But, at the same time, they note that an effective exercise of power has to involve the free assent of the members of the Church. The unwillingness of Catholics any longer to render simple obedience to Church authority was most tellingly demon-

32. Andrew M. Greeley, *Parish, Priest and People* (Chicago: Thomas More Press, 1981), pp. 100–35.

strated by their reaction to *Humanae Vitae*. If a date must be chosen to mark the end of the medieval authoritarian model of Church authority, it surely has to be the day that encyclical appeared: July 30, 1968.

Theologians may opine about what people expect from their ministers, but what do people really want? Some interesting answers to this question are found in a study, *Ministry in America*, which is a report based on an in-depth survey of forty-seven denominations in the United States and Canada, published in 1980. The study shows that what Catholics and most Protestants value in their clergy is an open, affirming and flexible style. Just as important for Catholics—though not, interestingly enough, for Protestants—is an appreciation of the great tradition of the Church, a point that might suggest many Catholics feel the clergy are presently too willing to throw away some cherished elements of the Church's liturgy and teaching. As can be discerned by the rankings they gave to the various functions of the ministry, it is clear that Catholics still are not very concerned about sharing authority with the pastor: in contrast with Protestants, Catholics gave a low rating to the need "to share congregational leadership." One significant change in Catholic expectations of their priests is evident in the much higher rating given to "competent preaching," as opposed to "sacramental ministry." It confirms what daily experience shows: that Catholics are now much more concerned with the quality of the homily than formerly. Finally, in spite of the efforts of Church leaders to awaken the Catholic social conscience, this aspect of the ministry (described in such terms as "support of unpopular causes, active concern for the oppressed, interest in new ideas and aggressive political leadership") is near the bottom of the list of what Catholics want from their priests.[33]

33. D. Schuller, M. Strommen and M. Brekke, eds., *Ministry in America* (San Francisco: Harper & Row, 1980), pp. 467–87.

# V

---

## The Christian Way of Life

# 23

## Morality Today

The task of moral theology is sometimes defined as providing the answers to the question "What ought I to do?" But, as James Gustafson points out, this is really the wrong question. "You cannot know what you ought to do, or can do, until you acknowledge what has been done for you and for the world. You must turn to Him who is the source, power, and goal of personal life and history. Jesus Christ is the starting point; Jesus Christ the Incarnation of God, Jesus Christ the judgment of God, Jesus Christ the elect of God, Jesus Christ the victor over sin and death. Jesus Christ is the reality of moral life."[1]

It is Jesus who reveals to us the true nature of creation; it is Jesus who reveals to us that we are both sinful and redeemed. It is Jesus who shows us that our vocation is to live in a spirit of faith and openness to God and to make love the inspiration and goal of all our actions. In Jesus we know that sin has been overcome, and though we remain sinners we are no longer slaves to sin but are being liberated daily through the power of his grace. "And for anyone who is in Christ, there is a new creation; the old creation is gone, and now the new one is here."[2]

This is the reality we are called to manifest in our lives.

Living in the light of the reality of Jesus Christ does not mean that we have precise answers to our moral questions; it means that we face these questions in a joyful, affirmative manner, trusting in God in spite of all our

1. *Christ and the Moral Life* (New York: Harper & Row, 1968), p. 12.
2. 2 Cor. 5:17.

perplexities and failures. "The ethical life is conformity to reality; that is, conformity to Christ in whom both the reality of God and the reality of the world are known."[3] Because of Christ we know that, while sin is an awful human reality, it is not as imposing as the reality of our forgiveness.

Bernard Häring agrees that the point of departure of Christian ethics must be the reality of God as He has revealed himself in Jesus Christ. As Häring says, to be a Christian means to be a disciple of Jesus Christ. As such, the Christian is committed to a life of freedom and faithfulness. Another key word to characterize the Christian life, he says, is responsibility. "We exercise and develop our creative freedom and fidelity by listening and responding."[4] Our whole lives should be a response to God the Father through the Spirit given to us by Jesus.

## AN ETHIC OF RESPONSE

What kind of response? It is first of all . . . faith. Faith tells us that God speaks to us in the events and the persons that fill our lives. ". . . radical faith becomes incarnate insofar as our reaction to every event becomes a response in loyalty and confidence to the One who is present in all such events."[5]

God speaks to us especially through other people. Our response, faith tells us, must be one of love, for they are created in the image of God, Who is love. Absolute reverence for every human person is an imperative for all who love God.

The aim, then, of Christian discipleship is to make our whole life a response to God. We are truly responsible when, by our actions, we give witness to the fact that we belong to God.

Self-fulfillment is not the ultimate goal of the truly responsible Christian but, rather, one finds one's true self in giving oneself totally to God. A sincere response to God, moreover, always includes concern for the needs of our fellow human beings. So in judging the import of our actions we will always take into consideration how our decisions, desires and undertakings affect others.

A Christian ethic of responsibility views life as a partnership with God,

3. James Gustafson, *Christ and the Moral Life*, p. 15.
4. *Free and Faithful in Christ*, Vol. 1 (New York: Seabury Press, 1978), p. 59.
5. R. Niebuhr, *Radical Monotheism and Western Culture*. Quoted in Bernard Häring, *Free and Faithful in Christ*, p. 48.

Who wants our response to be creative and free. As co-creators with God, our relationship with Him is dialogic. He has not predetermined the outcome but looks to us to enrich the history of salvation in a creative way.

This dialogic and responsive character of Christian life is brought out very well by Dietrich Bonhoeffer in his *Ethics:*

> It is the "yes" to what is created, to becoming and to growth, to the flower and to the fruit, to health, happiness, ability, achievement, worth, success, greatness and honour; in short, it is the "yes" to the development of the power of life. And it is the "no" to that defection from the origin, the essence and the goal of life which is inherent in all this existence from the outset. This "no" means dying, suffering, poverty, renunciation, resignation, humility, degradation, self-denial, and in this again it already implies the "yes" to the new life, a life which does not fall apart into a juxtaposition of "yes" and "no," a life in which there is not to be found, for example, an unrestrained expansion of vitality side by side with a wholly separate ascetic and spiritual attitude, or "creaturely" conduct side by side with "Christian" conduct. If that were so, the "yes" and the "no" would lose their unity in Jesus Christ; it is in tension between the "yes" and the "no" in the sense that in every "yes" the "no" is already heard and in every "no" there is heard also the "yes." Development of the vital force and self-denial, growing and dying, health and suffering, happiness and renunciation, achievement and humility, honour and self-abasement, all these belong together in irreconcilable contradiction and yet in living unity . . .
>
> In Jesus Christ, God and man became one, and therefore through Him in the actions of the Christians "secular" and "Christian" become one also . . . They are not opposed but spring from the unity which is created in Christ, the unity of God and world, the unity of life . . . We live by responding to the word of God which is addressed to us in Jesus Christ and since this word is addressed to our entire life—the response can only be an entire one.[6]

As Christians, then, we believe that God has called us to be co-creators with Him and to share in His freedom and love.


## AN ETHIC OF FREEDOM

We receive our freedom from Christ and in Christ, who shows us the way to a liberated and creative love.

What is the nature of this freedom that comes from Christ? To under-

6. Dietrich Bonhoeffer, *Ethics*, ed. E. Bethge (New York: Macmillan, 1964), pp. 190–91.

stand it, we must realize that Christ himself is the great event of freedom. As the Word of God, Jesus shares in the infinite freedom of the Father, Whose self-giving love is totally and absolutely free.

Jesus' whole life is a demonstration of this radical personal freedom—of his utter freedom from every form of human bondage. His totally free, self-giving love manifests itself especially in his complete availability for others. The sick, the poor, the disabled, the suffering find him always ready to help and to heal. Death itself only manifests the absolute depth of his freedom, while the Resurrection shows him to be in truth the Father's free gift for the liberation of all.

Christ communicates his freedom to us by liberating us from everything that cripples our spirit and enslaves us to the world. Through him we overcome all the enemies of our freedom. Through his gift of truth we are liberated from self-deception and illusion. "[T]he truth will make you free."[7] In knowing the divine love, we find the truth of life and learn that it is possible to love one another as he has loved us.

To know this truth is to be delivered from bondage to the law so that we no longer look to the law to save us, but we realize that all we have is a gift of God, and we find our true selves in surrendering to God and in openness to others.

To know Christ's truth is to be freed from the egotism that subjects us to the sin of the world and burdens us with the cumulative weight of falsehood, injustice and violence. Instead we are transported into saving solidarity with Christ and become capable of genuine loving relationships. We find the freedom to love each other in Christ, who enables us to see the other as gift instead of threat.

Guilt, anxiety and scrupulosity keep many from enjoying interior freedom, and the Church has often fomented these feelings by its legalism. But Christ wants us to trust in the Father and to put away anxious thoughts. "Do not be anxious about tomorrow." As St. Paul says, "The spirit you received is not the spirit of slaves bringing fear into your lives again; it is the spirit of sons, and it makes us cry out, 'Abba, Father!' "[8]

Jesus calls us to a freedom that inspires us to active participation in the struggle. Sloth and apathy are incompatible with his Gospel. Rather, we are moved to risk our freedom in the unforeseeable events of the future.

7. Jn. 8:32.
8. Rom. 8:15.

"A Christian who knows about God's power and forgiveness and his own finiteness will not dare to stay idle in order to avoid the burden of risk."[9]

Like Jesus, the disciple will find in his heart the courage to confront the terrible powers of the world that keep people in bondage. Liberated interiorly himself, he will battle against the demons of political oppression and godless mammon that exploit the powerless. One of the most insidious of these today is sexism, which is so deeply rooted even in the Church itself and blinds even its leaders to the oppression of women.

Disciples of Christ are also co-creators with God. Jesus gives us the freedom to be creative and open to the future and the possibilities that the unfolding of history offers us. The morality inculcated by the Gospel is not a static one, but it should encourage us to react imaginatively and creatively to change affecting human relationships. Past experience alone can never be a sufficient guide. We are constantly confronted with new situations and new developments of culture and history that should evoke new responses from us if we truly believe in the God of Jesus Christ, "who makes all things new" and constantly offers new possibilities for action. His disciple is given the courage and hope to break through established rigidities of social custom and pattern and tap the unrealized possibilities hidden in human nature.

Finally, Jesus helps to free us from the most oppressive of all our enemies: the fear of death. "After that will come the end, when he hands over the kingdom to God the Father, having done away with every sovereignty, authority and power. For he must be king until he has put all his enemies under his feet and the last of the enemies to be destroyed is death . . ."[10]

## JESUS' ETHICAL DEMANDS

We have discussed what Jesus has done for us. The next question is, What does he ask of us in return? The precise nature of Jesus' ethics as given mainly in the Sermon on the Mount is a most difficult question. Many interpretations have been given. As Hans Küng says, we can rule out one of them right at the beginning. It is certainly not intended to be a *new code of laws*. Jesus came to "fulfill the law" not by adding more precepts but by showing its deeper meaning and leading people to a trusting relationship with God and a radical obedience to His will that cannot

9. Bernard Häring, op. cit., Vol. 1, p. 136.
10. 1 Cor. 15:24–26.

be measured by a code of laws. Salvation, as Jesus insisted, is a gift, not something that can be achieved by conformity to law.

The favorite and even official Catholic explanation before the Second Vatican Council was to see the Sermon as implying two ways to heaven: the *way of perfection,* followed by those who observed the "counsels" of the Sermon (usually taken as vows only by those in the religious orders and some clergy), and the *ordinary way,* followed by those who obeyed the Ten Commandments but were not obliged by the counsels.

The great Russian Tolstoy tried to turn the Sermon on the Mount into a blueprint for a new social order and called for its literal application to all human relations. But Jesus didn't offer it as a program of social reform: the Kingdom he preached was not simply a better world. While the Sermon throws a powerful light on the evils of society and its dehumanizing structures, and powerfully motivates people to change them, it is not basically a platform for political or social reform.

Others, like Albert Schweitzer, saw the Sermon as so utopian that it made sense only in terms of Jesus believing in the imminent end of the world. Hence, they say, he delivered it as an interim ethic to prepare people for the perfect world about to be ushered in. But this view is hard to square with the way Jesus' demands presuppose the present messy world—for it speaks of litigation, marriages, enmities, etc. And though its framework is undoubtedly the apocalyptic idea of the imminent End, Jesus does not appeal to the coming End as a motive but bases his moral demands on the will and nature of God.

The question of whether Jesus actually thought the world was at an end is one that has aroused much controversy since the end of the nineteenth century. Schweitzer (as we just said) found the key to the Gospels in Jesus' belief that the End was near. Catholics to this day, on the other hand, have been most reluctant to admit it. But it seems certain today to leading exegetes that Jesus did expect the advent of God's Kingdom in the immediate future. The texts of the synoptics with this sense cannot be easily explained away and must belong to the first layer, for they must have been very embarrassing for the early Church. And how otherwise explain the belief of early Paul and the primitive Church that the End was near? Moreover, as Hans Küng points out, the undoubtedly authentic parables of Jesus surely are meant to prepare the way for the coming Kingdom of God.[11]

Must we say, then, that Jesus on this point was mistaken? The answer is not simple. As we become more aware of the time-conditioned character of so much of the imagery of the Bible—the story of creation, for instance —we are learning to extract the core of truth from the mythological framework that contains it. In this case, the fact that in expressing his message about God as the ultimate reality Jesus was dependent on the apocalyptic thought and imagery of his day does not necessarily invalidate his central point: that it is only by looking to the End that we can judge rightly about the present, that God is our absolute future and this reality should shape our attitude toward the present. "The polarity of the 'not yet' and the 'but even now' holds."[12]

It is in the light of God's absolute future that Jesus proclaims his moral imperatives. Radical obedience to God's will is what he calls for. All forms of legalism are to be put aside: he issues no new law or set of rules or code of conduct. There are to be no legal limits to the demands of God. God wants more than what can be prescribed by law. Jesus wanted to break down the wall of legalism that separates man from God.[13]

But how do we discover the will of God? "Do not model yourselves on the behavior of the world around you, but let your behavior change, modeled by your new mind. This is the only way to discover the will of God and know what is good, what it is that God wants, what is the perfect thing to do."[14] As Bonhoeffer says, the will of God may lie very deeply concealed beneath a great number of available possibilities. The will of God is not a system of rules established from the outset; it is something new and different in each situation in life, and for this reason a man must ever anew examine what the will of God may be for him. The heart, the understanding, observation and experience must all collaborate in this task. Our knowledge of God's will depends on grace; it is a grace that is constantly new, and we must constantly prove anew what the will of God is. The prime requisite for finding out the will of God is that we are transformed into the form of Christ, children of God living now in unity

11. *On Being a Christian* (Garden City, N.Y.: Doubleday, 1976), p. 217.
12. Ibid., pp. 221–23.
13. G. Bornkamm, *Jesus* (New York: Harper & Row, 1960), p. 105.
14. Rom. 12:2.

with the will of the Father. And only in Jesus Christ can man prove what is the will of God.[15]

What, then, does God will? Jesus summed up his ethical teaching in answering the question put to him by the Pharisees: "Master, which is the greatest commandment of the Law?" In answer he said, "You must love the Lord your God with all your heart, with all your soul, and with all your mind. This is the greatest and the first commandment. The second resembles it: You must love your neighbor as yourself. On these two commandments hang the whole Law, and the Prophets also."[16]

It is clear that Jesus' command to love is not simply a utopian dream. It obliges us here and now to a radical commitment to God coupled with a radical commitment to promote our neighbor's welfare and to be ready if necessary to sacrifice ourselves for the sake of human dignity. It functions as a norm by which all laws and societal arrangements should be judged. It forces us to live in a state of tension between the demands of love and the imperfect realities of our world as we continually seek to lessen the gap between what is actual and what is possible in life. Thus Christ's law of love becomes a norm: "a source of principles and axioms, a 'transcendent' point of criticism in living out the actualities and ambiguities of life in history."[17]

And though Jesus did not lay down rules that were absolutely authoritative and applicable to every situation, he did give concrete indications concerning our use of property, earthly status and power that point in a certain definite direction. Or as James Gustafson puts it, "The teachings of Jesus point to the kinds of behavior that will be consistent with the message of redemption."[18]

Take Jesus' statements on the use of property, for instance. Such sayings as "Lend, without any hope of return" and "Do not store up treasures for yourself on earth" and "Provide yourselves with no gold for the journey or spare tunic or footwear or a staff." As Karl Barth points out, these sayings are no call to realize an ideal or principle such as was incorporated into the monastic rules, nor does it offer a normative technical rule. Rather, the object was to liberate us from our deep-rooted attachment to our possessions and to liberate us so that we can let go of them when this is called for.

15. Dietrich Bonhoeffer, *Ethics*, pp. 161–63.
16. Mt. 22:36–40.
17. James Gustafson, op. cit., p. 234.
18. Ibid., p. 204.

Barth emphasized the point that Jesus' sayings were directed at specific persons in specific circumstances and therefore cannot simply be applied to other persons in different circumstances. We cannot merely reproduce the behavior recommended by Jesus in the Gospels, but we must render obedience in our own concrete way to the command of God as it comes to us here and now in all its concreteness. And we must be wary of any response on our part that is less demanding or less uncomfortable than that asked of the first disciples.[19]

One must keep in mind that the moral teaching of Christ must always be understood in the light of his offer to man of God's love and salvation. He can make such extreme demands only because the wonderful God Whom he preaches really exists: a God Who is all-loving and merciful. Trust in such a God surely should affect our behavior and give it the specific direction indicated by Jesus' commands.

How original was the ethical teaching of Jesus? It is certainly true that parallels, or at least partial ones, can be found in the various world religions and philosophies. If one scans the Old Testament, the Apocrypha and the Talmudic and Midrashic literature of Jesus' time, one can find parallels with every item of Jesus' teaching. But Jesus was original in the way he brought the great insights of the tradition together, developed and harmonized them, and above all, made them real in his own life with such unparalleled intensity. His object was not to formulate a new moral code but to bring home to people the reality of God, to make people so conscious of God and His goodness and their own status as His children that they would be enabled to do the good they already knew.

It is important to keep this point in mind: all Jesus' moral imperatives are founded on the reality of God's Kingdom. For Jesus, as we have mentioned above, this Kingdom was both a present and a future, a subjective and an objective, reality. It is realized subjectively in the heart of the individual who accepts God's claim on him and surrenders to God's rule in all he does. As L. H. Marshall says in *The Challenge of New Testament Ethics*, "So long as we regard our ideals as our own, in all our ethical endeavours we are simply trying to raise ourselves by tugging at our own bootstraps. But the initiative in the remaking of personality cannot come from within the personality that is to be remade. When, however, we recognize and surrender ourselves to God's transcendent claim upon us,

19. Quoted by James Gustafson, op. cit., p. 207.

our ideals are no longer our own, but His ideals for us, and we become conscious of His power working with us."[20]

What, then, does God will? Jesus sums up his whole teaching in one word: love. Love of God, and love of neighbor as oneself. Jesus combines the two in an indissoluble unity, but love of God comes first. And Jesus often warns us against making an idol of some creature, whether another person or money or power or pleasure. God alone must be adored, with every fiber of our being. "You must love the Lord your God with your whole heart, with all your soul, and with all your mind."

Intimately connected with our love of God is love of neighbor. Any love of God that is divorced from love of neighbor is a sham. This love must be real and sincere—not the kind of love that is extended grudgingly for the sake of God. It is a love that must embrace the neighbor wholeheartedly for his own sake. As the Gospel points out, those declared blessed at the Last Judgment are completely surprised to find that in serving the poor, the hungry, the dispossessed, they were actually serving the Lord.

Jesus makes it clear that he is talking about a down-to-earth, concrete love that here and now is embodied in practical deeds of mercy and compassion.

Our love of neighbor must be as far-reaching as our love of self. The tremendous concern we have for our own well-being, our own health, our own material interests, our own comfort, our own security, is the measure of how we should love our neighbor. We must be as concerned about her as we are about ourselves. We must be, as Jesus was, a person for others. For it is in the person of our neighbor that we most often encounter God.

But who is my neighbor? Jesus closes all the loopholes we might use to escape his radical demands: everyone is potentially a neighbor. As the story of the Good Samaritan points out, my neighbor is anyone in need. He annuls all the categories people use to exclude people from the ambit of their love: race, nationality, religion, social stratum, etc. No human being must be left outside.

Not even our enemy! This is the most original feature of Jesus' ethical teaching. In none of the ancient sages, nor in Judaism itself, do we find the command so clear-cut: "Love your enemies, do good to those who hate you, bless those who curse you, pray for those who treat you badly."[21] As in his other radical demands, Jesus makes sense only if we believe in

20. New York: Macmillan, 1947, p. 29.
21. Lk. 6:27–28.

the God Who makes His sun shine on the just and the unjust and His rain fall on the good and the bad.

Moreover, love as Jesus sees it demands that we do more than pray for our enemies. We should take the initiative in seeking reconciliation. In forgiving them, we manifest awareness of our own need for God's forgiveness and our gratitude for God's mercy.

A disciple of Jesus must regard himself as a servant. The game is not about honors, status and power. Anyone who follows him must be ready to undertake the lowliest tasks at the call of circumstance. In washing his disciples' feet, Jesus said, "I have given you an example." For those who wish to be the greatest should be the servant of all.

The demands of love reach their climax when he calls for renunciation even of our most basic right: self-defense. "To the man who slaps you on one cheek, present the other cheek too; to the man who takes your cloak from you, do not refuse your tunic. Give to everyone who asks you, and do not ask for your property back from the man who robs you."[22] Critics of Jesus' teaching find here the clearest evidence that his morality is impossible, suitable only in view of a near End of the world. But we must remember that Jesus is not enunciating a code. He is only giving illustrations (with no doubt a dash of Oriental hyperbole) of what might be possible in certain circumstances for one deeply imbued with the love of God. Moreover, the idea that nonviolence might be the most reasonable response to enemy provocations after all is gaining increasing credibility in the light of how successfully it has been used by such great and prophetic leaders as Gandhi, Martin Luther King and Cesar Chavez. So, in a world on the brink of annihilation, those who preach Jesus' doctrine of nonviolence are getting an increasingly attentive hearing.

Jesus demonstrated the meaning of love by his actions as well as by his words, as we have said. By action even more than by word, he drove home the lesson that true love is manifest especially in compassion for the poor and the sick and the oppressed. Women, for example, were an oppressed class in the ancient world, held in contempt and barred from participation in public life. But Jesus treated them as friends and equals, while they showered him with affection.

The same is true of his attitude toward the poor. He was no doubt poor himself. With no possessions, he depended completely on the hospitality of others. Most of his followers were drawn from the lower classes: the

22. Lk. 6:29–30.

poor, the uneducated. He saw great danger in riches and often warned against setting one's heart on mammon. He told the rich young man to sell what he had and give to the poor. He scored the absurdity of trusting in perishable riches and held up to scorn the arrogant rich, who live as though they, and not God, were the lord of life and death. Riches are often a curse, because they tempt one to worship mammon instead of God.

But while he was definitely on the side of the poor, he did not condemn the rich or preach a social revolution. He even accepted their hospitality on occasion, and some of his followers themselves were property owners.

His main point was that we should set our heart on the Kingdom of God and not on possessions. We should trust in the providence of God and not give in to worry and anxiety over material things, but take each day as it comes, relying on God to support us in whatever trials may befall us on the morrow. The God Who is our absolute future is a God of love, Who will keep His promise.

## AN ETHIC OF CONVERSION

The very core of the morality of Jesus is the need for conversion. As all exegetes agree, it was the main theme of Jesus: ". . . the kingdom of God is close at hand. Repent . . ."[23] The prophets of the Old Testament spoke often of the need for a complete change of heart on the part of their hearers—a turning away from sin and a total commitment to God. John the Baptist put the same message in tones of tremendous urgency as he announced the imminence of God's final judgment: the ax is already laid to the root; every tree that does not bear good fruit will be cut down and thrown into the fire. With John the mood is one of urgency and expectation, but with Jesus it is one of fulfillment. The Kingdom promised for long is now present in his offer of God's salvation, and his hearers are called to respond by a decision to turn to God with no reservations. What is called for is a childlike acceptance of God's gift of forgiveness and a decision to shake oneself loose from bondage to self and to the world.

Conversion, in essence, is to commit oneself wholeheartedly to the Kingdom of God as a disciple of Jesus. In his beatitudes, Jesus gives us a profile of the true disciple. His disciples are those committed to values

23. Mk. 1:15.

that stand in sharp contrast to those espoused by the worldly person. The worldly person seeks happiness in possessions, wealth, power, status, and is often domineering, unscrupulous, devious, prone to violence, and heartless. But true disciples find happiness only in complete surrender to the will of God and, making this their goal, do not cling to possessions, and so, if not actually poor, are at least poor in spirit. Meek, they have no need to dominate others, but instead seek to use whatever power they have to serve the well-being of others. Adversity and suffering do not crush them, but help them to be even more sensitive and compassionate, and so, although they grieve, they are blessed. Indeed, experience of evil in the world does not harden their hearts but only leads them to seek true comfort in the promises of God. They hunger and thirst for justice by not allowing complacency to soften their resolution but constantly yearn to be more faithful in promoting the Kingdom of God. Their purity of heart is manifest in the candid and straightforward way in which they deal with others, and though persecuted on account of the stands they take, they are not deflected from their chosen path.

In the writings of Paul and John, conversion is cast in different terms. It is now faith in Jesus Christ. To believe in Jesus Christ is to make a decision for God and against his opponents, for love and against hatred. It is to walk in the Spirit and to enjoy the new life in Christ.

## MODERN PSYCHOLOGY AND CONVERSION

New light has been thrown on the nature of religious conversion by recent discussions of "fundamental stance" and "fundamental option."

Fundamental stance, as used in Catholic moral theology, refers to the direction or orientation or meaning one gives to one's life. It is based on the findings of psychologists that at a certain point in our development we make certain basic decisions about what we want out of life and what explicitly or implicitly draw us either toward or away from God as our ultimate end. The decision or decisions that orient our life in a definite direction are termed the fundamental option.

As Timothy O'Connell puts it, ". . . a fundamental option does not exist all by itself . . . Rather it is the deeper meaning and significance of some of the decisions of our lives . . . nor is it final and definitive."[24]

24. *Principles for a Catholic Morality* (New York: Seabury Press, 1978), pp. 64–65.

One of the psychologists who has greatly contributed to our understanding of fundamental option is Erik Erikson. As Bernard Häring points out, Erikson is especially interested in the gradual unfolding of one's identity as one passes through the basic stages of life. At each stage of life, he claims, a person is called to make certain basic decisions, or fundamental options. It is these basic decisions that shape one's identity as he/she grows toward maturity.

Erikson found eight stages, with their specific crises and the basic decisions they called for: beginning with infancy, during which the child learns to trust or mistrust others, to the eighth, and final, stage—ego integrity versus despair—during which the aging person is confronted with the choice between accepting the course of his life and accepting those people who have become meaningful for it or of succumbing to bitterness and despair. As Häring says, one cannot simply equate fundamental option with Erikson's concept of identity, but they have much in common: "It is identity that gives the ego strength so necessary for a total commitment."[25]

Another psychologist, Viktor Frankl, offers hope for those who "missed the boat," so to speak. In their experience of existential dread and meaninglessness, they can find the inner strength to renew their dedication to truth and recover their identity by making a firm commitment to it. "In this wholehearted search there is already a contact, although unconscious, with the 'hidden God.' "[26]

The concept of the fundamental option can throw light on God's call to conversion and our response to freely commit ourselves to Him and to our neighbor. It must be a total self-commitment, so that it influences all of our actions. "The fundamental option decides about one's 'heart' which can overflow with love and goodness but can also harbour deeply rooted selfishness."[27]

Certain decisions we make are of such import that they profoundly affect our fundamental options, such as the choice of a spouse, of a career, or of a religious vocation.

25. Bernard Häring, *Free and Faithful in Christ,* p. 177.
26. Ibid., p. 181.
27. Ibid., p. 188.

# 24

## Sin Reconsidered

The New York *Times* recently noted that a course on the relationship of sin to society called "The Seven Deadly Sins" was offered at the New School for Social Research. "We're saving lust for last to keep interest high," the professor admitted. She also said that it was easy to relate the seven sins to New York City, since it has them in such abundance. Anger, for instance, is so prevalent that, as a New York police officer said, "Anything short of a shooting is a friendly argument."

Karl Menninger, the well-known psychiatrist, wrote a book, *Whatever Became of Sin?* in which he decries the modern trend to do away with the concept of sin. The author attempts to trace the steps leading to the disappearance of the word "sin" from the vocabulary of so many social scientists, psychologists and others concerned with human behavior.[1]

A harbinger of the changed attitude toward sin, he points out, was the change regarding masturbation. A moral taboo throughout the Christian era, it was looked on as a very serious sin. In the nineteenth century, many medical treatises were written which connected it with a whole host of physical and mental derangements including mania, stupidity, melancholy and even suicide. Then, suddenly, at the turn of the present century, this ancient taboo simply vanished. With the exception of Roman Catholics and a few other groups, people stopped regarding it as a sin.

Menninger sees this as a paradigm for what happened later in other areas of human behavior. The great advances made by the scientific study

1. Karl Menninger, *Whatever Became of Sin?* (New York: Hawthorn Books, 1973).

of human behavior beginning with Freud's discovery of the psychoanalytic method (about 1900), followed by Pavlov's conditioned reflex, the use of mood- and behavior-altering drugs, the development of psychology as a science—all led to new theories of behavior and motivation. Sin became questionable as an explanation for behavior which now appeared to be the result of numerous determining events over which the subject had little or no control. Bad children were maladjusted, criminals were simply ill, etc.

While Menninger is happy that many acts once thought sinful are no longer so considered (including masturbation), he deeply deplores the loss altogether of a sense of sin. Words like "delinquency," "deviancy," even "crime," he maintains, do not convey adequately the reality of human guilt and wickedness like the word "sin." There is, he almost shouts, immorality, there is wrongdoing; there is personal moral responsibility and there is culpable failure to exercise it! The guilt people feel can be cured only by their willingness to admit it and to be forgiven. And so he pleads fervently for a restoration of the concept, if not the word, sin. And he calls on the clergy to exercise their moral leadership by urging people to confess their sins and repent.[2]

There has, no doubt, been a great weakening of the sense of sin, for many reasons. There may have been too much emphasis on sin in many sermons in the past. There is also much more questioning of authority today by people who are more aware of human fallibility. They are no longer as ready, as they once were, to rely on the Church's definition of what is or is not a sin. They appeal more often to the dictates of their conscience—which is certainly better than the blind obedience of the past, but it can be abused when people confuse "doing what comes naturally" with acting according to conscience.

There is also a diminished sense of God's presence in the world as a technological civilization exalts the power of man over nature and tends to push God out of the picture.

Catholics have specific reasons of their own for a certain agnosticism in regard to sin. They were educated by the clergy to think of sin as something very definable and measurable, if not actually palpable. They memorized the various forms of sin: original and actual, mortal and venial. They were told that a mortal sin was committed when it involved a serious matter, sufficient reflection and full consent of the will. Serious matter was

2. Ibid., p. 228.

ascertained rather easily. Sermons and catechisms and other books abounded with complete lists of the serious sins.

This whole legalistic, materialistic presentation of sin has become increasingly problematic for intelligent Catholics over the past twenty years. The Second Vatican Council surely played a major role in the transformation of consciousness changing their attitude toward sin. Watching the bishops at the Council argue, they learned how much room there was for debate on matters involving Church teaching. The circumstances surrounding *Humanae Vitae* and the subsequent furor made them question the Church's teaching not only on birth control but on many other aspects of sexual morality. Many looked back partly in anger and partly in amusement at the taboo-ridden preachments of the nuns and priests on sex. And the whole question of sin became very confused in their minds.

Yet in spite of their willingness to question the Church's traditional teaching and their disuse of the confessional, many remained conscious of sin. Its effects were too obvious to ignore in the world around them. The ravages of human pride and selfishness confronted them daily in the polluted streams and air, on the dangerous streets where muggers lurked, in the courtrooms where white-collar criminals bribed their way to freedom, in the hospitals where so many victims of violence lay suffering, in the slums filled with the victims of a profit-mad society, in the families disintegrated by the failure of spouses to keep their sacred promises, on the TV screen with its daily depiction of terror and violence around the world, and above all in the mounting fear of a global nuclear war that would destroy the planet itself.

It is obvious, then, that there is need for a better understanding of sin, one that draws on the experience and insights of the Church while avoiding the oversimplified legalistic, static and privatistic emphases that were so characteristic of past teaching.

## SIN IN THE SCRIPTURES

The place to start is no doubt with the Scriptures. What do the two Testaments tell us?

The Old Testament has no special word for sin as a theological concept. There are four different Hebrew root words that may be translated by our word sin. They convey differing nuances of meaning, such as to violate a legal norm, to go astray, to rebel, to err. But the Hebrews used many other words to convey the meaning of sin: including disorder, foolishness, guilt. But however they described it, sin for Israel was always rupture of their relationship with God. For He had made a covenant with them; they were His people and were expected to act in accordance with His will, which they discovered through their experience and recorded in their laws. To disobey this sacred law, then, was to sin, to rebel against God, to break the covenant with Him.

Idolatry was the most heinous sin, forbidden by the First Commandment and denounced often by the prophets, who likened it to adultery. For Israel was "married" to God and experienced His ever-present love in its long and checkered history. Thus Jeremiah speaks for God in the tone of a husband who has been deserted. "If you wish to come back, Israel . . . it is to me you must return."[3] It was not only idolatry, however, that separated Israel from its God. Injustice, harshness, exploitation of one's neighbor were also targets of the prophet's wrath.

The reality of sin is central in the story of Jesus, who comes to call sinners to repentance and to accept the sweet rule of God. But the emphasis is on forgiveness and conversion. His Gospel is the good news that, in the person of Jesus, God is offering forgiveness to all, for all are in need of it. He has harsh words only for the self-righteous, who feel no need for God's mercy, while he associates with the disreputable and the outcasts of society to show that God's offer of mercy extends to everyone. He was most insistent in preaching that sin is rooted in the unregenerate heart. ". . . the things that come out of the mouth come from the heart, and it is these that make a man unclean. For from the heart come evil intentions: murder, adultery, fornication, theft, perjury, slander . . ."[4]

In the New Testament, the concept of sin takes on a different color, from its relation to the saving work of Jesus Christ. It is Jesus who most clearly revealed the true nature of sin as a rejection of God's invitation to share with him a history of salvation.

Jesus does not spend a great amount of time denouncing sin or in describing particular sins. He prefers to emphasize the wonderful goodness of God, Who in His mercy is always eager to welcome us home to His banquet of love and peace as the father welcomed his prodigal son, as the shepherd rejoices over the lost sheep or the woman rejoices when she finds the lost coin.

Paul has the most comprehensive theology of sin. For Paul, sin is not

3. Jer. 4:1.
4. Mt. 15:18–19.

only a transgression of the divine law, an act of disobedience, but it is a state, an all-embracing reality, that is a fundamental condition of existence. He speaks of the reign of sin: we are enslaved to the power of sin unless we allow Christ to rule over us. The old Adam and the new Adam struggle within us, the flesh lusts against the Spirit and often it's the flesh (our unredeemed nature) that triumphs. Because of sin's power, the world is an appalling spectacle: people are "steeped in all sorts of depravity, rottenness, greed and malice, and addicted to envy, murder, wrangling, treachery and spite. Libelers, slanderers, enemies of God, rude, arrogant and boastful, enterprising in sin, rebellious to parents, without brains, honor, love or pity."[5]

The struggle against sin, Paul says, must be unceasing. Even though we are baptized and converted we are not spared. To overcome sin we must live a life of constant mortification and crucify the "old man" and destroy the body of sin that dwells in us. Our life must be a constant dying as "we carry with us in our body the death of Jesus, so that the life of Jesus, too, may always be seen in our body."[6]

Among the Fathers of the Church, Augustine stands out for his profound analysis of sin. Having left behind him a dissolute life, he was well suited to enlarge the Church's understanding of sin. He saw it as turning away from God toward creatures so as to enjoy them in a way contrary to God's will. In his debates with the Pelagians, who championed the natural freedom and goodness of human nature, Augustine argued that without the grace of Christ we are nothing but slaves to our egotism and fleshly desires. Our freedom is an illusion, for though we retain the power to choose this or that, we are not free to change the overall sinful direction of our lives. It is only the grace of Christ that liberates us from the chains of our evil habits and orients us away from our obsession with self.

## ORIGINAL SIN

One of the most difficult of all theological inquiries is the one dealing with original sin. It is also one of the doctrines of the Church that currently is in a rather confused state as theologians vie with each other in offering revisions of the classic doctrine.

The classic doctrine was based mainly on the interpretation of two

5. Rom. 1:29–31.
6. 2 Cor. 4:10.

biblical passages: Genesis Chapters 2 and 3 (the story of Adam and Eve's disobedience in eating the forbidden fruit) and the epistle to the Romans, Chapter 5, verses 12–21 (where Paul connects the existence of sin and death with Adam's sin and also juxtaposes Adam and Christ inasmuch as while we inherited condemnation from Adam we receive the free gift of justification from Jesus Christ).

The history of the doctrine is extremely complex. The thought of the Greek Fathers, for instance, is already considerably at variance with that of their Latin counterparts. As George Vandervelde says, the Greek Fathers "left little room for an idea of original sin conceived of as a culpable reality in Adam's posterity, a reality that incisively qualifies man's will and moral capacities. Rather than original sin, the central idea is that of inherited evil and inherited (physical) corruption compounded by the legacy of social decadence."[7]

In the West, it was Saint Augustine who formulated the doctrine in a way that was to stand the test of time—at least until a few years ago. Some of the Fathers before him anticipated some of his ideas but at the same time differed considerably from him on certain points. Tertullian, for instance, introduced the idea of a sin inherited from Adam since all of us were in some way contained in Adam. But Tertullian insisted that human nature was still good and the will free. Cyprian saw baptism as necessary for the infant because of the legacy of inherited sin but held that the child itself was not guilty.

Ambrose (d. 397) and his contemporary Ambrosiaster had the greatest influence on Augustine's thought. Ambrosiaster's faulty translation of Rom. 5:12 had Paul say that "sin came into the world through one man *in whom* all have sinned" rather than what it should be: ". . . sin came into the world through one man *inasmuch* as all have sinned." The erroneous *"in whom"* became a pivotal passage in supporting the idea that all men have sinned *in Adam*—meaning that all share in his sin.

However, neither Ambrose nor Ambrosiaster drew the conclusion that Augustine did, namely, that all share in Adam's guilt and are therefore punishable for Adam's sin. Nor did they subscribe, like Augustine, to the idea that because of solidarity in Adam's sin mankind is totally corrupted in will and unable to love God.

Augustine worked out his doctrine of original sin in conflict with another theologian of genius, Pelagius, who landed on the shores of Africa,

7 *Original Sin: Two Major Trends in Contemporary Roman Catholic Reinterpretation* (Washington, D.C.. University Press of America, 1981), p. 5.

in 410, near Augustine's see of Hippo. Pelagius held very strong views on the essential goodness of human nature and its ability to surmount the evil effects of Adam's sin. His central idea was an intense conviction about human freedom: the certitude that in spite of the tremendous damage wrought in man's nature by Adam's sin and in spite of the fact that through force of habit sin becomes almost a second nature, man yet retains his freedom.

Pelagius acknowledged the importance of God's grace. In fact, he taught that all adults are in need of the new start given them as remission of their personal sins, a grace that God bestows on them without any merit on their part but which is received only by faith. He also insisted on two other major forms of grace: the Law, found in the Old Testament, and the example of Christ, who is the image of God.

The nub of Augustine's conflict with Pelagius lay in their differing conceptions of grace and human nature. For Pelagius, human nature remained basically good, while he identified grace in its most fundamental meaning as God's gift of man's good nature, consisting of being able to freely choose and do the good. But, for Augustine, nature itself was corrupted by self-love, and he rejected any identification of grace with human nature.

Also relying on Ambrosiaster's incorrect translation *"Adam . . . in whom all have sinned,"* Augustine stressed our involvement in Adam's sin much more emphatically than any theologian before him. And unlike Pelagius, who saw the will as still free in spite of the inroads of sin, Augustine saw the human will as completely enslaved to sin. Man retains his freedom in the sense that he sins willingly, but he is not able not to sin. Only those who receive the grace of God—which works interiorly and irresistibly in our will to redirect it to the good—are saved. Those who do not are damned. Why some receive it and others do not is a mystery hidden in the inscrutable justice of God: the mystery of predestination.

While his opponent Pelagius took refuge in the Holy Land, where he found bishops more receptive to his views, Augustine, in Africa, rallied the bishops to condemn the teachings of Pelagius at the Council of Carthage in 418.

Augustine decisively influenced the subsequent theology of original sin, and the Council of Trent reflected much of his thought in its decree on original sin, which is the most comprehensive and definitive statement ever made on the question. Basically the Council taught: a) that all are guilty of original sin, b) that it was transmitted from Adam, c) that because of Adam's sin all his descendants lost the holiness and justice he had received from God, d) that it was transmitted by "generation" and inheres in each of us, and e) that baptism is necessary for its removal.

## REINTERPRETATIONS OF THE DOCTRINE

The Tridentine doctrine of original sin remained a solid-rock foundation for Catholic theology until the 1950s. But then an earthquake occurred. The advance of knowledge about the origins of man began to shake the foundation, and cracks started to appear. Catholics found they could no longer ignore the modern evolutionary worldview, which differed so radically from the worldview presupposed in Trent's doctrine of original sin, that is, a static understanding of reality, a world created in one piece, an original paradise where God fashioned and placed one couple who failed humanity's first big test—a catastrophe that irrevocably spoiled creation and turned evil loose in human society.

This neat little picture could no longer be taken seriously as science uncovered overwhelming evidence for a dynamic and evolutionary universe. Life, it showed, was a developing force spewing forth new forms in a continuous stream over millions of years. The golden age does not lie at the beginning but may lie at the end. The evil in the world is a necessary part of an unfinished universe and can't be traced back to some primordial catastrophe.

Other developments also undermined Trent's doctrine. The study of biblical literary forms—encouraged by Pius XII's encyclical *Divino Afflante Spiritu*—showed how great a part myth played in the composition of the Bible. Genesis' account of the Fall was obviously not intended as history but, rather, as a way of expressing the biblical author's awareness of a basic flaw in human nature. And patristic studies uncovered Ambrosiaster's incorrect reading of St. Paul.

Catholic theologians at mid-twentieth century obviously had their work all cut out for them. For the Church had made its doctrine of original sin the keystone of its dogmatic teaching about man, sin and redemption. The question was, How could an "infallible" Church have committed itself to ideas that now seemed so outdated? A whole spate of books (the most notable being the *New Dutch Catechism)* appeared to show that Trent's dogma of original sin could be reinterpreted in a way that did not compromise the essential meaning of the doctrine and yet stripped it of its mythic and archaic features.

In this effort of reinterpretation, one can discern two main schools: the **situationists**, who focus on man's historical situation and see original sin as a way of speaking about a kind of moral ecology—the human moral environment so permeated with sin that everyone is spiritually conditioned and drawn to make sinful decisions. The other school, the **personalists**, take a much more radical approach and jettison the entire traditional baggage of myth and medieval concepts and hold that "original sin" means simply the factual universality of personal sin: everyone is willy-nilly a sinner.

The Dutch theologian Piet Schoonenberg has the honor of founding the situationist school, although he has acknowledged his indebtedness for some of his ideas to Karl Rahner, who likewise belongs to this school.

One of Schoonenberg's strong points is the great use he makes of Scripture. In an intensive analysis of the Bible, he finds two basic insights: human solidarity in sin and personal responsibility. The second idea developed very slowly but it is very strong in the later prophets.

Now, he maintains that both of these insights must be kept together in dealing with the question of human guilt, and the best way to link them together, he maintains, is with the concept of situation. As George Vandervelde says, Schoonenberg's main concern is to safeguard personal responsibility while maintaining human solidarity in sin. And while the human, interpersonal situation does not coerce a specific response from a person, it is in some way determinative: One of the best examples he uses is the situation in which someone tells you he is in love with you. You cannot avoid a response. Either you accept or reject the proffered love. You have been placed in a "situation" that becomes the content of your freely given response.[8]

Schoonenberg insists on the "awesome massivity and fixity of being-situated" (in a sin-saturated world that reaches into the very being of a person as a determination of his will).

One of the great difficulties facing the situationists is how to reconcile their theory with Trent's teaching that speaks of the guilt of original sin. Rahner and another situationist, Karl-Heinz Weger, improve on Schoonenberg's unsatisfactory explanation of this point by their concept of "original sin as the situational privation of grace, showing that it in-

8. Ibid., pp. 75–76.

volves a prepersonal unholiness counter to God's will . . . which in contrast to personal sin . . . does not involve culpability for the person deprived of grace."[9]

How did the world become situated in sin? Schoonenberg answers the question by appealing to the Johannine concept of the "sin of the world." Accepting human origins as polygenetic and taking an evolutionary view, Schoonenberg does not put much importance on the first evil human act, but proposes a history of sin as a continually intensifying reality. Sin, for him, is basically the refusal to get involved in the history of salvation. The refusal to accept Christ represents the climax—or better, the low point— in the history of sin.

The numerous unsolved problems created by the situationists in attempting a reinterpretation of original sin—problems we will not discuss here but which are well elaborated in Vandervelde's study—led other theologians to devise a more radical reinterpretation. The leader of this school (the personalist) is A. Vanneste, who calls his study a thorough renovation of the doctrine. He dispenses with the whole framework of the traditional doctrine—that is, the historical Adam, the primordial Fall, a monogenetic origin of the race and its biological unity. Unlike the situationists, he also abandons any attempt to posit original sin as some kind of prepersonal sinfulness. And so (some would say thank God) he clears the deck of the whole esoteric situationist terminology.

As Vanneste insists, sin must involve the voluntary free acts of the individual, and therefore this must be true of original sin as well. Thus original sin is nothing else than the universality of actual sins. "This, in his view, constitutes the indispensable kernel wrapped in the outdated, mythological husk of the traditional teaching."[10]

The only point of the myth of Adam was to teach that the first free and conscious act of every human being . . . is a sinful one. He sides with Augustine against Pelagius insofar as he stressed the absolute necessity of grace for a person to be capable of good. But he notes how the Council of Orange refused to accept Augustine's idea that the will was completely enslaved to sin and held instead that man's will is weakened.

So why the absolute necessity of grace? As creatures, he says, we are metaphysically dependent on God—which is only another way of saying we need grace—the first grace. But we also need a second grace—a heal-

9. Ibid., p. 184.
10. Ibid., p. 263.

ing grace—insofar as our wills have been weakened, but not (pace Augustine) totally corrupted.

What original sin means, then, in Vanneste's opinion is that *de facto* we all sin and we all need the saving grace of Jesus Christ. Even if we allow for exceptions, as in the case of the Virgin Mary, this only points up the possibility that some people could be righteous "precisely by virtue of grace they have already received from Christ."[11]

Vanneste believes that the doctrine of original sin is in harmony with human experience, but it is only in the Bible and the teaching of the Church that "the breadth and the length, the height and the depth" of human sinfulness is adequately revealed.

## LISTS OF SIN, DEGREES OF SIN

The Bible did not simply denounce sin, it also provided lists of specific sins to be avoided. (The most famous of these, of course, is the Ten Commandments.) By the time of Jesus, the Mosaic law contained a nearly exhaustive list of 613 precepts. Other lists of sins are found in the writings of the prophets. In the New Testament we find similar lists of sins. In his first epistle to the Corinthians, Paul lists those who will not inherit the Kingdom of God: ". . . people of immoral lives, idolaters, adulterers, catamites, sodomites, thieves, usurers, drunkards, slanderers and swindlers . . ."[12]

One point to keep in mind is the relative character of these lists. It is obvious they reflect certain historical circumstances and are conditioned accordingly. Even the Ten Commandments have to be reinterpreted in the light of the modern understanding of human relationships. For example, when Paul denounced homosexuals, as in the quote above, he obviously had no idea that a large number of the population were not responsible for their homosexual orientation.

One of the concerns regarding sins has always been their degree of seriousness. For Catholics, this concern was intensified by the mandate of the Council of Trent that all mortal sins be confessed in detail. This resulted in an unhealthy preoccupation with trying to define accurately and even quantitatively the boundary between mortal and venial sin. Such a preoccupation was certainly foreign to the spirit of the Bible, which

11. Ibid., p. 276.
12. 6:9–10.

spoke of sin not in terms of mortal and venial, but of fundamental option or conversion.

But under the influence of legalism and the rigorism associated especially with the Jansenists and also the advent of the exact sciences with their obsession with measurement, Catholic moralists of the seventeenth and eighteenth centuries often emphasized the quantitative and objective aspects of sin. The classic example of this kind of thinking is found in the Catholic theologians who taught that the theft of one to five ears of grain from a rich man's harvest was no sin; theft of from six to ten ears was a venial sin, while any amount beyond that constituted a mortal sin.[13] Older Catholics today will recall how extreme this tendency could become in the pre-Vatican II Church. A venial sin, for instance, was committed by voluntarily missing the first part or last part of the Mass (before the Gospel or after the Communion), but to miss both of these parts or the Consecration alone would be mortal. In matters sexual, this led to a dissecting of the human anatomy as to which parts, if touched, provided zones of mortal and venial sin, etc. Many Catholics brought up in this system still suffer from scrupulosity, being frequently tormented with doubts about whether a particular action or even thought was a mortal sin or not.

The quantitative and objective approach to mortal sin has largely been abandoned by Catholic theologians today, who prefer to think of mortal sin in terms of what they call the *fundamental option*. The theory of fundamental option is based partly on Scripture and partly on the insight of modern psychology which holds that human beings have the capacity to make basic decisions that determine the whole orientation of their life. Thus, from a religious standpoint they can choose a life-style that is fundamentally selfish and turns them away from God and others, or they can choose one that commits them to serving God and neighbor. Mortal sin, therefore, would be a fundamental option in favor of self as opposed to the demands of God and others. Such a decision would place one in the state of mortal sin. Actions taken in accord with this basic option would constitute mortal or venial sin depending on how much they reinforce this evil option. On the other hand, in the case of those whose fundamental option is for God and others, actions that deviate seriously from this option would be mortal or venial depending on how much they weaken one's option for God. Obviously, in this perspective there is no question of a

13. Bernard Häring, *Free and Faithful in Christ,* Vol. 1, p. 403.

simple categorizing of sin into mortal or venial. Nor is a venial sin to be taken lightly, inasmuch as it weakens one's commitment to God.

One of the questions often occurring is why my behavior is not always in accord with my fundamental stance. Theoretically speaking, if my fundamental option is for God and others, my actions should follow suit. But often they don't. My behavior contains an appalling mixture of good and evil, and so I can never be sure of my fundamental stance. This contradiction within my soul is one of the signs of original sin. It would explain why our fundamental stance never "succeeds in fully and unequivocally expressing itself in behavior."[14]

As Father Häring says, freedom in its "basic depth" is not just a matter of saying yes or no to a specific option; it is the power to mold and create ourselves, to become what we truly are. The fundamental option decides about one's "heart," which can overflow with love and goodness but can also harbor deeply rooted selfishness. "Self-realization in openness towards others—love—is the true moral commitment of a person's basic freedom. Withdrawal into oneself is the negative self-commitment."[15]

We must also remember, as Häring says, that while in the abstract our fundamental option should govern and influence all our actions, in fact, because of various factors such as genetic inheritance, the tug of evil in our environment, etc., our actions are often not in "synch" with our fundamental option. "It needs long and patient striving, attention and continuing conversion until that fundamental option is so embodied in fundamental attitudes, in virtues, that the whole life-style is a coherent and true expression of the unique self as God created it to be."[16]

Obviously from this perspective there is no question of a simple categorizing of sin into mortal or venial. However, one can safely say that a sin involving some relatively small matter should not be considered mortal. The important word is *relatively*, for the act is to be judged according to one's level of maturity, awareness and full use of freedom.

Scripture does not use the term fundamental option when speaking of sin. But it is clear that its description of mortal sin amounts to the same thing. The perspective of the Bible is always the call to conversion. To reject this call is mortally sinful. The degree of sinfulness of any act, according to Scripture, is in proportion to the danger it presents of turning one away from God. It makes no sharp distinction between mortal and

14. Timothy O'Connell, op. cit., p. 476.
15. *Free and Faithful in Christ*, Vol. 1, p. 188.
16. Ibid., p. 195.

venial. It recognizes there are grave faults which nevertheless are not mortal: "If anybody sees his brother commit a sin/that is not a deadly sin,/he has only to pray, and God will give life to the sinner . . . Every kind of wrong-doing is sin,/but not all sin is deadly."[17]

If we understand mortal sin, then, as involving a negative fundamental option, it is clear that it is not to be identified with any specific act. Rather, it is the "act of self-disposition occurring *through* and *in* that concrete categorical act."[18] But mortal sin never occurs except in connection with the doing of specific deeds.

Several conclusions may be drawn here. One is that the commission of a mortal sin would be a relatively infrequent occurrence. How often would the ordinary person change the fundamental direction of his life? As the most serious act of our life, it certainly cannot be something done casually, flippantly or accidentally.

Second, since mortal sin is not simply identifiable with the actual deed but, rather, the transcendental orientation of the deed, we cannot know for sure whether any particular deed involved a basic option for or against God, whether, in other words, we are in the state of grace or of sin. We may make a reasonable conjecture, but we can never have certainty about our ultimate standing with God. The only thing we have to fall back on is hope. For God alone, as St. Paul says, can bring to light what is hidden in darkness and manifest the intentions of hearts.[19]

The older moral theology tried to base the distinction between mortal and venial sin mainly on the gravity of the matter. But in the light of our understanding of mortal sin as fundamental option, the difference between the two would, rather, reside in how deeply the person's will is involved. In other words, Does the sin in question spring from the very core of consciousness or only from its periphery? In this perspective, mortal sin would be a rather rare occurrence, for modern psychology shows that many of our acts spring only from the surface of our consciousness. That we could fall in and out of mortal sin several times a day, as the older moralists seemed to imply, is a psychological absurdity. Nevertheless, there is some value to those lists of "mortal sins" and "venial sins" familiar to Catholics—for they at least provide some indication that one may be making a fundamental option in the commission of some act that is objectively very evil.

17. 1 Jn. 5:16–17.
18. Timothy O'Connell, op. cit., p. 71.
19. 1 Cor. 4:2–5.

In this connection it is interesting to note what Bernard Häring says about so-called "sins of weakness." "If the momentary failure, even in grave matters, is not preceded by a series of offences of infidelity to God's grace, and not followed by a substantial weakening of the good direction, then there is at least a high probability that the sin of weakness was not mortal, although it might have been a *grave* venial sin."[20]

## CONSCIENCE

The phenomenon we call *conscience* is a pivotal one in any discussion of morality. It is also so complex and used with so many meanings that some theologians advise against using the term at all. But in spite of the bewildering and conflicting variety of opinions, it seems better to retain the term, since it does at least point to a definite psychological reality.

The link between the concept of conscience and morality is very close. It is the operation of our conscience that provides the main focus in any discussion of morality.

The term conscience is not found in the Bible until the late Book of Wisdom, but the reality it refers to is found in many passages. The most favored term for it is "heart," as in the expression "God probes the heart." At first the Hebrew people thought of conscience as an objective, extrinsic and communal thing. But the great contribution of the prophets was the stress they put on one's interior dispositions and the responsibility of the individual. Jeremiah looked forward to the day when God would seal with his people a new covenant written "in the heart."[21]

The richest biblical treatment of conscience is found in the writings of Paul. As a cultured Roman citizen, he no doubt drew on the Stoic understanding of *syneidesis*, but he enriched it with insights from the Bible and his own Christian experience. For Paul, conscience is a God-given faculty resident in everyone that enables one to distinguish right from wrong. He also calls conscience weak when a person acts against it. But in any case it is sovereign, for even though it may be erring it must be followed.

Paul thus uses the term conscience rather loosely, but later Catholic theologians, following Aquinas, distinguished between **synderesis, moral science** and **conscience.** Synderesis consists of those basic principles which are innate, such as: Good should be done, evil avoided. One must

20. *Free and Faithful in Christ,* Vol. 1, p. 215.
21. Jer. 11:20; 17:10.

act according to nature; happiness must be pursued. **Moral science** provides the knowledge of less evident principles, which must be deduced from the first, or basic, principles. It also includes whatever else can be drawn from revelation or the authority of the Church. Finally, **conscience** is a practical judgment about the morality of a concrete choice I am about to make or have made in the light of my general understanding of morality.

Theologian Timothy O'Connell prefers to call all three of these "a general sense of value, an awareness of personal responsibility which is utterly characteristic of the human person," and he labels the three kinds mentioned above **Conscience 1, Conscience 2** and **Conscience 3. Conscience 2** derives from **Conscience 1** insofar as our awareness of value compels us to search among competing and apparent values for what is really good and worthwhile. **Conscience 2,** then, involves moral reasoning, and here is where a great difference of opinion occurs as people are faced with the ambiguities and ambivalences of human experience. For instance, some Christians argue for pacifism as an imperative of the Gospel, while others justify war, etc. **Conscience 2** is quite different from **Conscience 1.** It needs all the help it can get. It is by no means infallible; it must humbly and sincerely seek the truth.

**Conscience 3** is the practical judgment we make that we should do or not do something here and now. **Conscience 3** is the final norm of morality, and it is infallible in the sense that we must do what it commands. It may be objectively wrong because of an error made by **Conscience 2,** but it must here and now be obeyed. "It is the quintessence of human morality that we should do what *we believe* to be right and avoid what *we believe* to be wrong."[22]

Much of the confusion surrounding the subject of conscience stems from a failure to distinguish between **Conscience 2** and **Conscience 3.** The popular phrase "You must always follow your conscience" applies only to **Conscience 3.** As we said above, **Conscience 2** is not an infallible guide in itself. Its insights must be constantly checked and corrected in the light of new knowledge that we acquire. It must also take into account the teaching of Scripture and the Church.

What about the situation occurring when there is a conflict of conscience with Church authority? Sometimes Catholics are told in such a case they must follow the authority of the Church. Such a statement

22. Timothy O'Connell, op. cit., p. 92.

terribly oversimplifies, since it fails to make the distinction between **Conscience 2** and **Conscience 3**. If by conscience in conflict we mean **Conscience 3**, then it is wrong, for **Conscience 3** is superior to Church authority, since it is the final and infallible norm of conduct. This is the conscience referred to by Vatican II in its *Constitution on the Church in the Modern World* (16): "Deep within his conscience man discovers a law which he has not laid upon himself, but which he must obey. Its voice, ever calling him to love and to do what is good and to avoid evil, tells him inwardly at the right moment: do this, shun that. For man has in his heart a law inscribed by God. His dignity lies in observing this law, and by it he will be judged. His conscience is man's most secret core, and his sanctuary. There he is alone with God, whose voice echoes in his depths."

What is the role of Church authority in the formation of conscience (Conscience 2)? For most Catholics before the Second Vatican Council, a rather simplistic view prevailed. There was very little room for dissent. A good Catholic was one who submitted his conscience totally to the dictates of the Church. Any conflict between conscience and Church teaching was to be resolved in favor of the Church. This was expressed well in the attitude of certain priests during the birth-control controversy while the papal commission was deliberating. They would say, "Why don't they hurry up and tell us what to believe!"

However, the groundwork for a different view of conscience was laid by the bishops at Vatican II. They used the word "conscience" no less than seventy-two times, in eleven of the seventeen documents. They spoke eloquently of the sacredness of conscience as a person's most secret core and sanctuary, that one will be judged by fidelity primarily to conscience, that one must search with all persons of goodwill for the answers to one's moral dilemmas, that freedom is of the essence of conscience, that one is bound to obey even an erring conscience.

This long overdue recognition of the rights of conscience helped to intensify a crisis of authority in the Church. The real implications of the teaching on conscience became fully apparent only during the aftermath of the pope's encyclical *Humanae Vitae*. Conservatives called for blind obedience, while liberals appealed to Vatican II in upholding the right of conscience to dissent from the papal teaching.

Since then, much has been written about the relation of conscience to Church authority. A number of Catholic theologians have attempted to work out syntheses that accord due weight to both Church authority and the rights of the individual conscience. One of these is Bernard Häring, who describes this as "a reciprocity of consciences."[23] He sees the Church as a great school of conscience formation where all would search together for the answers to the terribly perplexing moral problems of our times. All must be open to the truth and ready to follow the inspiration of the Holy Spirit speaking especially through the lives of the saints and prophets among us. All must realize that nobody possesses a monopoly of the truth. The authority of the bishops and the pope will be in proportion only to their willingness to listen to the faithful. Authority is necessary and all should be willing to submit to the teaching of the Church, but to exercise this authority effectively the leaders of the Church must demonstrate their willingness to listen to the faithful, especially to those who "embody the moral and religious authority of life, competence and experience."[24]

There will always be those who try to escape the burden of freedom by a servile dependence on Church authority. These people need to be reminded of the limitations of Church authority as revealed in its history, which shows that it has often been guilty of grievous errors. There is need, as Avery Dulles says, of a theology of the fallibility of the Church. And as another Jesuit, Albert Hartmann, says, "By means of bloody martyrdom the church fought for the freedom of conscience against the pagan state, until it was proclaimed for the first time in the historic Edict of Tolerance at Milan in 311. But later the same church denied others that freedom and persecuted people for the sake of their faith."[25]

Dissenters have played an important role in pushing the Church forward. Häring gives the example of the prophetic dissent of Friedrich Spee, against torture and the burning of witches, which brought the official teaching of the Church more in accord with the demands of the Gospel and respect for human dignity and freedom. Without the dissent of those who courageously opposed various tenets of official teaching under Pius XII, Vatican II would have been impossible. The Jesuit John Courtney Murray, for instance, almost single-handedly forced the hierarchy to reconsider its medieval doctrine which denied full religious freedom to non-Catholics. And in the 1930s and '40s a few brave moral theologians paved the way for Vatican II's change in the teaching on marriage by challenging the prevailing Augustinian theology of sex, which saw the conjugal act

23. *Free and Faithful in Christ,* p. 282.
24. Ibid., p. 283.
25. Quoted by C. Ellis Nelson, *Conscience; Theological and Psychological Perspectives* (Paramus, N.J.: Newman Press, 1973), p. 110.

as shameful and only tolerable if performed with the intention to procreate.

## HOW FREE IS FREE?

The question of how much freedom we really have in making our moral choices is a much debated one. The thoroughgoing determinists deny any real freedom: a person is completely at the mercy of subconscious, instinctual drives. Others, like B. F. Skinner, put people on the level of the animals as a creature totally responsive to rewards and punishment and needing to be socialized by a system of external controls. For Durkheim, the influential sociologist, social conditioning is the key to human behavior.

There is no doubt a great amount of unfreedom. We are very much determined by biological, psychical and social constraints.

Consider, for instance, the recent discoveries of neurosurgery (modifications of the personality induced by lobotomies). Also the effects of various chemicals and drugs on the interior life of the person, profoundly influencing his decision-making powers.

Social pressures, if anything, seem even more telling. There is a widespread feeling today of being submerged in the anonymous mass, of being manipulated by the mass media, of being controlled subliminally by the seducing power of modern technology. But few can live happily with the theory of total human unfreedom. Our experience of freedom is too real. How else can we explain the conflict of conscience in the face of temptation and our ability to withstand compulsion and say, "No," to convention and authority. Moreover, there is the universal testimony of history that human beings have always been held accountable and responsible for their actions.

## GUILT AND THE SUPEREGO

Some would exalt human freedom to the utmost and, like Nietzsche, have us liberated from all constraints. They would discard antiquated notions of sin in order to restore us to a so-called primitive state of innocence, to what Norman O. Brown called the "unrepressed, shameless, guilt-free man."

But man without guilt would be a monster. As Dr. Willard Gaylin, a New York psychotherapist, says, "Guilt, the sense of anguish that we have fallen short of our own standards, is the guardian of our goodness. It is necessary to the development of conscience in children and to the avoidance of antisocial behavior."[26] The absence of guilt feelings is the mark of a psychopath, who can commit the vilest of crimes without remorse. The anticipation of guilt can inhibit unacceptable behavior, and it has been found that people with the highest level of guilt feelings are the least likely to engage in delinquent forms of behavior.

Guilt originates in childhood, when the child internalizes an "ego ideal"—some form of father figure who becomes the model of proper behavior. When the person betrays this ideal in some way, he feels guilt and will punish himself in order to obtain relief. Much antisocial behavior today is due to the lack of appropriate role models or father figures. People grow up without feeling guilt about their wrongdoing.

On the other hand, many people suffer from exaggerated and morbid feelings of guilt out of all proportion to their actual responsibility. This can be due to all sorts of influences, such as an insecure childhood; parents, clergy or teachers who emphasized fear and punishment in moral training and inculcated a legalistic type of morality; etc.

One of the principal factors in causing exaggerated guilt feelings is no doubt the superego, a term coined by Freud for a mechanism he discovered in his patients. It acts as an inner judge of actions and behavior. It is formed when the child internalizes the do's and don'ts "imposed on him at first from without by parents and other authority figures." Thus the parent slaps the child's hand and says "naughty" when the two-year-old reaches into the cookie jar. At age three the child will reach into the cookie jar, slap its own hand and say "naughty" to itself. By age four the child will reach into the cookie jar and now feel "guilt." The external prohibition is internalized into an experience of "feeling guilty."

The driving power of the superego comes from the subject's fear of rejection and his need to be loved, "a frantic compulsion to experience oneself as lovable," which is the most fundamental of the drives of a child. In order to feel secure and avoid rejection, the child internalizes the commands and prohibitions of the authority figures in his life. The guilt feelings experienced when the child goes against these internalized rules rep-

26. New York *Times*, November 29, 1983, p. 13.

resent the fury of the violated superego. This violence of the offended superego arises from the panic felt at losing one's right to be loved.

Growing to maturity of conscience means coming to terms with the superego—a task that takes a lifetime. One must here keep in mind that the commands and prohibitions of the superego do not arise from any kind of perception of the intrinsic goodness or badness of the action in question. The source of such commands and prohibitions is simply in the desire of the person to be loved or the fear of not being loved. The superego moreover operates mainly on the level of the unconscious.

The person of mature conscience is one who consciously chooses to be governed by freely chosen values. The mature person does not act primarily to be loved but to love and so doing experiences self-value.

There are several salient features that differentiate the person dominated by the superego from the person of mature conscience: the superego is static and fixated, whereas the mature conscience is open to change and grows in awareness of value and is able to confront new situations in a creative way; the superego is dependent on authority figures, but the mature conscience does not need support of authority in order to respond to value or disvalue. The excessive influence of the superego betrays itself also in individuals who experience guilt out of all proportion to the offense committed. Likewise it is evident in the person whose guilt feelings and sense of isolation are quickly relieved by confessing to an authority figure, as opposed to the mature person, who finds the solution in a process of growth.

Observation would seem to indicate that many people in society are dominated by the superego. They still see morality largely in terms of obedience to law and authority, which would place them in stage four of Lawrence Kohlberg's system of conscience development.

## KOHLBERG'S THEORY OF CONSCIENCE DEVELOPMENT

A distinguished contemporary psychologist and student of human psychological development, Kohlberg is famous for his theory that human beings normally pass through a number of stages in the development of their conscience. He distinguished six stages at three levels:

1. The *preconventional* level, in which one views rules and expectations as external to oneself.

*Stage one:* the egocentric point of view, marked by a strict obedience-and-punishment orientation. The child foresees the physical consequences of disobeying.

*Stage two:* a concrete individualistic perspective as the child begins to perceive certain values such as fairness and reciprocity but acts mainly to satisfy its own needs while letting others do the same.

2. The *conventional level:* one has internalized the rules.

*Stage three:* marked by mutual, interpersonal expectations and relationships—a good-boy or nice-girl orientation. One wants to earn approval of others by conforming to stereotyped images of what is acceptable behavior.

*Stage four:* a social-system perspective involving respect for authority and the necessity of maintaining order. The person judges from the point of view of the system.

3. The *postconventional level:* the autonomous level of self-chosen principles.

*Stage five:* contractual legalistic orientation. One is aware of the relativity of personal opinion and the need to follow laws built on consensus. There is also recognition of the need to change laws that are unjust and a violation of a person's rights. There is some sense of a moral good beyond law and awareness of the difficulty in some cases of reconciling the moral and legal point of view.

*Stage six:* conscience, or principle, orientation. One appeals to a higher law based on a decision of conscience guided by self-chosen principles of universal validity such as equality of human rights, respect for human dignity. When a law violates these principles, one acts in accordance with the principles.

The aim of all moral education should be to help the person reach the sixth stage, in which one acts in harmony with a conscience that freely decides, on the basis of values and norms to which one is freely committed. The Church, in particular, should not try to impose its moral values but, rather, teach its members how to deal with the ambiguities of life with integrity, fortitude and a willingness to accept the consequence of its choices.

Study has shown that exposure to moral dilemmas and differing types of reasoning will appreciably help a person grow to moral maturity. Thus a certain element of disequilibrium is valuable in stimulating moral growth. A person needs to hear all sides of an issue, digest a great deal of information and be exposed to new ideas in order to become more self-aware and morally mature. This forces one to examine and justify one's own assumptions and thus grow to greater moral maturity.

The family certainly plays a crucial role in the moral development of the child. The atmosphere most conducive to moral growth is one in which the child feels she really belongs and can risk experimenting with new ideas without fear of being rejected. In such a family there is mutual respect and recognition of the equality of all; and decisions are made with the participation of all, and each member's opinions, including those of the children, are respected. In this way, the child learns the give-and-take of problem solving. Moreover, in this type of family, which encourages the children to think for themselves, the child feels no need to adopt a blind nonconformist stance, but will be helped to learn much from giving a fair hearing to adult opinion.[27]

27. See William D. Boyce and Larry C. Jensen, *Moral Reasoning* (Lincoln, Neb.: University of Nebraska Press, 1978), pp. 103f.

# 25

# The Great Debate In Moral Theology: Revisionists vs. Traditionalists

Catholic moral theology has felt the impact of the Second Vatican Council as much as, if not more than, any other area of Catholic thought. It would be no exaggeration to say that a quantum leap has occurred, as tremendous changes have taken place in the way the majority of Catholic moralists see their task.

Possibly the most basic has been the change from the classical to the historical consciousness. Before the Council, Catholic theologians seemed to dwell in a world apart, safe from the corrosive forces of historical change. But the Council was a revelation of how relative much of Church teaching is and how much change is possible. This forced moral theologians to question many of the ideas and principles—such as "natural law" —which they had previously regarded as impervious to change, and to see moral concepts as the products of history and, perhaps for that reason, in many cases outdated.

Another big change was much more attention to Scripture. The great biblical renewal within the Catholic Church affected their *modus operandi* in many significant ways.

Another change is the abandonment of legalism. This was the most characteristic feature of Catholic morality in the past. One sometimes got the impression that morality was simply a matter of obedience to the law as promulgated by the Church. There seemed to be a law to govern almost every situation. People were warned against taking a drop of water before Communion or missing a small part of the Mass.

The new emphasis on the Bible made theologians more aware of how opposed Jesus was to all legalism and how he excoriated the religious leaders for making observance of the law the very touchstone of religion.

Perhaps the most impressive change is the pluralism that is now characteristic of Catholic moral theology. In the past there was a great amount of unanimity as theologians followed the same basic principles and held the same concept of the rights of authority. But since the Council, one finds great diversity of opinion. Fundamentally, however, one can distinguish two main schools of thought today among Catholic moralists: the **revisionists** and the **traditionalists**.

One of the main differences between the two schools is in their approach to the role of *norms,* or *rules.* The revisionists are willing to admit some truth in situation ethics, which in its extreme form—identified with Joseph Fletcher—questions all norms except "love your neighbor." The revisionists would not go that far, but they do espouse an approach often called "proportionalism," which considerably reduces the weight of norms in moral decision-making.

In their view, there are few if any moral absolutes. The function of norms and moral commandments, they say, is to inform us about the values at stake in certain actions. For example, "do not murder" informs us about the value of life; other norms and moral commandments concern human integrity, dignity, etc. Moral rules or norms are not infallible but serve to warn us that if we do the action prohibited without a **proportionate reason,** we may be guilty of sin. In other words, they point to behavior that should be avoided if at all possible.

**Proportionate reason** is the key word in their system. Another is **conflict,** for they see human beings as often involved in situations in which one is caught between the demands of conflicting moral norms. One cannot obey them both—as in the example of the soldier who kills in defense of his country or the one who uses violence to save another's life.

Classical theology (still generally adhered to by the traditionalists) recognized the possibility of such conflict situations, in which two results could be expected: one good and one evil; e.g., a doctor's killing the fetus to save the life of the mother in a case of ectopic pregnancy. But several conditions had to be fulfilled: the evil effect must not be directly intended, but only permitted. Nor could one ever perform an intrinsically evil act to secure a good effect. Nor could the good effect be obtained by means of the evil effect. Thus one could not *directly* kill an innocent person to obtain a greater good—since direct killing of an innocent would be regarded as intrinsically evil.

Thus, from the classical, or traditional, point of view, an intrinsically evil action could not be directly intended even as a means to a good end. Thus a doctor could remove the fallopian tube in an ectopic pregnancy to save the mother, but he could not directly abort the fetus even if the tube could be saved.

An even more curious example: the classical theology would allow a captured agent to pull a pin on a grenade attached to his belt to destroy important documents he had on his person for fear that he might reveal them under torture or influence of drugs. But he would be forbidden to pull the pin if the secret information was not in his belt but in his head. For, in this view, "if the evil physically precedes the willed good and so is the means to its achievement, then it is directly willed and makes the entire act evil, just as if the evil was intended by the act."[1]

For the revisionists, on the other hand, the directness or indirectness of the intention is not to be gauged by the physical relation between the good and evil consequences. They say, ". . . the justification or non-justification must come from an appreciation and estimation of all the values and disvalues in the total consequences of the behavior under consideration."[2]

Thus the revisionists have introduced several modifications into the theory of double effect. One, they reject the characterization of certain actions as intrinsically evil regardless of consequences and circumstances (e.g., direct sterilization). They also reject the distinction between *directly* and *indirectly* intending the evil effect, which, as they say, often involves mere semantics. They prefer another model summed up in the phrase "Is there a proportionate reason?"—not "Was it intended or caused directly or indirectly?" A classic example they give is the horseman who flees his enemies and in the process has to trample on some people occupying the road. Classical Catholic moral theology judged him not guilty of sin because he only *"indirectly"* intended, that is, only *permitted* their deaths (since the killing of the innocent did not *physically* precede the act of escape.) But as the revisionists say, the escaper cannot say he only "per-

1. Peter Knauer, S.J. "The Principle of Double Effect." In Richard McCormick and Charles Curran, eds., *Readings in Moral Theology* (New York: Paulist Press, 1979), p. 18.
2. Nicholas Crotty, O.P "Conscience and Conflict," in *Theological Studies*, Vol. 32 (1974), p. 222.

mitted" the deaths, for the deaths were means of his escaping, and the means as well as the ends are both directly intended.

The revisionists make an important distinction between **premoral** and **moral** evil. Killing, wounding, sterilizing, deceiving, etc., they say, are **premoral** evils, not necessarily **moral** evils. **Premoral** evil embraces all those **disvalues** involved in our human situation: physical injury, violence, ignorance, error, fatigue, poverty, etc. These **premoral** evils are inevitably present in the human situation because of the unavoidable limitations built into our human situation. But causing **premoral** (or ontic—another term they use) evil is not in itself an immoral action. It becomes immoral only when we cause the ontic evil without **proportionate reason.** We must realize that we cannot realize all possible values but have to sacrifice some in order to secure others. The doctor has to weigh telling an untruth in order to allow the patient peace of mind, The couple must weigh obedience to *Humanae Vitae* against the risk of jeopardizing the well-being and education of the children they already have, etc.

As the revisionists often point out, this is a world of ambiguity, and since we often face situations of conflict, we must often choose to permit a disvalue in order to secure a more important value. They give the example of the soldiers in World War II who took their own lives, rather than be drugged and tortured into revealing secrets that might endanger the lives of others. What they did was moral because they preferred a lesser premoral disvalue (their own death) in order to secure a higher premoral value (many lives and important military secrets).

For the revisionists, then, practically all norms admit of exceptions (that is, *material* norms, which prohibit certain concrete actions, as distinct from *formal* norms, which, rather, serve to motivate and inspire us; e.g., be honest, be chaste, etc.—this distinction they make, between material and formal norms, is important to keep in mind). They do, however, admit that some **material** norms are virtually exceptionless, for instance, "cruel treatment of a child which is of no benefit to the child."[3] Another one is given by Louis Janssens; "You shall render help to a person in extreme distress."[4]

In support of their case, they show how hard it is to appeal to the Bible as evidence of **absolute material** norms. Biblical studies indicate how relative the morality enshrined in the Old Testament is. It was a dynamic and

3. Richard M. Gula, S.S. *What Are They Saying About Moral Norms?* (New York: Paulist Press, 1981), p. 78.
4. Ibid.

evolving morality. The Ten Commandments, for instance, which predates Moses in fact, while beautifully expressive of Israel's desire to live in a covenant relationship with God, was not more enlightened than other moral codes of the day, e.g., Hammurabi's. Moreover, when examined in context, they actually demand much less than many people think. For instance, the fourth commandment prohibited cursing only one's parents, while the fifth forbade the killing of a fellow Israelite.

When it comes to the New Testament, it is not easy to prove that it contains a revealed set of material norms as absolutes. In fact, a growing number of Catholic authors hold that on the level of concrete behavior the New Testament inculcates nothing that could not be derived from human experience. They insist on the historical and cultural limitations of the morality taught even in the New Testament. And they remind us that the ethical content of the New Testament, for the most part, is not derived from Jesus, but from a variety of pagan and Jewish sources.

The traditionalists, or deontologists (a name they sometimes prefer), refuse to admit that morality is determined solely by consequences and contend there are many moral absolutes, such as the prohibition of masturbation, contraception, direct sterilization, artificial insemination, abortion, homosexuality, extramarital sex, etc. According to their theory, one must never act in a way that offends against a basic moral good: life, physical integrity of the sexual act, worship, etc. Abortion, for instance, they point out, strikes directly against the good of human life and therefore, they hold, is intrinsically evil.

An essential difference between the deontologists and the revisionists is in the kind of evil they claim is at stake in violating a basic good. For the deontologists, all direct killing is a *moral* evil. For the revisionists, direct killing considered apart from motive and circumstances can only be termed a *premoral* evil.

The deontologists, or traditionalists, accuse the revisionists of judging morality solely by the consequences—but the revisionists deny this. A leading revisionist, the Jesuit Richard McCormick, gives an example: betraying a secret. Betraying a secret, he says, is inherently a disvalue (premoral evil). One does not condemn such an action simply because of the evil consequences foreseeable. Rather, the question is, Can there be a **proportionate reason** for doing this *premoral evil*—that is, betraying a secret?[5]

5. *Notes on Moral Theology, 1965 Through 1980* (Washington, D.C.: University Press of America, 1981), p. 541.

Another charge against the revisionists is that their system of morality is individualistic and subjectivistic. But this is wrong, as McCormick says, for the revisionists insist that the weighing of values against disvalues must be done in conjunction with the whole community. Or, as Bernard Häring would put it: in terms of the *reciprocity of consciences.* There are many actions, for instance, that in the eyes of the community could never be justified by a proportionate reason. "Sorting out the claims of conflicting values is a community task subject to objective criteria."[6] McCormick gives the example of capital punishment. For centuries the disvalue of the killing involved was justified by the value of greater security for the community. However, the trade-off is no longer clear, and so many communities have done away with capital punishment.

One of the main reasons for the division in Catholic moral theology between revisionists and deontologists is their differing understanding of *natural law.* Deontologists, who claim that some actions are intrinsically evil regardless of circumstances, do so mainly on the basis of their interpretation of natural law. However, it is generally agreed that natural law is an ambiguous concept. According to one reading, natural law is supposed to provide norms that are applicable always, everywhere and for everyone. It is supposed to be discoverable by everyone by simple study of the human organism insofar as we can easily discover the purpose nature intends for our various organs: the eye's primary purpose obviously is to see, the ear to hear, the stomach to digest, speech to communicate, the genitals to reproduce, etc. Natural law, then, in this reading would oblige us to respect the finality of these organs. To be moral is therefore to act in accord with the blueprint provided us by nature. Natural law would thus indeed be a reflection of God's eternal law, as Aquinas and the classical moralists said, since He is the One Who has designed nature to operate in this fashion.

We realize today, however, that this very *physicalist* interpretation of natural law is a partial reading of the natural-law tradition. It basically derives from the Greeks via the Roman jurist Ulpian (d. A.D. 228), who had a paramount influence on medieval scholastic theories of natural law.

There is another approach to natural law that is less deterministic and was favored by such Roman thinkers as Cicero (d. 43 B.C.) and Gaius, a second-century-A.D. Roman jurist who took a much more hopeful view of the ability of human beings through the use of reason to subordinate and

6. Ibid., p. 599.

adapt the biological and physical facts of life in order to reach more humane ends.

It is most noteworthy that Thomas Aquinas vacillated between these two approaches to natural law. In some passages, he emphasizes the order of reason and with Cicero takes a dynamic, open view of human nature. In others, he seems to identify the demands of natural law with biological and physical processes.

This tension between the order of reason and the order of nature is very much evident in subsequent Catholic theology and explains much of the confusion in Catholic natural-law thought today.

In sexual and medical matters, the physicalist approach has held sway. Following Aquinas, who, for instance, considered masturbation more wicked than rape, since it was more abusive of the genitals' natural link with procreation, the modern popes have inculcated a physicalist doctrine of natural law. Pope Pius XII, for instance, leaned heavily on Francis X. Hurth, S.J. (1880–1963), a leading professor of moral theology at the Gregorian University who was largely responsible for Pius' major addresses on medical and sexual issues. Father Hurth saw an exact coincidence of the moral law and the biological law particularly in matters of sex. He regarded procreativity as the exclusive primary finality of human sexuality. This, he held, was "the intention of nature inscribed in the organs and their functions." Pope Paul VI in *Humanae Vitae* (1968) remained faithful to this tradition in his assertion that married couples must respect "the laws of the generative process" as ministers of the design established by the Creator.

This physicalist approach to natural law has been subjected to much criticism and has generally been rejected by the revisionist theologians. In their view, biological processes are not the final arbiter of morality but must be subservient to the total well-being of human life. They point out how Vatican II proposed as a general criterion of morality not "the intention of nature inscribed in the organs and their function" but the "person integrally and adequately considered." And as Richard McCormick says, "To discover what is promotive or destructive of the person is not a deductive procedure."[7]

---

7 "Therapy or Tampering? The Ethics of Reproductive Technology," *America*, December 7, 1985, p. 400.

# 26

## A New Morality of Sex?

As the foregoing shows, Catholic moral theology today is in a state of great ferment, or as some would say, anarchy. Deontologists battle with revisionists while the magisterium sides with the deontologists and tries to uphold the traditional principles. In no area is the conflict more intense and emotionally jarring than in questions of sex. Paul VI's *Humanae Vitae* served as a catalyst as many theologians and even some bishops contested its basic assertion that artificial contraception is not permissible.

There has been no letup since that epochal document appeared. Rome has continued to issue its stern condemnations of birth control, of extramarital sex, masturbation and other forms of unconventional sexual behavior, while Catholic theologians have continued to register their dissent.

The present pope, John Paul II, in particular, is not the type to equivocate. As a young bishop, he took a strong stand against liberal sexual morality in his book *Love and Responsibility*, which endeared him to the conservatives in the Curia. Then he stepped onto the world stage, firmly committed to the Church's traditional tenets on sex and determined to preach them in season and out of season.

The words of the pope and the Vatican commissions, however, fall for the most part on deaf ears, as is obvious from polls and other indications that even faithful Catholics no longer conform to Church teachings on sex. Vatican efforts against "artificial" methods of birth control have been in vain, and the Church has suffered such a general loss of credibility that its preachments on sex are ignored if not scorned by the overwhelming majority of Catholics. It is the rare Catholic today who confesses sins against the sixth commandment.

In the meantime, the pursuit of the perfect orgasm continues unabated. Queen Victoria may be uncomfortable in her grave, but the hedonistic pursuit of sexual pleasure has become a marked feature of most urban societies of the West. A glance at the bookstand in any airport reveals a startling array of erotica. Old "classics" like De Sade and Harris keep company with the latest manuals: *The Joy of Sex, More Joy of Sex* and *Fear of Flying.* X-rated movies abound, and the nearly undraped human anatomy leaps out at us as we spin the TV dial.

What is behind all this?

Christian fundamentalists see it, of course, as a clear indication of the devil's power over fallen humanity. But their hellfire-and-brimstone warnings reach only a tiny portion.

More rationalistic observers offer a better explanation of this great change in sexual mores, this huge release of sexual energy. They point to such factors as increasing control over fertilization combined with reduction in family size; women's drive for equality, with its rejection of traditional male sexual privileges; increased psychological knowledge, which calls into question traditional sexual values, and finally the enormous increase in the material standard of living, which allows people more freedom to experiment.

Questions previously unthought of now face the average parent: Should I allow my fourteen-year-old daughter to get on the pill? Should my church provide for homosexual marriages? Should I allow a sex clinic to provide a surrogate partner for my husband, who is having difficulties? Should I recommend masturbation to my pubescent daughter as a relief for menstrual tension?

It seems obvious that if the Church is to regain credibility to help people deal realistically with their sexual dilemmas and reach maturity, it will have to formulate a more convincing and intelligible approach than we find in its traditional doctrine.

This doctrine was summed up recently in the "Declaration on Sexual Ethics," issued by the Congregation for the Doctrine of the Faith on December 29, 1975, which focused on masturbation, homosexuality and premarital sex.

At the outset, the document laments the increasing corruption of morals and unbridled exaltation of sex and notes how Christians are confused because of the diversity of opinions contrary to the teaching of the Church.

The document asserts the existence of an objective moral order and speaks of precepts of the natural law that are absolute and of immutable value and can be grasped by reason. It is in the light of this objective order of nature that sexual acts must be judged. The use of the sexual act, therefore, must be in accordance with the finality inscribed in it by the Creator. This means that if the sexual act is to preserve its "full sense of mutual self-giving and human procreation in the context of true love," the partners must be married.[1]

Having enunciated its basic principle, drawn from natural law, that the sexual function has its true meaning and moral goodness only in marriage, the document goes on to rule out premarital sex, homosexual acts and masturbation.

Premarital sex is ruled out even when the partners are deeply committed to each other and are impeded from marrying only by adverse circumstances. No possible exceptions are admitted to the principle that every genital act must be within the framework of marriage, for it is only marriage that can protect the relationship of the couple from the corrosion of whims and caprices. Moreover, Scripture and Church tradition teach the necessity of marriage, while experience shows the importance of a stable union of parents for the well-being and proper development of children.

As to homosexuality, while allowing for the possibility that some homosexuals are fixed in their orientation "by some kind of innate instinct or a pathological constitution" and should be treated with compassion, the document still considers all acts of homosexuality as intrinsically disordered and not to be approved of. For they lack the essential and indispensable finality.[2]

Masturbation is likewise described as a grave moral disorder, for, once again, "the deliberate use of the sexual faculty outside normal conjugal relations essentially contradicts the finality of the faculty."[3] It rejects arguments drawn from sociological data showing the high incidence of this behavior, which in the eyes of the author only attests to the power of original sin. However, while refusing to accept the theory of psychology that masturbation forms a normal part of sexual development, it does

1. Text in *Catholic Mind*, April 1976, p. 55.
2. Ibid., p. 57.
3. Ibid.

admit the possibility that subjectively the person may not be guilty of serious fault, due to such causes as the pressure of habit.

The response of Catholic theologians to this document sheds much light on the current situation in moral theology. Those who were critical of it far outnumbered its defenders, as Richard McCormick says.[4] Its defects were many, according to the critics: outmoded theology and language, contempt for the empirical sciences, legalism and abusive authoritarianism, misuse of Scripture. Bernard Häring scored its rigorism, "which goes far beyond that of the past. It brings tightly together all previous rigoristic teachings and presents them simply as *the* tradition."[5]

Many of the theologians followed Charles Curran in decrying the document's physicalist approach to natural law, which evaluates sexual acts mainly in terms of the biological processes involved. But as Curran points out, modern knowledge shows that the psychological aspect is just as important and objective. Masturbation, for instance, viewed from the standpoint of the individual's psychological development, may be regarded more leniently than the Vatican document seems to do. While masturbation does not reflect the full meaning of sexual behavior, it should not be taken too seriously, "providing the individual is truly growing in sexual maturity and integration."[6]

Likewise as to homosexual acts, which the Vatican document excludes as "intrinsically disordered," Curran holds a theory of compromise which proposes that for the irreversible homosexual "these actions are not wrong for this individual provided there is a context of a loving commitment to another."[7]

In his *Issues in Sexual and Medical Ethics,* Curran draws up a comprehensive critique of the Vatican document. Its methodology he finds deficient inasmuch as it subscribes to an "essential order of nature." Its espousal of immutable principles and a deductive approach leaves little room for developing cultural and historical realities. Its methodology thus stands in sharp contrast with the methodology of the *Pastoral Constitution on the Church in the Modern World,* of Vatican II, which pays great attention to the signs of the times and follows a much more inductive type of logic. Second, the document bases its conclusions on the finality of the physical act itself without reference to the personal dimension and the

4. *Notes on Moral Theology, 1965 Through 1980,* p. 60.
5. Ibid., p. 148.
6. Ibid., p. 677.
7. Ibid.

connection between love and sexuality. This cold, impersonal approach leaves much to be desired. Third, the document upholds a legalistic version of morality by its emphasis on principle, norms and laws, whereas Curran thinks the Christian model should be one of relational responsibility that focuses primarily on the values that laws are meant to safeguard. Moreover, the document speaks with a tone of certitude that belies the difficulty of discovering "eternal and immutable laws" when one is dealing with the contingencies of human relationships—a difficulty that Aquinas himself recognized when he admitted the possibility of exceptions in particular cases. Fourth, the document gives insufficient attention to the actual life of people today and makes unsubstantiated assertions about what the Christian people today actually believe about such issues as homosexuality and masturbation. Finally, he scores its unhistorical approach to Scripture, which lifts texts out of their historical and cultural circumstances and applies them to entirely different situations. It unhistorically treats the Bible as a moral code with ready-made answers.[8]

As Curran's critique shows, the Catholic Church has reached a stage of intense crisis as far as authority in matters sexual goes. Its credibility is weak. The official statements of the Church still hand down the black-and-white prescriptions of the past with hardly any reference to advances in the human sciences or even to the latest findings in scriptural, dogmatic and moral theology.

## A NEW SEXUAL ETHIC?

The call for a new ethic of sexual morality has become clear and insistent. As Jack Dominian says in his *Proposals for a New Sexual Ethic,* ". . . the whole basis of Christian thinking on sexual morality needs fundamental reconstruction."[9]

The difficulty of effecting such a change is fully appreciated only if we realize how deeply rooted the traditional teaching is, with its basically puritanical and negative attitudes toward the body and sexual pleasure. We must not forget that, for many centuries, it was the constant teaching of the Church that intercourse was sinful unless performed for the explicit purpose of procreation, that intercourse during menstruation or pregnancy

8. Charles Curran, *Issues in Sexual and Medical Ethics* (Notre Dame, Ind.: University of Notre Dame Press, 1978), pp. 30–52.
9. London: Darton, Longman & Todd, 1977, p. 21.

was a mortal sin, that only one position (husband on top) was allowable, etc. The apostle Paul and the Fathers of the Church were deeply influenced by the prevailing Stoic philosophy, which exalted reason over emotion, and in consequence manifested a distrust of sexual pleasure which has marked the teaching of the Church down to our time. Jerome thought marriage justified only because it could produce virgins, while Augustine stamped the Catholic teaching with his own profound pessimism about human sexuality. Later authors continued in the same vein. Pope Gregory the Great taught that a person could no more have intercourse without sin than fall into a fire without getting burned. Adult Catholics can readily remember how fear-laden and sex-obsessed Catholic moral teaching was. Nuns and priests with little or no experience often descended into the most ludicrous particulars when giving instruction: girls were not to wear patent-leather shoes lest they afford a mirror view of their thighs, while the body was divided into the touchable and untouchable parts.

To dwell on the negative aspects of the tradition is not to deny its positive side. Certainly no one who looks out on the sexual anarchy rampant today can take a smug approach about the follies of the old method. It did help many people achieve stability in their married lives, and it was certainly not purely negative. It helped keep many people from making sex an idol. It curbed the human propensity to unreal expectations about sex. It maintained in spite of everything the basic Scriptural insight that sex was a gift of the Creator and its expression in marriage a sacrament. But a simple reiteration of the traditional teaching is no longer feasible, for as Jack Dominian says, ". . . the undeniable vacuum in Christian thought is being filled by alternative ideologies which have little respect for either Christian or human values."[10]

In this vacuum, the Catholic is often told just to follow his conscience, but how can one escape a pure situational ethics in the absence of any consensus in the Church on such matters as the significance of sexual pleasure, masturbation, premarital sexual intercourse, contraception, divorce and the role of love?

If we are ever to reach a new consensus, it seems obvious that we will have to explicitly disown the rigidity and pessimism of the past teaching, and confront the challenge of speaking meaningfully about sex in today's world.

It was out of such a concern that the board of directors of the Catholic

10. *Proposals for a New Sexual Ethic*, p. 21.

Theological Society established a committee to do a study on human sexuality in the hope of "providing some helpful and illuminating guidelines in the present confusion."[11]

The authors of this study at the outset recognize the need to take a much broader view of sexuality than the genital and generative one found in the traditional doctrine. They assert that human sexuality is only properly understood as a basic differentiation which defines the way a person experiences the world, that is, either as male or female. It is the reason why male and female feel incomplete and why they seek completion in one another. "Interpersonally, it calls each to reach out to the other without whom full integration can never be achieved."[12] The proper meaning of sexuality is not simply the satisfaction of an animal urge, but the means by which people break out of their isolation and attain communion with one another. Sex has the potential to bring people to the deepest level of intimacy. Sex serves the absolute need of people to reach out and to embrace others to achieve personal fulfillment. Sex plays a crucial role in the struggle to reach maturity, in becoming fully a man or fully a woman, through creative relationships with the opposite sex.

For these reasons, then, the authors feel it necessary to go beyond the traditional view which defined the purpose of sex as procreative and unitive. The norm they propose for defining wholesome sexuality is whatever "fosters a creative growth toward integration."[13] In other words, sexual behavior is moral if it contributes to the growth of the person toward integration. "Destructive sexuality results in personal frustration and interpersonal alienation."[14] The norm laid down in the traditional doctrine that sexuality must be *both* "procreative and unitive" restricts the meaning of sexuality to the context of marriage and procreation and does not sufficiently bring out the potential sexuality has for enhancing the total development of the person.

While rejecting any simplistic attempt to define specifically what concrete sexual acts meet the criterion they have just enunciated, they believe it possible to identify a number of values that may enable one to determine whether a particular sexual act is conducive to growth and integration. Seven of these they find particularly significant. Sex should be

11. Anthony Kosnik et al., *Human Sexuality: New Directions in American Catholic Thought* (New York: Paulist Press, 1977), p. xi.
12. Ibid., p. 82.
13. Ibid., p. 86.
14. Ibid.

1. *Self-liberating:* it must foster one's own personal growth as well as that of the other person.

2. *Other-enriching:* not only not manipulative, but one must be sensitive, considerate, thoughtful, compassionate, understanding and supportive of the other.

3. *Honest:* They recognize how difficult this requirement is, for human beings are infinitely complex and there are many differences between the partners. But true communion can occur only if both truly open their hearts to each other.

4. *Faithful:* This is necessary for the kind of unique, deep and enduring relationship that marriage should create.

5. *Socially responsible:* There is a social dimension to sexuality, and it should be used in a way that promotes the interests of society.

6. *Life-serving:* While most marriage partners should generously cooperate with God in transmitting life, some may decide they can serve life better by not begetting children.

7. *Joyous:* It is meant to be an extremely pleasurable act and a celebration of the life that it serves.

The authors note they took as their starting point Vatican II's recommendation that sexual behavior be evaluated in terms of the nature of the human person and his acts. Sexuality, they claim, should serve the human person and promote his creative growth and integration.

The reaction to *Human Sexuality* in the Catholic community was predictable. Brickbats and bouquets came flying at the authors from all directions. For the most part, the bishops found it an intolerable attempt to subvert the authority of the magisterium. The Committee on Doctrine of the National Conference of Bishops found much fault with the study: its treatment of Scripture, they labeled impoverished; its claim to provide pastoral guidelines, unwarranted; its normative criteria, too vague; and its appeal to empirical data, superficial.

One thing the controversy made clear: any attempt to supersede the traditional procreative-unitive norm was bound to meet tremendous opposition, since such efforts are immediately interpreted as an attack on the authority of the Church.

Critics of *Human Sexuality*, however, were not limited to the authoritarians. Liberal moralists such as Richard McCormick and Daniel Maguire, for instance, found the criteria for healthy sex rather unhelpful, since they do not address what is specific to sex itself. The same criteria could be applied to almost any human activity: dietary habits, athletics, study, etc.

In the same year that *Human Sexuality* appeared, another attempt to revise the traditional Catholic sex morality was published: *Sexual Morality: A Catholic Perspective*, by Philip S. Keane, S.S.[15]

Keane espouses a holistic understanding of sexuality which stresses the idea that sexuality is a gift of God that "touches human persons on all levels of their existence including the physical, the psychological, the spiritual and the social. It is fundamental to the way we relate to ourselves, to others and to God."[16] He notes that too often in the past the Catholic Church took an almost exclusively physical procreational approach to sexuality and failed to note how deeply sexuality conditions our whole range of interpersonal relationships and even opens us to the mystery of God himself.

Keane argues, therefore, that we must abandon the physicalist approach to sex and take a relational, responsible one. That is, in judging the morality of our sexual acts we should ask the question, How am I using God's gift of sexuality to relate most responsibly to myself, to other people and to the holy mystery of God?

Instead of trying to set up a new set of criteria, like the authors of *Human Sexuality*, Keane bases his evaluations of the sexual act on the revisionists' principle of **proportionate reason** and the distinction between *ontic (premoral)* and *moral evil*—ontic evil referring to the unavoidable evil we may cause but not intend in pursuing some course of action. Thanks to the nature of the world we live in, some disorder or ontic evil is often involved in our actions. But the ontic, or premoral, evil becomes moral evil only if we do not have a proportionate reason for positing the action. Thus masturbation involves some disorder, since it fails to realize the full possibility of sexuality, but viewed in the light of the total good of the person, it might be justified as a stage in adolescent development, for instance, or as a means of relieving intolerable sexual tension, etc.

Applying this logic to the problem of birth control, Keane sees contraception as justifiable in certain circumstances. While contraception certainly involves some ontic evil, since it precludes procreation and, in addition, often includes some concomitant problems such as certain physical or psychological drawbacks, it can be justified at times, for instance if prolonged abstention from intercourse would endanger the unitive pur-

15. New York: Paulist Press, 1977.
16. *Sexual Morality: A Catholic Perspective*, p. 4.

pose of marriage or if some physical disability necessitated the use of contraception or some serious economic factor ruled out the possibility of having more children.

Another important contribution to the debate has come from Jack Dominian in a series of books and articles that have appeared regularly over the past ten years or so. Like other revisionists, he considers the traditional sex doctrine of the Church obsolete, and like them also, he finds the key to a new approach in the concept of the human person and love. The fundamental drive of the human person, he says, is growth toward wholeness, which means the fullest realization of one's potential at every level: physical, psychological, spiritual and social. Like all activity, sexual activity should be judged according to how it affects this growth.

Now, he says, any acts that do not engage the whole person fall short of human potential and carry with them the danger of dehumanization. Thus if persons in acts of sex attend only to the physical aspects, they cheat themselves of its full meaning and potential for personal growth. For sexual activity has great significance in promoting growth insofar as it engages the whole person and attains its fullest realization in love.

Love meets two very important needs of the individual. One is the need for someone who can enter into our inner world and react sensitively and compassionately to our need for acceptance and our need for significance and meaning. The other is the need to be healed of the many wounds inflicted on us in the struggle for existence. We need someone who can share our pain, one to whom we can reveal our deepest hurts and sorrows, one who can heal us with love and whom we in turn can heal. And as Dominian says, "It hardly needs saying that healing cannot easily occur under circumstances of transient relationships . . . We need to trust the other sufficiently to feel that we can take the risk of exposing our painful wounds . . . to feel that he or she can take our pain and handle it with care and effectiveness. This needs time, *continuity, reliability* and *predictability.* (Our emphasis) The essentials of healing, that is, healing the whole person, do not occur in transient relationships . . ."[17]

Again, in a fruitful relationship, each partner acts as midwife to the other "by rendering conscious the unconscious, confirming talent in place of doubt and uncertainty, reinforcing initiative, encouraging experimentation, providing succour at times of pain, failure and despair, helping one to face and integrate the dark side of oneself."[18]

17 *Proposals for a New Sexual Ethic,* pp. 35–39.
18. Ibid., p. 40.

Now, while this can occur to some extent in any real friendship, only a permanent relationship, consecrated in marriage, can ordinarily facilitate growth to the fullest extent, for only such a relationship answers the human need for reliability, predictability and continuity.

Marriage must be, therefore, first and foremost a community of love between husband and wife. Children are certainly part of the picture, but their successful nurture depends on the quality of the relationship between husband and wife. In this sense, the procreation and education of children are subordinate to the formation of a true community of love embracing husband and wife.

## SPECIFIC QUESTIONS OF SEXUAL MORALITY

The first category has to do with sexual acts of the person with himself, and these include sexual fantasies or impure thoughts and masturbation. Traditional Catholic morality even in its updated version tended to be very severe on these matters. Impure thoughts (unless immediately connected with the marriage act) and masturbation if consciously and fully intended, were considered objectively serious sins. Any directly willed venereal pleasure not directly connected with the rightful exercise of the marital act was considered against nature, as a frustration of its purpose. In this physicalist understanding of the natural law, indeed there could not even be **parvity** of matter when it came to sins of sex—meaning that any directly willed and illicit venereal pleasure was considered mortally sinful no matter how trivial it might be. A lustful embrace, a passionate kiss, or an obscene thought (if it triggered erotic feelings that were consciously consented to) was regarded as a mortal sin. Theologians did tend to mitigate the harshness of this teaching by restricting culpability because of lack of sufficient reflection or full consent of the will, but it nevertheless tended to engender enormous guilt feelings about sex in the hearts of conscientious Catholics.

This rigid teaching has largely been rejected by the revisionists under the influence of the behavioral sciences. They reject it as a physicalist understanding of natural law. They point out how the behavioral sciences have shown how frequent casual and spontaneous erotic fantasies are, and how they actually help people cope with the sexual tension in their lives. Moreover, such thoughts do not as a rule affect the fundamental moral orientation of a person to the point that a question of mortal sin need arise.

Data from the sciences have also severely challenged the traditional condemnation of masturbation, which to some extent was based on out-moded views of human reproduction. At one time it was believed the male sperm was the only active factor in human reproduction, and the sperm was regarded as humans in miniature. Hence spilling it was tantamount to abortion as well as a waste of a precious element. Other myths also played a role. Masturbation was blamed for a whole host of physical and spiritual ills such as acne, asthma, heart murmurs, lethargy and even insanity.

Another factor in changing the minds of theologians was the finding of sociology that masturbation is very common among both males and fe-males, especially during adolescence.

Many Catholic revisionists in consequence take a somewhat benign view of masturbation, especially in one's adolescent phase, as part of a person's growth toward sexual maturity. For Jack Dominian it is even a necessary part of growing up, since it helps one to discover the new di-mensions of one's body and prepares one for heterosexual relationships.

A somewhat less benign view is taken by Philip Keane, who sees some ontic evil in every act of masturbation, since it does not realize the full potential of sexual experience. But Keane is hesitant about speaking of it as moral evil—certainly not in prepubertal cases and hardly in the case of adolescents as long as one realizes one should be moving to reach a higher stage of sexual maturity; but in the case of adults he considers the ontic evil more serious, since it can signal a certain amount of moral disorder. Like all expressions of human sexuality, it can be problematic. It might, for instance, be used compulsively as a substitute for more rewarding, interpersonal encounters.

The ontic evil of adult masturbation, according to Keane, has to be weighed against a variety of factors, depending on circumstances. For instance, one would be very lenient in judging a single person who has been addicted to masturbation since adolescence. And certainly masturba-tion may be employed to obtain sperm for medical reasons to improve a couple's chance of procreating.

In the past twenty years we have seen a tremendous change in the public attitude toward pornography. Several decisions of the United States Supreme Court helped to remove the barriers of censorship previously holding it in check. In consequence, nearly every city in America soon sported small theaters where one could see every imaginable variety of pornographic films. The report of the President's Commission on Obscenity and Pornography also favored the spread of pornography, since it concluded that there was no link between exposure to erotic stimuli and forms of sexual deviancy. It also recommended that federal, state and local laws prohibiting the sale, exhibition and distribution of sexually explicit material be repealed.

Many Americans were not convinced and see the deluge of pornography as a disaster. Pornography, they feel, is essentially dehumanizing and exploitative—most evidently in its consistent choice of themes showing people degraded and humiliated: through incest, the profaning of the sacred, flagellation, child abuse and bestiality. As D. H. Lawrence said, "You can recognize it by the insult offered, invariably, to sex and to the human spirit . . . the insult to the human body, the insult to a vital human relationship."[19]

## HOMOSEXUALITY

The gay liberation movement has forced people to confront this question, which many in the past preferred to ignore. As with other moral issues, one finds a great variety of Christian answers, ranging from the fundamentalists' outright and total condemnation of all homosexual acts to approval of homosexual "marriages."

Is there a clear condemnation of homosexual behavior in the Bible? Not if one does a critical reading of the main texts usually cited as evidence: Genesis 19:4–11; Leviticus 18:22, 20:13; and the formal condemnations of St. Paul in Romans 1:27, 1 Corinthians 6:9–10 and 1 Timothy 1:9–10.

The Book of Genesis relates how the men of Sodom tried to rape the guests of Lot and were punished by the Lord. But there is much that is unclear about the meaning of this passage. It is possible that the sin involved has to do with the violation of the sacred duty of hospitality.

Leviticus, on the other hand, is quite explicit: "You must not lie with a man as with a woman," and it imposes the death penalty for those guilty. But the context is the condemnation of idolatrous customs such as sacrificing children to the god Moloch. And it is difficult to see how Jewish law, which was relatively lenient in comparison with other codes, would pre-

19. Quoted in Charles Socarides, M.D., *Beyond Sexual Freedom* (New York: Times Books, 1975), p. 95.

scribe the death penalty here unless the homosexual act was considered idolatrous.

As to St. Paul's condemnation—if viewed in its context, it, too, seems to be mainly concerned with the inroads of Greek paganism as associated with certain sexual practices. Moreover, Paul certainly had no concept of homosexuality as a predetermined state of sexual orientation.

In summary, these passages do not close the case against homosexuality. The point of the condemnations may well be not the perversity of the act but the religious unfaithfulness manifested by the act. At least one cannot rule out such an interpretation. "Furthermore," as André Guindon says, "even if it were possible to establish that any one of these texts is a categorical condemnation of homosexual practices because they represent a perversion of human sexual behavior, the issue would still be unclear inasmuch as it would remain to be determined how applicable the biblical view, taken in its materiality, is to the contemporary scene."[20]

What is the position of the Church? The Scriptural story of Sodom has immensely influenced the Fathers, who were unanimous in condemning homosexual acts as deliberate perversion. Under the influence of Church teaching, it was prohibited by the Code of Justinian under penalty of death. In fact, there is no doubt that the Church bears some responsibility for the long history of civil persecution of homosexuals. In its *Declaration on Sexual Ethics*, the Church has continued to maintain the negative attitude toward homosexuality inherited from the Bible and medieval natural-law theory in condemning all homosexual acts as intrinsically evil.

This blanket condemnation of all homosexual acts (even though softened by its pastoral advice to confessors to treat the practicing homosexual with compassion) seems extreme to many Catholic theologians. They find the Vatican's use of Scripture inadequate and its natural-law theory untenable. Many of them prefer to see homosexual behavior as not necessarily immoral but as only incomplete, insofar as it lacks openness to procreation. Nevertheless most of them do not accept the idea of homosexuality as an equally valid life-style, and they appeal to philosophical arguments to argue that the man-woman sexual dialogue is essential to full humanity: "Neither femininity nor masculinity are self-sufficient realities . . . To the extent that the homosexual pattern represents a vain effort to become integrally human as a self-sufficient male or female, it is a practical denial

20. *The Sexual Language* (Ottawa: University of Ottawa Press, 1977), p. 322.

of the fact that being a human person is being a male or a female interdependently and not independently, in a sort of neuter fashion."[21]

But what about the supposed findings of anthropologists that homosexual life-styles were a fully accepted alternative in many societies? The facts actually are not so clear. As Guindon points out, if you rule out such cases as adolescent experimentation and the use of homosexual acts in puberty rites, there is no good evidence that primitive societies regarded homosexuality as an acceptable sexual alternative.[22]

Greece, for instance, is often singled out as a culture in which the homosexual was fully accepted and respected and given unlimited opportunities to gratify his desires. But the historical reality is much more complex. In most of the city-states there were laws to prevent the seduction of boys by older males, and Plato himself, whose *Symposium* is often cited for its celebration of the love of boys, later condemned pederasty in his treatise on *Laws*.

Certain factors no doubt endemic to Greek culture could dispose males to form homosexual relationships. Comradeship in arms could easily lead male warriors especially to some physical expressions and such love between an older and younger man was believed to enhance the pair's fighting qualities by exciting them to heroism and self-sacrifice. There was also the prevailing exclusion of women from public life and a male bias that treated women as incapable of real intellectual life. Such misogyny could easily foster homosexual tendencies.

Nevertheless, revisionist Catholic theologians accept the findings of the behavioral sciences that the homosexual preference is often irreversible. And in these cases they ask, Must homosexuals see continence as their only choice? No, they say. Homosexuals who seek to fulfill their sexual needs in the context of a stable, loving relationship are not acting immorally. Their decision of conscience should be respected by the Church and they should be welcomed to the eucharistic table.

The gay community generally finds even this liberal response unsatisfactory. What they want is recognition of their preference as a fully normal alternative. Only a few Catholic authors, such as Gregory Baum and John McNeil, seem willing to go this far—with arguments drawn from history and anthropology.

Actually the state of research is still rudimentary. Many theories, how-

21. Ibid., p. 338.
22. Ibid., pp. 324–26.

ever, have surfaced to explain the origin of homosexuality. It is due to the genes or the hormones or the parents. Some claim it is due to a kind of short circuit in the brain. One of the most popular theories supposes a passive, ineffectual father and a dominant, close-binding mother. But as Ray Arens, a California psychiatrist, says, it's equally possible that the child may itself be responsible for eliciting the disposing kind of behavior in the parent . . . "It is just as tenable to assume that the father of a pre-homosexual son becomes detached or hostile because he does not understand his son, is disappointed in him, or threatened by him, as it is to assume that the son becomes homosexual because of the father's rejection."[23]

But, according to *Human Sexuality*, the study commissioned by the Catholic Theological Society, "authorities disagree as to whether homosexuality should be seen as a disease, a disorientation, or simply a departure from a prevalent social pattern."[24]

In view of the Church's share in the curse that society has visited on homosexuals, it seems only just that it should be in the forefront of efforts to unveil the many myths that surround the topic and take the lead in ending discrimination against them.

## PREMARITAL AND EXTRAMARITAL SEX

Some interesting facts have turned up lately in sociological studies of these activities. One of these is that the incidence of premarital sex among males has not really increased that much since the beginning of the twentieth century. The increase in premarital sex since World War II is largely due to women. A high percentage of males (some 80 to 90 percent) throughout the twentieth century have indulged in this practice, while it was only after the Second World War that large numbers of women began to engage in premarital sex. (The percentage nearly doubled—from 36 to 65 percent). Another interesting fact is that promiscuity seems actually on the decline. Surveys show that youth today are more likely to have sex only with those to whom they are deeply committed.

Another significant fact shows no clear correlation between premarital

23. Quoted in Eugene Kennedy, *The New Sexuality* (Garden City, N.Y.: Image Books), p. 133, 1972.
24. Anthony Kosnick et al., op. cit., p. 211.

sex and the success or failure of the marriages of those practicing or not practicing it.

And, again, extramarital sex is much less frequently practiced than premarital sex.

Traditional Catholic theology and Church teaching condemn premarital and extramarital sex as gravely sinful. No distinction is made between casual or promiscuous sex and sex involving a couple strongly committed to one another. Not only intercourse but any directly willed venereal pleasure resulting from kissing or embracing is also regarded as gravely sinful. The recent Vatican document on sexual ethics underscores this position.

The arguments in its support are drawn from both Scripture and the so-called natural law. Recently, however, these arguments have been called into question by revisionist Catholic moralists.

The Old Testament, for instance, they point out, did not always condemn all forms of premarital and extramarital sex, as previously supposed. Polygamy and prostitution, if not idolatrous, were both countenanced in some parts of the Old Testament, though it is true that later Judaism took a stricter position.

The question of New Testament attitudes is moot. According to the Theological Dictionary of the New Testament, the New Testament is characterized by "an unconditional repudiation of all extra-marital and unnatural intercourse."[25] However, others claim that the sexual immorality condemned in the New Testament refers to adultery, incest and prostitution, in particular idolatrous temple prostitution, and so does not address the question of premarital sex between those deeply committed to one another with eventual marriage in mind.

Most Catholic theologians, however, it seems, today still hold that all premarital sex is wrong, although a few make allowances for the rather unusual case in which the couple are hindered, by circumstances beyond their control, from marriage and yet privately have made a full mutual commitment. This is the position of the authors of *Human Sexuality: New Directions in American Catholic Thought* and also of some revisionist authors such as Philip S. Keane.[26]

What are the main arguments against premarital intercourse? First, it is considered basically dishonest on the grounds that sexual intercourse is symbolic of total self-donation. People who refuse to make a public avowal

25. Vol. 6 (Grand Rapids, Mich.: Wm. B. Eerdmans, 1968), p. 590. Ed. by Gerhard Kittel and Gerhard Friedrich.
26. *Sexual Morality: A Catholic Perspective*, p. 107.

of their commitment in marriage are actually holding some part of themselves back from the total commitment which marriage publicly seals and reinforces in so many ways. Second, even if one were to admit that the unitive nature of the sexual act were respected by the putative couple, they would still be in violation of its equally essential procreative nature, since with the easy availability of contraceptive devices it is supposed that they would exclude children. Moreover, if for some reason pregnancy should ensue, the risk would be very great that the pregnant mother and her child would both suffer grave injustice: injustice to the potential child, who has the right to be raised in a stable and loving environment provided by two parents, and injustice often to the woman, who frequently has to fend for herself while facing many problems such as financial difficulties and lessened prospects for marriage. Moreover, the way out taken so often today—abortion—is not a moral option, from the Catholic perspective.

But what about the argument so often heard today "We have to experiment before marriage to see if we are really sexually compatible"? Some fallacies seem to be involved in this argument. If physical incompatibility is meant, then the argument is practically worthless, since this possibility is most remote. And even in the rare case where some physical impediment is discovered, it can be medically treated. Psychological or spiritual incompatibility? If a couple are truly and firmly committed to each other, how could they be sexually incompatible? Actually the argument based on fear of sexual incompatibility often masks more basic problems such as the lack of a truly firm commitment or a desire for sexual gratification on the part of the male who wants to satisfy his needs without paying the price demanded in any truly responsible relationship.

However, it is noteworthy that in spite of what has just been said, the authors of *Human Sexuality: New Directions* conclude that moral theologians have not yet succeeded in producing convincing proof as to why in every case sexual intercourse must always be matched by a total spiritual self-donation that can be expressed only in marriage. And they also question the physicalist interpretation of natural law involved in the argument, which requires that sexual intercourse always be ordained to procreation. Modern methods of birth control have made this ordination a matter of choice, rather than of nature. So they conclude, "Premarital sexual morality is largely a matter of drawing honest and appropriate lines. To this end, the characteristics of wholesome human sexual behavior outlined above (in Chapter IV) can serve as useful criteria for judging what kind of intimacy is honest and appropriate to a given relationship. Is it self-liberating, other-enriching, honest, faithful, life-serving, and joyous . . . To what extent, if any, is there selfishness, dishonesty, disrespect, promiscuity, the danger of scandal or of hurting or shaming family and loved ones? . . . using each other to prove their respective masculine, feminine attractiveness . . . and willingness to accept a child if one is conceived [for] no contraceptive device thus far invented is altogether foolproof."[27]

However, those Catholic theologians who depart from the classic doctrine generally insist on the need for deep and firm commitment on the part of the couple who engage in sexual intimacy. Polls show that a growing number of American Christians are moving in this direction. As of 1973, only 45 percent of them believed all premarital sex was wrong. *The Study Document on Sexuality and the Human Community*, presented to the United Presbyterian Church in the United States, argued for the morality of any form of sexual expression as long as it was proportional to the depth and maturity of the relationship. Some even go so far as to endorse sex as a needed form of recreation that should be available to everyone—married or not.

However, there is a danger in such trends, as Richard McCormick points out, for in a sex-obsessed culture such as ours, the sex exchange could be stripped of any meaning and totally trivialized, thereby depriving all of us of a most important form of sharing and growth.

## BIRTH CONTROL

This question must be put in the context of the mounting concern over the population explosion. Demographers show that at the time of Christ world population stood at some 250 million. It took sixteen hundred years for this number to double. Then, by 1830, at the beginning of the industrial revolution, it increased to 1 billion. But it took only one hundred years to double the world's population to 2 billion, in 1930. Only thirty years was needed for one more billion to be added and finally only fifteen more years for another billion, by 1975, to reach a total of four billion.

Projected population figures are hard to establish because of the variables, but an original estimate of 7.5 billion by the year 2000 has been revised downward by 20 percent since the growth rate continues to fall and is expected to be only 1.5 percent by that year.

27. *Human Sexuality: New Directions in American Catholic Thought*, p. 168.

This rapid rate of growth has intensified economic and social problems of the poor and developing nations of the world: shortage of food, depletion of nonrenewable mineral resources, increased rates of illiteracy, decline in the quality of education available, increased unemployment, etc.

Scholars are generally agreed that the rate of population growth must be curbed if we are to ward off mass starvation and economic and social chaos in large portions of the world. People simply have to be educated in responsible parenthood—which means adjusting the size of their families to the demands of the common good and the welfare of their own children.

Various methods of birth control have been used over the centuries. Some devices physically obstruct the union of the sperm and ovum, while certain chemicals are used to inhibit fertilization. Sterilization of either one or both spouses is another method. One of the oldest has been withdrawal before ejaculation. The rhythm method makes use of the female menstrual cycle, which leaves a woman fertile for only about six days in each twenty-eight-day period.

Contraception was no doubt widely practiced by many Christians over the centuries, but it became a paramount moral concern only in the twentieth, when, under the pressures of a highly industrialized society, many couples began its practice. The first religious proponents of birth control were the Universalists, Unitarians and adherents of Reformed Judaism. Other Christian bodies were very slow to give it their blessing, until around 1930, when the Lambeth Conference of the Church of England allowed it, as did the Federal Council of Churches in 1931 and the Conservative Rabbinical Assembly of America in 1935. Muslim, Hindu and Buddhist traditions, on the other hand, still do not favor using birth control.

The Roman Catholic Church literally made a life-and-death issue out of it when Pope Pius XI in *Casti Connubii* vehemently condemned the practice (although he did allow use of the infertile period for grave reasons). Opposition to birth control became an important part of Catholic identity, but Catholics were not immune to the pressures felt by other couples who made use of it.

Two developments accelerated a crisis over this issue within the Church. A Catholic, Dr. John Rock, in collaboration with several others, developed a progestin compound (the pill) and began to administer it to his patients. Second, Pope John XXIII called a council for the universal Church to meet in 1961.

We must remember that Dr. Rock's pill was the "first method of birth control which could make sexual intercourse fully satisfying psychologically and fully sterile physiologically."[28]

During the Council, Cardinals Suenens, Alfrink and Leger and the Patriarch Maximos IV spoke out for a change in the Church's teaching and were applauded by the majority of the bishops. But Paul VI immediately removed the issue from the Council and assigned it to a commission previously set up by Pope John, which he enlarged. In 1966 they submitted their report with a majority in favor of allowing artificial contraception. But after much agony of conscience Paul VI issued his encyclical *Humanae Vitae*, which ruled out any use of artificial contraceptives as intrinsically wrong.

The furor aroused was unprecedented in modern Church history. A wave of anger and resentment swept through large sectors of the Catholic community directed not so much at the person of the pope as against the papal office itself. The dissent was massive and involved many organizations of priests and lay people as well as some of the world's most prominent theologians. A statement signed by some six hundred American theologians took exception to the ecclesiology implied and the methodology employed in the encyclical and concluded that spouses may responsibly decide according to their conscience that artificial contraception in some cases is permissible and even necessary.

More remarkable yet, a number of the Catholic hierarchies around the world, including those of Canada, the Netherlands, Germany, Austria, Scandinavia and Belgium went on record as accepting the papal teaching but stressing the right of the individual to follow his or her conscience. The U.S. bishops themselves waffled: admitting the right to follow one's conscience but stressing that it must be formed according to the Church's teaching.

As time passed, it became clear that very few Catholics adhered to the teaching of the encyclical. A survey in the United States showed that nearly 77 percent of Catholic wives were practicing birth control in 1975, 94 percent of whom were using the forbidden methods. And another study showed that only 29 percent of the priests regard artificial contraception as morally wrong. Another study, of ten thousand Catholics in

28. Julian Pleasants, *The Catholic Case for Contraception* (New York: Macmillan 1969), p. 33.

sixty American parishes made between 1978 and 1982, showed that only 15 percent thought artificial birth control wrong.[29]

In a few words, the pope's position was that "it is necessary that every single marriage act remain of itself destined to procreate human life," that "each and every marriage act must remain open to the transmission of life."[30] The pope based this principle on "the inseparable link" between the unitive and the procreative meanings God assigned to the marriage act.

How, then, does the pope try to prove there is such a link which must not be obstructed artificially in any act of sexual intercourse?

To support his position, the pope refers to the tradition of the Church and also the natural law. But he does not develop the argument from either source. In fact, there is not much strict argument at all. He doesn't try to explain why the tradition of the Church precludes any change, nor does he explicate the argument from natural law but simply asserts his belief that "the men of our day are particularly capable of seizing the deeply reasonable and human character of this fundamental principle" (that is, the need for every act of intercourse to be open to the transmission of life).

Those who dissented from the papal teaching employed a number of arguments. Perhaps the most cogent was formulated by Karl Rahner: "Why is it unnatural for man deliberately to induce a condition which 'nature' itself produces constantly through infertile days?"[31]

Again, as some have pointed out, the papal encyclical offers no convincing proof of its main contention, namely, that biological integrity must be held as an absolute norm with absolute priority over all other values sought by married couples from their union. As twenty-one of Europe's most respected moral theologians stated after a public conference, "We believe we must state in conscience that we are unable to comprehend the validity of a view which considers 'the development of natural processes' as a law possessing a value in itself, that is to say, independently of the total finality of conjugal and family life. It is for this reason that we no longer understand the significance of a moral distinction between the use of the period

29. *The National Catholic Reporter,* September 30, 1983, p. 1.
30. Trans. in Julian Pleasants, op. cit., p. 220.
31. *The Tablet* (London), September 14, 1968, p. 918.

of infertility and the employment of means capable of being used for good as well as for evil."[32]

The division of opinion on this question is traced by these same moralists to two divergent theologies of marriage: one, the traditional and papal theology, which takes as its starting point the inviolability of natural processes; the other, a personalist theology, which takes as its starting point the human person considered as a totality. The former characteristically asks, "What is the generative process for?" the latter asks, "What is marriage for?"

The personalist does not understand why a person may not intervene in the generative process if he thereby makes his marriage more loving and vital. Biological integrity is indeed a real value and part of God's creation —but the same can be said of other values sought in married life: harmonious relations, some degree of economic security, the psychological equilibrium of husband and wife, a wholesome relation with the children. Are not such values equally as sacred to God? If our general moral experience indicates that we must sometimes sacrifice one value to secure another, they see no reason, when it comes to marriage, for placing a premium on biological integrity, especially since it is assumed that good Catholic couples intend to have children.

Some defenders of the papal position argue simply from the infallibility of the Church. They assert that artificial contraception has been universally condemned by the bishops and the popes in the exercise of their ordinary magisterium throughout history and therefore it is an infallible doctrine of the Church. However, the Vatican itself refused to attach infallibility to the teaching of *Humanae Vitae*, and while it is true that both the official teachers of the Church and Catholic theologians have consistently and unanimously condemned artificial contraception since at least the third century, this does not of itself constitute an exercise of infallibility. We are more aware than ever today of how past statements of the ordinary magisterium must be interpreted according to their historical context.

32. *The Tablet* (London), September 28, 1968, p. 973.

## STERILIZATION

This is a most complex question, and the differing approaches taken by Catholic moralists reveal the conflict of the two world views we discussed above. Traditionalist theologians condemn sterilization on the grounds that it frustrates the organ's natural purpose. They allow only indirect sterilization, such as an operation on a diseased organ that only *indirectly* leaves the person sterile. Most Catholic theologians today, however, as we said above, define "direct" and "indirect" not by the mere physical aspects of the action, but by the overall purpose in mind. Thus *direct* sterilization, for them, occurs only when the person desires sterility for insufficient reasons, such as to avoid the inconvenience of having children, etc. —which they would regard as immoral. On the other hand, sometimes sterilization might be justified. A woman may be suffering from a pregnancy psychosis or there may be a very high risk of having extremely defective children in a situation where caring for them would be psychologically and emotionally impossible, etc., or the very well-being of the family might be at stake. It is with such rationales in mind that Bernard Häring, for instance, holds that Catholic hospitals might be permitted at least material cooperation in forms of sterilization that are considered by many Catholic theologians and virtually all Protestant ones to be therapeutic in a broader and more holistic sense.[33]

Rome, however, is adamantly opposed to such views and only recently imposed its will in no uncertain terms.

The episode involved the Sisters of Mercy of the Union, sponsors of the largest group of nonprofit hospitals in the country. After a lengthy study was made of the theological and ethical aspects of tubal ligation, the General Administration of the Sisters decided to accept in principle a recommendation that tubal ligations be permitted when the overall good of the patient warranted it. Then the General Administration asked for a dialogue with concerned persons on the issue.

At this point the American bishops took cognizance of the matter and appointed a committee to initiate dialogue with the Sisters. But Rome intervened, quashed the dialogue and simply ordered the Sisters to accept the teaching of the magisterium. As Cardinal Eduardo Pironio, Prefect of

33. *Free and Faithful in Christ,* Vol. 2, p. 486.

the Sacred Congregation for Religious and Secular Institutes, said, ". . . there is nothing to be gained by dialogue on this issue." He ordered the Sisters to prohibit all tubal ligations, and each sister was asked to sign a statement that she would continue to study and reflect on the teaching of the Church with a view to accepting it. Richard McCormick, in his comments on the affair, finds the Congregation's action most disturbing. He wonders how they can rule out dialogue on the matter in "light of the very widespread theological questioning" of the Holy See's position by many established theologians throughout Europe and the United States?

## ABORTION

Human sentiment about abortion has never been uniform. Plato allowed it, while Aristotle approved of it only before "quickening": when the fetus' movements in the womb could be detected. Pagan Rome took a permissive stand until the second century A.D., when it began to campaign against it. Both the Jewish and the Christian traditions were always unanimously opposed.

For whatever reasons, the incidence of abortions greatly increased in the United States after World War II, reaching some 600,000 in 1972. This number more than doubled, to 1.4 million, in 1978, after the Supreme Court had legalized abortion on demand, in 1973. The number of abortions worldwide increased to 40 million in 1979.

The Supreme Court's decision, like *Humanae Vitae* (if two documents with such enormously different philosophies can be compared), did not settle the debate, but only intensified it. It has proved to be one of the most controversial decisions of the Court's history. The literature it has engendered would sink an ocean liner; the emotions it has generated would fuel a battleship.

As Richard McCormick said so well, "Abortion is a matter that is morally problematic, pastorally delicate, legislatively thorny, constitutionally insecure, ecumenically divisive, medically normless, humanly anguishing, racially provocative, journalistically abused, personally biased, and widely performed. It demands a most extraordinary discipline of moral thought, one that is penetrating without being impenetrable, humanly compassionate without being morally compromising, legally realistic without being legally positivistic, instructed by cognate disciplines without being determined by them, informed by tradition without being enslaved by it, etc. Abortion, therefore is a severe testing ground for moral reflection . . . and probably a paradigm of the way we will face other human problems in the future."[34]

In the debate over abortion, both sides often base their arguments on unproven assumptions. Here is where the social sciences have been able to render a real service in sifting the facts from the myths, viz.:

## SOME QUESTIONABLE ASSUMPTIONS OF THE PRO-ABORTIONISTS:

1. An abortion will often save the pregnant teenage woman from **disastrous long-range consequences** such as economic distress and other life disadvantages. But social-science researchers who have studied the negative impact of early or unwed parenthood have found this impact less severe than is often asserted.[35]

2. Children who are aborted are **unwanted**. Actually, evidence is sorely lacking that unwanted children are really unwanted in a sense that would be injurious to their chances for a happy life. A major study of Czech children published in 1975 showed no major differences in outcomes between children whose mothers were denied abortions and children who were "wanted."[36]

Also, a study exploring the effects on children having very young parents showed similar results. It would be difficult to conclude, Ms. Lamanna says, that these children of younger mothers suffer such disabilities that they would be better off not born.

3. Legal abortion is necessary to reduce **abortion deaths**. It is a fact that the maternal death rate from abortionists has taken a dramatic plunge since abortion was legalized. Abortion-related deaths dropped more than 40 percent in 1973 and continue to decline. But how much of this decline is simply due to the legalization and how much is part of a long-term decline in such deaths is difficult to establish. Moreover, a number of studies do indicate some risk of reproductive complications following abortion, especially in the case of repeated abortions.[37]

34. *Notes on Moral Theology 1965 through 1980.*
35. Mary Ann Lamanna, "Science and Its Uses." In James Burtchaell, C.S.C., ed., *Abortion Parley* (Fairway, Kans.: Andrews & McMeel, 1980), pp. 115–39.
36. Ibid., p. 135.
37. Ibid., pp. 138–39.

## QUESTIONABLE ASSUMPTIONS OF ANTI-ABORTIONISTS

1. Women who abort usually do so for **frivolous reasons**. It is true that the hard cases—those involving illness, potentially defective children, rape/incest, excessively large families or poverty—do not account for most of the abortions. There are many women who seek abortions for such reasons as an imminent divorce, family stress, conception in an extramarital relationship, etc. But whether these should be termed frivolous is a good question.[38]

2. Most women who have abortions are **promiscuous**. But empirical studies do not support this.[39]

3. The woman who aborts will suffer traumatic and crippling **guilt feelings**. Various studies, however, do not confirm this claim. One such was reported by Mary Lamanna at the Notre Dame conference on abortion in 1979. According to Ms. Lamanna, 94 percent of women report satisfaction with their decision to abort. She claims that "no obvious psychological trauma can be attributed to abortion." But, on the other hand, she emphasizes that while women who undergo abortion may not suffer mental illness or need a therapist, there is no doubt that it is a highly stressful experience for them. About 40 percent of women in one study regarded their abortion as too upsetting to think about, and many of them felt betrayed by feminists who led them to believe that having an abortion was as easy as having a tooth pulled.[40]

In conclusion, it seems fair to say that assumptions on both sides of the debate are often wide of the mark. The anti-abortionists have to realize that most people who seek abortion do so for reasons that appear to them, at least, as virtually insurmountable. Stereotypes of these women as promiscuous and irresponsible should be discarded. Another conclusion is that if the problem of abortion is to be solved, those opposed to it must come to terms with the social problems that lead people to resort to the practice. They should work to get support programs for those who choose to have their babies and for their acceptance by the community. They

38. Ibid., pp. 118–19.
39. Ibid., p. 120.
40. Ibid., pp. 121–30.

must also face the possibility that reducing the availability of abortion may cause an increase in deaths from illegal abortions.

Those favoring easy availability of abortion must also examine their assumptions, some of which, as indicated above, are not supported by factual studies. Even on their own terms, abortion is not as good an answer as they seem to think. Its personal costs are serious: if not crippling guilt, at least heavy emotional stress and risk to one's reproductive capacity. Its social costs are difficult to measure but certainly substantial.

The Catholic Church has always officially condemned—with a few vacillations—any direct abortion as an objective serious sin. In *Humanae Vitae*, Paul VI condemned any directly willed and procured abortion, even for therapeutic reasons. The only allowable abortion, in the eyes of the Church, is when the killing of the fetus is indirect and is performed to save the life of the mother, as in the case of a cancerous uterus or when an ectopic pregnancy occurs and the fallopian tube is removed, with consequent death of the fetus.

Among Catholic theologians today, however, there is a variety of dissent. In fact, as Charles Curran says, ". . . there is a sizable and growing number of Catholic theologians who disagree with some aspects of the officially proposed Catholic teaching that direct abortion from the time of conception is always wrong."[41] And in fact probably only a minority would hold that all abortions are immoral. They differ from the traditional teachings for a variety of reasons. Some revisionists no longer accept the classic indirect-killing approach. As in other tragic conflict situations, they would justify abortion as the lesser of two evils—if there is a proportionate reason—which for most of them would be only if the life of the mother is at stake or to avert grave psychological damage.

Some reject the traditional teaching because they differ on the question of when human life is present. Charles Curran, for instance, argues that individual human life is present only after twinning and recombination are no longer possible, that is, after the first fourteen days. Until then, cells are identical replications and any or each of them could become the nucleus of an individual human being—as happens in the case of twins.

Some Catholic moralists argue that there must be no direct killing of the fetus even though that be the only means of saving the mother. However, as Bernard Häring points out, it is no longer proper to say that

41. "Abortion: Law and Morality in Contemporary Catholic Theology," *The Jurist* 33 (1973), p. 183.

the life of the mother is preferred to the life of the unborn child, "for there are no cases in which the life of the fetus can be saved by taking the life of the mother . . . the sole choice is to let both die or to save the life of the mother." As he says, the almost common opinion of Catholic moralists is that in such a case it is better to interrupt the pregnancy to save the life of the mother.[42]

Some Catholic moralists have come to accept the morality of abortion not only where the life of the mother is at stake but when the birth of the child might create an inhuman situation or where the mental life of the mother would be seriously impaired.[43]

Roman Catholics have generally been associated with the demand for very restrictive abortion laws, and the Catholic bishops of the United States have devoted much energy to the movement for a constitutional amendment prohibiting abortion. It might come as a surprise, therefore, to many to hear there is no such thing as *the* Catholic opinion on the issue.

Evidence indicates how very divided Catholics are on this issue. According to a November 1982 Yankelovich poll of Catholic women, fewer than one fifth consider abortion immoral in case of rape, risk to health or a deformed fetus. A majority of them would allow abortion for a teenager, a welfare mother unable to work or a woman with a large family.[44] As studies show, a high percentage of anti-abortion sentiment exists only among Catholics who attend church frequently and fundamentalist Protestants.

As to the advisability of laws or a constitutional amendment to prohibit abortion, there is a wide range of opinion. Some, like the Jesuit and ex-congressman Robert Drinan, are opposed to any law, while others, such as Richard McCormick, favor moderate legislation that would witness to the importance of protecting the fetus and would allow abortion only where the life and health of the mother is at stake. A more restrictive law such as proposed by the backers of a constitutional amendment would not be feasible, they claim, for it would not have the support of a large portion of the citizenry.

Critics of the bishops' absolutist position on abortion point out the

42. Bernard Häring, op. cit., Vol. 3, p. 33.
43. See Richard McCormick, op. cit., pp. 493–515.
44. Daniel Maguire, "Abortion: A Question of Catholic Honesty," *Christian Century*, September 14–21, 1983, pp. 805–6.

# 27

## Social Justice:
## The Church's Call to Action

The most emphatic statement on the social ministry of the Church is found in the document issued by the Synod of Bishops in 1971:

> Action on behalf of justice and participation in the transformation of the world fully appear to us as a constitutive dimension of the preaching of the Gospel, or in other words, of the Church's mission of the redemption of the human race and its liberation from every oppressive situation.

This statement puts everyone on notice: The Catholic Church believes that religion belongs at the center of things. Concern for social justice must permeate the whole life of the Church. It is not enough just to mouth pretty words about peace and justice in the pulpit. The message must be put into action. The Church commits itself to the work of social change and the struggle against all forms of oppression. Nor is it a task devolving on the clergy alone or on the laity alone, but it is a ministry that must involve everyone. What is at stake is nothing less than the redemption of the human race.

Behind those words of the Synod lies an extremely complicated, two-thousand-year history of effort by the Church to relate the Gospel to human life. Surveying this history, one can discern several distinct stages in the development of Catholic social thought.

## JESUS AND SOCIAL JUSTICE

Jesus himself, we should note, was certainly not a social reformer, in spite of a spate of recent books that attempt to depict him as a revolutionary and one of the Zealots, who were fanatically devoted to expelling the Roman occupiers from Palestine. There is indeed a certain resemblance: like them, Jesus identified with the poor and the oppressed, and he offered reasons for hope with his message of the coming Kingdom. And, in fact, this resemblance caused his crucifixion by the Romans. But Jesus differed radically from the Zealots by his conviction that the source of evil is in the individual human heart and that true liberation begins with the intent of the individual to allow the Kingdom of God to take possession of his heart. The Zealot would spill the blood of his enemy, but Jesus appealed to the Father's love of all people and demanded love of enemies and renunciation of violence.

Jesus stood for human freedom, though he did not dwell on the theme. For him, freedom happened when the Kingdom of God came to people. People are truly free only where God is sovereign. The Kingdom of God is the power of God active in the world, challenging the powers of the world. And its power is most manifest in Jesus himself, the freest of humans, free with the freedom of love and goodness informed by the love of the Father, by unconditional openness and trust, as one not enslaved to any human passion or sin. His attitude toward the Torah brings out best his understanding of freedom. He did not emancipate people from the Torah, but urged devotion to it, and modified it only in order to serve God's will more authentically. For he taught that one is really free only when one's relation to God's will is right; that is, when one repents.

## PAUL AND LUKE

There is much in Paul and elsewhere in the New Testament to support a social-justice vision of the world. Sin, for Paul, is social isolation, whereas life according to the Spirit promotes those things which make human social life possible. Moreover, Paul sees the present world existing in a state of tension between slavery to the power of sin and death and, at the same time, in some sense sharing in Jesus' victory over the evil powers, so that the Christian lives *between* the times.

Evil and injustice still exert their sway over us as "we too groan inwardly as we wait for our bodies to be set free."[1] So Paul would have us struggle against the powers that enslave and oppress us—and hence we need to diagnose accurately what these powers are. At the same time, he upholds his eschatological vision that we are living between the times, always in hope and anticipation, meaning that the realization of justice will always be imperfect. As co-workers in the process of transforming the world, we must always bear in mind that no social system is final. God's saving justice can never be incarnated perfectly in any system.

Paul has also much to say about building community. As his "Second Adam" theology shows, in Romans 5, 1 Corinthians 15 and Romans 9–11, justification means more than individual acceptance and freedom. It also entails incorporation into a new social structure, the body of Christ. And Paul has much to say about how Christians should relate to one another. In their enjoyment of freedom, for instance, they must consider the weak and easily scandalized members of the community. They must respond to the needs of others by bearing their burdens so as to fulfill the law of Christ. They must be concerned especially with the needs of the poor in imitation of Jesus, who "was rich but . . . became poor for your sake, to make you rich out of his poverty."[2] Finally, Paul constantly exhorts his quarreling communities to live in harmony with one another by cultivating relations that are based on justice and concern for the felt needs of others. For Paul, the ministry of reconciliation and the work of justice is an integral part of preaching the Gospel.

Among the evangelists, Luke is the one who is most interested in social justice, and he portrays Jesus as a prophet on the Old Testament model. It is in Luke that we find those powerful words of Jesus heralding his ministry as he sees himself in the role of the servant prophet of Isaiah, who will proclaim release to the captives, recovery of sight to the blind and freedom to the oppressed.

Of all the biblical authors, Luke is most severe toward the wealthy. In general, the Bible sees wealth as spiritually dangerous if it causes us to harden our hearts and dominate others or if it becomes a substitute for God. But Luke goes further and even finds it incompatible with the Gospel. For Luke, the Gospel of Jesus is good news for the poor: Levi "leaves

1. Rom. 8:23.
2. 2 Cor. 8:9.

everything" in order to follow Jesus. In contrast to Matthew, Luke has Jesus say in the beatitudes, "Blessed are the poor" period—that is, the poor literally, not the "poor in spirit," as Matthew has it. For Luke, discipleship means renouncing all that you have.[3] Again, it is Luke who gives us the picture of the early Church as a community of disciples sharing their property and distributing it to those in need. "The study of the third Gospel should be a reminder that violence is done to the message of Jesus when it is severed from concern for man's social problems."[4]

## THE FATHERS OF THE CHURCH

The first Christian communities lived in expectation of the imminent arrival of the Kingdom of God. They also were strongly individualistic in their emphasis on the need for personal repentance and personal response to God's will, but at the same time they had a strong sense of their solidarity in Christ and their share in the universal love of God for all His children. Their expectation of the Kingdom and their rejection of everything superfluous sharply differentiated them from the world and fostered a heroic ethic which admitted of no compromise with the world.

The Church gradually realized that the end of the world was not at hand, and this, together with the increasing size and complexity of its membership, brought it into closer touch with the world. But it never saw itself as an agent of social reform. Its concept of salvation remained focused on the individual working out his salvation within a community of love and faith. A static view of institutions and a spirit of detachment from the perishable things of this world kept it from developing an ethic of social justice.

Thus the Fathers of the Church counseled almsgiving to relieve the needs of the poor but did not think in terms of social justice or reform. They showed no concern about economic inequality, for example, except when it involved private riches in excess of what was morally safe for the owners or when it was a sign of lack of compassion. They even took a tolerant view of slavery and in fact never took part in or advocated a mass enfranchisement of slaves. Some of them even owned slaves themselves. Slavery was accepted as part of God's plan and as a punishment for sin

3. Lk. 14:33.
4. John R. Donahue, S.J., "Biblical Perspectives on Justice." In J. Haughey, S.J., ed. *The Faith That Does Justice* (New York: Paulist Press, 1977), p. 108.

and, in some way, its remedy. However, unlike the pagans, they upheld the dignity of the individual slave, who in the eyes of God might be far superior to his master.

Nevertheless the social teachings of the Fathers contain elements that are still of value for us in our search for an ethic of social justice. There is, first of all, their insistence on the need to subordinate the desire for material goods to the love of God and the service of neighbor. As they realized, this demands an interior conversion and the purification of one's heart. Likewise is their stress on the need for a community of love and support as the basis of all human relationships, as well as the way they identified Christ most especially with the poor.

The insight of the Fathers into the selfish heart of man is also most instructive as a warning against entertaining utopian hopes about social reform. People who attempt to realize utopias end up on the ant heap—exchanging even more repressive structures for the ones they have cast off. But we should not despair of any progress at all. The very awareness of the boundless egotism of human beings should drive us in constant effort to reform and to seek what is better.

Perhaps most important of all to remember in this connection is that the early Church's profound commitment to a set of spiritual values gave it a standard with which to judge existing institutions. And so its submission to these institutions was conditional and not absolute, and in the long run it exerted a profoundly transforming influence on these institutions. So, without a deliberate revolution, it succeeded in destroying and breaking down evil institutions and inaugurating new ones.[5]

## MEDIEVAL SOCIAL THOUGHT

The social ethics of the Church during the Middle Ages was based on principles already developed during the earlier period. As the official religion of the empire, the Christian Church threw its weight behind a concept of social order based on keeping people in line and containing the always potentially explosive forces of social discontent. "Gradually an organic, functional, social theory emerged which upheld the given social

5. Ernst Troeltsch, *The Social Teaching of the Christian Church* (New York: Harper Torchbooks, 1960), pp. 89–164.

order as ordained by God and made clear the sinfulness of discontent and the futility of efforts at social change."[6]

Aquinas, one of the Church's chief architects of social theory, drew on the philosophy of Aristotle and the Stoics as well as on tradition in elaborating a social ethic that canonized the *status quo*. Social obligations were stressed at the expense of individual human rights. It was predicated on a firm belief in the divinely willed hierarchical structure of society and of society as an organism whose members each contributed to the well-being of the whole by each remaining in his or her state in life and fulfilling the duties thereto ascribed. Thus the serf as a serf owed certain definite duties to the feudal lord, who in turn as lord owed certain duties to the serf.

The medieval Church therefore remained virtually untouched by any impulse toward social reform and played very little part in such movements as the emancipation of the serfs. For the Church, the principles of a proper social order were discoverable by human reason and unchangeable. The actual situation of man was idealized and rationalized. A host of social evils—slavery, male domination, war, poverty, etc.—were all considered part of immutable natural law, which regulated human relationships in a world corrupted by original sin.

## THE REFORMATION

The Reformation did not mean a dramatic break with the medieval social morality. Most of the Reformers continued to uphold the basic principles of the Christian tradition, with certain modifications. Like their medieval predecessors, the Protestant divines adhered to an organic conception of society, and Luther and Calvin were even more emphatic than the medieval theologians in demanding social responsibility of all and in asserting the claims of the Church and community over those of the individual. Some have argued that Protestantism favored an unrestrained economic capitalism, but this is not true. Luther was more conservative on the issue of usury than his Catholic opponents, while Calvin added nothing to what the fifteenth-century theologian St. Antoninus taught on the subject. In sum, Luther and Calvin agreed wholeheartedly with the medieval Church that all worldly endeavors should be subject to the scrutiny of both Church and state in the light of the demands of the Gospel.

6. David O'Brien and Thomas Shannon, eds., *Renewing the Earth: Catholic Documents on Peace, Justice and Liberation* (Garden City, N.Y.: Image Books, 1977), p. 18.

## THE  ERA  OF  REVOLUTION

With the advent of the Enlightenment, a big intellectual shift occurred as regards the relation of the individual to society. Social and intellectual trends favored individualism, and the leading theorists of the seventeenth century, Hobbes and Locke, championed the rights of the individual on the basis of a theory of a social contract. According to this theory, the individual was endowed with certain inalienable rights which society must respect. But how to reconcile the rights of the individual with his social obligations? This problem was left unresolved.

The French Revolution exalted the rights of the individual and ushered in a period of great turmoil as revolutionaries across the continent challenged the old order in the name of liberty, equality and fraternity. After some hesitation, the Catholic Church finally identified with the parties of order and authority. Under Pope Pius IX (1846–78), this policy reached its climax as the pope managed during his long reign to condemn nearly every conceivable form of liberalism.

The Industrial Revolution also brought tremendous social disruption into the life of Europe. The exploited and oppressed factory workers, many of them women and children, were forced to live in abominable circumstances, cramped into squalid tenements while working fifteen or more hours a day, seven days a week, in order to earn wages that kept them on a starvation diet of potatoes and cabbage.

The Church's response to this "social question" was like its response to the political question: extremely conservative and even reactionary. A few perceptive liberal Catholics such as Lamennais, Ozanam and Charles de Coux saw the need for a new approach, but they were dismissed by most Catholics as impractical visionaries.

A German bishop, Wilhelm von Ketteler (d. 1877) had more success in his campaign to alert the Church to the gravity of the social question. He sketched out a Catholic solution that he marked off from both socialism and sectarian liberalism, pointing out the dangers in both the unlimited competition of liberal capitalism and the exaggerated state control of the socialists. Above all, he insisted on the right of workers to form their own associations, and he called for a whole series of reforms including profit sharing, reasonable working hours, sufficient rest days, factory inspection, and the regulation of female and child labor. In most countries, however, the Church remained wedded to a medieval approach to the problem and in consequence lost permanently the allegiance of a good part of the European working class.

However, a number of Catholics following in Ketteler's footsteps refused to accept the loss of the workers; they came to the fore in the 1880s with more realistic ideas and with programs calculated to compete with those of the socialists. In contrast with the prevailing Catholic paternalism and authoritarianism, they favored the new democratic procedures. Many of them, especially those from Germany, Austria, France, Belgium and Italy adhered to the Fribourg Union, which met annually in Switzerland from 1884 under the presidency of Bishop Mermillod to pool their ideas. They agreed on the need for workers to have separate unions instead of the joint unions of employer and worker favored by conservative Catholics; they also affirmed every person's right to work and to a living wage and called for insurance against sickness, accidents and unemployment. In this way there emerged in the eighties a profound Catholic sociology offering a powerful alternative to the other major ideologies of the day: economic liberalism and Marxian socialism.

Another school of Catholic social thought also emerged at this time, one that espoused a conservative philosophy arguing that the social problem was primarily a moral one that could be remedied only by Christian charity. Its best-known leaders were Charles Perrin in Belgium and Bishop Freppel of Angers, in France. Unlike the Fribourg Union, they were generally opposed to state intervention except in special circumstances, since they thought it would lead to socialism.

## RERUM NOVARUM

However, in his epoch-making encyclical *Rerum Novarum,* Pope Leo XIII endorsed the Fribourg school's demand for state intervention.

In spite of Leo's alliance with the progressive Catholic position at the time, there is a tendency today to belittle the encyclical. Some Catholics insist, and rightly so, that Leo seriously distorted the Thomistic teaching by his emphasis on the rights of private property, that he was too abstract and vague in proposing remedies, and that he failed with calamitous results to discriminate between moderate and extreme-left-wing socialism and thereby helped plunge Italy into fascism. But it's well to realize what a great service the pope did for the cause of labor at that point by insisting on the right of the workers to organize in unions of their own at a time when this right was only reluctantly recognized by the powers of the world. As Professor Aubert says, "While there is no denying that the workers' movement was under way well before *Rerum Novarum* or that the credit for launching it belongs in essence to the socialists, this was the first time it had received a stamp of approval from any of the great forces of order in the world."[7]

Another point to remember is that the encyclical provided a major impetus in moving Catholics away from their fascination with medieval-type solutions to social problems and getting them to face modern problems realistically. Moreover, though Leo himself didn't intend it, since he himself was not a democrat, the encyclical indirectly assisted those Catholics who had launched the Christian Democratic movement.

Pope Leo's forceful statements on social issues set a strong precedent for his successors, and in fact, as Richard Camp says, "With the possible exception of Pius X, no pope since Leo XIII has repudiated the social conscience and the social mission of the Vatican."[8] It is surely inconceivable that any future pope would do so.

## LEO XIII TO PIUS XII

Taking a comprehensive view of the Church's social teaching since Leo, one can discern two distinct periods: from Leo to Pius XII (1878–1958) and from John XXIII and the Second Vatican Council to the present (1958– ).

As we have seen, Leo upheld the right of the workingman to organize. He also defended the right of the worker to a wage that would enable him to support himself and his family and to become a property owner. This theme—the need of the worker to become a property owner—was often reiterated subsequently by the popes.

Another consistent theme of social Catholicism for more than a half century was a strong anti-Communist message. Pope Leo XIII himself set the tone for this campaign in his encyclical *Quod Apostolici Muneris* (1878), in which he denounced the Communists as a "sect . . . known by the barbaric names of Socialists, Communists, and Nihilists . . . tied

---

7. Roger Aubert, *The Church in a Secularized Society* (New York: Paulist Press, 1978), p. 151.
8. Richard Camp, *The Papal Ideology of Social Reform* (Leiden: E. Brill, 1969), p. 23.

together in an iniquitous pact . . . to overthrow the very foundations of the civil order."9

The next pope to advance Catholic social thought was Pius XI (d. 1939), who like Leo was fiercely anti-Communist. And in fact in fighting communism he helped push Italy into the arms of the Fascists. For him, communism was the greatest of all evils and he attacked the Communists with increasing fury as he witnessed their barbarous treatment of Catholics not only in Russia but in Spain and Mexico.

Pius was not satisfied with simply condemning communism, for once again, as with Leo XIII, a pope had to choose between two opposing schools of Catholic social thought—in German, the *Sozialpolitik* school and the *Sozialreform* school. The former school basically accepted the capitalist system but wished only to alleviate its harsher features by various forms of social welfare such as insurance against sickness, old age and unemployment, as well as securing the right of the worker to organize. There was nothing really distinctive about this form of Catholic social thought, for its main ideas were favored by most European democratic politicians.

The *Sozialreform* school, on the other hand, was much more radical and called for a whole revamping of the capitalist system. These Catholic intellectuals felt that the system was vitiated by an exaggerated individualism which promoted selfishness, greed, unjust distribution of wealth and the brutal upheavals of the trade cycle. Unlike the socialists, however, they did not call for revolution, which they felt would only exacerbate the evils. Instead they stood for harmony between the classes, which they felt could be strengthened by making use of the natural and organic groups in society. Thus they called for corporations or industry councils in which employers and employees of every branch of industry could associate and determine policy for the industry as a whole, with each industry council represented in a national council that would determine general economic policy. The state would have the power to intervene only when the public good demanded it.

The pope came down decisively on the side of the latter school in *Quadragesimo Anno.* 10

However, his prescriptions were so vague and indefinite that his plan was given a bewildering variety of interpretations.

9. *Actes de Léon XIII,* Vol. 1, p. 27. Trans. in Richard Camp, op. cit., p. 51.
10. John R. Whyte, *Catholics in Western Democracies* (New York: St. Martin's Press, 1981), pp. 83–84.

His successor, Pius XII, was fully committed to the social-justice mission of the Church, and though he never produced a social encyclical equal in importance to *Rerum Novarum* or *Quadragesimo Anno*, he often made pronouncements on social issues. While he endorsed Pius XI's call for social reconstruction, he interpreted it in a very moderate sense. He even looked askance at the comanagement plans recommended by Pius XI and implemented in Germany, France and the Netherlands, which allowed the workers a share in the making of managerial decisions. And, in fact, his teaching amounted in practice to acceptance of the capitalist system as the only feasible alternative to communism and fascism.

Pius' major concern was the omnipresent threats he saw to the dignity of the human person. He saw people being torn from their native lands and regions because of wars and revolutions. He saw families broken up and people separated from their friends and relatives because of economic and social dislocations. In consequence he saw the individual swallowed up into anonymous and bureaucratically controlled mass society. The totalitarian states were merely the worst examples of a process occurring everywhere. Human beings were becoming mere objects to be used and if necessary discarded by those who directed society. So Pius constantly insisted on the need to respect basic human rights, and he offered support for democratic political structures.

With the death of Pope Pius XII, ". . . the classical period of Catholic doctrine abruptly ended."[11] Its limitations and weaknesses have been pointed out recently by a number of Catholic scholars. It was often marked by unsophisticated moralizing. Its solutions to terribly complicated economic problems were sometimes oversimplified. Pius XI, for instance, blamed the depression too much on moral evil "and not enough on universal ignorance as to how to keep a complex, modern industrial economy functioning at top speed."[12] According to another scholar, the encyclicals were not only too European in outlook and too "'curial' in style but were also too theoretical or abstract and did not adequately reflect the actual diversity of opinion within the universal Church."[13] The ecclesiology presupposed by the encyclicals was also one that now appears outdated. The ultramontane emphasis on the sheer authority of the pope encouraged the view that the Church had all the answers, and tended to lend exaggerated authority to papal opinions that in the nature of things

11. George Higgins, "Issues of Justice and Peace," *Chicago Studies* 20–21 (1981–82), p. 195.
12. Richard Camp, op. cit., p. 100.
13. George Higgins, op. cit., p. 195.

could only have limited validity. Their doctrinaire hostility to all forms of socialism was unfortunate and prevented cooperation that might have benefited both sides. The papal encyclicals were also pervaded by a general antimodern world attitude that was pessimistic about any movements not connected with the Church.

But, as Richard Camp says, much remains that is praiseworthy in the social teaching of the Leos, Benedicts and Piuses. "On subjects such as the labor problem and state social intervention, the popes showed time and again that they could be realistic, could learn from past mistakes, and could adjust to changing circumstances. In proposing social reform, they tried to be both humane and universal; they never ignored the issue of human dignity, nor did they consider the welfare of one nation only, or one race, or one social class, as did many reformers in the twentieth century."[14]

In mid-twentieth century the papacy enjoyed a new prestige, and Christian Democratic governments, which derived their social ideas from the papal encyclicals, became the chief agents in the rebuilding of Western European society.

## POPE JOHN XXIII AND THE SECOND VATICAN COUNCIL

Most scholars would agree that a new era of Catholic social thought opened up with the advent of Pope John XXIII. John was able to win the hearts of millions around the world, believers and nonbelievers, by his simple, humorous, affectionate, down-to-earth attitude toward people. If anyone might pull the world back from its headlong plunge into the nuclear inferno, it would be John, they seemed to think.

Chosen, no doubt, as an interim pope, at the age of seventy-six, he surprised everyone by taking a firm hold on the helm of the ship and steering it into uncharted seas, far from its familiar shores. His most dramatic act was to call an Ecumenical Council, which opened up a whole new chapter in the history of the Church. But his social encyclicals, *Mater et Magistra* and *Pacem in Terris,* were also highly significant documents that rank among the most important papal pronouncements of the twentieth century.

With his encyclicals and the convocation of the Council, John turned

14. *The Papal Ideology of Social Reform,* p. 163.

the Church in a new direction—a change that is clearly reflected in the social teaching of the Church. This is clear if we look at the other major pronouncements since *Mater et Magistra: Pacem in Terris* (1963), the *Pastoral Constitution of the Church in the Modern World (Gaudium et Spes)* of the Second Vatican Council (1964), *Populorum Progressio* (1967) of Pope Paul VI, *The 80th Year Letter* (1971) of Pope Paul VI, *Justice in the World* (1971) of the Synod of Bishops and *Laborem Exercens* (1981) of Pope John Paul II. In these documents it is no longer a triumphalist Church but a Church that wants to humbly serve the world; a Church no longer dubious about the value of human progress but one that applauds every human effort to build a better world; no longer a Church with all the answers, but a Church that seeks dialogue and admits that it can learn as well as teach; no longer one that looks longingly to the past, but one that faces the unknown future in a strong spirit of optimism and hope. It is a Church that no longer speaks ambiguously about human liberty, but commits itself wholeheartedly to the struggle for greater human freedom and liberation of the oppressed.

By 1960, the northern third of the human family had reached previously undreamed-of levels of mass abundance. Pope John, in *Mater et Magistra*, welcomed this progress. In fact, he seems to be the first pope who appreciated the possibilities of the modern economy. However, it distressed him to note the enormous gap between the rich and the poor nations—the most difficult problem of the modern world, in his view. He urged the richer nations to come to the aid of those in need.

*Mater et Magistra* addressed a number of other concerns: the rights and duties of capital and labor, the growing need for greater state ownership of property, the peculiar problems of agriculture (the first time a papal encyclical took up this theme in depth) and also the phenomenon he called "socialization," meaning the proliferation of organizations, voluntary and otherwise, that connected members of society with each other. Most significant was the way the *Mater* shifted the focus of Catholic social thought. John refused private property the privileged position it had previously held in Catholic thought, and he disengaged the Church from its customary alliance with the Right by espousing the "welfare state model" of society. Little wonder that conservative Catholics felt betrayed and cried *"Mater si, magistra no!"*

*Mater* was still a very Catholic document, intended mainly for Catholics and discussed chiefly by them. But *Pacem in Terris* came at an appropriate time at the height of John's popularity and with the Council already in session and attracting the attention of the whole world. John was therefore able to get a tremendous hearing for his message, which focused on the rights and duties of the human person. In the aftermath of World War II and the horrible assault on human rights by the Nazi criminals, human rights were at the forefront of consciousness, as shown by the 1948 "Universal Declaration of Human Rights" of the United Nations. John found his doctrine of human rights on the dignity of the human person as a being endowed with intelligence and free will, a dignity that is tremendously enhanced by redemption through the blood of Christ. And he takes a comprehensive view of the worldwide struggle for human dignity and rights: workers seeking a greater share in the political process, women refusing to tolerate discrimination, people throwing off colonialism, oppressed races emancipating themselves. He applauds all these movements but at the same time delivers a salutary reminder that to every right there corresponds a duty, "for every fundamental human right draws its indestructible moral force from the natural law, which in granting it imposes a corresponding obligation."[15]

The pope also condemned the arms race and called for the banning of nuclear weapons. He noted the need for some form of public authority that could operate on a worldwide basis and prayed that the United Nations might become more effective as a protector of basic human rights for every member of the human race.

*The Pastoral Constitution on the Church in the Modern World (Gaudium et Spes)*, issued by the Second Vatican Council, was undoubtedly the most ambitious project of the Council, in its length and scope as well as in its objective, which was to begin a realistic dialogue with the modern world. It builds on Pope John's two great encyclicals but actually commands greater authority as the voice of the universal episcopate. It shows an openness to the world that reflects very well the amazing change wrought in the Church by Pope John and the events of the Council.

Why should the Church occupy itself with the social, economic and political problems facing humanity? This is the question it dwells on at good length in the first part of the document. The Church, it says, cannot stand by, indifferent to the tremendous waves of change sweeping over the world. Humanity, in fact, seems to be at a critical turning point in its history as it experiences a tremendous social and cultural transformation. The Church cannot stand by indifferently, because man's earthly endeav-

15. *Pacem in Terris* 30. In David O'Brien and Thomas A. Shannon, eds., *Renewing the Earth* (Garden City, N.Y.: Doubleday/Image Books, 1977).

ors are of vital concern to the Kingdom of God. For it is man's divine vocation and task to bring about a more human world by nurturing the values of human dignity, freedom and devotion to truth.

While invested with no mission in the political, social or economic order, the Church has a vital part to play in fostering human progress. It has a profound commitment to the cause of human dignity based on its belief in man as created in the image and likeness of God. Therefore it desires to lend its support and encouragement to every effort to promote human freedom and dignity and "therefore by virtue of the gospel committed to her, the Church proclaims the rights of man."[16]

The Council states very clearly that the Church does not have a mission in the political, social or economic order. Its mission is entirely religious. But because of its religious conviction about the dignity of the human person, it cannot stand aloof from the struggle for greater human dignity and human rights. It is committed to a distinct set of values, and it must test every societal arrangement in the light of these values. And it will speak out in support of laws and policies that promote these values and in opposition to laws and policies that endanger these values.

The Council, as one sees, bases its social ethic on the principle of **personalism**, rather than on the **natural-law** concept, which previously dominated Catholic thought. According to personalism, morality begins and ends with the needs and rights of the human person. The person is the crown and center of reality, absolutely unique as the locus of freedom in the world. It is this understanding of the person which undergirds its doctrine of inalienable human rights.

Respect for the rights of each individual demands that each person be treated equally. And the Council lends its support to all those contemporary movements seeking equality. "There must be made available to all men everything necessary for leading a life truly human, such as food, clothing and shelter; the right to choose a state of life freely and to found a family; the right to education, to employment, to a good reputation, to respect, to appropriate information, to activity in accord with the upright norm of one's own conscience, to protection of privacy and to rightful freedom in matters religious too."[17] Elsewhere it defends the right of the worker to organize and to have a greater share in the decision making of the enterprise.

If, in the past, papal encyclicals overemphasized the right of private

16. *Pastoral Constitution on the Church in the Modern World,* 41.
17. Ibid., 26.

property, the Council rectifies the imbalance by stressing in accord with *Mater et Magistra* the social aspects and stating that the right to private property is not absolute but limited by the fact that temporal goods were given us by the Creator for the use of every human being and people.

It favors movements aimed at achieving participatory democracy and reminds all citizens of their right and duty to vote freely.

It stresses the connection between justice and peace. In spite of the horror and perversity of war, it refuses to condemn all wars as immoral, but it pays respect to those who for reasons of conscience refuse to bear arms. The arms race must be stopped, it insists, for it is an "utterly treacherous trap for humanity and one which injures the poor to an intolerable degree."[18]

## PAUL VI: DEVELOPMENT OR LIBERATION?

*Gaudium et Spes* touched only briefly on the question of economic development and the duty of advanced nations to come to the aid of the underdeveloped. Paul, however, devoted a major social encyclical, *Populorum Progressio*, to this theme. Paul urged all to realize that peace and justice in the world depend on the willingness of the advanced nations to foster the full self-development of the poor nations of the world. In many ways the most radical of papal encyclicals, it deplored the type of capitalism that "considers profit as the key motive for economic progress, competition as the supreme law of economics, and private ownership of the means of production as an absolute right that has no limits and carries no corresponding social obligation."[19] It called for "bold transformations, innovations that go deep . . . urgent reforms" and, most astonishing of all, even seems to say that the poor retain the right to revolution when all else fails.

Another noteworthy feature of the encyclical was its implied recognition that the Church did not have the competence to propose concrete solutions to social problems. Its social mission was limited to being a moral critic and prophet, to securing from its members a strong commitment to basic human values and encouraging them to participate actively in the struggle for a more humane world.

Was "development," however, the answer? Many leaders in the under-

18. Ibid., 81.
19. In *Renewing the Earth*, p. 322.

developed nations, especially Latin America, thought not. In view of the stranglehold imposed on them by a multinational system of trusts and technology, they preferred to think in terms of *liberation*. A number of Latin American theologians in agreement with this point of view have developed a "theology of liberation"; many of its ideas surfaced in the Latin American Bishops' Conference (CELAM) at Medellín, Colombia, in 1968. The documents of this conference entitled *Justice and Peace* constitute charter documents for all those working for social justice, not only in Latin America but elsewhere as well. They adapt the social teaching of the Church to the specific problems of Latin America, focusing on the unjust situations caused both by neocolonialism and imperialism as well as by the internal oppression of dominant groups and privileged sectors within the individual Latin American countries. One of the most significant steps forward that they make in Catholic social thought is in the active role they attribute to poor people themselves. Whereas Pope Paul VI seemed to envisage social reform as something to be accomplished by the elite for the benefit of the poor and oppressed, the Latin bishops see no possible improvement unless the poor themselves take part in the political process and unless measures are taken to awaken the social conscience of individuals of every class.

This means educating especially the illiterate and marginal poor (conscientization), who as they become more aware of their plight may turn to violent means of securing their rights. The bishops face this problem of violence squarely. They cite many reasons why violence should not be employed—the Christian preference for peace, the disruptions caused by civil war, the terrible logic of violence as it spawns ever more savage atrocities, the risk of provoking foreign intervention, the difficulty of building a regime of justice in its aftermath—but they do not rule it out altogether, while expressing the hope that peaceful solutions may be found.

In view of the intractable character of the problems and the failure of previous approaches, some are beginning to wonder if Marxism may not be the answer after all. Even within the Catholic Church there has been a noticeable softening of attitudes toward communism. Pope John XXIII helped to mitigate the almost fanatical hostility of the Church toward communism when he allowed for the existence of "good and commendable elements" in movements that originated in a false philosophy of the nature, origin and purpose of men and the world." Everyone knew John was referring to the Communist movement, and since then many Catholic activists especially in Latin America have espoused some of Marx's ideas. But Pope Paul VI, in his second major social encyclical, *Octogesima Adveniens*, refused to endorse any Catholic alliance with the Marxists. However, he did admit that one can distinguish various elements within Marxism, not all of them equally pernicious. In fact, the Pope said, as "a rigorous method of examining social and political reality, and as the rational link, tested by history, between theoretical knowledge and the practice of revolutionary transformation," it can appear attractive to the modern mind. Ultimately, however, Paul rejected the use of Marxism even when restricted to a tool of social analysis.[20]

Since then, the question of Marxism has become more pressing, as many Catholics in other lands openly espouse some form of socialism. The 1972 "Christians for Socialism" meeting in Santiago, Chile, was a dramatic indication of this trend, while a commission of French bishops concluded in 1972 that "there are major elements of Marxism which have been adopted by Christian workers, and which do not seem to be incompatible with their faith."[21]

## JOHN PAUL II

The present pope comes from a country run by Marxists and can therefore speak with more than a little authority on the subject. His encyclical *Laborem exercens (On Human Work)*, issued on September 14, 1981, is in fact a critique of Marxism as well as of liberal capitalism.

"Rigid" capitalism, the Pope says, must be reformed if the rights of the workers are to be respected. But, at the same time, he sees some grave deficiencies in the Communist system, with its excessive bureaucratic centralization, which makes the worker feel he is nothing but a cog in a huge machine. The truth that must be emphasized in opposition to both systems, the Pope says, is the priority of the individual person over the means of production. This doctrine of the primacy of the person is one deeply rooted in the Christian tradition. Any system must be judged by whether or not it promotes the rights and dignity and self-realization of the individual person. One of the basic aims of all industrial reform, he says, should be to enable the individual worker to gain more control over his work, a

20. Ibid., 369–70.
21. George Higgins, op. cit., p. 204.

greater sense of ownership over "the great workbench," at which he is working with everyone else. To this end, the Pope recommends various forms of profit sharing and co-management. Collectivist forms of socialism are not the answer, because "merely converting the means of production into state property is by no means equivalent to 'socializing' that property." Any socialization of the means of production must ensure that the human person can preserve his awareness of working "for himself."

There are some important points on which the Pope can agree with the Marxists. For one thing, like them the Pope emphasizes the nature of man as a *worker*. And while the Pope rejects a crude interpretation of Marxism which sees class war as an inevitable law of history, scientifically interpreted, so today do the more critical Marxists. They simply focus on the fact that much history has been as a matter of fact a history of class struggle, and here the Pope would certainly have to agree. Both Pope and Marxists could also no doubt agree that past injustice has often crystallized in concrete social structures that oppress the poor and that must be dismantled.

In fact, as Donal Dorr says, a review of current Catholic social thought —especially as exemplified in recent papal statements—shows the need for a good deal of "study, reflection and dialogue on the relation between the new current in Vatican social teaching and the more liberal and critical strands in the Marxist tradition." Just as there is likewise need for dialogue with the more moderate schools of liberal capitalism. Catholics are becoming increasingly aware that one cannot look for some ideal social system embodying all the values cherished in their tradition, but only a variety of systems each of which more or less successfully incorporates these values. However, in evaluating any social system a Catholic will give special attention to how open to self-criticism the system is and therefore how open it is to improvement.[22]

Besides his critique of Marxism and liberal capitalism, the Pope made so.ne other important points in his encyclical. He stressed the need for labor unions as "an indispensable element" of modern industrialized society and as a "vehicle for the struggle for social justice."

John Paul also emphasized the differing roles he believes clergy and laity should play in the work for justice. Speaking in Brazil, he warned the clergy against engaging in partisan struggles or in strife among groups and

22. *Option for the Poor* (Maryknoll, N.Y.: Orbis Books, 1983), pp. 270–71

systems. They must not abandon, in favor of political commitments, what is essential to their vocation: total consecration to God, prayer, testimony to a future life, the quest for holiness.

The clergy should project a vision of a just social order but not try to offer specific, concrete programs, since they lack the expertise. Rather, it is incumbent on the laity to work directly for the renewal of the temporal order. It is their duty to infuse a spirit of justice into the laws and arrangements of society. The laity's competence in secular affairs should enable them to deal wisely with the specifics of implementing the Church's vision of social justice. The bishops, for instance, might insist on the right of all citizens to health care, but it is up to the laity to find ways of achieving this either through private or public funding.

One of the most noteworthy aspects of John Paul's social teaching is his recognition of the need of the poor to take responsibility for their own advancement. As we have seen, this point was consistently neglected by previous popes, who still held to an elitist conception of social action. The bishops at Medellín remedied this with their insistence on the necessity of the poor taking part in the struggle, and in Brazil and Mexico Pope John Paul also addressed himself to this issue. He, too, insisted that the poor must be the main agents of their own liberation, struggling together to improve their conditions. "In the encyclical *Laborem Exercens* this point was taken further: great stress was laid on the solidarity of the poor and oppressed, and they were encouraged to struggle to overcome the disadvantages imposed on them."[23] The Pope's idea of solidarity allows for confrontation of the oppressed with the oppressor—which constitutes a significant contribution to the social thought of the Church, which previously played down this aspect of the struggle for social justice.

## THE MINISTRY OF JUSTICE IN THE AMERICAN CATHOLIC CHURCH

Social Catholicism became a major force in the U.S. Church only after the First World War, with the founding of the Social Action Department of the National Catholic Welfare Conference. Its first major statement was the bishops' *Program of Social Reconstruction*, issued in 1919. Popularly known as the *Bishops' Program*, it became more widely known than

23. Ibid., p. 259.

any of the other sixty or so postwar proposals for social reconstruction. It called for legislation to guarantee the rights of workers to bargain collectively, a minimum-wage act, social security, and health and unemployment insurance. Though denounced in the New York State legislature as socialistic, it proved astonishingly on target: all but one of the proposals were incorporated into the New Deal legislation of the thirties.

The 1920s represented a period of dormancy for Catholic social action, but the depression aroused the slumbering Catholic social conscience. And Pius XI's encyclical *Quadragesimo Anno*, of 1931, calling for structural changes in the economic system, met with an enthusiastic response. Monsignor John A. Ryan, chairman of the Social Action Department and the major Catholic spokesman on social issues, saw a close agreement between Roosevelt's New Deal and the papal program, while Roosevelt deliberately wooed Catholics by a number of ceremonial gestures. However, Roosevelt's attack on the Supreme Court lost him many Catholic supporters.

Catholic leaders wholeheartedly supported the Wagner Act, of 1935, which gave unions legal protection and made possible the formation of the CIO. A sizable number of priests began to educate themselves in industrial problems. A new type of priest appeared, the labor priest, who picketed with the workers and set up schools to instruct labor organizers in the basics of Catholic social doctrine. In time, more than a hundred of these schools made their appearance. Catholics formed a high percentage of union members, and 40 percent of the leaders of the CIO were Catholic.

One of the most significant movements of social Catholicism that appeared in the 1930s was the Catholic Worker movement, founded by Dorothy Day and Peter Maurin. They were heralds of the personalist ethic, which has now become the basic principle of Catholic social doctrine.

Their profound belief in the value of the individual and their desire to identify with the poor led them to open their first "House of Hospitality," in the Bowery in 1933, where the hungry and the homeless could find a warm welcome and a warm meal. In the pages of their paper, *The Catholic Worker*, Dorothy and Peter and their colleagues protested against the impersonal, mechanistic character of a technological society and stressed personal responsibility for injustice. They spread the message of the papal social encyclicals far and wide by their writings and lectures and by their presence in demonstrations and picket lines wherever people were taking a stand for the poor and the oppressed. Numerous communities of Catholic

Workers sprang up around the country modeled on the original one in the Bowery and dedicated, like it, to a deep sacramental spiritual life combined with social action. The Catholic Workers played a prophetic role in the American Church. By challenging the prevailing narrow Catholic mentality that equated morality with opposition to indecent movies and birth control, they helped many of their coreligionists to adopt a more profound view of social reconstruction.

With the end of the Second World War and the beginning of the Cold War, much of the Catholic community's energy and attention were devoted to crusading anticommunism. Spearheading this fight for Catholics was the Association of Catholic Trade Unionists (ACTU), organized in New York on the eve of World War II. In numerous unions, the ACTU served as a ready nucleus around which anti-Communists could gather.

The American Catholic Church in general took up the anti-Communist line and moved away from the social and economic goals of Catholic social action of the 1930s. Now it became tantamount to disloyalty to attack the system. Some Catholic leaders reverted to wholehearted acceptance of capitalism, while the great majority at least espoused the idea of reforming the system, with such ideas as profit-sharing plans, extension of unionism and labor participation in management. Only the Catholic Worker remained essentially anticapitalist.

It was not until the 1960s that social Catholicism and Catholic radicalism were revitalized. Many Catholics participated in the black civil rights movement and joined the peace marches and the demonstrations for amnesty. Such priests as the Berrigans and James Groppi, and many nuns, braved the wrath of conservative Catholics by their nonviolent demonstrations against social evils. The bishops and clergy gave tremendous help to Cesar Chavez in his efforts to organize the migrant farmworkers.

The American bishops have tried to outline a program of social action embracing the complete spectrum of pro-life issues, linking abortion to a host of other social evils, including nuclear weapons, hunger, poverty and unemployment. Since 1972 they have taken strong stands in favor of arms reduction, human rights in places like Chile, Central America and Rhodesia, the food-stamp program, health insurance and decent housing. They have endorsed gun control and opposed capital punishment. On most of these issues they are very progressive and well in advance of national policy and public opinion.

On May 3, 1983, the U.S. bishops approved a national pastoral letter on war and peace in the nuclear age, "The Challenge of Peace: God's Promise and Our Response." It was an extraordinary document in many respects. For one thing, the bishops grappled, under the public spotlight, with the most terrifying issue ever to face the human race: the possibility of nuclear war. The public attention and controversy this intervention aroused was enormous.

Moreover, it was issued only after the most exhaustive process of consultation with a host of diverse groups including top officials of the Administration as well as leading experts from the military and academic communities. Every effort was made to give a hearing to all viewpoints. It was a unique effort on the part of the bishops to build consensus on an extremely complex problem.

The objective is to commit the Church to a peacemaking role and to make the Church a peace Church. In constructing its theology of peace, the conference drew from many sources: biblical studies, systematic and moral theology, ecclesiology, and the experience and insight of members of the Church engaged in the peace movement.

As the bishops point out, Jesus himself is the supreme example of a peacemaker. His message of God's forgiveness and his demonstration of God's love as well as his call to love one's enemies and his own refusal to defend himself by force provide the greatest inspiration to all who are striving to convert the world to nonviolence.

They note also that while for most of its history the Church has sanctioned war as a last resort on the basis of the "just war" theory, there have always been prophetic Christians who have espoused a nonviolent lifestyle and witnessed to the truth of Jesus' teaching that we should all be peacemakers.

They see the present moment, with the prospect of nuclear annihilation of the human race hanging over us, as forcing all of us to make a fresh appraisal of war.

After reviewing the data establishing the fact that nuclear war constitutes a direct and immediate threat of mutual suicide, they lay down several conclusions. First, they rule out all use of nuclear weapons targeted at population centers. They do not allow even retaliatory action which would "strike enemy cities after our own have already been struck."

Next, they rule out a first strike as morally unjustifiable—a judgment based on their "extreme skepticism about the prospects for controlling a nuclear exchange." However, they do allow the possession of nuclear weapons as a deterrent until the time when alternative modes of defense can be developed. However, any strategy of deterrence, they say, is morally allowable only if it is kept limited to a "sufficiency" to deter; the quest for nuclear superiority must be rejected. Moreover, deterrence must be considered only a step on the way to progressive nuclear disarmament.

The bishops followed up their peace pastoral with another forthright challenge to the establishment in 1985 with their pastoral "On Catholic Social Teaching and the U.S. Economy." They call the current level of poverty and unemployment in the United States a "social and moral scandal." They urge a renewal of the war on poverty at a time when most Americans would rather forget all about it. Our economy, they argue, is biased in morally unacceptable ways against the poor and must be reformed to redress the balance. The measures they call for include a reduction of unemployment to 3 to 4 percent by the use of public service jobs, a reform of the welfare system that would provide a national minimum benefit for welfare recipients and a revamping of the tax system to eliminate taxation of the poor. No doubt the most arresting feature of the pastoral is its hard-hitting critique of current American cultural and economic values.

An interesting and important point about these pastorals is the recognition that sincere Catholics may differ with the bishops. They point out that in laying down these concrete moral norms they are not attempting to make them binding in conscience, since, as they say, one cannot achieve the same degree of certainty about specific moral judgments as in the case of universal moral principles. "The church's teaching authority does not carry the same force when it deals with technical solutions involving particular means as it does when it speaks of principles or ends."

For the average American, unaware of the great range of social issues addressed by the bishops over the past twenty years, these two pastorals came as a surprise. They were accustomed to associating the Catholic Church mainly with its stand on abortion. One of the reasons for this, no doubt, is that the bishops have approved and funded programs intended to make Catholics aware of the Church's stand on abortion, while they have not done a whole lot to implement their statements on other issues.

However, the pastorals have undoubtedly opened up a new chapter in the American Church's quest for social justice. Much effort is being expended to bring home their teachings to the average Catholic, and it is just possible that out of it may come a whole new image of the Church as a force for peace and justice.

# 28

## Bioethics and Ecology

On July 26, 1978, news broke of the birth of the world's first test tube baby, Louise Brown, of England. Two physicians, Robert G. Edwards and Patrick C. Steptoe, had succeeded in fertilizing an ovum of Mrs. Brown's in a petri dish *(in vitro)* and implanting the embryo in her uterus. The birth of healthy-looking Louise nine months later was hailed as a significant triumph of medical science. Since then, more than two thousand such births have been recorded.

Progress of this kind in the life sciences has generated a great number of ethical questions in regard to eugenic engineering, genetic screening, *in vitro* fertilization, cloning, etc. Obviously, an adequate treatment of all the ramifications involved would take us far beyond the scope of this volume. The intention here is merely to give a summary view of how moralists approach some of the more important issues raised by the new discoveries.

The pure consequentialists (or situation ethicists) take a very benign view of most of these developments. Joseph Fletcher, for instance, seems very happy to foresee the day when babies will regularly be spawned in test tubes from sperm and ova donated by anonymous donors, and the day when semihuman clones will perform the difficult and dangerous tasks of society such as testing for pollution or investigating threatening volcanoes or snowslides. He dismisses those who have moral objections to such possibilities, as people captive to aprioristic, metaphysical and religious scruples. Fletcher seems eager to give his blessing to almost anything the genetic engineers may come up with, as long as it gives man more control over his world. Other moralists, however, like Richard McCormick, see grave defects in such an approach insofar as it fails to deal with such crucial questions as what might be the personal and social costs: how dehumanizing, etc.?

The other end of the spectrum, away from Fletcher, is occupied by Paul Ramsey, of Princeton, and members of the deontologist school. These scholars take a very negative view of AID (artificial insemination by donor), *in vitro* fertilization, cloning (when a fetus is produced that is the exact genetic replica of another human being) and other forms of experimentation on the unborn, infants, children and the mentally defective.

One of Ramsey's basic principles is the duty to respect certain biological structures that God intended to be permanent. The link between procreation and marital love, for instance, he holds divinely ordained. On this principle alone, Ramsey rejects AID, reproduction *in vitro*, and cloning. Ramsey also rules out experimentation such as genetic surgery on the fetus or infant, since such procedures, performed without the child's consent, reduce the child to an object. A similar approach is taken by another deontologist, Leon Kass, who argues against *in vitro* (fertilization insofar as it involves the prospective child in risks of deformity without its consent. Moreover, this procedure sometimes involves discarding unimplanted embryos, which may very well be human life.

A mediating position between the Fletcher and Ramsey-Kass schools is taken by James Gustafson and Charles Curran. They hold in high regard the values defended by Ramsey and Kass—inseparability of marital love and procreation, right of the unborn and infant not to be exposed to risks that are nontherapeutic—but they refuse to regard these as absolutes and speak of possible circumstances in which they might be sacrificed for greater values such as the good of society.

Many Catholic theologians oppose *in vitro* fertilization and cloning, since they agree with Ramsey and Kass that they are dehumanizing insofar as, by removing procreation from the bodily union of the spouses, they subtract a very important human element from the marital relationship. Married partners, as he says, are not only reason, freedom, emotions, they are also bodies, and when they procreate, all of these elements should play a role. Otherwise, we make procreation less human. Moreover, biological parenthood helps to strengthen the family. To relegate it to the laboratory tends to undermine the family.

Some of the objections made by other moralists who oppose *in vitro* fertilization include: the use of precious medical resources that could more profitably be used in more urgent health-care programs; appeal to Pius XII's authority, who had condemned even artificial insemination by the husband, since it violated the God-given design of nature; the likelihood that scientists would escalate such interventions and perform all sorts of experiments on embryos *in vitro;* the fact that *in vitro* fertilization often involves the destruction of many embryos that may well be considered human; the possibility of producing fetal monsters; the undermining of the family as its link with biological parenthood is severed, with consequent confusion about the identity of one's parents; etc.

However, many revisionists, including Richard McCormick, argue in favor of *in vitro* fertilization. They reject Pius XII's natural-design argument as inconsistent with the Church's acceptance of other medical technologies such as kidney dialysis and respirators. They also reject the argument that the procreative and unitive aspects of intercourse should not be separated: there is no need for every act of intercourse to be open to procreation. The unitive aspect of sexuality, they say, is the fundamental one, and so sexuality serves its purpose of uniting two people in love even if the procreative aspect is postponed. Moreover, while love is essential to reproduction, it is the total relationship of the couple that matters and not whether each act, itself, of reproduction expresses this conjugal love.

As the revisionists see it, procreation *in vitro*, as artificial, is a disvalue, but disvalues can be permitted for a proportionate reason—which in this case would be the need of the spouses for a child. The escalation argument also is recognized as weighty but not decisive. And as to the destruction of many fertilized ova (zygotes), this need not happen. It is possible, as recent research shows (at the Eastern Virginia Medical School), to implant all fertilized ova that show signs of life in the woman's uterus. Moreover, even where ova showing signs of life are destroyed in the process, many moralists question whether they should be regarded as persons with rights—and therefore, they claim, their destruction may be permitted for a proportionate reason, such as the good of the spouses (helping a couple to have their own genetic children), a value that should not be readily dismissed, since the genetic link does bind children to parents in a special way and the parents to each other. Finally, as to the risk of injury to the test-tube baby, it now seems apparent that such risks are no graver than those involved in normal conception (but this is a disputed point).

It should be noted here that the Ethics Advisory Board of the Department of Health, Education and Welfare, on March 16, 1979, after months of hearings and deliberations, issued a statement that labeled *in vitro* fertilization "ethically acceptable" under certain conditions. They allowed experimentation on a fertilized ovum not intended for implantation as long as the ovum was not sustained in the test tube for more than fourteen days—the time at which it is believed the ovum is first firmly established on its way to full human development.

Artificial insemination by donor (AID) involves impregnating a woman with sperm that is not her husband's; it is often drawn from commercial banks and chosen for the physical, intellectual, etc., qualities described on an attached label. This is almost universally condemned by Catholic moralists, the main reason being that it seems to threaten the stability of the marriage on account of the feelings of inadequacy it may engender or intensify in the husband or the danger of the wife's fantasizing about the identity of the surrogate husband as well as the confusion of the child as to its real father. The possible benefits do not seem proportionate to these risks.

The same objections have been leveled against the use of ovum banks, which make it possible for a donor's ovum to be implanted in the infertile woman. But some argue that the drawbacks of AID or ovum banks can be overcome: in the case of AID, by sensitive counseling and maximum participation of the male partner during the insemination process; in the case of the woman receiving another's ovum, the fact that she experiences pregnancy and the birth of the child would seem to ensure her sense of sharing with her husband in the begetting of the child. But Catholic moralists would rule out any use of embryo banks, since in this case neither genetic parent is involved in the total life-generating process.

The possible Xeroxing of many of the best specimens of the human race has tempted many people to advocate a practice called cloning, which is already practiced with animals. It involves removing the nucleus of an animal's ovum and replacing it with the nucleus of a somatic cell obtained from the donor animal chosen to be a stencil. The ovum is then implanted, and the offspring of this operation would be a carbon copy of the donor, carrying its identical genetic package. In this way, frogs and toads have already been reproduced as exact copies of a single parent donor, and it is even claimed, by David Rorvik, that a human clone—a carbon copy of an eccentric millionaire—has been produced in a laboratory somewhere in Southeast Asia, though many suspect the whole story is a hoax.

The moral objection to this practice: it would be tantamount to using human beings as guinea pigs or objects.

## DEATH AND DYING

The moral issues involved in care for the dying have become extremely complex, thanks to the advent of sophisticated technology that enables doctors to keep people alive who previously would have succumbed. One of the questions most often asked is whether it is moral to "pull the plug" when the person artificially kept alive has little or no chance of recovery.

A number of recent events have focused public attention on this issue. Karen Quinlan, a twenty-one-year-old woman living in New Jersey fell into a coma in April 1975. When it became apparent that she had no chance of regaining consciousness, her parents asked the hospital to remove the respirator keeping her alive. The hospital refused, and it was only after a lengthy court battle that the parents' request was honored. Ironically, Karen did not expire, but has continued to survive in a vegetable state. More recently, we have the case of twenty-six-year-old quadriplegic, Elizabeth Bouvia, paralyzed since birth and kept alive by intravenous feeding against her will. She has sued her hospital, in Riverside, California, to allow her to starve to death and to ease her way with hygienic care and pain-killing drugs. "Let me die with dignity," she said in an interview. But a superior court has ruled that the hospital staff could not be compelled to let her starve.[1]

Some other recent rulings indicate how muddled the law is on this issue. An appellate court in New Jersey overturned a lower court's decision to allow a hospital to withdraw life support from an eighty-three-year-old woman nearly unconscious and unable to communicate because of a brain disorder. But, on the other hand, a California court upheld a lower court's ruling that dismissed murder charges against two physicians who withdrew life-support equipment from a patient in a deeply comatose state and unlikely to recover. According to the court, the burden of the treatment outweighed the benefit likely to be gained.[2]

Catholic moralists used to approach this issue in terms of *ordinary* and *extraordinary* treatment. One was obliged only to use *ordinary* treatment

1. New York *Times*, January 3, 1984, p. 18.
2. Ibid., p. 10.

to maintain life. But with the many advances in medical technology, it is no longer easy to distinguish ordinary from extraordinary means. What was extraordinary a few years ago may be quite commonplace today.

Hence many theologians prefer to use the terms *beneficial* and *nonbeneficial*. We are obliged to use beneficial means; that is, treatment that has a good chance of restoring the patient to a reasonable state of well-being. Treatment that would merely prolong the life of the patient in a physically and mentally deteriorated state would be described as nonbeneficial and therefore not demanded.

Another question altogether is the morality of so-called active euthanasia; that is, the patient is not merely allowed to die, as in the preceding examples, but his death is directly caused, for example by a lethal injection or overdose of sleeping pills, etc. It may be either voluntary or involuntary inasmuch as death is caused with or without the patient's knowledge and consent.

Often these cases involve deformed babies, crippled adults or elderly and senile persons. Though guilty of a criminal act, those responsible are often treated very leniently by the court. A United States citizen, Lester Zygmaniak, for instance, walked into the hospital with a sawed-off shotgun and killed his brother, who was totally immobilized by a motorcycle accident and had pleaded to be put out of his misery. Lester was acquitted on the ground of temporary insanity. An Englishwoman, Mrs. Elizabeth Wise, pleaded guilty to causing the death of her nine-month-old blind and deaf daughter by mixing barbiturates in her milk. She was found guilty of manslaughter and placed on probation.

Movements have been launched in various countries to have euthanasia legalized—without much success so far. Its supporters have mustered many arguments in its favor, including the idea that a terminally ill patient who has nothing more to contribute to family or society should not be compelled to endure meaningless suffering, especially if the patient's faith system does not involve the existence of God and the value of redemptive suffering; when faced with a conflict of two evils, one should choose the lesser—which in this case would be death, rather than useless suffering; one's right to die should be respected, since personal rights should be restricted only when their exercise involves injury to another's rights; why burden family and society with the labor and costs of keeping a terminally ill person alive against his or her will—using scarce resources that could be more beneficial to others? What proof is there that God wants us to suffer unnecessarily?

Catholic moralists generally—though not unanimously—condemn active euthanasia for reasons drawn from tradition and Scripture: notably the doctrine that God alone has dominion over life. They also contend that modern methods of alleviating pain weaken the argument based on the unbearable suffering of the terminally ill. Moreover, as they point out, there are grave social dangers in crossing the line between allowing to die (passive euthanasia) and actively intervening to cause death. If active euthanasia were legalized, those who are ill and elderly, for instance, would have to live in fear that someone might use their illness as a pretext for putting them to death. Unscrupulous family members or relatives might connive to exploit an elderly person's confused and weakened state to pressure her into agreeing to voluntary euthanasia.[3]

## THE LIVING WILL

With modern technology, doctors can often keep people alive indefinitely even though their chance of recovering any significant degree of health is minimal. Unfortunately, too many doctors, fearing malpractice suits, prolong the lives of their patients beyond all reason. To protect oneself it is now possible to draw up a living will, which notifies those responsible of one's desire to die when there is no reasonable expectation of recovery. It is signed in the presence of witnesses and is distributed to the family, physicians, clergy, etc. To date, a number of states have legalized living wills.

## ECOLOGICAL ETHICS

At a conference titled "the Global Possible," in Washington, D.C., on May 5, 1984, a group of scientists and scholars called for concerted international action "to protect the global environment and the biological systems that support human life."[4] Meeting under the auspices of the World Resource Institute, a nonprofit group devoted to seeking solutions to environmental and resource problems, they took note of "the erosion of the planet's renewable resource base—the forests, fisheries, agricultural

3. Andrew C. Varga, *The Main Issues in Bioethics* (New York: Paulist Press, 1980), pp. 183–86.
4. New York *Times*, May 6, 1984, p. 12.

lands, wildlife and biological diversity." Pointing out how this generation has the unprecedented power of altering the environment on a global scale, they insisted on the need to plan and manage our use of the environment.

As we become increasingly aware of the frailty of our Spaceship Earth and of how perishable is our environment, it is obvious that we need a whole new approach to ethics. An important task of ethics today, it seems, should be to sharpen our sense of moral responsibility for saving the planet. Mankind must learn to maintain a "universal ecological balance," which will demand a whole new set of moral values based on preserving the environment for future generations.

A basic moral imperative today, then, is to develop a new life-style that will meet the real needs of human nature and be compatible with the healthy condition of our environment and with the limited resources of the earth.

Looking at the first requisite—a life-style that meets the real needs of human nature—it is obvious that modern technology has taken over much of the labor formerly performed by individuals. Many people no longer have the opportunity of doing productive and creative labor that employs their brains and their hands in working on the various forms of material. Yet people need and enjoy this kind of work. Why, then, should we let technology take over completely? Much of our production could be left to individuals in workshops creating and making many of the accoutrements of daily life. This is especially true in the Third World, where there is a lack of sophisticated technology and capital but a lot of manpower. Instead of trying to increase mass production, they should be devising methods of production by the masses, as E. F. Schumacher says in his *Small Is Beautiful.* [5]

Next, as we said, the new life-style should be compatible with the healthy condition of the environment. It is becoming quite clear that we can no longer afford to pollute our air and water and wreak havoc on our surroundings by wanton destruction of many species of plants and animals.

The hazards of our reckless use of chemicals is finally beginning to dawn on the average citizen, as hardly a week goes by without news of some new threat from a careless use of chemicals. The link between cancer and a chemically polluted environment is well established. The National Cancer

5. New York: Harper & Row, 1975.

Institute estimates that 60–90 percent of cancer is caused by the polluted environment and that one fourth of the population will suffer from some form of cancer. Also, environmental factors account for nearly one fifth of the physical and mental defects found in newly born infants. The pesticide DBCP has been found as a contaminant in the milk of nursing mothers. The most vicious of all pollutants are the radioactive chemicals, which as they move through the food chain become ever more concentrated. Thus a small dose of strontium 90 discharged in a pasture becomes more concentrated in the cows eating the grass and even more concentrated in the child that drinks the cows' milk.

Another frightening possibility is that with our aerosol sprays we may be destroying the ozone layer in the stratosphere, which protects us from ultraviolet rays.

The dominant atmospheric problems, according to the recent conference of the Global Possible, "are acid precipitation, ozone depletion and the risk of disruptive climate change from the buildup of carbon dioxide and other greenhouse gases and urban air pollution."[6]

Another ominous fact is the damage we are doing to the complex network of organisms and plants that constitute our ecosystem. As was stated at the Global Possible conference, we lose a species a day—very bad news, for as science shows, the diverse organisms of the ecosystem live together in orderly fashion and form a whole whose parts are extremely interdependent. Interference with this smoothly functioning system can have unforeseen and devastating effects. A parable illustrating this point is found in the story of the health workers in Borneo who sprayed the huts of the villagers with DDT in order to exterminate a malaria-carrying parasite. Lizards ingested large quantities of the DDT sprayed on the walls and died. Cats ate some of the moribund lizards and they, too, died, while the caterpillars, which were kept in check by the lizards, were now free to go to work chewing on the thatched roofs of the huts. As a result, the villagers lost the roofs of their homes and suffered from a plague of rats.

Research has also turned up many examples of the damage we are doing to the plankton in the ocean with our use of synthetic chemicals. Since the plankton forms the basis of the food chain of the ocean, we are putting this entire food chain in jeopardy.

Thanks to our reckless attitude, many species of birds and animals have already been irretrievably lost, while many others are endangered. On the

6. Ibid., p. 12.

other hand, other species of birds, plants and mammals have been introduced into new ecosystems lacking natural predators or controls—which has allowed them to multiply and cause great damage to the environment. This happened when the cotton culture was introduced in the South, causing the reduction of many species of plants and animals. One result was infestation by the boll weevil.

At the present state of knowledge, it is difficult to predict with certainty what damage may be done by our thoughtless extinction of rare species. We do know that species once thought of little use have proved to be extremely valuable. The South American cinchona tree, for instance, was believed worthless until the discovery of quinine's antimalarial properties. It is estimated that some fifty thousand new chemicals with diverse medical and scientific applications could be derived from plants many of which might be lost if wholesale extinction of plant life continues to occur.[7]

The third ethical imperative we mentioned is to shoulder the responsibility for conserving our limited and diminishing energy resources. The constant need to increase our GNP (gross national product) has meant a constant increase in our consumption of energy—as if we had an unlimited supply. True, we have reached an unparalleled level of affluence and "the American dream" has been realized for many, but it is slowly becoming apparent that we cannot keep going at this pace. It is calculated that if we stay at the present rate of increase, the demand for energy will double by the year 2000.

The hard truth is that we are rapidly depleting our energy sources. Some figures indicate that our domestic supplies of natural gas and petroleum will be used up by about the year 2000. Some expect coal to become the main source. But the problems associated with dependence on coal are staggering. Full exploitation of our resources of coal would mean a tremendous increase in strip-mining, with resulting destruction of arable and forested land. The amount of water alone needed for the operation of power stations and liquefaction or gasification plants would amount to more than three or four times the total amount of water now used throughout the entire country. With water already in short supply in various parts of the country, there is no way that much water could be allocated. Add to this the ecological and pollution problems, and it becomes obvious that "the amount of coal we can reasonably expect to

7. Albert J. Fritsch, *Environmental Ethics* (Garden City, N.Y.: Anchor Press, 1980), p. 20.

obtain and use is far less than the amount theoretically available in the ground. At best, coal offers only a temporary, stopgap satisfaction of our short-term energy requirements . . ."[8]

Will nuclear energy provide the answer? This is an exceedingly complex and controverted issue. Without mentioning the problem of inefficiency (70 percent of uranium 235 is turned into waste heat, to dissipate which requires enormous amounts of water, already in short supply in many places), the question of safety is fraught with dilemmas. As William Ophuls says, "Nuclear power generation can be *safe* only if the design and construction of the reactor are flawless; there are no accidents or operating errors; reactors, fuels, and other nuclear installations can be perfectly protected from acts of God, terrorism and sabotage, criminal acts, and acts of war, civil or foreign; and the release of radionuclides during all other phases of the fuel cycle (mining, processing, transportation, reprocessing, disposal) can be rigidly controlled. As critics point out, this is a rather alarming list of *ifs*. In fact, the infant nuclear industry has run into trouble in almost every one of the areas mentioned."[9]

Perhaps the thorniest of all the problems connected with nuclear energy is that of finding suitable sites for disposal of the extremely dangerous wastes. To date there is simply no satisfactory disposal method available. Even salt-bed repositories, which were once regarded as a solution, are now looked on less optimistically: there could be contamination of water-laden rock formations below the salt floor and also possible human intrusion. The waste-disposal problem alone should forbid pinning any great hopes on nuclear energy as a panacea.

Another consideration to keep in mind: energy is always needed to produce energy, and the gains from nuclear energy have to be balanced against the amount of energy that has to be invested. The net gain is subject to the law of diminishing returns.

It is thus becoming more and more obvious to many observers that the era of cheap and abundant energy is over, that we are on the threshold of a postindustrial age, when we will have to depend very much on such resources as solar energy, wind and water power, etc., with all their inherent limitations. The "full speed ahead" economy will have to give way to a steady-state economy based on keeping a balance between our material needs and the limits of our environment.

8. William Ophuls, *Ecology and the Politics of Scarcity* (San Francisco: W. H. Freeman, 1977), pp. 88–89.
9. Ibid., p. 92.

Adapting to scarcity will present a great moral challenge. We must abandon the dream of achieving technological mastery over nature and find ways instead of living in harmony with it.

This will mean adopting a life-style reflecting a sense of responsibility about conserving our precious resources. This ethic of conservation would affect our decisions regarding the type of jobs we look for, the type of recreation we take, the kind of food we eat, the way we heat and furnish our homes. It would inspire us to seek ways of reducing waste and inefficiency in our use of energy and to question the values of our society, which still idolizes consumption and growth.

More specifically, an ecologically conscious way of life would mean attention to proper nutrition, preferring, for instance, as far as possible, natural to processed foods. It would also mean avoiding dependence on drugs, alcohol and tobacco and developing our creativity in recreation by choosing the kind that draws on our personal talents and enhances our creativity. It would mean devoting time and energy to movements seeking to build community both locally and globally to foster social justice— prophetic communities that could demonstrate that there is more satisfaction in sharing spiritual goods than in material consumption and expenditure of physical resources.

Some environmentalists have pointed to Christianity and the Bible as a major cause of the mentality that led Western man to rape and ravage his environment. They quote the Book of Genesis: "Be fruitful, multiply, fill the earth and conquer it. Be masters of the fish of the sea, the birds of heaven and all living animals on the earth."[10] And they note that it was the Christian West that spawned the Industrial Revolution. However, there is on the other hand much in the Bible and in Christian faith to inspire an ethic of conversation. We read in the Book of Genesis that God has entrusted His creatures with a garden, "to cultivate and take care of it."[11] The Bible also reminds us constantly of our sinfulness and the need to reform. It inculcates an ethic of sharing and community. It emphasizes our responsibility as stewards and not owners of the earth. It tells us that the earth is for everyone and that its fruits must not be alienated for the enjoyment of a few. Finally, the biblical prophets were extremely vehement in denouncing those who deprived the poor of the necessities of life.

10. Gen. 1:28.
11 Gen. 2:15.

The conference on the Global Possible offered a number of proposals to protect and preserve our environment. A tenth of the earth's land, said the participants, should be preserved for parks. Better management of fisheries and forests is needed, as are energy policies that remove subsidies for consumption. Also, we must pursue the development of renewable-energy supplies. Global assessment of resources and life-support systems is likewise a most urgent necessity.

Some practical suggestions for the individual committed to an ethic of conservation: Learn about plants and birds and take hikes to enjoy the wilderness; participate in discussions of power-plant and coal-conversion-plant locations. Help to preserve the natural beauty of wild rivers and seashores. Find out what chemicals are being used in your vicinity and alert fellow citizens to the need for monitoring emissions and checking on hazardous-waste disposal. Help form committees to advocate solar-energy research. Be sparing in the use of nonrenewable resources. Prefer natural materials and practices to synthetic and artificial ones: biological versus chemical pest controls, natural birth control and birth practices, etc.[12]

12. Albert J. Fritsch, op. cit., pp. 271–72.

# 29

# Human Destiny

"Death, judgment, heaven and hell" is the traditional formula of the Church which summarizes its teaching on human destiny. The Scriptures portray these faith realities in the most graphic imagery: at the end of the world the Son of Man will come on the clouds of heaven dispatching his angels with a mighty trumpet blast, while the moon darkens and the stars fall from the skies. On the earth the nations will be in anguish, distraught at the roaring of the sea and the waves as men die in panic at what is happening. Then the Son of Man will sit on his royal throne and judge all the nations assembled before him, separating people as a shepherd separates sheep from goats, placing the sheep on his right hand and the goats on his left. The good people, on his right hand, who have lived lives of self-giving active love, he will welcome into the Kingdom prepared from the creation of the world, but those on the left, the hard-hearted and the merciless, will be thrust into Gehenna, a place of unquenchable fire where, with the devil and his angels, they will suffer everlasting torment.

One of the first questions that present themselves in interpreting these passages is how much of this is derived from the historical Jesus and how much is due to the early Christian community. There is no easy answer. But what is certain is that the imagery itself is largely colored by Jewish apocalyptic thought—a strong current of ideas and feelings running through Judaism in the two centuries before Christ which nurtured the great hope that God would intervene in cataclysmic fashion and rescue his people from their oppression. It would mean a final separation of the good from the wicked, as those faithful to God would receive their reward and the wicked would be eternally punished.

The obvious derivation from Jewish apocalyptic thought and especially the vindictive character of the sentiments expressed in these images should caution us against ascribing them directly to Jesus himself in the light of other statements of his which stress mercy and compassion, viz., "Be compassionate as your Father is compassionate. Do not judge, and you will not be judged yourselves; do not condemn, and you will not be condemned yourselves; grant pardon, and you will be pardoned."[1]

However, if Jesus himself did not utter the apocalyptic prophecies exactly as recorded in the Gospel, there can be no doubt that his whole message was strongly future oriented, or *eschatological*. He taught that the Kingdom of God—already a mysterious reality present in his ministry—would be consummated in God's future. Salvation is still to come, but it is certain to come and it requires decision and obedience. "The new world may be depicted in bizarre imagery but there can be no mistake about what is really meant: the world of salvation is a wonder, an object of hope, the realization of which transcends all imagination."[2]

The Kingdom is still not visibly present; it can and must be proclaimed, but it is very near. We must pray for its coming in the hope that God will establish it in spite of the resistance of men. Above all, we must repent—forsake our sinful ways and surrender our will to the rule of God.

The New Testament doctrine of the last things is expressed in imagery and symbolism, therefore, which at least in part is derived from Jesus' own teaching. Its main elements are the Second Coming, or Parousia, the resurrection of the body, the Last Judgment, and Heaven and hell. In interpreting them we must keep several things in mind. One is that they were not meant to give us factual information about actual events of history. Eschatology partakes of the character of myth. Just as Genesis does not intend to describe the actual history of human origins, so the eschatology of the New Testament should not be taken as literal descriptions of the End, but as imaginative conceptions of ineffable transcendent realities: the ultimate purpose of history and the primal force that undergirds it.

Another point to keep in mind is that the Church has constantly had to wrestle with these symbols in terms of its unfolding experience. The first

1. Lk. 6:36–37.
2. Hans Conzelmann, *An Outline of the Theology of the New Testament* (New York: Harper & Row, 1969), p. 23.

Christians believed that the End was near and expected Christ to return at any moment. But already we see Paul coming to grips with the delay of the Parousia and focusing the attention of his followers on the present spiritual blessings they enjoy. This reinterpretation of the original eschatology is carried even further in John's Gospel, which defuses the urgency of the original expectancy of the End by replacing it with a so-called realized eschatology: Christ's promise to return is virtually fulfilled by the descent of the Holy Spirit. The believer already enjoys eternal life, which is simply to know God and Jesus. One is already judged by the decision to reject or accept Jesus.

When the Gospel was brought to the Greek world, which was unfamiliar with Jewish apocalyptic imagery, it was not always easy to maintain a balance between the original Hebraic and Christian hope and the thought forms of Greek culture. One tendency, the predominant one, interpreted the Hebraic symbols in a literal pictorial and chronological fashion, while the opposite tendency, inspired by Greek philosophy, lost all contact with the Jewish apocalyptic and produced an almost completely noneschatological version of Christianity.

The pictorial interpretation of the New Testament sometimes took rather crude forms, as in millennialism, which fostered belief in a future millennium, to be inaugurated by Christ at his Second Coming, when he would reign for a thousand years on earth in company with his saints, who would be raised in their identical earthly bodies. At its end they would be taken up with him into heaven.

In their efforts to explicate the full import of New Testament eschatology, the Fathers of the Church came up with a number of ideas that entered into the mainstream of tradition. Thus the idea of an intermediate state between the death of the individual and the Final Judgment originated with Jerome, it seems, and was also favored by Augustine. Closely connected with this view was the doctrine of purgatory as a place or state after death where a person might still make atonement for sin. It is found already in Clement of Alexandria (d. c. 215). Augustine, too, taught the reality of purifying pains in the next life, and Gregory the Great held that privation of the vision of God was one form of purgative suffering. The doctrine was also implied in the Church's constant practice of offering Masses and prayers for the dead. The problem of what happened to good people as well as infants who died unbaptized and therefore presumably ineligible for Heaven was solved by later theologians with the idea of "Limbo," a place of merely natural happiness and contentment.

The official teaching of the Catholic Church always avoided the pictorial apocalyptic imagery. Simply stated, the doctrine proclaims that the blessed in Heaven enjoy the beatific vision of God, while the damned are punished with the torments of hell. No change is possible, for the states of both the blessed and the damned are fixed for eternity. But the torments of hell are not specified; presumably, the fires of hell mentioned in Scripture are to be interpreted as symbolic.

Modern attempts to interpret the eschatology of Jesus include principally the fundamentalist, the liberal and the existentialist views. The fundamentalist expects a literal fulfillment of the apocalyptic imagery of the New Testament and identifies the coming of the Kingdom and the resurrection exclusively with otherworldly hopes which leave no room for the terrestrial aspirations of humanity. The liberal interpretation reverses the previous one and puts the whole emphasis on the hope of a better future in this world. This school admits that Jesus used apocalyptic eschatological imagery, but they reinterpret this language in terms of the emergent forces that work in history.

The existentialist interpretation is represented notably by Rudolf Bultmann and his followers, who demythologize the eschatological language of the Gospels, which they say is predicated on such myths as the three-story universe and a conflict between God and Satan. For them, the eschatological language is taken as the symbol for an absolute value or a realized eschatology without sequence or fulfillment of a divine plan. According to Bultmann, "Jesus sees men as imprisoned in their own self-assertion and clinging to the false security of their 'world' of vanity and death."[3] Jesus offers them instead the possibilities of freedom and true security in God's Kingdom.

Each one of the above interpretations fails to do full justice to the eschatology of Jesus and the New Testament. The fundamentalist focuses exclusively on the next world, while the liberal neglects the transcendent aspect altogether. And Bultmann's existentialist interpretation completely ignores the corporate and social character of human destiny, which is so profoundly inscribed in New Testament thought.

On the other hand, the bishops at the Second Vatican Council, in revising Catholic eschatology, skillfully keep these various elements in a

3. Amos N. Wilder, *Eschatology and Ethics in the Teaching of Jesus* (Westport, Conn.: Greenwood Press, 1978), p. 65..

creative tension. In *Lumen Gentium* they recognize the individual's responsibility to work out his salvation, but at the same time they emphasize the link between the individual and the corporate destiny. Moreover, they relate the terrestrial future of mankind to its ultimate destiny, insofar as human progress is said to be "of vital concern to the kingdom of God." For, as they say, the values that we struggle to promote on earth, "human dignity, brotherly communion, and freedom . . . we will find . . . once again cleansed this time from the stain of sin, illuminated and transfigured, when Christ presents to his Father, an eternal and universal kingdom."[4]

How, then, in the light of new insights and in view of the symbolic character of the traditional imagery, should we interpret the traditional last things: death, judgment, Heaven and hell?

Death must be seen in the light of Christ's Resurrection, which, however interpreted, stands for his transformation into a new mode of existence.

So how, in union with Christ, will we be transformed into a new mode of existence? We must realize that death will uncover our true spiritual state. In this life we become the kind of self we want to be—we can deceive ourselves and shape ourselves according to a set of false values that are illusory since they have no root in the creative will of God. Or we can live in openness to God and neighbor and choose values that reflect eternal reality. On earth we live in tension between these two possibilities—experiencing a foretaste of Heaven as we share in God's peace or experiencing hell as in alienation from God and neighbor we are tormented by frustration and despair. Death, however, fixes our spiritual state and reveals our true self. Whatever in us, in our lives, our relationships and our work and achievements is rooted in divine reality will constitute our eternal self. Whatever was false and illusory will simply cease to exist. Insofar as we led a life of selfishness, in alienation from God and neighbor, there will be nothing left of eternal significance and value; but insofar as we have been open to God and neighbor, we will participate in the eternal life of God. "At death we shall for the first time experience fully the immediate self-presence of our true eternal selves."[5] Heaven therefore represents the fulfillment of the eternal possibilities that human life offers, while hell represents the ultimate failure to achieve that fulfillment.

Judgment therefore merely stands for the revelation of our true self,

4. *Pastoral Constitution on the Church in the Modern World*, 39.
5. Patrick Fanon, "And After Death . . . ?" *Catholic Mind* (April, 1974), p. 21.

which we will experience at death as we are made aware of what in our lives and our selves has eternal value in the light of the Gospel of Jesus Christ.

The other traditional concepts also need to be interpreted symbolically. Purgatory, for instance, in light of the above, would mean the pain involved in facing how much falsehood and unreality we have built into our selves and which therefore must be annihilated. The resurrection of the body would stand for the truth that our earthly struggles, relationships and achievements will somehow be taken up into the eternal life we share with God, for "creation still retains the hope of being freed, like us, from its slavery to decadence, to enjoy the same freedom and glory as the children of God . . . we too groan inwardly as we wait for our bodies to be set free."[6]

6. Rom. 8:21, 23

# BIBLIOGRAPHY

BASIC REFERENCE WORKS

*Encyclopedia of Theology: The Concise Sacramentum Mundi.* Edited by Karl Rahner, S.J. New York: Seabury Press, 1975.
*A History of Christian Doctrine.* Edited by H. Cunliffe-Jones. Philadelphia: Fortress Press, 1978.
McKenzie, John, S.J. *Dictionary of the Bible.* Milwaukee: Bruce, 1965 (paper).
*The Christian Faith in the Doctrinal Documents of the Catholic Church.* Edited by Joseph Neuner and James Dupuis. Westminster, Md.: Christian Classics, 1975.
*The Jerome Biblical Commentary.* Edited by Raymond Brown, S.S., et al. Englewood Cliffs, N.J.: Prentice-Hall, 1968.
*The New Catholic Encyclopedia.* 17 vols. New York: McGraw Hill, 1967–79.
*The Oxford Dictionary of the Christian Church.* 2d ed. Edited by F. L. Cross and E. A. Livingston. London: Oxford University Press, 1974.
*Vatican Council II: The Conciliar and Post Conciliar Documents.* Edited by Austin Flannery, O.P. Collegeville, Minn.: The Liturgical Press, 1975.


GENERAL WORKS

Berger, Peter. *The Heretical Imperative: Contemporary Possibilities of Religious Affirmation.* Garden City, N.Y.: Doubleday Anchor Books, 1980.
Bokenkotter, Thomas. *A Concise History of the Catholic Church.* Garden City, N.Y.: Doubleday Image Books, 1979.
Carmody, J. T., and D. L. Carmody. *Contemporary Catholic Theology: An Introduction.* New York: Harper & Row, 1980.
Gilkey, Langdon. *Reaping the Whirlwind: A Christian Interpretation of History.* New York: Seabury Press, 1976.
Hellwig, Monika. *Understanding Catholicism.* New York: Paulist Press, 1981.
Hitchcock, James. *Catholicism and Modernity: Confrontation or Capitulation?* New York: Seabury Press, 1979.

Küng, Hans. *On Being a Christian*. Garden City, N.Y.: Doubleday, 1976.

Lonergan, Bernard J. F. *Method in Theology*. New York: Seabury Press, 1979.

McBrien, Richard. *Catholicism*. Minneapolis, Minn.: Winston Press, 1981.

Macquarrie, John. *Principles of Christian Theology*. New York: Charles Scribner's Sons, 1977.

Pelikan, Jaroslav, *The Christian Tradition: A History of the Development of Doctrine*. Chicago: University of Chicago Press. 4 vols. 1971–84.

Rahner, Karl. *Foundations of Christian Faith*. New York: Seabury Press, 1978.

Schoof, Mark. *A Survey of Catholic Theology, 1800–1970*. New York: Paulist Press, 1970.

Tracy, David. *Blessed Rage for Order: The New Pluralism in Theology*. New York: Seabury Press, 1975.

## 1. RELIGION: DO WE NEED IT?

Cavendish, Richard. *The Great Religions*. New York: Arco Press, 1980.

Jung, Carl. *Man and His Symbols*. New York: Dell Publishing, 1964.

*The Essential Jung*. Selected and introduced by Anthony Storr. Princeton, N.J.: Princeton University Press, 1983.

Macquarrie, John. *Twentieth Century Religious Thought*. New York: Charles Scribner's Sons, 1981.

Smith, Huston. *The Religions of Man*. New York: Harper & Row, 1965.

Toynbee, A. *An Historian's Approach to Religion: Christianity Among the Great Religions of the World*. New York: Oxford University Press, 1957.

## 2. THE QUESTION: IS GOD THERE?

*Dogmatic Constitution on Divine Revelation*. In Austin Flannery, O.P., ed. *Vatican Council II: The Conciliar and Post Conciliar Documents*. Collegeville, Minn.: The Liturgical Press, 1975.

Hick, John. *Evil and the God of Love*. New York: Collins Fontana Library, 1968.

Kaufman, Gordon. *God the Problem*. Cambridge, Mass.: Harvard University Press, 1972.

Küng, Hans. *Does God Exist?* New York: Random House, 1981.

Neville, Robert C. *Creativity and God: A Challenge to Process Theology*. New York: The Seabury Press, 1980.

### 3. CHANGING CONCEPTS OF REVELATION

Achtemeier, Paul J. *The Inspiration of Scripture: Problems and Proposals.* Philadelphia: Westminster Press, 1980.

Dulles, Avery, S.J. *Models of Revelation.* Garden City, N.Y.: Doubleday, 1983.

———. *Revelation Theology: A History.* New York: Herder & Herder, 1969.

Latourelle, René. *Theology of Revelation.* New York: Alba House, 1966.

Niebuhr, H. Richard. *The Meaning of Revelation.* New York: Macmillan, 1962.

Schleiermacher, Friedrich. *The Christian Faith.* Edited by H. R. Mackintosh and J. B. Stewart. Edinburgh: T. & T. Clark, 1956.


### 4. FAITH: POSSIBLE TODAY?

Gutiérrez, Gustavo. *A Theology of Liberation.* Maryknoll, N.Y.: Orbis Books, 1972.

Haughey, John C., S.J., ed. *The Faith That Does Justice.* New York: Paulist Press, 1977.

Monden, Louis. *Faith: Can Man Still Believe?* New York: Sheed & Ward, 1969.

Mouroux, Jean. *I Believe: The Personal Structure of Faith.* New York: Sheed & Ward, 1959.

Tillich, Paul. *The Courage to Be.* New Haven: Yale University Press, 1952.


### 5. THE MAN AND THE MESSAGE

Balthasar, Hans Urs von. *The Glory of the Lord: A Theological Aesthetics.* Vol. 1: *Seeing the Form.* Edited by J. Fessio, S.J., and John Riches. Translated from the German by Erasmo Leiva-Merikakis. San Francisco: Ignatius/Crossroad, 1983.

Bornkamm, Günther. *Jesus of Nazareth.* New York: Harper & Row, 1960.

Bultmann, Rudolf, et al. *Kerygma and Myth.* Edited by Hans W. Bartsch, New York: Harper & Brothers, 1961.

Cook, Michael, S.J. *The Jesus of Faith.* New York: Paulist Press, 1981.

Dodd, Charles H. *The Founder of Christianity.* New York: Macmillan, 1970.

Grant, Michael. *Jesus.* London: Sphere Books, 1978.

McKenzie, John L., S.J. *The Power and the Wisdom.* Milwaukee: Bruce Publishing Co., 1965.

Perrin, Norman. *Rediscovering the Teaching of Jesus.* New York: Harper & Row, 1967.

Senior, Donald. *Jesus.* Dayton: Pflaum Press, 1975.


## 6. DEATH AND RESURRECTION

Fuller, Reginald. *The Formation of the Resurrection Narratives.* New York: Macmillan, 1971.

O'Collins, Gerald. *The Resurrection of Jesus Christ.* Valley Forge, Penn.: Judson Press, 1973.

Sloyan, Gerard. *Jesus on Trial.* Philadelphia: Fortress Press, 1973.


## 7. CHRIST THE GOD INCARNATE—MYTH OR MYSTERY?

Bracken, Joseph. *What Are They Saying About the Trinity?* New York: Paulist Press, 1979.

Fuller, Reginald. *The Foundations of New Testament Christology.* New York: Charles Scribner's Sons, 1965.

Grillmeier, Aloys, S.J. *Christ in Christian Tradition.* New York: Sheed & Ward, 1965.

Kasper, Walter. *Jesus the Christ.* New York: Paulist Press, 1977.

Kelly, J. N. D. *Early Christian Doctrines.* New York: Harper & Row, 1960.

Knitter, Paul. *No Other Name? A Critical Survey of Christian Attitudes Towards World Religions.* Maryknoll, N.Y.: Orbis Books, 1985.

Lane, Dermot. *The Reality of Jesus: An Essay in Christology.* New York: Paulist Press, 1975.

Schillebeeckx, Edward. *Jesus: An Experiment in Christology.* New York: The Seabury Press, 1979.

Thüsing, Wilhelm, and Karl Rahner. *A New Christology.* New York: The Seabury Press, 1980.


## 8. THE CHURCH TODAY

*Dogmatic Constitution on the Church.* In Austin Flannery, O.P., *Vatican Council II: The Conciliar and Post Conciliar Documents.* Collegeville, Minn.: The Liturgical Press, 1975.

Dulles, Avery, S.J. *Models of the Church.* Garden City, N.Y.: Doubleday, 1974 (Image Books Edition, 1978).

Küng, Hans. *The Church*. New York: Sheed & Ward, 1967.

Maritain, Jacques. *On the Church of Christ*. Notre Dame, Ind.: University of Notre Dame Press, 1973.

McBrien, Richard. *Church: The Continuing Quest*. New York: Newman Press, 1970.

Minear, Paul S. *Images of the Church in the New Testament*. Philadelphia: The Westminster Press, 1960.


## 9. THE QUESTION OF AUTHORITY

Brown, Raymond. *The Community of the Beloved Disciple*. New York: Paulist Press, 1979.

Dulles, Avery, S.J. *The Survival of Dogma*. New York: Crossroad Publishing, 1982.

McKenzie, John L. *Authority in the Church*. New York: Sheed & Ward, 1966.

Schnackenburg, Rudolf. *The Church in the New Testament*. New York: Herder & Herder, 1965.


## 10. THE CHURCH IN DIALOGUE

*Decree on Ecumenism*. In Austin Flannery, ed. *Vatican Council II: The Conciliar and Post Conciliar Documents*. Collegeville, Minn.: The Liturgical Press, 1975.

Dulles, Avery, S.J. *The Resilient Church*. Garden City, N.Y.: Doubleday, 1977.

Kilmartin, Edward. *Toward Reunion: The Orthodox and Roman Catholic Churches*. New York: Paulist Press, 1980 (paper).

Lindbeck, George. *The Future of Roman Catholic Theology: Vatican II—Catalyst for Change*. Philadelphia: Fortress Press, 1970.

*The Unity We Seek: A Statement by the Roman Catholic/Presbyterian-Reformed Consultation*. Bishop Ernest L. Unterkoefler and Dr. Andrew Harsanyi, eds. New York: Paulist Press, 1977.


## 11. THE POPE—MONARCH OR MINISTER?

Brown, Raymond E., et al. *Peter in the New Testament*. New York: Paulist Press, 1973 (paper).

Cullmann, Oscar. *Peter: Disciple, Apostle, Martyr; A Historical and Theological Essay*. 2nd. ed. Philadelphia: Westminster Press, 1962.

Empie, Paul, and T. Austin Murphy, eds. *Papal Primacy and the Universal Church*. Minneapolis, Minn.: Augsburg Publishing House, 1974.

Granfield, Patrick. *The Papacy in Transition*. Garden City, N.Y.: Doubleday, 1980.

McCord, Peter, ed. *A Pope for All Christians*. New York: Paulist Press, 1977.

Tillard, J. M. R., O.P. *The Bishop of Rome*. Wilmington, Del.: Michael Glazier, 1983.

## 12. INFALLIBILITY REVISITED

Chirico, Peter. *Infallibility: The Crossroads of Doctrine*. Shawnee, Kan.: Sheed, Andrews & McMeel, 1977.

Dulles, Avery, S.J. *A Church to Believe In*. New York: Crossroad Publishing, 1982.

Empie, Paul, et al., eds. *Teaching Authority and Infallibility in the Church*. Minneapolis, Minn.: Augsburg Publishing House, 1978.

Hasler, August. *How the Pope Became Infallible*. Garden City, N.Y.: Doubleday, 1981.

Küng, Hans. *Infallible? An Inquiry*. Garden City, N.Y.: Doubleday, 1971.

Tierney, Brian. *Origins of Papal Infallibility, 1150–1350*. Leiden: Brill, 1972.

## 13. IMAGES OF MARY

Brown, Raymond E. *The Virginal Conception and Bodily Resurrection of Jesus*. New York: Paulist Press, 1973.

———. *The Birth of the Messiah*. Garden City, N.Y.: Doubleday, 1977.

——— et al., eds. *Mary in the New Testament: A Collaborative Assessment by Protestant and Roman Catholic Scholars*. Philadelphia: Fortress Press, 1978.

Congar, Yves. *Christ, Our Lady and the Church*. Westminster, Md.: Newman Press, 1957.

Graef, Hilda. *Mary: A History of Doctrine and Devotion*. 2 vols. New York: Sheed & Ward, 1963.

Laurentin, René. *The Question of Mary*. New York: Holt, Rinehart & Winston, 1965.

Suenens, Léon Joseph. *Mary the Mother of God*. New York: Hawthorn Books, 1959.

### 14. THE SAINTS

Brown, Peter. *The Cult of the Saints: Its Rise and Function in Latin Christianity.* Chicago: University of Chicago Press, 1981.

Cunningham, Lawrence. *The Meaning of the Saints.* New York: Harper & Row, 1980.

Delehaye, Hippolyte. *Legends of the Saints.* New York: Fordham University Press, 1962.

Weinstein, D., and R. Bell. *Saints and Society.* Chicago: University of Chicago Press, 1982.

### 15. LITURGY—SACRAMENT OF CHRIST

*Constitution on the Sacred Liturgy.* In *Vatican Council II: The Conciliar and Post Conciliar Documents.* Austin Flannery, O.P., ed. Collegeville, Minn.: The Liturgical Press, 1975.

Cullmann, Oscar. *Early Christian Worship.* Philadelphia: Westminster Press, 1978.

Dix, Gregory. *The Shape of the Liturgy.* London, Dacre Press, 1946.

Guardini, Romano. *The Spirit of the Liturgy.* London, Sheed & Ward, 1930.

### 16. SACRAMENTS—CHRIST'S LOVE MADE VISIBLE

Champlin, Joseph. *The Sacraments in a World of Change.* Notre Dame, Ind.: University of Notre Dame Press, 1973.

Erikson, Erik H. "The Development of Ritualization." In *The Religious Situation.* Edited by Donald R. Cutler. Boston: Beacon Press, 1968.

Guzie, Tad. *The Book of Sacramental Basics.* Glen Rock, N.J.: Paulist Press, 1981.

Martos, Joseph. *Doors to the Sacred.* Garden City, N.Y.: Doubleday Image Books, 1981.

———. *The Catholic Sacraments.* Wilmington, Del.: Michael Glazier, 1983.

Schillebeeckx, Edward. *Christ the Sacrament of the Encounter with God.* New York: Sheed & Ward, 1963.

Segundo, Juan Luis, S.J. *The Sacraments Today.* Maryknoll, N.Y.: Orbis Books, 1974.

### 17. THE SACRAMENTS OF INITIATION

Cullmann, Oscar. *Baptism in the New Testament.* Philadelphia: Westminster Press, 1950.

Davis, Charles. *Sacraments of Initiation: Baptism and Confirmation.* New York: Sheed & Ward, 1964.

Ganoczy, Alexander. *Becoming Christian.* Transl. by John Lynch, C.S.P. New York: Paulist Press, 1976.

Kavanagh, Aidan. *The Shape of Baptism: The Rite of Christian Initiation.* New York: Pueblo Publishing, 1978.

Lampe, Geoffrey. *The Seal of the Spirit.* New York: Longmans, Green, 1951.

Murphy Center for Liturgical Research, The. *Made, Not Born: New Perspectives on Christian Initiation and the Catechumenate.* Notre Dame, Ind.: University of Notre Dame Press, 1976.

### 18. EUCHARIST

Duffy, Regis, O.F.M. *Real Presence: Worship, Sacrament and Commitment.* New York: Harper & Row, 1982.

Jenson, Robert. *Visible Words.* Philadelphia: Fortress Press, 1978.

Jungmann, Josef, S.J. *The Mass.* Collegeville, Minn.: The Liturgical Press, 1976.

Keifer, Ralph. *Blessed and Broken.* Wilmington, Del.: Michael Glazier, 1982.

Kilmartin, Edward J., S.J. *Church, Eucharist and Priesthood.* New York: Paulist Press, 1981.

————. *The Eucharist in the Primitive Church.* Englewood Cliffs, N.J.: Prentice-Hall, 1965.

Klauser, Theodore. *A Short History of the Western Liturgy.* New York: Oxford University Press, 1979.

MacLeod, Donald. *Presbyterian Worship: Its Meaning and Method.* Atlanta, Ga.: John Knox, 1980.

Nichols, James Hastings. *Corporate Worship in the Reformed Tradition.* Philadelphia: Westminster Press, 1968.

Swidler, Leonard, ed. *Eucharist in Ecumenical Dialogue.* New York: Paulist Press, 1976.

### 19. and 20. PENANCE AND ANOINTING OF THE SICK
### (THE SACRAMENTS OF HEALING)

Empereur, James L., S.J. *Prophetic Anointing.* Wilmington, Del.: Michael Glazier, 1982.

Hamlin, L. *Reconciliation in the Church: A Theology and Pastoral Essay on the Sacrament of Penance.* Collegeville, Minn.: The Liturgical Press, 1980.

Hellwig, Monika K. *Sign of Reconciliation and Conversion.* Wilmington, Del.: Michael Glazier, 1982.

Poschmann, Bernard. *Penance and the Anointing of the Sick.* New York: Herder & Herder, 1964.

Tentler, Thomas. *Sin and Confession on the Eve of the Reformation.* Princeton, N.J.: Princeton University Press, 1977.


### 21. MARRIAGE—STILL FOREVER?

Curran, Charles. *New Perspectives in Moral Theology.* Notre Dame, Ind.: Fides Publishers, 1974.

Dominian, Jack. *Marriage, Faith and Love.* New York: Crossroad Publishing, 1982.

Haughton, Rosemary. *The Theology of Marriage.* Butler, Wis.: Clergy Book Service, 1971.

Schillebeeckx, Edward. *Marriage: Human Reality and Saving Mystery.* New York: Sheed & Ward, 1965.


### 22. HOLY ORDERS: THE MEANING OF MINISTRY TODAY

Cooke, Bernard. *Ministry to God's Word and Sacrament.* Philadelphia, Fortress Press, 1976.

*Decree on the Ministry and Life of Priests.* In Austin Flannery, O.P., ed. *Vatican Council II: The Conciliar and Post Conciliar Documents.* Collegeville, Minn.: The Liturgical Press, 1975.

Greeley, Andrew. *Parish, Priest and People.* Chicago: The Thomas More Press, 1981.

Mitchell, Nathan, O.S.B. *Mission and Ministry,* Wilmington, Del., 1982.

Mohler, James. *The Origin and Evolution of the Priesthood.* New York: Alba House, 1970.

O'Meara, Thomas, O.P. *Theology of Ministry.* New York: Paulist Press, 1983.

Schillebeeckx, Edward. *Ministry: Leadership in the Community of Jesus Christ.* New York: Crossroad Publishing, 1981.

————. *The Church with a Human Face.* New York: Crossroad Publishing, 1985.

Schuller, D., M. Strommen and M. Brekke, eds. *Ministry in America.* New York: Harper & Row, 1980.

Schweizer, Eduard. *Church Order in the New Testament.* London, SCM Press, 1961.


## 23. MORALITY TODAY

Bonhoeffer, Dietrich. *Ethics.* New York: Macmillan, 1964.

Curran, Charles. *Contemporary Problems in Moral Theology.* Notre Dame, Ind.: Fides Publishers, 1970.

————. *Transition and Tradition in Moral Theology.* Notre Dame, Ind.: University of Notre Dame Press, 1979.

Grisez, Germain, with the help of Joseph Boyle, Jr., et al. *The Way of the Lord Jesus.* Vol. 1: *Christian Moral Principles.* Chicago: Franciscan Herald Press, 1984.

Gustafson, James. *Christ and the Moral Life.* New York: Harper & Row, 1968.

Häring, Bernard. *Free and Faithful in Christ.* 3 vols. New York: The Seabury Press, 1978–81.

Maguire, Daniel. *The Moral Choice.* Garden City, N.Y.: Doubleday, 1978.

McCormick, Richard. *Notes on Moral Theology, 1965 through 1980.* Washington, D.C.: University Press of America, 1981.

O'Connell, Timothy. *Principles for a Catholic Morality.* New York: The Seabury Press, 1978.


## 24. SIN RECONSIDERED

Fairlee, Henry. *The Seven Deadly Sins Today.* Washington, D.C.: New Republic Books, 1978.

Kohlberg, Lawrence. *The Philosophy of Moral Development.* New York: Harper & Row, 1981.

Lyman, Stanford. *The Seven Deadly Sins: Society and Evil.* New York: St. Martin's Press, 1978.

Menninger, Karl. *Whatever Became of Sin?* New York: Hawthorn Books, 1973.

Piaget, Jean. *The Child and Reality.* New York: Viking Press, 1973.

Tennant, F. R. *The Concept of Sin.* Cambridge, England: University Press, 1912.

Vandervelde, George. *Original Sin: Two Major Trends in Contemporary Roman*

*Catholic Reinterpretation.* Washington, D.C.: University Press of America, 1981.


## 25. THE GREAT DEBATE IN MORAL THEOLOGY: REVISIONISTS VS. TRADITIONALISTS


Connery, John, S.J. "Catholic Ethics: Has the Norm for Rule-Making Changed?" In *Theological Studies* 42 (1981), pp. 232–50.

*Doing Evil to Achieve Good: Moral Choice in Conflict Situations.* Edited by Paul Ramsey and Richard McCormick. Chicago: Loyola University Press, 1978.

Gustafson, James. *Protestant and Roman Catholic Ethics: Prospects for Rapprochement.* Chicago: University of Chicago Press, 1975.

Keane, Philip, S.S. "The Objective Moral Order: Reflections on Recent Research." In *Theological Studies* 43 (1982), pp. 260–78.

McCormick, Richard. *Ambiguity in Moral Choice.* Milwaukee, Wis.: Marquette University, 1973.

Milhaven, John Giles. *Toward a New Catholic Morality.* Garden City, N.Y.: Doubleday Image Books, 1970.

*Readings in Moral Theology No.1: Moral Norms and Catholic Tradition.* Ed. by Charles Curran and Richard McCormick. New York: Paulist Press, 1979.


## 26. A NEW MORALITY OF SEX?


Boswell, John. *Christianity, Social Tolerance and Homosexuality: Gay People in Western Europe from the Beginning of the Christian Era to the Fourteenth Century.* Chicago: University of Chicago Press, 1980.

Dominian, Jack. *Proposals for a New Sexual Ethic.* London: Darton, Longman & Todd, 1977.

Hanigan, James P. *What Are They Saying About Sexual Morality?* New York: Paulist Press, 1982.

Keane, Philip S., S.S. *Sexual Morality: A Catholic Perspective.* New York: Paulist Press, 1977.

Kennedy, Eugene. *The New Sexuality.* Garden City, N.Y.: Doubleday Image Books, 1972.

Kosnik, Anthony, et al. *Human Sexuality: New Directions in American Catholic Thought.* New York: Paulist Press, 1977.

May, William. *Sex, Marriage and Chastity: Reflections of a Catholic Layman, Spouse, and Parent.* Chicago: Franciscan Herald Press, 1981.

McNeil, John. J. *The Church and the Homosexual.* Shawnee Mission, Kan.: Sheed, Andrews & McMeel, 1976.

Ostling, Richard N., and Bernard N. Nathanson. *Aborting America.* Garden City, N.Y.: Doubleday, 1979.


## 27. SOCIAL JUSTICE:
### THE CHURCH'S CALL TO ACTION


Bigo, Pierre, S.J. *The Church and Third World Revolution.* Maryknoll, N.Y.: Orbis Books, 1977.

Boff, Leonardo. *Liberating Grace.* Maryknoll, N.Y.: Orbis Books, 1979.

Camp, Richard. *The Papal Ideology of Social Reform.* Leiden: E. Brill, 1969.

Greinacher, N., and A. Müller, eds. *The Church and Human Rights.* New York: Crossroad Publishing, 1979.

Gudorf, Christine. *Catholic Social Teaching and Liberation Themes.* Washington, D.C.: University Press of America, 1980.

Gutiérrez, Gustavo. *A Theology of Liberation.* Maryknoll, N.Y.: Orbis Books, 1972.

Holland, Joe, and Peter Henriot. *Social Analysis: Linking Faith and Justice.* Washington, D.C.: Center of Concern, 1980.

Hollenbach, David. *Claims in Conflict: Retrieving and Renewing the Catholic Human Rights Tradition.* New York: Paulist Press, 1979.

Lernoux, Penny. *Cry of the People.* Garden City, N.Y.: Doubleday, 1980.

McGinnis, James B. *Bread and Justice: Toward a New International Economic Order.* New York: Paulist Press, 1979.

Miranda, José. *Marx Against the Marxists: The Christian Humanism of Karl Marx.* Maryknoll, N.Y.: Orbis Books, 1980.

O'Brien, David, and Thomas Shannon, eds. *Renewing the Earth: Catholic Documents on Peace, Justice and Liberation.* Garden City, N.Y.: Doubleday Image Books, 1977.

Overberg, Kenneth. *An Inconsistent Ethic? Teachings of the American Catholic Bishops.* Washington, D.C.: University Press of America, 1980.

*The Pastoral Constitution on the Church in the Modern World.* In Austin Flannery, O.P., ed. *Vatican Council: The Conciliar and Post Conciliar Documents.* Collegeville, Minn.: The Liturgical Press, 1975.

*To Do the Work of Justice.* The National Conference of Catholic Bishops. Washington, D.C., 1978.

Whyte, John R. *Catholics in Western Democracies.* New York: St. Martin's Press, 1981.

## 28. BIOETHICS AND ECOLOGY

Carmody, John. *Ecology and Religion: Toward a New Christian Theology of Nature*. New York: Paulist Press, 1983 (paper).

Dedek, John. *Contemporary Medical Ethics*. New York: Sheed & Ward, 1975.

Fritsch, Albert J. *Environmental Ethics*. Garden City, N.Y.: Doubleday Anchor Books, 1980.

Kelly, David F. *The Emergence of Roman Catholic Medical Ethics in North America: An Historical-Methodological-Bibliographical Study*. New York: Edwin Mellen, 1979.

Ophuls, William. *Ecology and the Politics of Scarcity*. San Francisco: W. H. Freeman, 1977.

Varga, Andrew C. *The Main Issues in Bioethics*. New York: Paulist Press, 1980.


## 29. HUMAN DESTINY

Baillie, John. *And the Life Everlasting*. London, Oxford University Press, 1934.

Braaten, Carl E. *The Future of God*. New York: Harper & Row, 1969.

Carse, James P. *Death and Existence: A Conceptual History of Human Mortality*. New York: Wiley Interscience, 1980.

Cullmann, Oscar. *Christ and Time*. Philadelphia: Westminster Press, 1964.

Lifton, Robert Jay. *The Broken Connection: On Death and the Continuity of Life*. New York: Simon & Schuster, 1979.

Moltmann, Jurgen. *Theology of Hope*. New York: Harper & Row, 1976.

Robinson, John A. T. *In the End God*. New York, Harper & Row, 1968.

# APPENDIX

## The Creed

You may remember the flap, not too long ago, over the book *Christ Among Us*. The controversy that raged over this popular Catholic catechism highlights the tension in the Church today about what a Catholic should believe. The text was used by thousands of religion teachers in the United States who considered it an effective tool for teaching Catholic doctrine today. Other people, however, complained about the book's positions on certain teachings, and Rome eventually determined that it should no longer be used as a text in classes on Catholic doctrine.

There is, no doubt, a wide range of opinion on many points of Church teaching today. Liberals are often opposed to conservatives and sometimes the conflict gets pretty testy. Some fundamentalist Catholics are even organized to save the faith from those they call "modernists." The average Catholic often feels confused—especially if his or her previous religious education was limited to the *Baltimore Catechism*.

One may speculate about the reasons for the turmoil but it is obvious that the Second Vatican Council's call for change in many areas of Catholic life is the biggest factor. We must especially keep in mind that the Council endorsed a new critical approach to the Bible. Some theologians took this new spirit of openness as a green light to reexamine such traditional doctrines as infallibility, original sin and sanctifying grace. Such theologians as Hans Küng, Karl Rahner and Edward Schillebeeckx became famous for their bold speculations on these and other topics.

### WHAT ARE THE ESSENTIALS OF OUR FAITH?

The average American Catholic was not very well prepared, to put it mildly, for this invasion of liberal-thinking theologians. Many were very bewildered by all the "new ideas."

One thing is clear. Many Catholics have a hard time distinguishing between essentials and nonessentials in matters of faith. Too many put everything on the same level. If they are told, for example, that the account of Jonah and the whale should be seen as a story teaching God's mercy rather than as historical fact, they often exclaim: "What can I believe anymore? Are we to throw out the whole Bible?"

The question of what is essential and what is not essential to Catholic belief is not a new problem by any means. It existed from the very beginning of the Church and that is why the various creeds of Christianity (brief statements of the essentials of the faith) were issued.

The creed we recite at Sunday Mass, popularly called the Nicene Creed (since it is based in part on the Council of Nicaea, 325 A.D.) is a developed form of an early baptismal creed. Regarded as an ideal statement of Catholic orthodoxy, the Nicene Creed soon spread through East and West. It has lately even been recommended as an ideal basis for agreement between Catholics and Protestants.

For those who are confused today about what to believe, a brief, point-by-point reflection on the Nicene Creed might help refocus our attention on the essentials of our faith. To assist in this worthy endeavor, let me offer the following.

*We believe in one God . . .*

The first article and the basis of everything else is belief in God. The use of "we" rather than "I" reminds me that my faith in God, though a very personal act and rooted in my own experience, is something I share with the community, and it is strengthened and enriched by its contact with the tradition and the life of the community.

Belief in God is a free choice, an act of fundamental trust. Atheism cannot be refuted purely on a logical basis, for the evidence regarding God's existence points both ways. Charles Darwin himself never denied the existence of God, but many regard his theory of evolution as eliminating the need for a God who created all things.

Others, while still believers, have experienced the "death of God" insofar as they feel the absence of God rather than his presence. They are haunted by images of people suffering terrible pain and degradation, human beings flayed alive by the atom bomb at Hiroshima, Jews tortured to death in the Nazi camps, starving Ethiopian babies with bloated bellies. If God exists, they ask themselves, how can he allow such enormous, senseless evil?

Archie Bunker, in heated argument with his agnostic son-in-law, was asked, "Archie, if there's a God, why is there so much suffering in the world?" He replied, "I'll tell you why . . . [pause] . . . Edith, if there's a God, why is there so much suffering in the world?" There is only a blank silence, so Archie yells, "Edith, would you get in here and help me? I'm having to defend God all by myself."

Only a fool, of course, can give a ready answer to the problem of pain and evil. Jesus himself did not live in a fool's paradise. He was terribly familiar with human suffering and degradation. He saw all around him the brutal results of plague, war, Roman occupation, famine and earthquake. But in spite of it all, he proclaimed the nearness of God whose glory shines through all the murkiness of sin and evil in the world, and he staked his life on God's ultimate victory over all that is anti-life.

Take courage, he said. Be stouthearted. Trust in God who numbers the hairs on your head and watches over the flight of sparrows. He is your heavenly Father and his fantastic love for you makes the love of an earthly father look poor indeed.

*The Father, the Almighty, maker of heaven and earth, of all that is seen and unseen.*

In saying this we are really answering the questions that nag constantly at any thoughtful human being: Why am I here? What is the meaning of it all?

As I saw on a T-shirt recently, "Life is tough. And then you die."

In Joseph Heller's novel *Something Happened,* the main character works for a huge insurance company and presides over an unhappy family which is falling apart. At one point he asks, "Is this all I can expect from life?"

The need for meaning, for some kind of answer to "Why?" can't be permanently put aside. In the very first pages of Scripture, the Book of Genesis gives us an answer: God created us to be happy in a wonderful universe in a life of communion with him and with each other.

Above all, in saying, "We believe in God, the Maker," we are saying that we believe in the eternal destiny and sacred dignity of each human being, that life has meaning, that we are not just human flotsam and jetsam lost in an empty universe.

*We believe in one Lord, Jesus Christ, the only Son of God, eternally begotten of the Father, God from God, Light from Light, true God from true God, begotten, not made, one in Being with the Father. Through him all things were made.*

This whole passage reflects the ancient controversies of the Church as to the precise relation of Jesus to God the Father. The main point is the affirmation that Jesus is "one in being" with the Father, which was the Council of Nicaea's answer to those who denied that Jesus was divine. Belief in Christ as divine and as Lord of creation is undoubtedly the central dogma of the Church.

What should accepting Jesus as Lord mean in our everyday life? Everyone needs a faith of some kind to live by. Many simply have faith in life. They believe it is worthwhile to struggle against injustice, to work for a better world. And they will make great sacrifices in order to serve the victims of poverty and oppression. Their choice about life is not something strictly provable by reason. It's a form of faith, a gut feeling they have that this is the way life should be lived. They could not rebut the arguments of those who favor the opposite life-style.

Christians, however, rely on more than gut feelings. They commit themselves consciously to Jesus Christ as their Lord, as the Shepherd who leads them along the path of righteousness and reveals to them the goodness at the heart of things —Jesus Christ who manifests God as Creator and Redeemer of the world. It is this trust in Jesus and in Jesus' God that activates our hope for this world and draws us into the struggle for peace and justice.

*For us and for our salvation he came down from heaven . . .*

How did Jesus bring us salvation? To get the answer we have to start with the Bible's realistic description of the human condition: Human history is a history of sin—it is a record of crime, bloodshed and wars of incredible ferocity. The normal state of man and woman is alienation. People are alienated from each other: There is hatred, lying, injustice, oppression and open or covert hostility, not to mention ignorance and sheer folly. War after war has drenched the earth in blood and now our propensity to violence threatens the very future of the planet.

The sheer tragic character of our solidarity in evil was brought home forcefully to me recently while reading an article in *The New York Times* about the U.S. government's "Star Wars" concept. While the plan is supposedly intended to diminish the threat of a nuclear holocaust, I, for one, fear that it may be just another spiral in human distrust and another reminder of our hopeless sinful condition apart from Christ's saving love.

Human experience certainly testifies to human solidarity in sin and alienation. Left to ourselves the human race is powerless to change this state of affairs. But as Walter Kasper professes in *Jesus the Christ:* "Through the Incarnation of God in Jesus Christ the disastrous situation in which all men are caught up and by which they are determined in their inmost being is changed. It has broken through at one point and this new beginning from now on determines anew the situation of all men."

Christ calls people out of the old solidarity in evil into a new solidarity, a solidarity of love and caring. The power of original sin—our solidarity in sin—is broken. Jesus is the "one for others," the firstborn of many brothers and sisters, the New Adam. For our salvation and liberation, Jesus establishes the new People of God and is the beginning of the new history of humanity.

*By the power of the Holy Spirit he was born of the Virgin Mary, and became man.*

The basis for this article is found in Matthew and Luke who describe how Jesus was conceived in Mary's womb through the action of the Holy Spirit. The question many Scripture scholars—including some Catholics—ask today is whether the primary intention of Matthew and Luke in asserting Mary's virginity was historical or theological. Nevertheless, official Church teaching continues to uphold Mary's virginity in both senses.

In any case, the theological meaning of the virgin birth is clear: Jesus' birth does not belong to the ordinary course of human history. He represents a new beginning for the human race. And his being conceived by the Spirit means that the power of God rather than that of humanity is what brings forth a savior and a new creation.

*For our sake he was crucified under Pontius Pilate; he suffered, died, and was buried.*

It is striking that the creed says nothing about the message and way of life of Jesus. But in stating that he was crucified—an atrocious death reserved for slaves and criminals and for politically dangerous persons—the creed tells us what is most important: Jesus' message, way of life and love for humanity were a radical and tremendous challenge, as they still are, to all systems that seek to thwart the genuine good of God's children.

*On the third day he rose again in fulfillment of the Scriptures . . .*

Important to keep in mind: The Resurrection does not prove the truth of Christianity. The Resurrection itself is an object of faith; it is not historically verifiable. History only testifies to the faith of the first witnesses. This is evident if we consider how various are the accounts of the Gospels: They differ about how, when, where and to whom Jesus first appeared. No effort was made to tidy up these often conflicting details, no doubt, because the experience of the Resurrection they were trying to relate was an experience that transcended all normal human limits. It was an experience of the presence of Jesus, an experience of conversion and an awareness of the ultimate, definitive meaning of his life and death.

It was a vision of Jesus that transformed their lives and launched the Church. In fact, the reason Christians began worshiping on Sunday is that it was the day of the Resurrection. The belief that Jesus is risen and present among us becomes the central motivating force of our faith.

*He ascended into heaven and is seated at the right hand of the Father. He will come again in glory to judge the living and the dead, and his kingdom will have no end.*

The risen Jesus now lives with the Father and watches over and guides his Church. We are reminded of this regularly in the Eucharist when we pray, "You plead for us at the right hand of the Father."

Fundamentalists, in a literal rendition of Scripture, pictorialize Christ's Second Coming on clouds with angels blowing trumpets summoning all the risen dead before his throne of judgment. The imagery is no doubt derived from the apocalyptic (end-of-the-world) literature of Christ's time and is not essential to the basic message intended—namely, that the purpose of God revealed in Christ will be fulfilled, the Kingdom of God will be fully realized and Christ and his Gospel will stand forever as the standard by which we all will be measured.

*We believe in the Holy Spirit, the Lord, the giver of life, who proceeds from the Father and the Son. With the Father and the Son he is worshiped and glorified. He has spoken through the Prophets.*

Paul, above all, testifies to the reality of the Holy Spirit as one of the three Persons of the Trinity when he says that the Spirit works in a unique way in believers through the gifts it imparts to each. Through the Spirit, faith in Christ is made possible while hope is sustained. And the Spirit builds up the Church through the love it pours into each heart. The distinction of the Spirit from Christ is suggested by the fact that the Spirit "dwells" in the believers now while the Lord will only return in the future (1 Thessalonians 4:16). The insight here somewhat faintly indicated—that, in the interim before the End, the Spirit is given to the Church in the absence of Christ—was developed gradually by the Fathers of the Church into the doctrine of the Trinity.

Devotion to the Holy Spirit is changing the lives of many Catholics today and is the hallmark of the charismatic movement, one of the most visible signs of the current Catholic renewal. The charismatic movement has spread widely throughout the world, as I realized last summer in Borneo. The charismatic movement is very strong among the natives there. Missionaries told me how their previously rather unresponsive parishioners were stirred up by what appears to be almost a new Pentecost. People who previously refused to participate actively in the liturgy are now entering into it with great gusto, singing and clapping and joyfully praising the Lord, "Puji Tuhan," as they say in their native Iban language.

The charismatic movement is only one manifestation of the way the Spirit is renewing the Church today. We see the Spirit alive in many other areas of the Church as well: in those taking courageous stands on issues of peace and justice; in those laboring quietly for Christian unity; in those seeking more effective forms of liturgical renewal, to name a few. The Holy Spirit continues to be the "giver of life" to the Christian community today through a great variety of gifts.

*We believe in one holy catholic and apostolic Church.*

These are the four main "marks" or qualities of the Church (one, holy, catholic, apostolic), according to the venerable tradition. The meaning of these marks seems obvious at first view but historically they have been interpreted in very diverse ways. Older Roman Catholics will remember how the word *Church* here was identified with one visible institution—the Roman Catholic Church. The marks accordingly were interpreted in a visible, concrete, statistical way to show that only the Roman Catholic Church clearly possessed all four of them and therefore it was the only true Church. For example, it alone was supposed to be *one* (unified under one visible head, the Pope); it alone was *holy* (having many saints within its membership); it alone was *catholic* (that is, universal or spread throughout the world); it alone was *apostolic* (or able to trace its leaders back to the apostles).

The Second Vatican Council, however, moved away from this narrow view of the nature of the Church and the emphasis on proofs and arguments. In the Council's documents the "Church" is no longer strictly identified with any one society or institution. Rather, the Council begins with the biblical view of the Church as primarily a "mystery," and the four marks therefore are regarded primarily as spiritual gifts which are not easily measured and which, in fact, are shared to some degree by other Churches. No one Church exhausts the reality of the Church or has a monopoly on the marks. In fact, in this dynamic view taken of the marks, each Church is called to become more fully one, holy, catholic and apostolic.

*We acknowledge one baptism for the forgiveness of sins.*

Christian Baptism is derived from the baptism of Jesus. We may recall that when he was baptized by John the Baptist in the Jordan River, Jesus was anointed by God's Spirit which descended in the form of a dove. The Spirit possessed him entirely, indicating Jesus' permanent unity with the Father. A voice from heaven proclaimed him God's Son in terms that suggested he would carry out the role of God's suffering servant, as described by Isaiah in his four "suffering servant" songs (chapters 42–53). Through his suffering Jesus would atone for the sins of many.

The baptism of Jesus thus symbolized the new relationship that would be established between God and the human family through Jesus' saving work. With that work fulfilled, his followers are baptized to show their response in faith to this work of reconciliation prefigured in his baptism. The Sacrament of Baptism also accomplishes union with Christ and forgiveness of sins because it brings one into the Church, which is his resurrected Body.

*We look for the resurrection of the dead, and the life of the world to come.*

One of the most exciting adventures on my recent trip to Borneo was my visit to the caves of Niah located deep in the jungle. There in one of the caves were discovered the remnants of small canoe-like boats used as coffins, and nearby on the walls some paintings 40,000 years old. Depicted in these paintings are people sitting in these coffin-like boats and crossing a river to the next world. The paintings indicate a belief in some shadowy form of life after death, a belief found in most primitive cultures and reflected faintly in the earlier parts of the Old Testament.

In the Hebrew Scriptures the idea of life after death only gradually came into focus as Judaism arrived at an understanding that communion with God would not be broken even by death. It is only in the Christian Scriptures, however, that this belief is fully revealed by Christ. Jesus proclaimed it when he said, "God is the God of Abraham, Isaac and Joseph. He is not the God of the dead but of the living." Faith in resurrection was given conclusive force by Jesus' own resurrection. As Christians we believe we will share in his resurrection and glory.

In conclusion, the creed reminds us that what we believe is important. Historically, the Christian Churches almost without exception have insisted on the necessity of correct belief. But, on the other hand, one can become too concerned with *orthodoxy* (right belief) and forget that *orthopraxis* (right living) is even more important. Christ, after all, came not only as the *truth* but as the *way* and the *life*. And he said we would be finally judged by how we carry out his great commandment: "You shall love the Lord your God with your whole heart, with your whole soul, and with all your mind. . . . [And] you shall love your neighbor as yourself" (Matthew 22:37, 39).

# INDEX